MEMOIRS OF A GEEZER:
FROM THE TIMBER WOODS AND BACK

by

E. LUTHER COPELAND

International Standard Book Number 0-87012-660-1
Library of Congress Control Number 2001117472
Printed in the United States of America
Copyright ® 2001 E. Luther Copeland
Raleigh, NC
All Rights Reserved
2001

Camera-ready material provided.

McClain Printing Company
212 Main Street
Parsons, WV 26287

www.mcclainprinting.com

To
Louise
Our Children
Judy, Joy, Beth, Becky, and Luke
and Our Grandchildren
Sarah, Joe, Mike, Dave, Hannah, and Ella

TABLE OF CONTENTS

LIST OF ILLUSTRATIONS

PREFACE

This book is published primarily for my children and grandchildren, but it is also for any persons who may have an interest in it. Directing it toward members of my family may help protect me from the charge that anyone who writes about his own life is egotistical. Anyway, who should be concerned with my career? Since my life has been a varied one, added to the fact that it has spanned almost a century, and a very eventful one at that, it may be sufficiently interesting to enough people to justify its publication without overburdening me with guilt for egotism!

Some readers may wish to read selectively. For example, those who are related to Japan may wish to read the chapters on Japan only, while Southeasterners may want to read the section on my life as a Faculty member in that Seminary. Others may wish to read only the chapter which pertains to their school. However it is read is okay with the author!

In the use of Japanese names, I have followed the usual Japanese practice of presenting the surname first and the given name second. This ordering, the reverse of that which is usual for Westerners, should be more natural for Japanese readers without unduly disabling persons who are more familiar with English.

Speaking of names, I have changed some of them to protect the innocent. In such cases, I have aimed to inform the reader that I have given to certain people fictitious names.

Although the title has the word "Memoirs" in it, and although I am generally aware of the distinction made nowadays between autobiography and memoirs, I have not sought to conform to either genre: chronology suggests autobiography while interpretation favors memoirs.

Now a further word is in order concerning the title, *Memoirs of a Geezer: From the Timber Woods and Back.* Obviously, this title is a take off on the title of the book by Arthur Golden, *Memoirs of a Geisha.* Readers will recognize (1) that for the purposes of this manuscript, the definition of a geezer is "a male human being of advanced age," (2) that there has been a long detour between my growing up in the timber woods and my return to the woods in later life, and (3) that my calls to be a minister and a missionary have been taken with great seriousness. Moreover, unlike the volume by Golden, the book aims to be factual and not represent the musings of a creative imagination. Mostly, I have relied upon my memory, with certain exceptions. For the early years and for the heritage previous to my birth, I have used the well-written autobiography of a sister, the late Vernice Trimble, entitled *From My Point of View*. Unfortunately,Vernice's work concludes with her graduation from high school. In addition, I have utilized some very newsy letters, mostly written by my wife, Louise, from Japan during the early period of our missionary service. Some-times I have wished for the extensive diary which I do not have. Only for Chapter12 have I employed a somewhat sparse journal which I kept on the two-months trip from Japan back to the States in 1956. But, as I have indicated, usually, the volume is constructed from my remembrances.

Now I wish to make some heart-felt acknowledgments:

To my daughter, Beth Copeland Vargo, for expert proofreading, though the author alone is responsible for any errors.

To my niece, Louise Fox, for providing a number of photographs.

To Joe Sherwood, for allowing me to take photos in his hardware store in Mountain City, Tennessee, and to use an old catalog of the Summers Hardware and Supply Company.

To my wife, Louise Copeland, for tracing objects in Illustrations 4 (Miner"s Cap), 6 (Miner's Pick), 14 (Grabs), and 20, from items in Sum-mers Hardware and Supply Company, Johnson City, Tenn., *Catalog* No. 40 (1928?), pp. 63, 49-50, and 284.

To Ray M. Henderson, for photos in Illustration No. 5., (particularly, the Coal Auger and Tamping Bars).

To my grandson, Joe Vargo, for sketches used in Illus. Nos. 14 (Crosscut Saw) and 21.

To Alicia Tyler for photos in Illus. No.11 and 12.

To Forest History Society, Inc., 701 Vickers Avenue, Durham, NC 27701, for photographs in Illus. Nos. 10 and 15.

To Bill Wilkerson, 2102 Sprunt Avenue, Durham, NC for making several photographs acceptable for publication.

To Ms. Jean Porter, Patent and Trademark Librarian, North Carolina State University Libraries, for her helpfulness.

To Alvin Sellens, compiler, *Dictionary of American Hand Tools* (Augusta, KS:1990), pp. 77, 516, 29, and 108 for photographs in Illus. Nos.4 (Carbide Lamp), 5 (Auger and Bits), 14 (Logging Wedge and Double Bitted Axe),and 18 (Cant Hook and Peavey).

PART ONE
THE GROWING UP YEARS, 1916-1940

Chapter One
FOREBEARS AND FAMILY

On May 11, 1976, I was seated on the platform of a spacious auditorium on the campus of Seinan Gakuin University in Fukuoka, Japan. This large Baptist school was celebrating its sixtieth anniversary. As Chancellor, I was to deliver the Founder's Day address. I, too, was sixty years of age and in my second stint as a missionary to Japan, 1976-1980. For the second time, also, I was Chancellor of Seinan. For the almost twenty years between my two periods of missionary service, I had taught courses embracing the concerns of the Christian mission in relation to various cultures and religions. My travels had taken me around the globe more than once. I had lived both in Japan and in India.

What a strange coincidence, I reflected, had brought forth Seinan Gakuin and me in that same year, sixty years ago, obviously quite unknown to each other! What a singular providence had drawn us together. What a remarkable beacon had guided me from the relative isolation of the timber woods of Appalachia to an international ministry.

At the same time, I was aware that some mysterious fate had pushed me beyond what I could actually bring off. I have never believed that I was an over-achiever. The situation may be more complex than that. It was as if some heavy hand was behind me, pushing me on. People always seemed to expect more of me, and I expected more of myself, than I ever was able to perform. I suspect that I appear to have great self-confidence. Actually, for a long time I have been tormented by doubts. But enough of this! It certainly gets me ahead of my story.

I entered this world early in the twentieth century; thus I lived through most of that tumultuous one hundred years. Born in the midst of World War One, I survived the Great Depression, and World War Two, and I belong in what Tom Brokaw, apparently with permissible exaggeration, calls "the greatest generation."

I was born January 24, 1916, in Drennen, Nicholas County, West Virginia. My birth certificate, evidently filled out a few weeks after the event by the country doctor who had come to my home to deliver me, left a bit to be desired with regard to adequate recording of information. The certificate listed the date and place of my birth correctly enough, according to a very good authority, my mother, but informed the world that I was "Luther Copeland, son of Luther Copeland and Mrs. Luther Copeland." One would think that the certificate would have given my mother's name, or most of it, Nannie Cleveland Hurt Copeland. My father was Winfield Luther Lowell Copeland. The "Winfield" in my dad's name was the name of his father, which he never used, simply becoming Luther or, formally, L. L. Copeland.

Though my name was different in that I was Edwin Luther Copeland, the Edwin deriving from the name of one of my mother's brothers, Jubal Edwin Hurt, I, too, was called "Luther"-- or "Little Luther" or "Luke"--to distinguish me from my dad. Sometimes I am mistakenly called "Junior." Always when I am introduced to Lutherans, they perk up, thinking they've found another Lutheran. Their faces fall when they learn that I'm only a lowly Baptist.

The Copelands, of Scots-Irish derivation, came to West Virginia from Tennessee a few decades before the Civil War. Probably they had migrated to Tennessee from North Carolina, since Copeland is a common name in that state to the east. Almost certainly they arrived here from the British Isles in the eighteenth century. The story is told, true, no doubt, that Hezekiah, my great-great-grandfather, after making his way to West Virginia (then Virginia) from Tennessee, met the young woman who was to become his wife, Annie Kincaid, in the village of Gauley Bridge. The couple lived for a time in a large hollow tree until they could get more permanent quarters on Big Creek, a tributary of the Gauley River.

Such was the pioneering spirit of my forebears--not to mention the fact that this particular ancestor seems to have been a rascal as well as a pioneer: He left home to sell some of his father's hogs in a Virginia market, kept the money, journeyed to West Virginia and never returned home, for which insubordination and thievery he was practically left out of the will of his father David, a copy of which is in my possession.

A story has been passed down in our family for lo these several generations, to the effect that our ancestor Hezekiah had developed a reputation for uprightness by the time of his death.

At the moment he died, however, with several persons at his bedside who observed this strange phenomenon, a jet-black dog was said to have emerged from under the deathbed and escaped from the room, never to be seen again. You make whatever you want of this story. I suggest that it means that Hezekiah's early misdeeds, and possibly some later ones, dogged him until the moment of his death! So if you find any rascals on the Copeland family tree since Hezekiah, please know that they came by their meanness naturally.

Illustration No. 1

My Grandpa Copeland

My paternal grandfather Winfield Copeland, a grandson of Hezekiah and a vigorous and healthy man, lived until he was almost ninety and might have gone on for a few more years had he not been stricken with cancer. He worked as a lumber grader and as a "cruiser," one who walked over tracts of timber to estimate how many board feet of lumber they would produce. He was reputed to have been good at these tasks.

Grandpa remarked more than once that he became a Baptist by conviction, though his people were Methodists, and several stories circulated about his piety. For example, it was said that the ice had to be cut so that he could be baptized in the Gauley river. My father has indicated also that when

Grandpa had to have an appendectomy, a dangerous operation back then, he repeated a childhood prayer just before he inhaled the ether:

> Now I lay me down to sleep;
> I pray thee, Lord, my soul to keep.
> If I should die before I wake,
> I pray thee, Lord, /my soul to take.
> This I ask for Jesus' sake. Amen.

Grandpa Copeland was an earnest Christian, puritanical in action and attitude and apparently lacking in humor. He always seemed to have a judgmental attitude toward us who were the children of his son, Luther, compared to our cousins, the Grosses, children of his other offspring, Lettie. I found him easy to respect but difficult to like, though I gladly admit his influence on me.

Illustration No. 2

My Paternal Grandma

My paternal grandmother was Emma Hill Copeland who had some admixture of American Indian with her English blood. We Copelands have always taken some pride in our Indian heritage, though evidently we are not overly endowed with it. Since Grandma Copeland died of what was then called "childbed fever" shortly after my father was born, he never knew her. Neither did I!

After Grandma's death, Grandpa Copeland remained single and lived with their daughter Lettie (they only had the two children) where he created problems for Aunt Lettie's husband, Uncle Henry Gross, by taking an active role in disciplining their several children.

Pop used to say "When I married Nan, I got Hurt for life." My mother's family, the Hurts, came to West Virginia more recently than did the Copelands, waiting until after the Civil War. They came from Bedford County, Virginia. Though my mother and her siblings were born in West Virginia, her father, a native Virginian, was a Confederate soldier. The Hurts have been traced all

Illustration No. 3
My Maternal Grandparents

the way back to England, where they may ultimately have been Welsh. Certainly the name sounds Gaelic or Celtic rather than Anglo-Saxon.

One of their characteristics was that more than once first cousins married each other, the union of my maternal grandparents being one example of this practice, possibly due to the fact that eligible marital partners were somewhat scarce in those days. This phenomenon of intermarriage may help account for the psychological abnormalities in my family, though I am loath to lay such a burden on my ancestors!

My mother's parents were considerably older than Grandpa Copeland, and although they lived to an old age--death came to Grandpa Hurt at ninety and to Grandma at eighty-four--I hardly knew them. I remember fairly well how they looked in their advanced years but can recall little more about them. Grandma's maiden name was Field. Grandpa Hurt had married and had a son before his first wife died. Of course the son was a half-brother of my mother and her siblings, of whom there were several. Uncle Jube was the unstable one, suffering from what would be diagnosed today as manic depression. As he grew older, he became more and more withdrawn and dependent upon my parents until they were no longer able to care for him physically.

At this time, my older brother, Lowell, and I felt that we had to take responsibility to get him in a county home for the poor. We took him to the institution for a visit, and he agreed to move there. Soon after the move he died, and I have always felt somewhat guilty for my part in that tragic episode.

My parents were "Poppy" and "Mommy" to us children and "Pop" and "Mom" as we grew older. There were seven of us siblings who lived to adulthood, four girls and three boys, in that order. The oldest was Bertha Ellen, born in 1904. Daisy Dell was born two years later, in 1906, and Vernice Delora after two more years, in 1908. Rita Faye came along in 1911, Lowell Ellis in 1914, Edwin Luther in 1916, and Robert Warren in 1920. Warren, the youngest of the children, died in 1968, and Faye, the youngest girl, died in 1986. Two children died in infancy before I came upon the scene: Daisy's unnamed twin and a little boy who entered the family roster between Vernice and Faye. So I grew up with four older sisters, one older brother and one younger brother.

Pop was not a large man although he was of large stock.

He used to tell us that when he was nineteen he weighed 95 pounds. His height was little more than five feet, ten inches, and he usually weighed about 140 to 150. There was family speculation that he was small because of the well intended but inadequate care he had when a baby. Being left as a tiny infant without a mother, he was raised by an aunt (Aunt "Sissy," Octavia Copeland Simpson) who had to care for him while she was still young and unmarried. If Pop's infant care affected his size, it must not have diminished his strength. As an adult, he was muscular, exceedingly agile and unusually powerful for his size: even his sons, all three of whom were more than six feet in height, large, and strong, were amazed at his physical prowess.

Pop had almost no formal schooling, but he read avidly and was quite smart. Although his work was rough and ready, mostly in the coal mining and lumber industries, he became a good bookkeeper and he loved to keep accounts, whether for himself or for others. He was a hard worker and found laziness very difficult to tolerate. He had a good sense of humor and was a great raconteur. Pop seemed to have an inexhaustible store of interesting and often funny narratives, many of them about his own childhood and in not a few of which he was the hero. I sat enthralled with his stories, especially when we had company, even though I had heard them many times.

Pop was known for his hot temper, his fearlessness, and readiness to fight. My sister Vernice relates that Pop often became angry and walked off his job with Flynn Lumber Company, only to think better of it and be welcomed back to his work because he was very industrious and skillful. But these episodes were before I knew him. I noticed that he was well liked by his fellow workmen and unusually patient with them. However, I have known him to have a fit of anger, toward a person, an animal, or a situation, and then seem to be depressed for two or three days, as if remorseful for having lost control.

On one occasion while we lived at Hookersville, Pop had a famous fight with a fellow by the name of Shell Spinks, a large, rawboned man, about six feet tall and weighing more than two hundred pounds. The occasion of the altercation was an election at our polling place, which was the public school house across the highway from our home and filling station. The location of the fight was just outside our door. Shell's family were famous for bootlegging and on this particular day he seems to have imbibed too freely in their illicit product. Since he was using profane language in front of women and children, Pop told him respectfully that if he wished to speak like that, he would have to vacate our premises.

This admonition seemed to enrage Shell, and he attacked Pop. One of Shell's younger stepbrothers tried to join in the fight, jumping Pop from behind, but Pop threw him off and knocked him down. Cecil Craig, a young and able neighbor, took care of the stepbrother, insisting that the fight be confined to the two combatants. Shell hit Pop in the face, knocking his glasses off and lacerating his upper nose where the glasses had rested. Pop then knocked Shell through the medium-sized window of our lunchroom, with Shell landing on the inside. Shell came out, procured a rock from somewhere and came at Pop with the rock in his hand. Neighbors then grabbed Pop before they restrained Shell. Infuriated at this injustice, Pop broke away from their grasp and rushed inside to get his revolver.

At that juncture, Don Jarrell, my brother-in-law, Daisy's husband, and my older brother, Lowell, still a teenager, arrived upon the scene and persuaded Pop to give up his gun. Their most convincing argument was that Pop was about to get himself a prison sentence which would take him away from a family which very much needed his presence and his work. Finally, and tearfully, Pop surrendered the gun. By that time, Shell had departed and there was peace once more. (For some reason, I was gone, though it is very doubtful whether I would or could have done anything even if I had been present. I have heard the story so many times that I almost know it by heart.)

Pop related that some time later, when he saw Shell Spinks on the street in Summersville, the county seat town, he told Shell that the next time he decided to fight somebody he should be sober. "Because," said Pop, "if you try to fight drunk, you're liable to get hurt." Shell responded in good humor, "Luther, I don't mind payin' for any damages I caused, but I'll be damned if I'll pay for that window you knocked me through!"

Pop was a fairly strict disciplinarian, though not entirely consistent. When he had time, Pop would play with us. I have fond memories of his going swimming or fishing with us children in the Muddlety Creek, and of his accompanying me, on huckleberry picking jaunts during the Depression, and sometimes on night hunting excursions. Of course, he had close associations with Lowell and me as his partners in the logging business. He had good relations with all of us children except his youngest, and his problems with Warren seem not to have developed until after Warren reached the teenage years. Most of all, he found it difficult to tolerate Warren's laziness and refusal to accept responsibility.

When Lowell and I were little fellows, maybe six and four, Pop took us with him to the coal mine on the farm of a grocer at Enon, where we lived at the time. Pop dug coal to pay off a grocery debt incurred while he was ill and off from work in the timber industry. In Nicholas County, although there were almost no professional coal mines, many farmers had small tunnel mines on their property from which they supplied coal for themselves. The vein of coal in this particular mine was quite shallow: Lowell and I could almost stand up straight--at least I could--but Pop would have to bend over from the waist down.

Light for the tunnel was provided by a carbide lamp attached to the miner's cap. In the top compartment of the lamp was water and in the bottom, fastened by screwing it on, was calcium carbide. The drip of the water into the carbide, regulated by an adjustment on the lamp, produced the acetylene gas that served as fuel for the light. Each compartment was about two inches in diameter and both together were about four inches, meaning the lamp was about four inches high. The lens was not more than three inches in width. On it was a flint that made the

Illustration No. 4

Miner's Cap   Carbide Lamp

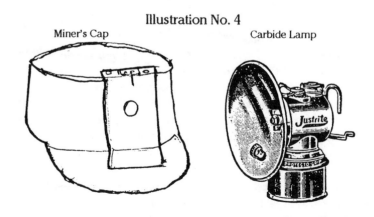

sparks for lighting the flame. These carbide lamps were super-ceded by the much safer electricity.

For several days Pop mined coal, which he could do quite professionally. With a two-bitted pick he would make a cut at the bottom of the face of the coal, digging with the pick as far as he could reach. Then, he would drill a hole with a hand auger (held against his shoulder) about three or four feet back into the face of the coal, near the top of the mine. Next, he would insert in the far end of the hole, a cartridge, about ten inches long, that he had made with special paper filled with black blasting powder. He would tamp the hole full of coal dust with a tool which was of two parts: a rod-like instrument which left a hole about the size of a man's little finger and a tamping rod which fit over the smaller implement. When he had completed tamping, he would have filled the large hole and left the tiny passageway open.

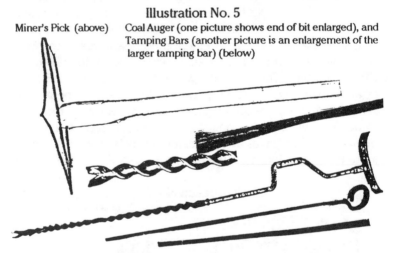

Illustration No. 5

Miner's Pick (above)   Coal Auger (one picture shows end of bit enlarged), and
Tamping Bars (another picture is an enlargement of the
larger tamping bar) (below)

Then, after ushering us boys to a safe hiding place, he would place a squib in the small hole and light it. Then Pop him-self would run to a place of safety. Then, when the fire he had lit burned back to an inflammatory substance on the squib*, the

---

*A squib was a small fuse, or detonator, preceding electrical devices which were safer, about five or six inches long and about the size of a pencil in diameter.

latter, like a tiny jet plane, would propel itself back through the channel left by the tamping bar to the powder cartridge, setting off the explosion that brought down the coal for Pop to load into the wooden car.

Lowell and I loved to "help" Pop push the car from the mine on its wooden tracks and dump the coal into the bin, which was called a "tipple." Underneath were drop gates from which wagons could be loaded. We also enjoyed sharing the lunch which Mom had prepared for Pop and breathing into our nostrils the unusual odor of the damp hollow, the mine, the coal, and the blasting powder, a pungent scent which I can yet recall.

Pop was deeply religious though not very demonstrative or vocal about his faith. One of my treasures is a marked Bible of Pop's, though the one into which he wrote many more notations was taken by Lowell, as the oldest son, upon Pop's death. For most of the time that I knew him, he was a loyal member of our local country churches of the Northern (later American) Baptist Convention. Pop was not given to rough language beyond an occasional "darn" or "shit." He was a very humble man, grateful for every blessing and accepting of various hardships. As he grew older, it was quite satisfying to observe him as he became calmer and more self-controlled.

In his late 50s, Pop had some health problems, which are something of a mystery to me. He developed some symptoms similar to diabetes, sores on his neck, giddiness, difficulty in healing a bad abrasion on a foot, and the like. About this time he wrecked one of our cars on the top of Little Elk mountain above Swiss, supposedly because of a spell of dizziness. Our family doctor, Flavia Brown, gave Pop a urine test for diabetes which established to the physician's satisfaction the presence of the disease. Then the doctor said that he thought the diabetes could be treated by diet, and he suggested that Pop emphasize vegetables, go light on meat, avoid most sweets, and eat no bread except whole wheat. Since, for some reason which I have never understood, Dr. Brown permitted Pop to eat as much honey as he wanted, after I left home and went to college, he began to keep bees.

Some years later, after Pop had entered his 80s, he took a urine analysis, which showed no diabetes at all. Long accustomed to his diet, he continued it. I have speculated that he did not have the diabetes to begin with (for instance, in the automobile accident I have mentioned, he may have suffered an injury to his pancreas which later healed). In any case the diet seemed to agree with him and to help prolong his life.

Pop's final illness with cancer was characterized by some humor and by much more pathos. Rather quickly, at the age of 85, he became quite diseased and had to enter the hospital in Beckley, West Virginia, near Crab Orchard, where he and Mom lived in their declining years. An exploratory operation revealed that he had an advanced cancer of the duct system connected to the liver and that there was nothing doctors could do except make his final days as free from pain as possible. Although Pop wished to die at home and not in the hospital, unfortunately he could not return home, because Mom was not physically able to care for him and we children were scattered and busy with our own work. We spent as much time with him as we could.

One day when I was with him and while he was quite in control of his faculties, he said something to me which I did not understand. I asked him to repeat it once and then again. At the second repetition, he became quite irritated and yelled out in a loud voice, "I said, git my britches, B-R-I-T-C-H-E-S!" Sadly, I had to explain to him that he could not go home.

The ravages of the cancer were quite rapid, including, among other things, jaundice, and the end was fast approaching when we children discovered, to our consternation, that Pop had prepared no will. We knew that he wished his very modest estate to go to Mom. So we hastily had a lawyer draw up a will to that end, and then it fell my unhappy lot to get Pop's signature on the document. Since he no longer had the strength to write, I had to hold his hand and direct it in as near a reproduction of his familiar signature as I could manage. I do not know whether he was fully conscious, and although I considered this an onerous duty, I am sure we did what he wanted done.

I am certain, also, that we followed his wishes when, several days later, we asked the doctors to end his intravenous feeding. His tissues were rapidly deteriorating, and wherever the needle had pierced his flesh previously, the fluids which had been injected into his veins were flowing out. As nearly as we could tell, he had been completely unconscious for some time.

Meantime, in the few hours which I was able to share with him, even when I was quite sure he was comatose, I spoke to him metaphorically of the new world he was about to enter. Among other things, I told him that in heaven there were vast tracts of virgin timber, clear, gurgling streams, singing birds, and friendly creatures of the forest. The Lord himself was in charge and everybody was treated with tenderness and fairness, both by the Lord and by each other.

Mom was quite different from Pop. She was taller, in fact she was unusually tall for a woman of her day, at least five feet eleven. When young she was willowy, but when I knew her she was somewhat overweight--increasingly so as she grew older. Even more than other members of her family, she was prematurely grey, and while she was still relatively young her hair turned a beautiful white. She was strong, very intelligent, outgoing and funny. She enjoyed a good laugh, even at her own expense, and her children loved to tease her.

Mom had a high school diploma, a somewhat rare accomplishment for women of her era, and was a school teacher in Marting, West Virginia, when she met Pop, who was a coal miner in the same town. They were married in Sanger in 1903, when Mom was 19 and Pop was 23. Like Pop, she was rather strict with us kids and could spank with her hand or wield a switch.

Mom had an insatiable interest in people and things. In 1969, when she was a widow and 85, she visited in my home in Raleigh, North Carolina, on her way to Valparaiso, Indiana, to live for a while with my sister, Faye. The night Mom stayed with us happened to be the time that the first human being touched foot on the moon. She stayed up for most of the night, awake and alert, to witness the historic event on television.

Mom was a good administrator, exceedingly frugal, as she needed to be in order for us to make it financially! When for a few years we operated a country store and filling station, Mom was mostly in charge. She became an excellent judge of animal furs, opossums, skunks, minks, muskrats, foxes, and raccoons, and of ginseng and other roots bought and sold in country stores. A representative of one of the large trading companies, came every month or so to our store to buy her stock of hides and roots. Very rarely did he differ with her judgment.

In my estimation, Mom's managerial skills were superior to Pop's, a fact which must have been a bit intimidating to him.

Since he was a strong individual, however, he seems not to have minded over much. The two were very fond of each other, and theirs was an excellent marriage.

We were poor, but there were always neighbors who had less than we, and Mom was the champion of the underdog--Pop too, but not as obviously so as Mom. As operator of our store, she became known as a kind of savior of the poor. When Negroes, as they were called then, came through our community and found it difficult or impossible to be waited upon in restaurants, Mom insisted that they should be served in our lunch room the same as anybody else.

In this way, and from both of my parents, I learned to respect all races, though in my growing up I never knew any African Americans. (It was not until some years later that I learned that the reason there were no African Americans in Nicholas County was that they were carefully excluded because of economics: white workers feared that the blacks would take their jobs.) Because of what I knew of my mother's attitude, it came as something of a surprise to me, therefore, to learn that Mom, in her final hospitalization in Titusville, Florida, had indicated fear of blacks who were on the hospital staff and seemed not to understand them.

Mom was a hard worker, whatever her chores might be, but she especially loved to work outdoors and was glad to leave the housework, as much as possible, to my sisters. One year, between eighth grade--which I had already repeated because of my young age--and high school, I stayed home and helped my mother who at that time was in charge of our store on Muddlety. I often had to do the washing, and I remember well heating water in a large kettle in our back yard, washing the clothes with a scrub board, wringing them out by hand, and hanging them on the line. (My wife is quite surprised to learn this, since I have shown no inclination to wash clothes since, even though the whole operation has become highly mechanized!)

After my father died, Mom sold the place they owned in Crab Orchard, near Beckley, West Virginia, and lived first with one daughter and then another, finally settling in with the oldest, Bertha, in Titusville, Florida, where she died at the age of 91. At that time I had been back in Japan for the second time less than a month and was very busy with school affairs. Even so, I have had some feeling of guilt that I did not return for Mom's funeral. When I came back from Japan four years later, I went to the lonely Appalachian hillside where she was laid to rest beside Pop, and finally told her goodbye. Mom was a fine Christian. She attended Sunday School and worship services whenever possible. It was from her and Pop, and especially from Mom, that I first learned about Christian faith. Both of my parents gave me encouragement and support in my Christian life and in my ministerial and missionary career.

When I last visited her in Titusville in the summer of 1975, my last visit with her before her death the next February, Mom told me of one of her experiences. "You will call it a dream," she said, "but I know it was real." What she related was the following --never mind that the "vision" involved youth and health which Pop had long left behind, even before his death, and which Mom also had outlived by many years, being old and a semi-invalid.

Her husband, Luther, came to see her, she told me, and she was overjoyed. He seemed just like always, and he asked if she had anything to eat. "Yes," she replied, "what would you like?" "Anything will be all right," he said, for, as Mom indicated, he was always easy to please. So she prepared him some bacon and eggs and they had a wonderful visit together. Then he announced that he must go. "No, no," Mom said, "please don't go." "I must," replied Pop, "for I have to help Warren with the babies." So he departed.

I thought it quite significant that in this remarkable dream which Mom related, her husband and their youngest son, both of whom had preceded Mom in death, were now caring for the infants whom Mom had lost long ago but whose memory remained vivid with her, and the little grandson, Warren's oldest child, who had died many years previously, presumably of Sudden Infant Death Syndrome.

Bertha, the oldest of the children, was artistic and poetic in temperament, a bit dreamy and absent-minded. She was also argumentative in her youth and rather hard to get along with, though very sweet in disposition as she grew older. She married Cecil Bays, a sort of mechanic and jack of all trades. Like the rest of my family, she was a strong Republican while Cecil was a Democrat. They didn't get along very well, and eventually divorced, after having a baby girl, Louise. Though neither remarried and they tried to get together again, the marriage was quite incompatible and failed once more. Bertha taught in the public schools for a long career, first in West Virginia and then in Florida. She has written many poems and has published several, some of them very good.

After Bertha retired from teaching, she started painting and demonstrated considerable talent in this area before she developed bronchiectasis, a severe lung ailment, and had to give up painting because of the fumes from the paints. After overcoming this dread disease, she became vigorous again and wrote several poems in her old age. She moved with her daughter to a farm near Luverne, Alabama, where she died in February 2000 at the age of 95.

Daisy was my favorite sister when I was little. She was a school teacher also, accepting an assignment in Raleigh County, West Virginia, while still quite young. There she was the first of my sisters to marry, choosing as her life partner a young coal miner, Don Jarrell. Don was a good fellow, quite enterprising, and easygoing. He did not share Daisy's education and he was always irrationally jealous of her. Nevertheless, he was a kind and generous man and they had a strong and enduring marriage. They reared an unusually good family. Among other things, Don was a coal miner, deputy sheriff, and highway maintenance superintendent. He and Daisy bought two or three places on Coal River, ran or rented a store for a time, and in general did very well financially. Some years after retirement, Don died of cancer.

Meanwhile, except for a brief interlude at Birch River, Don and Daisy lived on the Coal River in Raleigh County, where Daisy bore six children and never missed a semester of teaching! Actually, in order to help Daisy out, we kept the third child, Betty, in our home for one year while Betty was a toddler who had a baby sister. I was a teenager at the time and had much of the care of Betty, who soon became a favorite of mine. Daisy is now 94 and lives in Florida with one of her daughters.

Vernice was the largest of my sisters--though all were pretty big for girls--very religious, highly responsible and sweet natured. She prided herself on being able to lift like a man (actually she was stronger than several men I knew!). She was the favorite of all the disadvantaged fellows of our neighborhood-- of whom there were several--partly because she insisted on being very kind to them. She married Farley Trimble, a dashing fellow a few years younger than she. He was handsome but generally irresponsible. Obviously, Farley was manic depressive, and he probably had other psychological aberrations, all of which together at least help to excuse his meanness. He grossly neglected his two sons, was untrue to Vernice, and finally left her for a younger woman. This rejection came after the many years of Vernice's unselfish service to him and almost did her in phys-ically.

Meanwhile, in addition to being a housewife and mother, Vernice taught in public schools a while, was editor of the Nicholas county newspaper, *The Nicholas Chronicle,* for a few years, later operated a Krispy Kreme Donut business, and otherwise busied herself. She was quite a gifted writer. Just before her 91st birthday she had a stroke which left her paralyzed on the left side and unable to speak. In late October of 2000, at the age of 92, Vernice died of a second stroke suffered in a nursing home in Valparaiso, Indiana, near her older son's home.

Faye was a cheerful sort, closer in age to us boys and more of a companion to us. One of the favorite stories of my family is about Faye putting her own life in severe jeopardy to rescue me from a fishing hole in the Peters Creek when I fell in. I was

Illustration No. 6
The Family, Including the Four Girls
(From Left: Daisy, Pop, Faye, Bertha, Mom, Vernice)

only a toddler at the time, and Faye was probably no more than 6. I have always been grateful to her, though I was too young to remember much about the episode.

Like my other sisters, Faye went to college for a while, aiming to be a public school teacher. However, she married Paul ("Buck") Hanna, a large, strong West Virginian who was bright, though he had no more than a high school education. They moved to upper Indiana because of his asthma, where he worked as an electrician, developed his own business, and did well financially. They had four children, the second of whom, George, was severely handicapped by cerebral palsy.

Maybe because of George, Faye lost much of her carefree disposition. For several years, she sought cures for George, finally turning more seriously than before to religion and becoming charismatic and almost fanatical. In 1986, both Paul and Faye died in their 70s, within about a month of each other, he of a massive heart attack and she of cancer.

Lowell was the oldest of the boys who survived infancy, and perhaps because of his place in the family he was given much responsibility at an early age. When he was no more than 10, he took our sister Bertha to her teaching post in Marting by horse, an overnight trip, and he returned, after a harrowing flood, riding one horse and leading the other. He always bore these added responsibilities well, had excellent reflexes and a fair amount of courage. He was quite large and in his early years developed some obesity. So he had the nickname, "Fatty," and at the age of fifteen weighed two hundred and fifteen.

He was always agile, however, and did well at football. In fact, he could have had an athletic scholarship at King College, Bristol, Virginia, but for the fact that he broke his foot in spring tryouts. After some early work in the logging industry, Lowell became involved in the strip-mining of coal and before long a superintendent of strip-mining operations.

Meantime, Lowell married Hilda O'Dell, a fine and capable young woman, and they had two boys. Hilda died in 1979, after they had been married for more than 39 years. After a few years Lowell married Ruth Wilson Chafin, a widow. Though Ruth is quite different from Hilda, she, too, is a good woman and has cared for Lowell devotedly. He was fortunate in both marriages.

Lowell always had a way with children, probably in part because he was fond of them. Our children, when he visited us and they were little, always asked him to remove his shoe and show them where the big toe had been excised by a log train. He seemed to have no embarrassment whatever in complying.

Illustration No. 7
More of the Copeland Family
(left to right, Lowell, c.4, Faye, c.6, and me, c.2)

In his later years, in spite of the fact that Lowell was plagued by ill health, he always maintained a positive attitude. In September of 2000 he died on the way to the emergency room of the hospital near his home in Abingdon, Virginia, presumably of a heart attack. At the time of his death, Lowell was 86 and had been married to Ruth for more than eighteen years.

Warren was the youngest of the family, quite cute as a little boy, spoiled, and lazy. He had a fine sense of humor and would go to most any length to escape doing chores. On one occasion, Warren finally was persuaded to fetch a bucket of water from our well at the Muddlety house. Having counted the steps to the pump, he proceeded to do the chore with his eyes closed. The special porch where the pump was located had no railing around it, and it was rather high, about seven feet as I recall. Unfortunately, Warren had miscounted the paces required, and so he walked off the porch! In spite of the height of his fall, he escaped with no serious consequences except a severe case of embarrassment mingled with anger.

Illustration No. 8
The Boys of the Copeland Family
(Left to right: me, Warren , and Lowell)

Warren repeated his senior year of high school, just to prove to everyone concerned that he could make good grades. Since militarism was already in the air by that time, which was 1940, he joined the Army and stayed until the War was over. After returning, he married and eventually got a job as a security guard at Cape Canaveral near Titusville, Florida, where he lived.

Warren was big and strong, like Lowell, reaching a stature of six feet, four inches, and weighing considerably more than 200 pounds, but he seemed from an early age to have had some physical problems. After his marriage, doctors sometimes irritated him by finding no cause for his various complaints. Eventually, he died, in 1968, while still young at 47 years, of what was said to be the clogging of his arteries with cholesterol. Some of us think that he was subjected to radiation in New Mexico while in the U. S. Army following World War Two.

Warren's wife was Louvern McClung of Nicholas County and they had three lovely daughters, all of them quite artistic and attractive. However, the family has been beset with tragedy; for example, Warren's widow, Louvern, since her early seventies has been suffering from dementia and is in a nursing home.

The year 2000 was not a good year for the Copelands. We started the year with five of us siblings still living, and ended it with only two of us remaining, Daisy, next to the oldest, and I, next to the youngest. Bertha, Lowell, and Vernice all died in 2000.

Illustration No. 9
The Copeland Siblings at the Family Reunion in June, 1998
(front: Daisy, 92, Vernice, 90, Bertha, 94; back: Lowell, 84, and me, 82)

Chapter Two
LIVING AND WORKING

Drennen, where I was born and like the other places where I lived in my upbringing, was little more than a post office. The usual pattern for these little country sites was to have a post office, general store, and--when they came into being--a filling station, often in the same building! Drennen was named for a family of Drennens, but Biblical names were common in the region. Nearby were Enon, Zela, Gilboa, and Salem, usually with a little country Baptist church bearing a corresponding name. Like their Scriptural counterparts, in the vicinity of Enon and Salem there was "much water,"at least enough for Baptists to immerse, but unlike the Biblical situation (John 3:23), the water was not the Jordan River but the Peters Creek, a tributary of the Gauley River. (Was Peters Creek named for the famous apostle? or for a Peters family?) Across the Gauley River from the county seat town of Summersville, was Mount Nebo, in the Wilderness District, and beyond was the Promised Land; near Mount Nebo was the Gilgal Methodist Church, which I often attended. All of these names of places or churches, beyond the Gauley, were of Biblical origin.

I had plenty of religious influences upon me, but I am not sure whether these Biblical appellations (some of them rather obscure) had any part in this process. In any case, they certainly had ample opportunity, for we lived in or close to the places or churches bearing this Biblical nomenclature during my growing up. Before I can remember, we had moved twice, first to the Jim Drennen house in Drennen and then to the McCutcheon house in Zela. When I was about three years of age we moved to the Pettigrew place in Enon and about six years later to Muddlety-- well, the name of the post office was Hookersville, but the community was better known as Muddlety from the name of the creek which flowed nearby.

At the age of 11, I was baptized in the Muddlety Creek and thus became a member of Beulah Baptist Church. Other than the name of this church, I am unable to find any Scriptural connection to Muddlety and certainly not to Hookersville! After I finished high school, we moved to Mount Nebo where we were living when I went away to college at the age of 24. All these places of my birth and upbringing were in Nicholas County.

I was born in a mobile home. Of course, you're knowingly shaking your head, saying "He's trying to pull my leg. They didn't *have* mobile homes in 1916!" Well, we didn't have the modern kind. What we had were known as "shanty cars," little houses built for the employees of big lumber companies, and it was in one of those that I first saw the light of day.

The lumber operations constituted a big business indeed. The large companies had mills with band saws that could cut very much more lumber than the smaller circle saws that were generally portable. For their logging operations, the big band mills built their own railroads into the woods, often into huge tracts of virgin timber. In 1911, five years before I was born, West Virginia led the nation with about 3,000 miles of logging railroad.

Illustration No. 10
"Shanty Cars": Ready to Be Unloaded and Set Up for the Crew

Their shanty cars were portable; they could be moved wherever the lumber company wanted to locate their crew. A little shanty was about the size of a box car and could be lifted on or off a log car (which had a skeleton bed) by a crane-like log loader by simply placing a cable around the middle of the little house. Obviously, the roof of the shanty could project but little or the cable would damage it, so one semiliterate citizen of Nicholas County remarked that "the only thing wrong with the shanty cars is that they don't have enough objection to them."

These little structures were simple but sturdy. Like most country or mountain homes in those days, they had no running water and no inside toilets. Therefore, wherever we lived we had to have a spring or well for our water, and an outside toilet, usually a two-holer which my dad would construct, for other urgent business. Some of us children referred to our outhouse as "Pop's Summer Resort," because of his lengthy visits there; we accused him of perusing the Sears Roebuck catalog or the pulp magazines we used for toilet paper. He responded indignantly, and probably truthfully, that the reason he lingered was his "piles" (hemorrhoids).

In fact, until I went away to college in 1940, we never lived in a house with running water; and we only had electricity, that is, a Delco home electric system of our own, for part of the time we were in the house that we built on Muddlety (for the sake of the ice cream and soda pop that we sold in our lunchroom). In the winter time, we bathed once per week in a round washtub in the kitchen where the cook stove heated the place. In the summer, we could bathe a bit more often by using a nearby swimming hole. In those days living conditions were rather primitive, at least in rural areas in our part of the world.

Usually, in addition to shanty cars for family living, a lumber company would have one or more log camps where lumberjacks who were single or did not find it convenient to live at home with their families could board in shanty cars or other temporary buildings with special provisions for them to sleep in bunks. In these camps, one building was arranged for cooking and eating. The cook was usually of the masculine gender, with however many assistants he required, and the food was nourishing, tasty, and abundant, for lumberjacks were noted for their ravenous appetites.

Our last shanty car residence was at Hookersville, during which time, with a hint of economic betterment, my folks were able to buy a small piece of land. On this property we built a house out of rough oak lumber. The jack leg carpenter whom we employed was a fine man but almost illiterate. He had a proclivity for making ludicrous mistakes in his exaggerated attempts to speak properly. For instance, his Sunday School lessons--and he was a Sunday School teacher at the Beulah Baptist Church--were "lessings." He never got our name straight: he always called us "Copenders." One of our favorite quotations from him was "As I was caming across the mounting to Mr. Copender's, I met a game rewarder."

After we built the house, Tom O'Toole (a real character, but a fictitious name), the owner of the property where our former shanty cars were located, came to our new location to claim his "screen doors." Pop firmly believed that he owned the screen doors since he had bought them with his own hard-earned money and installed them on the shanty cars. So he had removed them and attached them appropriately to our new house. Tom made his first trip while Pop was away, and he accosted Mom and threatened her about the screen doors, whereupon she advised him to come back when Pop was at home, which he did.

Now Tom, though not much taller than Pop, was stocky of build and weighed something more than two hundred pounds. He was a hard-drinking Irishman, florid of face, and with a bit of a belly produced no doubt by his ample consumption of rotgut whiskey. Unscrupulous and overbearing, he had a reputation as the neighborhood bully.

When he appeared on our property and mentioned the screen doors, Pop lost his temper, grabbed a short piece of two-by-four, accused Tom of trying to intimidate Mom, verified his own claim to ownership of the screen doors, and dared Tom to bring his gun out of his pants pocket. Tom pulled his hand out empty, held both his hands over his head, and started backing away, all the while apologizing to Pop profusely. Pop ordered him off our property and told him never to set foot on it again. All of this took only a few seconds, but as a boy I savored the scene as I watched with rapt attention.

The U. S. highway went through our property, leaving our house with its back to the new road; so we moved the building down a rather high bank and across the highway. For this purpose we used a team of horses and an arrangement with a large block and tackle somewhat like a cane mill, by which the horses, walking in a circular motion, pulled the house. In a large room inside the house we had a country store, usually operated by my mother, and, after the move, we added smaller quarters for a lunchroom, staffed by my older sisters. Outside we constructed a small building for a grist mill which I ran on Saturdays, and a garage for our car. In addition, we put in gas tanks for a filling station, in the running of which all of us shared, especially the children.

At first I operated the grist mill with a stationary one-cylinder engine which would "put put," then pause, and then "put put" again, but when this exotic antique soon played out Pop, Lowell, and I replaced it with the motor of an old Star automobile (which, if we had kept, no doubt would have been a valuable antique by now). On Saturdays I ground corn for farmers who lived in the vicinity. I had a toll box and dipped out grain for each bushel I ground. Evidently the grinding stones, which I sharpened occasionally, did very good work, for people complimented me on the meal our mill produced. Once in a while I ground buckwheat and Mom made pancakes out of the flour which I made from the buckwheat toll, mixing it with corn meal. Ummm, those fritters were delicious!

When I was about 20, and we weren't quite so pinched by poverty, we sold the Muddlety property and bought a small farm at Mount Nebo. After a few years, while I was in college, my parents disposed of this property and purchased two other farms there in succession. In their old age, they bought a little place in Crab Orchard, West Virginia, where my sister Vernice and her family lived at the time, and where for the first time they had running water. When my father died there of cancer in March 1966, just short of 86, he had raised a garden the previous summer.

As you may have gathered, before we bought the Muddlety place, and when we weren't living in shanty cars, we were renting small farms. This was in order that my mother and the children could raise some crops and have some farm animals for drayage, milk, and meat. We usually had a horse, at least one cow, some hogs, and a number of chickens. So I learned to milk a cow and to churn butter.

You see, my father was engaged in "public works," labor which included most anything which was done by companies. For several years he had worked in the coal mines, but by the time I came along he had become involved in the lumber industry. He worked for the Flynn Lumber Company at Swiss, then for a subcontractor of the Birch Valley Lumber Company in Tioga, and finally as the manager of a small contracting firm in which his partners were Lowell and I.

When he worked for the timber industry, sometimes Pop was a log scaler, measuring logs with a rule to see how many board feet they would produce; or he was a timber cruiser, which, as I have explained, involved walking over some uncut timber to estimate how many board feet the tract would yield when cut.

Usually, however, he worked on a log train, in the various roles of fireman, engineer, brakeman, and tongs hooker. The last

Illustration No. 11
Log Cars and Loader
(Pop Is Standing on the Log Car with His Rule in His Hands)

of these involved throwing the heavy tongs attached to the cable of the log loader into a log, balancing the log's weight as much as possible by the location of the tongs in order that the log might be horizontal as it was lifted. In this way the operator of the log loader might more easily and efficiently place the logs on the log cars. Another workman was needed to unhook the tongs with a peavey (about which more later), another task sometimes performed by my dad.

The log loader, a crane-like machine fired by coal, ran on

steel rails--its own railroad--on top of the log cars, which were skeleton cars with large cross timbers about three feet apart. Thus the loader could begin by loading the first car behind the loco-motive and then backing up until it had loaded all the cars except the last one on which it could rest, travel, or wait for the next job. Or the order could be reversed for convenience.

The log trains were pulled by Shay or Climax locomotives, both fairly well adapted to the steep and crooked mountain railroads . These were powerful steam engines, usually fired by coal, with direct drive to each wheel for an even flow of power.

To see one of these locomotives in operation was an awesome experience for a boy, and to be permitted to ride in one of their cabs was a thrill beyond words. After all these years I can still hear the chugs and hisses of the engines, the clanging of their bells, and the piercing screams of their whistles, see the black smoke billowing from their smokestacks and the steam rising from their overflow pipes, and smell the coal smoke and the greasy odors of the oil and cotton waste used in the train's wheels to prevent "hot boxes," or overheating of the hub of the wheel.

Illustration No. 12
A Log Locomotive
(Uncle Henry Gross, The Engineer, in the Center, Foreground)

Eventually, I was to get considerably involved in the logging business myself. When I finished high school in 1933, my first employment was as a member of a crew of men building and maintaining railroad for the Birch Valley Lumber Company. Although the company itself was located several miles distant in Tioga, West Virginia, my work was in the general vicinity of my home on the Muddlety. By the time I started working I was about 18 and was approaching my adult height of 6 feet and 3 inches. I had no discernible body fat and weighed about 180 pounds. Already, with encouragement from my family, I was beginning to pride myself on my physical strength.

The steel rails were heavy, of course, and the wooden crossties were not light. An instrument which we used for carrying the rails was metal rail tongs. Two men would lift with one pair of tongs, one on either side of the rail. A minimum of four men, usually six or eight, would carry one steel rail.

Illustration No. 13
Railroad Tongs (about 18" on each side)

A certain member of our crew belonged to a bootlegging family, of whom there were several in Nicholas County in those days. Like others of his family, this employee not only made whiskey but also drank his own product, especially on weekends when he engaged in various forms of dissolute behavior. Since I was known as a Christian and a "clean liver," I was not surprised to hear my fellow worker exhorting our colleagues: "On Monday mornin', don't pair up on the tongs with Copeland. There's nuthin' to him but the runnin' gears." I have often used this Appalachian expression myself, to refer to someone who was slender and unimpeded by excess fat.

Sad to say, the effects of the Great Depression were hanging over us like a storm cloud, and when, with unwise timing, the crew organized a union and called a strike, the Birch Valley Lumber Company simply shut down for the duration of the Depression, as their manager had said they would do, leaving all of the crew unemployed. I had no success getting a job at other places, including the Ely/Thomas Lumber Company which was located near our home and which was paying one dollar a day. So I spent my summers digging ginseng and other roots and picking blackberries and huckleberries, and my winters trapping and hunting. I have often remarked that my family didn't notice the Depression much because we were already poor and the Depression didn't add all that much to our poverty.

Gradually, the economic situation eased a bit, and my father and my older brother, Lowell, began to do some logging on their own. At the age of 19 or so I joined them, and we formed a small logging contract firm called "L. L. Copeland and Sons."

It was while we were living on Muddlety that we began this company, and shortly thereafter we moved to Mount Nebo. Our equipment included a team of horses, a crawl tractor, two log trucks, and various smaller items. For all this equipment we contracted huge debts. We usually employed at least one team of timber cutters, a tractor operator, a teamster, another man to "jim" behind the tractor or horses--that is, drive grabs and such-- and sometimes one or two road builders, though most of us helped build the roads, with the exception of the timber cutters who often were paid by "piece work," that is, by the number of board feet they cut.

Illustration No.14
Some Logging Tools

Grab
(the bar was about 7" long
and the bit about 5")

Grab Hammer
(the handle was about 36" long)

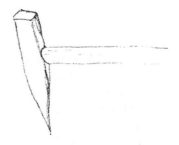

More Logging Tools

Header Grabs
(one grab to be driven into each side of
head log of the trail; ring to be attached to
the rigging of team of horses or tractor)

Coupler Grabs
(Center chain link is swivel;
one grab driven into rear
of front log, the other into
front of rear log,
to make up trail)

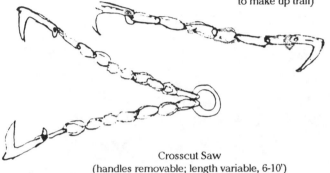

Crosscut Saw
(handles removable; length variable, 6-10')

Logging Wedge
(to be driven into the kerf behind
the saw to keep it from binding)

Double Bitted Axe
(handle of axe is about 36" long)

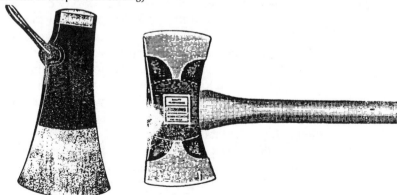

Illustration No. 15
Men Logging Up a Tree
(If you look carefully, you will see on the log, wedges and hammer
and double bitted axe.)

Lowell and I drove the trucks, which were moderately long wheelbase, no trailers, usually 2 to 3 ton Internationals, which, in spite of our dad's protests, we consistently overloaded. Sometimes Lowell also ran the crawl tractor, as he was quite good at operating machinery.

We constructed "skidways" from which to load the logs onto the trucks. A skidway was a pier-like contraption made of logs approximating the level of the truck bed, with two straight, long, and strong timbers, called "skids," upon which the logs would be rolled after they were pulled into position behind the skidway. The construction of the skidway took advantage of the gentler slope of the mountain in the valley before it became too steep. In order to facilitate loading the second tier of logs on the truck, often we built a kind of two-layer skidway, by using two more timbers set back a few feet from those built at truck level.

After loading the first layer of logs on the truck, we would use two "spiked skids," one on either of the skidway timbers, to load succeeding tiers. A spiked skid was a sturdy timber, commonly made of oak, with sharp metal spikes, about the size of a pencil in diameter, protruding upward about 1 ½" to keep the logs from spinning as they were rolled up the skids. Other metal spikes faced downward on plates on the end of the skid to keep the latter anchored in place on the tier of logs already loaded on the trucks and on the skidway timber.

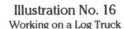
Illustration No. 16
Working on a Log Truck

Illustration No. 17
Skidway with Spiked Skid

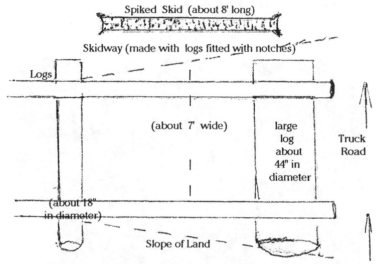

Spiked Skid (about 8' long)

Skidway (made with logs fitted with notches)

Logs

(about 7' wide)

large
log
about
44" in
diameter

Truck
Road

(about 18"
in diameter)

Slope of Land

All lumberjacks had to be proficient in the use of a peavey, but this was especially true of those loading logs onto trucks. The peavey was a straight instrument designed for rolling logs. It was usually from four to six feet in length and consisted of a round handle, usually hickory, sloping upward to smaller size and a nob on the end for easy gripping. On the bottom of the handle a metal sleeve was attached with a movable hook on it. The lower end of this metal hook had to be sloped just right and filed to acute sharpness so that it would bite into the log to be rolled. A metal spike at the end of the peavey was inserted into the wooden handle and the sleeve.

Illustration No. 18
Peavey (top) and Cant Hook (bottom)

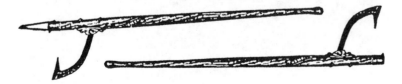

This spike was very useful in sticking into the skidway, or the ground, and cutting the rolling log to regulate its direction. The spike distinguished the peavey from the much less useful cant hook, which was similar to the peavey but without a spike--though the two terms were sometimes mistakenly used interchangeably.

All of us Copelands were pretty skillful with a peavey: Lowell and I, our dad, and Donald Copeland, a distant cousin who worked for us. Donald was like a brother to Lowell and me. I am still saddened to remember that he was killed in the Battle of the Bulge in World War Two. Lowell was a big fellow, still slightly inclined to obesity, six feet four in height and weighing about 220 pounds. After I attained my full growth, I was pretty big but not that big. Pop was relatively small, as I have indicated, about two inches short of six feet and weighing about 150 or so, but very powerful for his size and quite agile. Donald was not even as big as Pop, but like Pop he was quick on his feet. Men who worked for us also were adept with their peaveys

Illustration No. 19
Donald Copeland (as a G.I.)

It is remarkable what skill a good peavey man could develop, in rolling, determining the direction of, or stopping logs. Or what strength he could manifest in rolling a log, setting the peavey hook in the log and lifting with the peavey handle in his hands and then shifting the handle to his shoulder. Lowell and I often boasted about how big a log we could roll, since either of us could hold as much of a load as both of us together could lift in rolling a log with our peaveys. At one time or another I did most of the tasks of the timber woods at least briefly, but I never developed much facility in the use of an axe or saw.

I prided myself, however, both in my skill in using a peavey and in my considerable physical strength. I could break most any peavey handle, and sometimes did, including a favorite of Lowell's--much to his disgust--for pure macho enjoyment. Since both my strength and my skill are now largely gone, I realize that both were gifts from God with which I had very little to do, and that I should have been much more humble about them.

On at least one occasion, however, I made a dismal failure with my peavey, and the mishap which I caused is graphically etched on my memory. Lowell and I were behind a log, easing it down the slightly inclined skidway, preparatory to rolling it up the spiked skids and onto the load of logs on the truck. It was a fairly large oak log which was traveling rather fast, but not too large or too fast for both of us to stop it if we threw our peaveys into it backwards at the same time.

When Lowell yelled "Catch!" which was the signal for me to catch the log with my peavey together with him, for some reason which to this day I do not understand, I did not even try to catch the log. Unfortunately, Lowell did, and the log threw him over it and through the air, with his peavey flying--I don't remember where. His hand came down on one of the spiked skids and a steel spike grated upon the bone as it tore his palm open. I can still hear the sickening sound of that spike ripping into his hand and feel the hot shame for my inexplicable failure.

In at least one situation we were involved in "ball-hooting" because of the extremely steep terrain. This method, also known as "bruting," involved cutting a tree straight down the mountain. Usually, the top would break out and the tree would run off the steep incline like a blacksnake. In this case, one oak tree had refused to run and our timber cutters, as was usual in bruting, had logged it up. A log was temporarily caught behind a stump, so we had peeled it in preparation for sending it down the mountain. One of our employees, Bill Snyder, was down below the log doing something, I don't recall what, when the log suddenly slipped, glided from behind the restraining stump and rolled with lightning speed down the mountainside before turning endwise to run all the faster.

When the log lurched out from behind the stump, Bill started to jump out of the way, only to slip on a piece of slick bark. He fell downhill on his belly and the log rolled completely over him from his feet to his head. We thought Bill had been killed, but fortunately the ground was soft and Bill was small. We could see the print of his body in the pliable soil. Lowell and I ascertained that although Bill was still entirely conscious and aware, he was unable to walk. So one of us picked Bill up and the two of us took turns carrying him piggyback over the mountain to our camp. The backs of his legs became quite blue from the bruising and he couldn't walk for a while, but no bones were broken and Bill was back at work within a few days.

Often, in reflecting upon our logging days, I have felt considerable remorse for our recklessness and the arrogance which accompanied it. Donald, who sometimes rode with Lowell, shared our conceit. I could claim that the two of them influenced me and that they were worse than I, but that would not excuse my own prideful attitude. One of our habits was to lift a hand in what appeared to be a wave at friendly country people and halfway through the wave divert the hand on a head scratching expedition. By that time the person we had met was returning our wave only to find, to his or her discomfiture and embarrassment, that the wave was not really a wave.

When we logged above the little town of Quinwood, we would let our loaded log trucks roll rapidly down a mountain toward Quinwood on an unpaved road. Sometimes when we would meet a car, the driver in terror would steer his car into the bank in order to give us plenty of room. Privately, we, especially Lowell and Donald, found this behavior very funny. During this same logging operation, most of the road we traveled was paved. Once we had passed the last sharp curve on a certain mountain, we would let our brakes off and shift the loaded truck to high gear. This meant that our speed would approximate 75 or 80 miles per hour. When we were reported to the Highway Patrol, a friend at a filling station tipped us off. For a while we drove circumspectly until the danger passed.

In the meantime, some two or three dump trucks were hauling limestone chips on that same paved highway for a road building job. These trucks, like those driven by the Copeland boys, habitually were driven excessively fast. One of them, a driver whom we knew, came to the foot of the mountain I have mentioned at a very high rate of speed, only to find that at the top of a rise a slower vehicle was in his way. Rather than to try and brake behind it, he attempted to pass this vehicle, illegally of course. In the process, the hapless driver met the patrolman who was out to catch the Copeland boys, and crowded the police car completely off the pavement onto the shoulder, that, fortunately for the patrolman, happened to be wide at that point. The lawman turned around, overhauled the miscreant and arrested him.

I think we were incredibly lucky. Earlier, when I was driving an older truck, empty at the time, I was passing a one room school at recess time. Fortunately, I was not driving fast, when a little boy, probably a first or second grader, suddenly darted toward the dirt road in front of the school. Before I could stop, and while the front disk wheels were still skidding, the little boy collided with the nearest front wheel of the truck and knocked himself out. Of course, I quickly got out of my truck and helped the teacher revive him. I remember that we poured a pan of water over his face. When he came to, the little fellow cried, the most welcome crying I have ever heard. We took him to his nearby home for recovery, and fortunately, he was relatively unhurt.

On another occasion, I was hauling a 50 gallon drum full of gasoline on an empty truck. The truck had only a skeleton bed for hauling logs, with a short space floored for carrying tools and log chains. The floor was in the narrow area between two of the heavy cross timbers, or bunks, on its ends, and between the two four-by-four wooden stringers on top of the channel irons of the chassis on its sides. It was here that I had placed the gasoline drum, not bothering fastening it because it fit snugly.

Since an empty log truck has a low center of gravity and

is almost impossible to turn over, we steered our unloaded vehicles around curves--of which there were many on West Virginia roads--at high speed. In this case, I negotiated a right hand curve at such a velocity that the gasoline drum was thrown off, crossed the other lane of the paved road and settled several yards distant in the woods below. I have often thought, with a sobering sense of shame and relief, what if another vehicle had been in the opposite lane when the full gasoline barrel rolled off?

On still another job, Lowell and I were moving our crawl tractor on an unpaved road to where we needed to use it. Having placed a flat bed on one of our log trucks, we had loaded the tractor onto the truck. To unload it near where we were to use it, we had to choose a location where we could back the truck up to a bank of the unpaved road to a place approximating the height of the truck bed. The only suitable site we could find was on the mountain road and sloping somewhat sharply to one side. Since it was winter time and snow was on the truck, it was hazardous to back the tractor off.

Lowell and I both examined the situation and decided that the tractor could be unloaded, especially if the motor was gunned so that it would back off rapidly. Lowell, of course, was the one to operate the tractor. He started the motor, warmed it up, put the tractor in reverse, revved the motor, and let the clutch pedal out. Immediately and rapidly the tractor started to slide off the truck. In an amazing feat of agility for a big man, Lowell put a hand on each side of the seat, threw his legs up, jumped, landed on his feet, and outran the tractor as it turned completely over onto its tracks and backed up against the bank of the road where it killed its idling motor. Our tractor was now safely unloaded with practically no damage, but I still get goose bumps when I remember my brother's close call.

Nor did I merely cooperate in getting Lowell into trouble. Once in a while I helped get him out of it. In the vicinity of one of our log camps was a mountain school, and we learned that on a certain night there was to be a pie social there.

Now pie socials were big in those days, with pies made by pretty girls auctioned off to the highest bidder, who would then have the privilege of eating the pie with the attractive young woman who allegedly had baked it. There were also cake walks in which couples who had bought tickets walked in a circle, with the couple nearest to a mark when time was officially called, winning the cake. Sometimes, in addition, there were ugly man's contests, in which a candidate's backers supported him by paying money for the privilege of voting for him. And there might be other such activities, all for the benefit of the school.

Most of the small crew boarding in our camp decided to attend the social in a nearby school. But there was one major problem: the Copeland boys, all three of us still single at that time, were not particularly welcome in that community, since there was fear that these outsiders would steal the affections of the local young ladies.

It turned out that I was a candidate for ugly man, along with a certain young fellow of the community (who some time after this event proved that he was a pretty mean hombre by killing a man). This guy sent word to me that "If Copeland wins, he'll have to eat my fist." Not knowing his true nature, I interpreted his remark as an attempt at humor. Also I figured that he wasn't too dangerous if he sent his threats by someone else. So I responded in kind: "Tell him that I'd eat all of him if he wasn't so dirty." I don't remember who won the contest, though I thought I was pretty well qualified.

While I was still in the school house, I learned that some of the locals, including my erstwhile rival, were threatening Lowell and Donald outside. I made my way out, along with our tractor operator, Bill Snyder, who was not only small but also wiry and very tough. All four of us were able to get our backs against the building, and evidently the community young fellows were not up to challenging these ostensibly dangerous lumberjacks under the disadvantage of having to launch a frontal attack. The peril soon passed and we returned safely to our camp.

One night, during our stay in this same camp, the weather was mild and, as was our custom, we were sitting outdoors by a campfire exchanging stories, some of which were quite inane and a few of which were funny. On this particular night, our three timber cutters, a father and his two sons, spent some time enlightening us about a certain situation in their community. None of the three had much education. The older son was a rather silent type, while the younger one was quite voluble. The father, who had a good sense of humor, was inclined to be meditative and philosophical.

The three of them told us about a certain villain who lived in their neighborhood, evidently quite a rascal, though none of us knew either the bad man or the community being discussed. After they had talked about this wicked man's evil doings for some time, the younger son, who had carried the burden of the conversation, bravely announced that if that so-and-so did such-and-such to him, "I would tell him to kiss my ass!" Whereupon the father looked long into the darkness and spat amber juice from his dip of Copenhagen snuff into the camp fire. All eyes were upon him, especially those of his younger son, as we waited for some response, some gem of wisdom, to proceed from his mouth. Finally, he broke the silence. "He wuddn't do it," he allowed.

Chapter Three
CHURCH AND SCHOOL

From infancy, I learned the simple stories of the Bible from my parents and from the oldest three of my sisters, who were 12, 10, and 8 years older than I. Soon, also, I was aware of Jesus and his saving work. After we moved to Enon when I was about 3, Sunday School and monthly worship at the Enon Baptist Church supplemented this Biblical knowledge.

Religiously, I was thought to be precocious. Like primal peoples, unconsciously I even created a myth. My dad smoked a pipe, often filling a room with tobacco smoke. One day when I was out in the yard, I noticed some bluish-white, billowy clouds in the sky. "Gee whiz," said I, "look at the smoke! Jesus and God and Peter must all be smoking!" Never mind the scrambled Trinitarian theology and the sanction upon tobacco. That was a rather natural myth for a boy in my circumstances.

When, as was the practice in those days, (though I certainly would not condone it now, because of the different situation in our pluralistic society) the public school dismissed for the morning services of the "protracted meeting" at the Enon Baptist Church, I attended. At the first gos-pel invitation I can remember, I responded, with tears running down my face, saying that I wanted to belong to Jesus. I was not more than 5, I suppose, since I started school at the age of 4. I wasn't smart enough to know what the pastor meant by the later invitation to "unite with the church." Accordingly, I did not present myself for church membership.

I do not recall whether my response to this invitation to Christian discipleship was in the morning or evening service, but I remember riding home on a horse behind my brother Lowell, probably the evening of that same day. This particular horse did not like to be passed by automobiles, which were mostly Model T Fords in those days, so he would set out in pursuit of a car when it went by. Another peculiarity of this unusual steed was his ability to return the favor of a rider who had kicked him. That is, he could kick the heel of the offending rider, at no matter what speed, and never miss a stride. Riding on this gelding--and trusting Lowell since I was afraid of horses myself--my heart was singing, because, at such an early age, I had found the friendship and pardon of Jesus. Today in my advanced years I still view this event as the most important of my entire life.

In those days I must have been strongly influenced by our pastor, S. E. Brown, for I developed a fondness for preaching. In fact, I cannot recall a time when I did not feel called to preach. I remember exhorting my siblings and the chickens in our yard. My specialty seems to have been funerals. If a chicken met an untimely demise (except a sacrificial death for a Sunday dinner), I preached the funeral. When the community villain expired, I conducted for him a fearsome funeral in which I consigned him to the nether regions.

It was not until after we moved to Hookersville that I joined the church, in this case, the Beulah Baptist Church. I was eleven, and our then pastor (Enon and Beulah were in the same "field" of four or five churches, of which the Summersville congregation, the town church, was central), Joseph E. Brown, usually called "Joe" or "J. E.," baptized me in our familiar swimming hole in the Muddlety Creek. I did not have the same feeling of exultation which had accompanied my earlier decision, possibly because I was already a Christian.

Although I have had to bring my faith up to date at various junctures in my long life, I still judge that earlier experience, when I was about five, to have been valid. And I think most every day not only that I wish to live up to the high pledge of my baptism, but also, with Martin Luther, to rest myself in God's promise to me in that experience.

Beulah Baptist Church was located near the Muddlety Creek. Closer to this stream was a Methodist Episcopal Church. Since both of these churches had white frame buildings which were similar, they were known as the "Twin Churches." There was the familiar old saw that when the Baptists were singing "Will there be any stars, any stars in my crown?" the Methodists were responding, "No, not one." Actually the two churches got along very well. Since neither had a full time ministry, some of us Baptists attended the Methodists' worship services and vice versa.

On a hill about half-a-mile distant was the Methodist Episcopal Church, South. The two Methodist congregations were heirs of the slavery controversy of the nineteenth century, of which the

Civil War had been a crucial episode. Although the Methodists of both churches had some truck with each other, and although the community was not nearly big enough for the two, they were not about to unite. Differences between them, not only religious but political, ran pretty deep. After I left West Virginia, the M. E. Church, South, burned to the ground, and the two finally united. Some local wag, I am told, called the fire an "act of God."

Joe Brown, the pastor who baptized me, was quite a character. He was about average size, athletic in build, and an avid hunter and fisherman. Although he was in early middle age when I first knew him, his abundant head of hair was white as a sheet of fine muslin. His bluish-grey eyes were especially piercing. His voice was a deep, mellifluous baritone, but soon after he launched into his sermon he would become so agitated that his voice would almost fade out. His sermons were much more distinguished for fervor in delivery than for theological or other kinds of profundity.

When I was a teenager, I would go hunting with Brother Brown sometimes. I remember that on one beautiful autumn day, we had gone hunting together but had separated until time to return to the car. In addition to two or three squirrels, I had killed three ruffed grouse ("pheasants" to us mountaineers) by surprising them on their drumming logs. As we returned home, Preacher Brown said, "Luther, please trade me a pheasant for two squirrels. I have killed more squirrels than the law allows." I readily acquiesced. This story illustrates the fact that the best of us Appalachian dwellers had little respect for the game laws.

Brother Brown often referred to me as his "preacher boy," a title which I came to accept with increasing ambivalence as I entered my teen years. I had begun to think that my sense of a vocation to preach was but a childhood fancy which needed to be outgrown. When I objected to the pastor that I felt one should have an awareness of a call to become a preacher, he responded that if I would but listen to what I had already heard, I would know that I was called.

After a few years, Brown left for another pastorate. He was succeeded by an older man who had absolutely no rapport with the young people in the various churches in his field. I remember that when a contingent of us young folk of the Beulah Baptist congregation gathered in someone's house to listen to the

Joe Louis-Jim Braddock boxing match by radio, the preacher rebuked us from the pulpit, for having gone "to hear two brutes pound one another, and one of them was a nigger." At this point in my life, I think the pastor was right to oppose boxing, but what about his blatant racism? I vaguely remember that this man's preaching, defended by some as Biblical, consisted mostly of Scriptural verses strung together by a narrow, fundamentalist mind set. When, after a year, the churches of the field decided to act upon whether to retain the pastor, in spite of my youth, I was a member of the pulpit committee of our church. Along with others, maybe all of the committee members, I voted not to continue him.

The brief and unhappy tenure of this incompatible pastor was succeeded by a much more satisfactory era. Our next pastor was Rufus B. Nelson, from near Greensboro, North Carolina, but having cast in his lot with Northern (American) Baptists instead of the Southern Convention. He was known as "R. B." Nelson (I don't know why the pastors of my youth went by their initials rather than by their names). Nelson was a rather large man, a little short of six feet in height, and somewhat stout. His hair was between blonde and brunette with a tendency toward redness, and his face was florid and his complexion in keeping with red hair.

Nelson's voice was a high tenor, and he spoke with a controlled enthusiasm. His sermons were well organized and prepared, and with pretty good exegesis and theological (modified Calvinist) content. He was a graduate of the old Baptist Bible Institute in New Orleans, later to become a seminary of the Southern Baptist Convention.

Pastor Nelson loved to fox hunt--not to kill the foxes but to listen to his dogs run them--and for this purpose he bred registered Walker hounds. He also had been a good butcher and meat cutter before he entered the ministry, and he sometimes helped farmers with their butchering as a kind of hobby.

After we moved to Mount Nebo, we became acquainted with a neighbor who was one of Nelson's friends, Alf Dooley, a doughty old mountaineer. Nelson and Alf sometimes hunted together, and Nelson helped Alf with butchering. Alf remarked that "When the Lord called Brother Nelson into the ministry, he spoiled a good butcher and made a hell of a poor preacher."

Actually Nelson was a good butcher *and* a good preacher,

and he had a crucial influence upon me. He stayed at the Summersville circuit several years and was my pastor when I decided to enter college to study for the ministry. I sought his counsel about college; however, since the only Baptist college in West Virginia, Alderson-Broaddus, was not accredited at the time (though it became accredited later and currently enjoys a good reputation), Nelson did not recommend that I go to that school. Rather, he suggested that I go to Mars Hill College, a junior college in North Carolina. He had not attended Mars Hill, but he had sent a son there, and he was high on Mars Hill. "Go there for two years," he told me, "and I don't care where you go after that."

One thing that Preacher Nelson said impressed me so greatly that I have not forgotten it after all these years. "When I die and come face to face with the Judge of all the earth," said Nelson, "I can say but one thing. In the words of William Cowper's hymn, I can only plead, 'Nothing in my hand I bring. Simply to thy Cross I cling.'"

I have taken Nelson's words to heart. He was a good man, a good pastor, a good Christian. But, I reflected, no matter how good I am, no matter how unblemished my theology, how earnest my zeal, how unselfish my service, and I can claim none of these, and no matter how many miles I have on my spiritual odometer--and I've even been an international missionary!--when I come to face my Judge who is all perfection, I certainly have nothing to offer which will merit my salvation. I too must say, "Nothing in my hand I bring. Simply to thy Cross I cling." I believe Nelson was correct. I think that Will Campbell had it right also when he said that the gospel is simply this: "We are all bastards and God loves us." I'll let you speak for yourself.

The renewal of my awareness of the call to the ministry came in something of a dramatic fashion. The early "call to preach," as we termed it in the mountains, tended to fade from my consciousness as I became a teenager. When I was in high school, I thought I wanted to be a chemical engineer--though at this point I have no earthly idea why. The resurgence of the conviction that I was to be a preacher was the result of a very serious truck accident. My younger brother, Warren, and I had gone 'coon hunting, with our two hounds, Bob and Joe, chained on the skeleton bed of the 1936 International log truck which Lowell usually drove, where we had a small floor for our tools.

We had followed the paved highway over across the Gauley River from where we still lived on Muddlety.

Having hunted all night and caught nothing, we had returned in the early morning hours to the truck for the trip home. The morning was frosty and chilly, and when we got the truck's heater operating, Warren immediately went to sleep. I must have done so soon after and shifted to the dream world of automatic pilot, for I have no memory of passing through the town of Summersville, where there was not only a reduced speed limit but also a very sharp curve to negotiate.

We were traveling up the Muddlety, about five miles north of Summersville and about two miles from home, when the wreck occurred, evidently with the truck traveling at a high rate of speed, of which it was quite capable since it had an overdrive gear. After the accident we discovered that the speedometer was stuck at about sixty, and the road up the Muddlety valley was pretty straight, so I must have been traveling quite fast. In any case, I woke as I realized that the truck was leaving the pavement and hitting the shoulder, and I saw what appeared to be a blurred telephone pole coming at me with unbelievable speed.

It was fairly easy to reconstruct what happened from that point. I tried to miss the pole and almost succeeded. The right front wheel hit the pole, and the truck grazed by it with a metal strip from the truck piercing its way through the pole. Then the first of the "bunks" protruding crosswise beyond the cab, heavy six-by-eight inch timbers which made up the skeleton truck body, hit the telephone pole and clipped it off about four feet above the ground. Next the dual rear wheels hit the stub of the pole and climbed it, causing the truck to turn over in the air. I remember a quiet, peaceful feeling while the truck was airborne. Then *Wham!* The truck landed on its top. Since there was nothing at all to protect it, the cab was crumpled back even with the instrument panel. All became quiet, this time for real.

Both doors were sprung open and somewhere beneath the mangled cab were Warren and I. We had both remained conscious and both were awake! First of all, I said, "Warren, are you all right?" He answered, "I think so. What about you?" I said "I'm okay. Can you get out?" He said "Sure," and proceeded to do so. Then he came around to my side of the truck and asked, "Can you get out?" "Yeah," I said, "if you'll take this seat off me." When he started to pull the seat out, I discovered that a spring in it had penetrated the flesh of my rear end, so I hastily said "Wait! Wait!" stopping him until I could wiggle enough to get the metal out of my flesh. Then at my signal he pulled out the cushion, taking the seat of my pants with it.

I expected to step out, only to discover that I could not do so. You see, characteristically, I drove with one hand at the top of the steering wheel, and with the truck inverted, the steering wheel was its lowest point. My hand was under it, and the wheel was imbedded in the soft ground of the meadow where we had landed. To make matters much worse, the gasoline tank, normally under the seat, was now above me and gasoline had drenched my clothes. A short in the windshield wiper--which even then was electric--was smoking and threatening fire.

As we used to say in the mountains (an impressive understatement), at that point things were only "tol'able." "I can't get out." I told Warren. "Get a peavey if you can find one and try to pry this wheel off my hand." Somehow in our wreck, he found a peavey, placed the spike of it under the wheel and lifted. All he could do was tighten the wheel on my hand.

By that time it was getting daylight, and neighbors had heard the noise of our wreck and were assembling. I heard someone ask, "Who's under there?" And the reply, "It's 'little Luther.'" I was rather humiliated, since I was quite a bit bigger than Pop, who presumably was 'big Luther,' but I didn't linger long on this grievance.

A certain Mrs. Johnson was one of the neighbors who had gathered, a big fat woman weighing about 250 pounds. Someone suggested that they get a piece of timber, actually one of the bunks that had split, put it through the spokes of the steering wheel, put a heel under it, and ask Mrs. Johnson to sit down on the timber. They did just that, and when Mrs. Johnson sat down, the wheel came up immediately and I stepped out free. (I have always been thankful that some people inclined to be obese don't manage to do anything about it!) Miraculously, the truck never did catch fire.

So the two of us were out, and the neighbors began to ask us how badly we were hurt, since, as more than one of them said, they couldn't see "how anybody could come out of there alive." The truth is, neither one of us was hurt to speak of. Warren, a teenage boy of about 16, began to notice that he had some liquid in one of his shoes. He discovered that it was blood from a superficial cut on his leg. When because of shock he began to shiver, some women put a blanket on him, thinking he was cold, and he was profoundly embarrassed. Like Warren, I also had no more than a scratch or two.

We insisted that we were not injured, but we were told, "Just wait till tomorrow, after the excitement is over. You'll discover that you can't walk." Tomorrow came, and we were almost entirely unhurt. There was safety glass from the windshield in the hole where my hand had been, but there was no abrasion on my hand nor were any bones broken. The hand was stiff for a while, but by the next day it was pretty well back to normal. Fortunately, we had landed in the soft soil of a meadow.

Some of you are wondering about the dogs. Well, they were not killed in the accident. Their leather collars were broken by the impact and both of them were thrown off the truck. After we got out of the wreck, we heard Joe running a rabbit--he was none the worse for his ordeal at all. Bob ran away in fear and perhaps pain, but he came back after a bit, dragging his hind legs. It appeared that he had broken his back. I hasten to say that Bob recovered most of his previous ability as a hunting dog.

Of course, the truck was out of commission for repairs. It had to be fitted with a new cab, some new springs for the right side and other assorted parts. The repair was quite expensive, but before long the truck was hauling logs quite normally.

I never knew what effect the wreck had upon Warren, but it influenced me quite decisively. At that very time, we had a revival beginning in our church, and the evening sermons gave me an opportunity to reflect seriously upon the meaning of my life. It was not that I was scared. I was accustomed to living rather dangerously, and even though this accident was quite dramatic, it was not all that different from the usual occurrences of my life. Nevertheless, I knew that I had come face to face with death. My life so very easily could have been extinguished. So I began to ask myself, "Luther, why were you spared? Why are you here? What is the meaning of your life? Are you always going to follow the logging business? What does *God* have in mind for you?"

All at once, my awareness of the call to preach, which, as I have already recounted, had been somewhat vivid in my childhood, came flooding back like an ocean tide, clearer and more convincing than ever. But there were obstacles. One was the fact that I shared a debt for logging equipment with Lowell and Pop. How could I get out from under this responsibility?

A deeper problem was the sense of my unworthiness. Although I was generally known as a good Christian, I thought that I knew rather well my weaknesses. Especially was I troubled since puberty by sexual desire, though I was heterosexual and had carefully avoided intercourse. In my rather strict upbringing, I assumed that although God might well forgive such a sin as lust, it certainly was unworthy of the Christian ministry. In these circumstances, it seemed wise to keep my newly discovered awareness of call to myself, and I did. I shared it only with a Methodist preacher, who had spent several years as a farmer before becoming a minister. I do not remember his counsel.

Some time after this wreck we moved to Mount Nebo, where there were a number of small, mostly Methodist, churches in reach even by walking, and only one Baptist church, the Fowler's Knob Baptist Church, which was all but dead. Some of the Methodist churches were quite lively, and I began to worship with the Methodists. The testimony meetings I had known in the Baptist churches of my growing up, the Enon and Beulah Baptist Churches particularly, were even more prominent and familiar in the Methodist churches. I often gave a word of exhortation or testimony, usually with deep emotion and with noticeable effect.

Later, while in college, I would say that during this period the log camps where I worked became a theological seminary. I gave my leisure time to Bible study. It seemed that I was lifted above the humdrum of daily life and focused upon my calling, though before long I had come down to hard reality.

In the usual situation in West Virginia, Methodists were more given to shouting than were Baptists. Indeed, this whole matter of charismatic expressions of the Christian life had been exacerbated for the Methodists by the annual visits of a woman evangelist. According to my memory, she taught a doctrine of holiness, or sinless perfection. As one result of her meetings, a Holiness Tabernacle had been built at Mount Nebo, and the holiness doctrine, with the various charismatic mani-festations that accompanied it, tended to divide the Methodists of the area.

I and other members of my family often heard a Methodist neighbor, John Hughes, praying, crying and shouting in his fields. In evangelistic meetings in the Methodist churches of the area, Lawrence Bailes could always be counted on to shout when "Keep on the Firing Line" as sung. If a meeting was a bit dead, someone would ask for that song, and Lawrence would come out shouting and the meeting would liven up. When annual assemblies were held at the Tabernacle, people would run up and down the aisles and outside for a lap or two around the building, dancing and shouting.

I was a teacher of a Sunday School class in the Black's Chapel public school house quite near where we lived in Mount Nebo, and when the Tabernacle meetings were going on sometimes visitors would attend my class. In the center of the room was a Burnside coal heater, and on one occasion, whenever in my presentation of the lesson I made what a particular visitor deemed to be a good point, he would assume a crouching position, rapidly circumambulate the stove and then return to his seat. This kind of behavior was a bit disturbing--almost discouraged me from making a good point!

Illustration No. 20
West Virginia
Burnside Heater

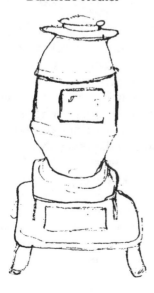

By and large, however, the Methodists were admirable people and they contributed significantly to my Christian development. It may well be that my ecumenical convictions are rooted in those experiences with Methodists in the Wilderness District of Nicholas County.

In any case, it was in the Hickory Grove Methodist Church that I first confessed that I was a minister of the gospel. A revival was in progress at this Church, and on a certain day I decided to walk the few miles from my home in Mount Nebo to the Church for the evening meeting. All day I was rehearsing what it seemed to me God was instructing me to say--assuming that I would be given an opportunity. As I had anticipated, the minister, whose name was Purtzer, invited testimonies or exhortations before his sermon. My presentation proved to be so moving that Brother Purtzer, sensing the spirit of the meeting, set aside his own prepared sermon and gave the invitation immediately. Several people responded, and one of them was my older brother, Lowell, who indicated tearfully that he wanted to rededicate his life.

This occurrence happened in December 1939, and I was 23, a few weeks away from 24. Buoyed up by that high moment, and assured that God could use me just as I was, unworthiness and all, I made known to that congregation before the benediction that I was called to preach. I recall that, among other things, I said, "Here is one clay vessel which is in the hands of God."

This same church, Hickory Grove Methodist, a few miles from Mount Nebo, invited me to preach my first sermon--not counting, of course, those sermons I had preached as a child in our yard at Enon! Although I was given several opportunities in those days to preach in Baptist churches, I am very thankful to those gracious Methodists.

It was not long before the debts of L. L. Copeland and Sons had cleared up, and I felt free to enter Mars Hill College in the fall of 1940. But I'm getting too far ahead of myself. I must tell you about my early education.

I am told that I was precocious intellectually and that I learned to read by the time I was about three, my older sisters teaching me. It was convenient to call the coldest room in our house at Enon "Alaska," because it was entirely unheated and snow blew in through its cracks in the winter. Alaska was a bedroom whose walls were papered with newspapers, which aided me in my attempts at reading. By the time I entered school, I seem to have been able to read some in the Bible--though it's difficult to separate fact from fancy in this regard.

I entered the Enon public school at the age of four, since, until the birth of Warren, I was the youngest of the children, and I begged my mother to let me accompany my older sisters and brother. Maybe in order to get me out of the house, she acceded to my entreaties. My first teacher, Lena Ransbarger, was showing some of us children pictures in one of our textbooks, probably a "primer," as reading books preceding the first grade reader were called back then. When I saw a snake, and before the teacher could identify it, I cried out, "There's a copperhead!" Miss Ransbarger, in surprise, said, "Luther, how did you know that's a copperhead?" I replied with some indignation, "Well, it says so right here. Didn't you know I can read?"

The Enon School was a one-room school, in which the grades primer through eight were taught by one teacher. Actually, although in some years there were forty or more pupils, younger students were taught by older; so, all in all, it made for a pretty good learning process. There were times when some students in attendance were older than the teacher. In those days teachers could start teaching very early and without college degrees, provided they could pass the teachers' examination and thus get a certificate. This usually meant that some pupils were older than their teacher. Also, there were students who, through no fault of their own, were hindered in their educational progress, for example, because school was too inconvenient for them to reach while small, because parents held them back to help with farm work, or for other reasons. Sometimes distances from school and bad roads meant that attendance was intermittent and grades were failed. In other cases, older students used these schools for refresher courses before launching their own teaching careers.

Through secondary school the system was 8+4. There were no junior highs or middle schools, and the only two elementary schools I attended, at Enon and Muddlety, were one-room schools. In both instances there were rather formidable bullies. At Enon we walked about a mile from the Pettigrew place where we lived, and on the way, much nearer to the school house, lived the Hinkle family. The big Hinkle boys, Lemon, and his brother, Ben, loved to pick on the younger kids. We smaller Copeland children were fortunate in that we had an older sister to protect us. Vernice was still in elementary school and she took care of the Hinkle boys quite well.

Unfortunately, the teacher sometimes would punish all students who fought on the way home, regardless of who started the fight, an obvious display of injustice. Punishment usually was switching, sometimes spanking, and in any case corporal.

Because of my tender age and consequent smallness of size, I was often selected as the teacher's pet. Even so, I was sometimes punished for infractions of the rules or else got by because I did my mischief in secret. I remember being reproved when I was four for displaying my private parts while sitting at my seat, and for sneaking below the girls' two-holer toilets for a upward look at their bottoms. When I was five or six, I was spanked for submersing my head on a hot day in the Peters Creek which flowed nearby. I'm sure I was guilty of other infractions which I no longer recollect. And far from being able to recount my educational progress year by year, I can hardly recall the names of my teachers.

When we moved to Hookersville (or Muddlety), I was in the fourth grade and found a school situation similar to that of Enon but with important differences. There was no older sister to offer protection--Faye was already beginning high school--and the O'Toole children were the community bullies. Unlike the Hinkles, there was a very large family of O'Tooles, two of whom were younger than I, Summers and Filmore, one about my age, General, and two girls and a boy, Meg, Ivalene, and Alec, who were older. There were other O'Toole children, a family of fourteen, of whom thirteen lived to adulthood. The ones I have not mentioned were already out of school and, to my knowledge, not belligerent. The ones named above were especially dangerous, I thought, when they could get me separated from my brother Lowell and gang up on me. I assiduously avoided trouble with them.

The O'Toole children were aided and abetted by their father, Tom, himself a bully, whose run-in with Pop I have described earlier. These kids made it their aim to run off any teacher, in my experience always a man, who had enough courage or poor judgment to accept a teaching assignment at the Muddlety school.

One teacher whom I will call Fullerton, a man lacking an air of authority and assertiveness, suffered much at their hands. Not only was he subjected to the indignity of being pelted with rocks when he tried to leave the premises at the end of the school day. Also, Meg and Ivalene would sometimes pad their bottoms with pillows to hinder Mr. Fullerton's attempts to discipline them. These girls would put on, over their padding, coveralls fastened with wire--I kid you not--so that a man teacher could not undress them sufficiently to make his whippings effective.

The best teacher at the Muddlety school while I was a student there, at least so far as keeping discipline is concerned, was a rather small fellow to whom I will give the name John Dabney. Mr. Dabney had the reputation of being an alcoholic. He was mild in demeanor but something of a terror when he became angry. One of his characteristics was that when he lost his temper he mumbled so that his speech became unintelligible. On one occasion he had punished Alec O'Toole, a big boy about fifteen or so, for some serious misbehavior by drawing a small circle on the chalkboard and forcing Alec to tiptoe to keep his finger in this circle for a specified number of minutes. The instant Alec's finger came out of the circle, Mr. Dabney put the whip to him.

The next day, Alec's father, Tom, appeared at the school-house door, ostensibly to threaten Mr. Dabney with dire consequences for disciplining his boy. Just the sight of Tom there to censure him infuriated Mr. Dabney. Before Tom had an opportunity to speak, our teacher began to mumble as he grabbed the iron poker from the coal scuttle, which was in its wonted place in front of the Burnside heater that used coal for fuel, and gestured toward the door.

None of us children got Mr. Dabney's message, but evidently Tom O'Toole did. He hastily pulled his right hand from his pocket where characteristically he had inserted it threateningly as though he held a gun there, he raised both hands aloft, and he sputtered explanations and apologies as he speedily withdrew from the school grounds. To my knowledge he never returned--certainly not so long as John Dabney was in charge.

After we moved to our own property across the highway diagonally from the schoolhouse, it was natural that the Copeland boys, in succession, be the janitors of the school. The employment of students to take care of the school building was common practice in those days. For a time, I don't remember how many years, I was the janitor. This meant that I swept up after school, sprinkling the oiled wooden floors of the school house with water before applying the broom, built fires in the coal-fired Burnside heater after the weather turned cold, and kept the heater stoked during school hours.

One time my mother saw me at a little shed outside the school house talking to Alec O'Toole with a hatchet in my hand with which I had split some kindling. She assumed, somewhat to her satisfaction, that I was threatening Alec with the hatchet. It is true that Alec richly deserved some intimidating, but I can't say that I was anything less than friendly to him. Probably I was the one who was scared.

There was a hill across the fence in the Porter Herold property, which we used for sleigh-riding when there were snows, a frequent occurrence in West Virginia winters. On one occasion, I poured several buckets of water on the sled road, letting the water flow down the slope freezing as it ran. This made for a very fast ride indeed! At the bottom of the slope, to make the ride more interesting, we pupils had constructed a kind of chute for the sleds to pass through, using for the sides of the narrow passage huge snowballs which we had rolled up while the snow was wet.

My own sled was wooden and homemade, since our family had no money to buy such unnecessary items, but I had nailed metal strips on the wooden runners to make for a right speedy sled. At the first recess, I took my sled to the top of the slope, mounted the sled on my stomach in my usual posture and let her go.

The sled went off the icy slope like a streak of light, and though I tried desperately to keep on track, I missed the constricted path between the frozen snow obstacles, hit one of them and suffered a bad accident, which, of course, could have been a lot worse. I'm sure I fractured a rib or two, because for some time I had severe pain when I breathed, but I never really thought of consulting a doctor for such a minor matter. The sled was sturdy enough to escape damage.

I was 11 when I finished eighth grade at the Muddlety school, and my parents deemed me too young to enter high school. So I repeated the eighth grade. Then I stayed out another year to help my mother operate the store and filling station and do the house work. I entered Nicholas County High School at the ripe old age of 13.

Meantime, my dad had installed a Delco home electric system so that we had some electric lights and appliances for the store and filling station—especially an appliance to keep the ice cream from melting and another to keep the drinks cold. The system was set up in our basement, which, since the house sat on a slope, opened to the outside under our back porch. The Delco Plant consisted of a gasoline fired motor with a whole spate of glass batteries lined up beside it, sixteen, I believe. It was easy to see when the batteries needed water since their sides were transparent. Included in my chores were filling the motor with gasoline daily and checking the water level of the batteries periodically.

It so happened that lightning, which was a rather common visitor on Muddelty, was striking our house rather frequently. It appears that the reason was some faulty wiring which before long we got corrected. While we were having this succession of lightning strikes, I entered the basement with my can of gasoline to fill the tank of the Delco engine. Just as I was prepared to pour the gasoline, the lightning hit with blazing force. Several batteries exploded, and I was thrust back against a corner of the wall. I ran from the basement in considerable confusion and fright. I assumed that battery acid was all over me and my clothes, but to my amazement I could find none! My life seemed to be charmed!

During that same year, after Pop had returned from work and others whom I wanted to hear me were present, I entered the basement for my usual chore of servicing the Delco plant and began to utter profanity as loudly as I could. People in the house above could not fail to hear me. As I see it now, my uncharacteristic behavior as a 12 year old was a bid for attention. I was feeling somewhat put upon having to stay home and help my mother while Warren, Lowell, and Faye, who were still in the home, were in school.

When Pop entered the basement, he seemed to show some understanding of my situation. He expressed keen disappointment in me, especially since I was a professing Christian, and indicated that I would have to be punished. I was relieved when he finished his low-key but effective lecture and switched me.

It was in the fall of 1929 that I entered Nicholas County High School (NCHS). Faye was repeating the last year, not because her grades were poor—they were always quite good--, but because it was not convenient for her to go on to college yet. Lowell was one year ahead of me. The school was located in Summersville, the county seat of Nicholas County, about 7 miles from where we lived on Muddlety.

Since school buses had not yet been introduced in our part of the world, we rode, with some neighbor children, in a succession of our cars, with Lowell driving. Although only 15, already Lowell was a good driver. A car I remember best was an old square bodied sedan with a shelf on the back behind the spare tire on which various objects might be hauled. It was a Gardner, a car which was produced only briefly and then permitted to slip out of automotive history.

For the first time I was in a school with many rooms and many teachers. NCHS was one of only two high schools in the county. The other was at Richwood, a lumbering town about 30 miles from where we lived. The NCHS building was located upon a hill overlooking the town of Sum-mersville. The campus was quite beautiful, especially after some of us students helped the custodian, "Farmer" McClung, in a New Deal program of setting out rhododendrons, procured from the nearby Gauley River canyon.

The four-year education provided by NCHS (in an 8+4 system) was good. In addition to the usual subjects, algebra, geometry, English, economics, general science, history, chemistry and such, I also took commercial subjects, shorthand, typing, and bookkeeping. I still remember a great deal of the Gregg shorthand, though I used it very little in later education. I enjoyed the bookkeeping (maybe it runs in the family; my dad taught himself to be a bookkeeper, and my son is a CPA).

As for the typing, I always made many mistakes, chiefly because my hands and head don't always seem to work together. To make matters worse, early in the first semester, I developed a bone infection on my left index finger and got impossibly far behind. Quite unreasonably, I think, my typing teacher, Ben Turpin, would not permit me to drop out but shamed me into continuing, with the result that I eked out a D on the course. I believe that I was graded A on all my other classes, so I turned out to be salutatorian of my class. If I had not had the D, I might have been valedictorian, though I never knew for sure.

In all my education, I remember cheating only once, and that lone incident--which, by the way, did not affect my grades--occurred while I was in high school. I had a history teacher who evidently was afraid that some of her pupils would cheat. Accordingly, she kept telling us that if we cheated on a test, she could certainly detect it. I got so tired of her *ad nauseam* claim that I decided to try her out. So it was that on one of her tests I cheated--I don't remember how--, and didn't get caught. Of course, I am in no way blaming her for my perfidy.

During high school days, my soul mate was Dexter Dotson, a Methodist boy who, like me, grew up the hard way. After college he began teaching at NCHS and made a career of it. From all accounts, Dexter was a good teacher. I kept up with him through the years and treasured this early friendship. Another associate from high school days was Lowell Siebert, though he was one year ahead of me in school. Our friendship became much closer after I had graduated and moved to Mount Nebo, near where Lowell lived. Our common Christian commitment and our participation in Methodist meetings of various kinds deepened our friendship. While in the armed service, Lowell sent me a silver dollar, which I have cherished through the years and have passed on to my son, Luke, to add to his coin collection. Sad to say, both Lowell and Dexter are dead.

You may wonder how my brother Lowell and I graduated together in 1933, since he was 2 years older than I and had entered high school a year ahead of me. The reason was that he had a very serious accident and had to stay out of school a year.

In the summer of 1929, just before I entered high school and when Lowell was a rising sophomore, he and I went from our home at Hookersville to Birch River, about 11 miles away, to bring home a pony for which our dad had exchanged an Atwater Kent radio. Lowell, who was 15, had driven our 1928 Whippet sedan to where we had to walk on the Birch Valley Lumber Company's railroad for some distance to where the company was logging.

When we returned with the pony and started to follow the railroad back to where we had left the car, Lowell opined that there was no sense in both of us accompanying the pony to the automobile, since only one of us could ride the small steed. Rather, he suggested, he would catch the log train which was just about to depart.

Lowell's plan seemed reasonable enough, since ordinarily to catch the train would not be too difficult. On each car, a steel ladder extended down fairly near the rail and one could climb up on the car in front of or behind the logs. However, for some reason, which Lowell himself seemed not to understand, his foot slipped down upon the track and one wheel of the log car ran right across the top of it. Lowell fell back into the ditch beside the track, probably, like me, in a state of shock.

Fortunately, some of the trainmen saw what had happened and stopped the train. They loaded Lowell into the pickup-like rear bed of Superintendent Frank Fiddler's Model A Ford which had railroad wheels on it for conveying Frank from job to job. Mr. Fiddler took Lowell to the house where we had left our car.

By some good circumstance, the housewife there was a practical nurse. She cut off Lowell's shoe, which the trainmen had been afraid to do because they thought if they did his foot would fall off. He was wearing a sixteen-inch leather boot with a thick composition outer sole that remained intact though the insole was completely severed. Flesh oozed from the burst top of the shoe like hamburger. The shoe was removed and the foot was in one piece, but surely every bone in the upper part of it was broken.

By the time Lowell reached home (with someone else driving of course), our family doctor, Flavia Brown, was waiting there to examine him. He set the bones the best he could, treated the wound with a potassium permanganate solution and put on a dressing (these were pre-miracle drug days). After a daily visit or two, he taught my mother how to dress the wound. "Let's not take him to the hospital," said Dr. Brown, "for I know exactly what they'll do. They'll amputate the foot at the ankle and Lowell will always be crippled. Maybe with some luck we can save the foot. Let's dress it twice a day and see what happens."

Lowell hobbled about on crutches, and Mom faithfully dressed the foot. Eventually, the big toe turned black as coal, obviously due to gangrene, though by that time the rest of the foot had vastly improved. At this time Dr. Brown suggested that Lowell be taken to the Roman Catholic Sacred Heart Hospital in Richwood (which, as I have indicated, was only about 30 miles from our home, though it seemed a world away). There they removed Lowell's big toe--as well as his tonsils on the other end! Lowell fought the anesthesia, administered by a nun, and in the scramble knocked the sister's cap off, revealing her shaven head!

Until Lowell had fairly well recuperated, it was deemed best that he should stay out of school. That's how we ended up graduating together.

Chapter Four
SEEKING MANHOOD AMID CHARACTERS

There were several of my teachers who thought that I was precocious and therefore encouraged my expectations of myself quite unrealistically. Now as to precocity, I have my own theory, which is supported by my sparse reading in the field. I believe that some of us develop earlier than others, and that a slower starter may actually have a higher intellectual ceiling than someone who is much more precocious. It is the height of the ceiling that matters, not the early manifestation of precocity.

At any rate, along the educational pilgrimage, especially after graduate school and a few years of teaching, I came to recognize that there were many people who were smarter than I. So my problem with precocity came later than the period I am now discussing. It became the profoundly disquieting feeling that I had not lived up to my potential. I will discuss it more at length later, since it has stayed with me.

Another very troubling aspect of my growing up was my seeming cowardice. I was nourished in a culture of violence, the Appalachian culture, and within my family I was known to have a very hot temper, though in this regard reputation outran fact. Though high tempers were somewhat lauded in our family, the truth is that I was always afraid of physical combat. I suspect that my starting to school at the unusually early age of four contributed to my unwillingness to fight. My classmates were always bigger than I, though eventually I outgrew most of them and became a rather large man. Even after I began the rough and ready life of the log woods and became unusually strong, I still carefully avoided physical altercations.

Meantime, when I was small, oftentimes life was miserable because of my fears. When we lived on Muddlety, and after Pop had bought a little piece of land and built our own home, it was often my responsibility to walk the three-quarters of a mile or so to the post office, or to Frame's grocery store, housed in the same building and operated by the same couple. The problem was that to reach this store, I had to pass the O'Toole place, a house on the hill, with a big, mean collie dog named Bull. In this home there were also several children whom I have already identified as bullies. They not only loved to hiss Bull onto me but also to threaten me otherwise.

Many times I have gone a circuitous route in the edge of the woods behind the O'Toole house in order to avoid these little tormentors. As I look back on it now, all I needed to do was to show some courage, and the O'Toole kids, who were not unusually brave, would have left me alone.

Also, when I was small, I was ready to cry at the hint of a hurt—not physical but mental, for actually I had a pretty high level of pain tolerance. I was known then, and still am, for being tender-hearted, an evaluation not fully justified. The inability to control my emotions has remained with me and has often caused me embarrassment and shame.

Sometimes, however, my crying stood me in good stead. One time when I was probably about ten years old, the O'Toole children threw our dog Jack, one half mostly collie and the other half a duke's mixture, off a trestle of the Birch Valley Lumber Company's railroad into the Muddlety Creek. The trestle certainly was not more than fifteen feet above the water, and the dog suffered no injury except possibly to his self-esteem.

There were three of us Copeland children present when this episode occurred, Faye, Lowell and I, but we were outnumbered by the O'Tooles. As I remember it, Faye and Lowell joined Jack's tormentors in their amusement at the dog's plight. When my mother learned about it, she scolded Faye and Lowell for not taking Jack's part. When they remonstrated that Luke also should be reproved, Mom asked how I had reacted. When informed that I had cried, she said, "Well, at least Luke cried." This was but one of many instances in which my own culpability was overlooked and the other children were blamed, especially my brother, Lowell, of whom, as I have stated, considerable responsibility was required.

I was athletic, in that I was strong and had good coordination, but for most games I had a significant flaw: I tended to be erratic, perhaps because my reflexes left something to be desired. I could bat fairly well at baseball and very well at softball, but I was notoriously inaccurate at throwing the ball. This failure made me a very unlikely choice for either the infield or the outfield. It was embarrassing not to be chosen for a team. Because people respected my judgment, I sometimes was asked to umpire, a kind of face-saving device.

I could do better at football, since physical strength is of such vital importance to that game. When I went out for football in high school, however, I injured my knees to the extent that I could hardly walk for a time, much less play football. Maybe it was because the ground was hard and my uniform pants were too short, or maybe it was because of the stage of my growth. Possibly it was both, or something else. I never could run very fast in spite of my height and my slender build. I excelled only at "duck-waddling," an exercise we performed as a part of football practice and in physical education classes. In either case I could always outrun the whole field at duck-waddling!

I am sure that my alleged precocity caused others to look upon me as different from the usual child, and I readily accepted their estimate. I certainly understood myself as distinctive. I had great dreams of how the world would recognize my superiority. Especially as my call to the ministry began to mature, I visualized myself as a great evangelist, indeed the greatest. I could hardly see how God could get along without me, even though, as I have related, I had plenty of doubts and feelings of my unworthiness. There was a certain ambiguity here, delusions of grandeur accompanied by a gnawing awareness of unworthiness, though this apparent contradiction in no way obliterated my sense of distinctiveness.

I suspect that this feeling of superiority has been even more difficult to disabuse myself of than my pride in my intellectual ability, though the two are interrelated. They have tended to merge and then to evolve into the general disillusionment of knowing that I had early potential, the promise of which I never realized, a disillusionment which has been very difficult.

Yet this conviction of distinctiveness was not without its values. I did not enter the usual world of dating and involvement with girls which could easily have led to marriage. I seemed to know that there was a destiny waiting for me out there somewhere, and I had best not get too attached to my local environment.

Of course, I did not refuse to enter into the social life of my community. On Muddlety, this took the form of youth groups, usually related either to church or to school. I vigorously played games such as *Skip to My Lou* which were nothing more or less than folk dances. Square dances, however, were strictly taboo for Baptists and many other Christians. We played card games such as Rook, but almost never used "gambling cards." Movies were permitted, except on Sunday, but the theater was in Summersville and therefore inconvenient. At Mount Nebo, the social life I enjoyed was almost entirely related to the activities of the Methodist churches of the area and therefore kosher.

Nor did the sense of my distinctiveness prevent my infatuation with a series of girls. In high school, I was smitten by Daisy Jackson, Alma Grose, and Alma's younger sister, Gertrude. After we moved to Mount Nebo, I had a particular liking for Thelma Dorsey, a member of Hickory Grove Methodist Church, who later married my good friend Lowell Siebert. Likewise, I had my eye on Thelma McClung of Mount Lookout and Kathleen Stanard of Enon. Both were Baptists, and either, I believe, would have made a good preacher's wife. As a matter of fact, Kathleen married a Cuban who was a minister and she performed well as a missionary. I was never quite interested enough, however, to ask any of these three for a date. Maybe a divine providence was looking out for me—or for them!

What I most enjoyed doing was hunting and trapping. I had a succession of dogs and I greatly enjoyed their fellowship, though at times I was a bit ill-tempered and impatient with them. I loved to hunt at night, for opossums, skunks, and raccoons, all three of which were primarily nocturnal. I caught more 'possums than any of the three. 'Coons somehow eluded me, though I usually had dogs that would tree them. My brother Lowell went hunting with some other fellows, using my dogs, and they caught a 'coon. I used to think that God kept me from catching 'coons so that I would not get overly attached to hunting!

As for the skunks, I'm ashamed to say that I caught them in spite of their very effective defense mechanism of a foul odor, which they did not hesitate to spray on me and my dogs. I used special clothing for skunk hunting which I hung separately so as not to infect the other items of clothing, and I smoked my hands with coffee grounds burned on top of a hot coal or wood kitchen stove to try and remove the offensive smell. Even so, I sometimes carried the skunk odor to school with me, a fact which certainly did not win friends and influence people on my behalf.

Skunks were usually "bayed" by dogs in the open, that is, dogs would rotate round and round the skunk, barking, or the skunk would take refuge in a burrow underground, and I would dig it out with my trusty mattock. Once in a while a skunk might be found by the dogs in a hollow log, 'possums and rabbits also, in which case it could be "twisted" out, by imbedding a withe or briar in its fur.

Usually raccoons would climb trees where at times they hid themselves in holes in the trees. On more rare occasions they would escape into dens under rock ledges. Opossums, like 'coons, are arboreal animals, and were usually treed by the dogs. In such cases either animal might be shot out of the tree, or the tree might be cut down so that the dogs could catch the animal that had sought refuge in it. 'Possums usually favored small trees, while 'coons chose larger ones. In addition, 'possums were sometimes caught by dogs on the ground, or they might crawl up hollow trees or into hollow logs or burrows.

In the day time, I often hunted rabbits or squirrels to put meat on the table. Also, I loved to hunt minks, not for their meat, of course, but for their fur, and I usually had dogs which could track them to a burrow. Often a mink would catch a bird or small animal and then enter a hole in the ground to eat it. The burrows I have mentioned thus far were very infrequently dug by the animals that used them, though sometimes rabbits, skunks, or opossums would dig a hole. In most cases others took advantage of the prolific digging habits of ground hogs (or woodchucks) and would seek out burrows abandoned by the animals who had first created them.

My trapping was closely related to my hunting, though not requiring the services of a dog. I set some deadfalls, that is, traps in which a large rock would fall on the hapless animal seeking to take the bait under it, usually a 'possum or skunk. More often I used steel leg traps to catch animals along the creeks, especially minks and muskrats. Usually a muskrat caught in a trap would try to swim, in which case the trap would pull it beneath the water and drown it. I would examine my traps in the day time, a practice called (at least by West Virginians) "running" or "looking" my trap line.

I became quite adept at skinning animals, and, for fur-bearing ones (excluding rabbits and squirrels whose hides were of little commercial value), making boards upon which to stretch and cure their pelts. A good mink pelt was the most valuable in those days, fetching a price of more than twenty dollars, which was a handsome price then. Muskrats and skunks were next, a number one pelt of either bringing three or four dollars. Opossums were rated lower.

I still have twinges of conscience about the cruelty of my lifestyle in those days. Of course, explanations can be made about the ethics of the particular era or culture, the inability to control the cruelty of hunting dogs, and the necessity of contributing to the limited income or to the meager diet of my family. I am sure that all these factors are relevant, especially the last.

Our system of family finance was very similar to that of communism: "from each according to his or her ability, to each according to her or his need," and needs were modestly met--insofar as they were met at all. For example, I never owned a bicycle, though you may be sure that I longed for one. And so we were pretty poor, though we were not so aware of our poverty.

No explanations, however, can assuage the pangs of remorse I feel for the unnecessary cruelty I imposed upon the animals of the field and forest. Let me give you one example: The usual method of killing a 'possum was to place a stick or mattock handle on the back of the animal's neck and then pull up on it by its hind legs. This was supposed to be a relatively painless method of breaking the neck. However, I have had the experience more times than I like to remember of severing the spine in the lower back instead of the neck of the opossum. In those cases it was difficult to break the neck, and there must have been some excruciating suffering before death brought a merciful end, usually by a shot between the eyes from a .22 caliber rifle.

But let me turn to a subject which is not so morbid. I consider myself fortunate to have grown up in a day before cultures had been homogenized by television and while individualism was still prized. This was certainly the case in Nicholas County. I have often stated that there were probably more characters per square mile in Nicholas County than anywhere else I have known. Even the dogs seemed to have an unusual degree of individuality.

For instance, there was a guy whom I will dub Carl Newsome and his dog, Ranger. It is convenient and seems appropriate to treat man and dog together. Carl was a member of one of the more respectable families of Muddlety, and presumably he had some education. According to the community's interpretation of things, Carl had gone off to Ohio and had become involved in the use of drugs, "dope," as it was called then, seriously impairing his health. In any case, Carl had returned to Muddlety in his forties, extremely thin and with something like eczema on his face. His rear end was absolutely flat (a condition to which his dope habit seems unrelated) as if his trousers had been vacated by their renters. Though Carl was not beyond middle age, he walked like an old man, except that he kept his hands clenched beside him as he trudged along.

Carl used to come to our country store, immediately hoisting himself to a seated position on our wooden counter and saying "Gimme a Coke." If he happened to have a chew of Mail Pouch tobacco in his mouth, which he usually did, he would lay the cud on the counter while he drank the Coke and talked incessantly. At times he would empty the Coke bottle and return to the chew, all the while continuing his stories. He might tell, for example, how a friend in Akron had rescued him from a much stronger opponent by the name of Connell. When Carl and his assailant squared off to fight, just as Carl unleashed his fist, his friend hit Connell in the head from behind with a billiard cue. After a while Connell came to, looked at Carl, and said, "Newsome, I didn't know you had such a punch."

Now as Carl talked, his Mail Pouch would stimulate his salivary glands and his mouth would become fuller and fuller. As he continued to talk without interruption, his head would tilt back farther and farther to accommodate the spittle until finally the latter would begin to trickle down his chin. At this point Carl would jump from our counter and head for the nearby door to the back porch where he would spit forth a lusty amber glob. We boys, the Copelands and our neighbors, the Hutchinson boys, loved to imitate Carl, running to the back porch to spit loudly, while Carl was oblivious to the whole affair. On one occasion Aubrey Hutchinson ran to the back porch with hands clenched and head held back as though his mouth was full of spittle, only to find that Carl had run out behind him and almost unloaded on him!

Unfortunately, at least from our perspective, Carl "went native," taking up with a single woman who lived with her brother and his family in a real backwoods situation. This woman bore a son who was presumably Carl's. She and her sister-in-law, availing themselves of the only access from their home to our store, would walk the several miles. Usually, they had huge dips of snuff in their mouths, and if they found no convenient place in our building to expectorate, they would pull open the front of their dresses and spit into their bosoms. I remarked that it was no wonder that the children started using tobacco early since they got it on the breast.

However, Carl was not without his good qualities. One example of his kindness was his teaching Lowell and me how to night hunt, that is, hunt with a kerosene lantern for 'possums and 'coons. Lowell and I must have been about eleven and nine at the time. Ranger, Carl's huge Walker hound, who must have weighed 100 pounds or more, was a good tree dog (that is, good at treeing 'possums and 'coons), a silent trailer who would open up and bark with a deep, booming voice when he treed. When Carl walked the half mile or so to our store at night, old Ranger would frequently amble off to the woods and tree a 'possum. Whereupon Carl would take Lowell and me with him as he carried his kerosene lantern to the spot where Ranger was barking to see what his hound had treed. Under Carl's tutelage we learned to cut small trees to catch 'possums or to dig them out of the groundhog burrows where they had made their home.

In this connection I had a rather amusing experience--amusing to me, I mean, but probably not to Ranger. We had butchered hogs, and I took the lights (lungs), which we would not eat, to the nearby woods, attached them to a huge log which was lying on the forest floor, and set three steel traps in front of them, hoping to catch a 'possum. That evening when Carl came to our store, we heard old Ranger barking up in the woods and figured that he had a 'possum treed.

When we went to investigate, the closer we got to where Ranger was barking the more it appeared to me that he was very near to my traps. Indeed he was near, he was caught by the traps! Ranger had tried to get the bait, which would be attractive to a dog as well as to a 'possum. I had caught him in all three traps, both of his hind legs in two and his tail in the other one. Since the traps were small and Ranger's appendages were very large, he probably was not in much physical pain, though undoubtedly he was humiliated. So he was just sitting there barking.

Which reminds me of another dog, of which I was the proud owner when I was in my teens, who was something of a character. His name was Bill, and he was mostly yellow cur. Now "cur" when used of a dog usually means a mongrel or dog of mixed breed. Actually, there is a breed of dog known as cur, and this was Bill's identity. He was a large-bodied, short-eared and yellow dog of high intelligence. Bill was a very good squirrel dog, in that he would tree a squirrel and then when the hunter would make his stealthy approach with his gun, Bill would move to the other side of the tree and proceed to make noise in order that the squirrel would switch over to the hunter's side so that the latter could shoot it. Bill was also a good dog for night hunting, especially good at treeing 'possums and 'coons.

Bill had at least two distinctive traits which justified my calling him a "character." One was his unusual toughness. On one occasion Bill was standing on the shoulder of the paved highway, U.S.19, which went by our store on Muddlety, perpendicular to the road, waiting patiently for traffic to pass so that he could cross. A car came along on the same side as Bill and traveling at a rather high rate of speed. The driver deliberately--and sadistically--drove over onto the shoulder where he could strike Bill in the head with the right front wheel of his vehicle. Bill spun around in the air two or three times, shook his head as if to clear it, then trotted on across the road as though nothing had happened.

Another time, I was night hunting with Bill when he bayed a skunk in a fence corner. I approached and readied my mattock

Illustration No. 21
Mattock
(top: cutting bit; bottom: digging bit
handle: about 36" long)

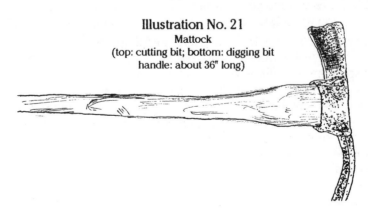

for a swing at the skunk. I aimed carefully at the skunk's head and brought the mattock down with all my strength. The problem was that Bill decided to charge just when I came down with the mattock . The result was that, to my chagrin, I hit Bill in the head with this heavy tool. I am sure Bill was surprised, and I wonder if he marveled at that skunk as had Cornell at Carl Newsome. Maybe he thought, "I had no idea that skunk had such a wallop!" In any case, he merely shook his head and attacked the skunk with renewed vigor.

The other unusual characteristic about Bill was his amorous nature. From a great distance, he could catch what was to him the distinctive scent of a bitch in her brief period of heat. When this happened, as it did more frequently than I wished, Bill would simply take off, even if he were hunting, and I would have no idea of his whereabouts--unless I knew about the particular, and temporary, object of his affections. This weakness for female dogs did not mean that Bill did not love to hunt. He did. But his sex drive was stronger than his joy of the chase.

To return to *homo sapiens*, the neighbor living nearest to us was Russell Hutchinson, whose home was about a quarter of a mile from our store. Russell was a rather natty dresser for a farmer. He wore twelve-inch leather boots, and blue denim overalls with one fold of about four inches at the bottom of each leg secured by a huge safety pin, about five inches long. To see these large safety pins was a rather common sight in those days. They were characteristically used for dressing up the attire of lumberjacks—though Russell did not work in the woods. His shirt had long sleeves, with folds above the elbows held in place by elastic bands which closely resembled garters, another item of male attire which was not too unusual for that time and place.

Russell's medium-brimmed hat sometimes had a greasy perspiration circle around its sweat band, which indicated that at least sometimes he was like Longfellows's blacksmith, whose "brow was wet with honest sweat." Russell lifted his feet several inches when he walked, a habit to which he himself called attention, criticizing others for stumbling on objects in their paths precisely because they did not pick up their feet. Russell was of medium size, his eyes were milky blue, and he had a moderately long handle bar mustache.

But the really unique thing about Russell Hutchinson was that he would walk into our store every few days, cock his head sideways, twitch his mustache, and look whoever happened to be in the store up and down. This process would continue for an embarrassingly long time and during it all Russell would remain utterly silent. You might say, "Good morning, Mr. Hutchinson. How are you today?" The response would be twitch, twitch, stare, stare, and silence. Finally--at which point the object of his gaze would breath a sigh of relief--Russell would complete his up and down survey and go about his business quite normally, making purchases or small talk, as the mood struck him. But I do not recall that he ever gave any greeting such as "Good morning."

The differences which some of the characters of our community manifested were due to mental or physical handicaps. There was a neighbor to whom I will refer as Tom Stewart, a middle-aged fellow who, as I have long since realized, was a victim of cerebral palsy. He was rather short of stature, had some spastic movements, especially of his head, and was quite strong for a man in his condition. He walked like a drunk man, and in fact had been accosted by policemen more than once for public drunkenness. In such instances, Tom proceeded to curse the unfortunate official black and blue, as he could do very well, in spite of the fact that his speech was a bit affected by his cerebral palsy.

According to the cruel ignorance of the day, people poked fun at Tom, teased him, and assumed that his mind, as well as his body, had been affected. Some even claimed that he had been "marked by a drunk man," that is, his mother, during her pregnancy with Tom, had been frightened by a fellow who was soused. To all such unjust indignities, Tom had developed an exaggerated sensitivity.

On one occasion, Tom was asked to be the janitor for our annual revival at Beulah Baptist Church, with special responsibility for building and maintaining the fires in the two potbellied stoves, Burnside coal heaters, which kept the building warm. After the first night of the revival, some complained to Tom that the church building had been too cold. The next evening he frequently attended to both heaters, noisily stoking them with fuel from the coal hods and generally making a nuisance of himself.

When gently reproved afterwards, Tom responded, "Fire is what they want, and, by God, fire is what they're gonna git!"

Looking back on the situation now, I believe that Tom had normal intelligence and could have learned in school if given a chance. This judgment is in part validated by the following anecdote, which, if it doesn't prove Tom's good sense surely demonstrates his sense of humor! There lived in our Muddlety community a family who were farmers, but whose daughters had gone off to school and had returned home for a while quite sophisticated.

One day a group of us were standing outside our country store wasting time when one of the girls from this family rode by on a horse. Two things were unusual about her, to say the least. One was that she was wearing shorts, something unheard of in those parts in those days. Secondly, a big collie dog was perched on the horse behind her. All eyes followed her as we gawked at her while she passed. Then someone broke the silence by asking, "Tom, how'd you like to be that big old dog?" Whereupon Tom replied, "I wouldn't give a damn about bein' the dog, but I wouldn't mind bein' in his place!"

Then there were those whom I will call the Pegram boys, Gerald and Bob. There was a most unfortunate strain of mental illness in their fairly large family, and these two boys, though very different from each other, were not normal. Both were tall when they got their growth, more than six feet. Gerald was called "Dancer" because of his peculiar walk. He was the very religious one. After he "got religion" at the age of about twenty-one, he was a very difficult problem for our Pastor, because he was always wanting to exhort the congregation of Beulah Baptist Church. The Pastor handled him very well by such strategies as carefully limiting his time, since Dancer never made sense. Also, Dancer thought he could sing and play the guitar, when, as a matter of fact he could neither carry a tune nor play a chord.

The girls liked to tease Dancer, and one day they asked him at church to recite the Ten Commandments. Dancer proceeded to do so, getting them right until he came to the command which bans coveting. This one he recited correctly except for one letter, one letter which made a significant difference. Intoned Dancer, "Thou shalt not cover thy neighbor's wife." The girls tittered in profound embarrassment, but they ceased their teasing, at least for the time being.

My sister Vernice, who was unfailingly kind to such as Dancer Pegram and Tom Stewart, and for her pains was the unwilling object of their romantic intentions, told me several years later of the very tragic manner in which Dancer died. Some sadistically cruel stranger came upon Dancer and decided to rob him. Not content with merely taking Dancer's modest possessions, this incredibly violent person stuck a shotgun up Dancer's anus and then pulled the trigger. Poor Dancer lived for a while but died in the hospital where he had been admitted.

Bob was younger than Dancer and of a very different sort. Bob could sing and play a guitar almost normally--almost. He was younger and not quite as tall as Dancer, and certainly not religiously inclined. He was moody, perhaps depressed, and seemed to have little to do with Dancer. He went swimming with the rest of us local boys in our favorite swimming hole in the Muddlety Creek. When Bob dived from the white oak tree which overhung the water, we would brag on him and exaggerate the number of somersaults he had made before hitting the water (actually he did well to make one and usually he landed on his tummy for a belly buster). He would then climb higher and higher and try for more flip-flops, to our considerable amusement.

One day Bob was shucking corn for Russell Hutchinson, and since the autumn weather was a bit nippy, Bob had dressed for the occasion. The Hutchinson women, as was their wont, had prepared a big midday meal for the workmen, and Bob went in with the others to enjoy the sumptuous repast. He came into the parlor where Mabel Hutchinson, the teenage daughter, was sitting, and proceeded to take off his overalls (kids today call them "hogwashers"). Mabel screamed and ran from the room. Then Bob, who, unbeknownst to Mabel, had on trousers under the overalls, remarked in great glee, "Can't a feller have lots of fun when he has two pair of britches on?"

Now I owned a number of dogs, usually one or two at a time, and most of them distinctive individuals. I have already told you about Bill, but I must introduce you to Joe as well, though I have already mentioned him as one of the riders on the back of the truck which I wrecked as a very crucial event in my call to the Christian ministry. Joe was a fairly good sized hound, mostly bluetick, who somewhere along the way before I knew him had suffered the loss of one eye. This handicap, however, slowed him up but little if at all, though he had been known to run into an occasional tree when on a hot trail.

Joe was a pretty good utility dog, who loved to chase something, most anything, day or night. During the daytime he was a good rabbit dog and he also loved to run foxes. At night he was a good 'possum and 'coon dog, though if he couldn't find an animal which he was supposed to run, he would chase a rabbit or fox at night, to my disgust. If snow were on the ground, as often occurred in the rigorous West Virginia winters, I could put him on the trail of a mink where it had been the night before; he would then track the mink to a groundhog burrow, and when I dug it out he would catch it. Joe was very devoted to me, and our affection was mutual.

During the winter season, Joe helped me catch many 'possums. I would skin them, make boards to stretch their pelts on and dry and sell the furs. Since we almost never, even at our poor-est, ate a possum, my mother, who, as I have told you, was a very frugal woman, was reluctant to see all this meat go to waste. So she said to me, "Why don't we cook up those 'possums and feed them to Joe, since we have trouble feeding him anyway?"

So I caught a big fat 'possum, skinned him, put his hide on a board, and turned the carcass over to my mother. She cooked the 'possum in the big black kettle in our backyard where she usually heated wash water. Having boiled the 'possum until tender and then cooled it appropriately, she offered it to old Joe. Seem-ingly taking a bit of umbrage at what he considered an indignity, Joe circled the 'possum a time or two sniffing it. Then he hiked up his hind leg and (to use a good King James Bible word) pissed on it. We never let my mother forget old Joe's evaluation of her cook-ing!--though she took our ribbing in good grace.

I will cease and desist discussing characters, though I assure you there were many more in Nicholas County, especially of the human variety! And I didn't even get to Summersville!

I believe that my almost frenetic outdoor existence which this chapter has described was a means of escaping from the reality of a life to which I did not really belong. Neither of my two brothers was such a zealot as I for the life in nature. In my heart of hearts I knew that I was destined for some calling of God which would take me away from my home and family and from the manner of life to which I was giving myself with such abandon. Finally, I had an inkling, at least, of what my future would be, and I was ready to proceed to another stage, led, I believed, by the Holy Spirit.

But I had at least one more problem. A Methodist lady, of holiness leanings, had warned me that if I went to college "they would take my religion away," and I had fears myself that gradually I would lose my faith. I knew that in higher education I would face a much larger world and would encounter many aspects of human experience that I had never faced before. Would my faith be equal to the test? I was somewhat troubled by this unresolved question. One day as I felt some anxiety about this matter, it seemed to me that I heard a voice saying, "Luther, stay near the cross, and you will be all right." I felt relieved, and have always taken comfort in that experience.

Even so, I was loath to leave West Virginia. I was to return only briefly, to drive a log truck for Pop for the summer of 1941. So my memories of Nicholas County are just that, the remembrances of an old man who dreams more of the past than he sees visions of the future. In my mind's eye I see vividly the little freshets rushing wantonly down the mountain sides in the early spring; later in the year I breathe again the seductive fragrance of the crab apple blossoms near the Rock Quarry at the mouth of Herold's Branch on the Muddlety; I catch the delicious aroma of the green corn, especially when it tassels in late summer; I am rendered almost ecstatic by the rich colors of the hardwoods in autumn with the backdrop of the green hemlocks; and I glory in the silence of the snows of winter, covering all the drabness and human-made junkiness of the various aspects of Appalachian civilization. So you can understand my reluctance to leave.

PART TWO
HIGHER EDUCATION: 1940-1949

Chapter Five
GRITS AND ZIP

In the fall of 1940, I arrived on the campus of Mars Hill College, Mars Hill, North Carolina, a few miles north of Asheville. I had in my possession only twenty-five dollars with which to enroll. More money than that was required, but the financial officer recognized my special circumstances and admitted me. My parents were able to help me with no more than five or ten dollars.

Illus. No. 22
c. 1942

When I left the college two years later, the Business Office paid me forty dollars. Meantime, I had worked my way, doing almost every kind of work that students did at Mars Hill College, and had come out fifteen dollars in the black--which I thought was very good. I discovered that the vast majority of the students worked to pay at least part of their school expenses, and so I had no reason to feel different or economically inferior on those grounds. Also, National Youth Administration (NYA), one of the New Deal programs, was a big help to the college as well as to me and other needy students. Usually, I was paid twenty cents per hour for this NYA work, twenty-five cents for the more skilled.

Although at 24, I was older than all except a handful of the students, I actually did not feel older. I was in an academic environment worlds away from the log woods situation in which I had been immersed for the past several years. Therefore I had a rather keen sense of cultural deficiency which caused me to think of myself as younger than I was--possibly less mature.

My lack of maturity seems to have been confirmed by a silly episode in my relations with the opposite sex. From Mars Hill I wrote to a young woman named Lucy Wiseman whom my sister Faye had met in college in Glenville, West Virginia. Faye had thought that Lucy would be a good match for me. I had visited in the Wiseman home once to see Lucy. She was an earnest Christian and a member of the Christian and Missionary Alliance. Lucy was short, had red hair, and was attractive enough, though certainly no beauty, as I remember her. In my letters from Mars Hill, though actually I hardly knew her, I proposed to her.

She replied that she really did not know what to say, since she did not know herself, let alone me. I took that as a negative answer, and I have since been grateful that Lucy seemed to have better judgment than I. I believe a marriage would have been a disaster for both of us, let alone the fact that I had no way of supporting a wife and family. Perhaps a kind providence saved both of us.

For living quarters at Mars Hill College, I was assigned to Wharton Cottage, just across the street from the back of the Library Building on the main campus. Cottages were still used at Mars Hill in those days to house male students. Of the several cottages on the campus, Wharton must have been the oldest; certainly it was the most dilapidated. I was told that it did not escape the razing crew for more than a year after I left. Each cottage had its monitor, a student chosen to keep order in the cottage, for which he was given some remuneration in the form of reduced or free rent--I don't remember which. In my senior year (first year students were juniors and second year students were seniors in junior college) I was elevated to that exalted status in Wharton.

I lived in one of the few remaining cottages which was heated by means of a wood stove in each room. With this kind of heating system I was in my element, though the fuel for stoves and fireplaces with which I was more familiar was not wood but coal. At Mars Hill, fuel for these heating stoves was supplied in the form of poles and small logs from the nearby woods, which were then sawed into firewood lengths by a small buzz saw powered by an automobile engine. The larger pieces of firewood were then split to appropriate size. Helping to supply this wood was one of my many jobs.

My roommate was Stuart Hepler, a fellow ministerial student, from Thomasville, North Carolina. Since Stuart was short in stature, we gave a "Mutt and Jeff" appearance as we walked together on the campus. Stuart was a very nice fellow and quite compatible. Like most of the students, he was a few years my junior. He said later that he sort of took it upon himself to tutor this

West Virginia wood hick in his subjects, until he soon perceived that I was brighter than he, whereupon he left me on my own. Stuart dropped out later to serve in the U. S. Army and then finished college and seminary. Several years later I helped him in a meeting in the South Carolina church of which he was pastor. I still have fond memories of him, though I no longer keep up with him.

Soon after arriving at Mars Hill, I read a book called *Manifest Victory* written by Rufus Mosely. Mosely was a native of Georgia. He was professor of philosophy at Mercer University until, as I was told, his free-wheeling ways got him into trouble and cost him his job. From then on, he functioned as a kind of free-lance man of God. He remained unmarried, and he and his brother had a pecan orchard which provided him an independent income. This remarkable man seemed to have no inhibitions. He went wherever the Spirit directed him and did whatever the Spirit told him to do. For example, when a neighboring black woman was quite ill, Mosely went to her home and served as her practical nurse, something entirely unheard of in the South, especially in those days before civil rights had emerged.

Mosely also had a fine sense of humor. Since I have not seen the book for many years, I will have to depend upon my memory to convey a bit of its contents. As I remember it, one of the experiences which the book recounts is Mosely's visit to a church--it sounds like a Mormon church or something similar--in which an invitation was given for people to come forward to volunteer to be baptized for some dead person or persons. Mosely went forward, and when he was asked for whom he wished to be baptized, he said, "I'll be baptized for Adam and take care of the whole business!"

Mosely's book made a profound impression upon me at the time. One thing which I learned from Mosely I have never forgotten. He indicated that if you have trouble discerning what the Holy Spirit wishes you to do, you should simply do what love requires. Though I have tried, I must confess that I have not done very well at following this admonition. I have had plenty of experience not knowing what the Spirit wanted me to do, but I have not been a good example of one who follows the law of love.

Mars Hill was in the North Carolina Appalachian Mountains, "a jewel in the emerald crown of the hills," and, since I was from this same chain of mountains though farther north, the culture was not unfamiliar to me. The principal differences were few. First was the absence of coal. Though I never worked in the coal industry in West Virginia, this business loomed very large and influenced even areas such as Nicholas County where there were few professional mines.

A second cultural distinctive was racial segregation. The separation of the races was characteristic of the Appalachians where I had grown up, but it was much stronger in the South, and Western North Carolina, though mountainous, was still part of the South. In my home county I had not really known black persons, since, as I have indicated, they were almost nonexistent there because of economic reasons. In Mars Hill College, there were no African American students, and outside the school the practice of segregation kept whites and blacks apart even if we had wanted to relate to each other. My awareness of racial injustice developed gradually, and I don't remember that it bothered me very much in my Mars Hill days.

Southern food, also, was somewhat different, especially hominy grits, to which I was introduced for the first time. I knew something about hominy and had actually helped my mother make it by using lye to take the hulls off grains of corn. The result was hominy: swollen, soft, white grains of corn. Obviously, hominy grits are made differently, but I had never even heard of such. Also, at the Dining Hall at Mars Hill we always had corn syrup, which we called "Zip." If food became a little scarce otherwise, which sometimes happened, you could fill up on bread and Zip--and maybe peanut butter.

At first I was somewhat nervous about my table manners and tried to be very polite. Unfortunately, I ended up at a table where most of my fellow diners were football players. As a result I almost starved and had to drop my scruples about manners. In one of President Hoyt Blackwell's chapel addresses, he told how he opened his eyes after the blessing in the Dining Hall only to find that during the prayer someone had speared a pork chop for himself! "Daddy" Blackwell characteristically spoke with his right hand inside his coat jacket over his heart. In relating this dining room episode, he may not have meant to be funny, but some of us found it hilarious.

All in all, the culture was reminiscent of Appalachia

farther to the north. With another student, I began a mountain mission under the auspices of the Mars Hill Baptist Church. When I became pastor of a little community (interdenominational) church at Linville Falls at the end of that first school year, I turned the mountain mission over to a fellow resident of Wharton Cottage, Dick Heller from Maryland, and it later became a church.

Heller was a fine guy, though he annoyed me by lying on my bed and putting his shoes on my quilt until I stopped him from it. Unlike me, Heller was from an urban environment and evidently didn't get dirt on his shoes. I deemed him to be a bit flippant. I remember his singing a parody of a song: "South of the border, she's built like a truck." We developed a friendship and he later became an effective pastor in Florida. We will encounter him again in the next chapter.

Mars Hill was an excellent junior college and was so recognized. The student body was relatively small, about six hundred, I believe, and we got to know almost all of our fellow students. The atmosphere was like that of a large family. As my pastor in West Virginia had anticipated, it was a very good environment for a person in my situation. Some years after I left, Mars Hill became a four-year college. I had mixed feelings about this change and said at the time that Mars Hill was a splendid junior college but would struggle to be an acceptably good senior college. My prophecy, which required no special insight, has proved to be true.

There were some outstanding teachers at Mars Hill when I was there. Some of them I did not have, notably Vernon Wood who taught chemistry. Of those whom I did have, Raymond De Shazo and John McLeod stand out in my memory--for very different reasons. Mr. De Shazo taught me first year English, and he was a stickler for correct English usage, especially punctuation. You could hardly pass his course without knowing how to write a term paper. I often remembered Mr. De Shazo with gratitude some years later when I tried to teach seminary students, college graduates, who had no idea how to report their research.

Mr. McLeod, who taught me English literature my second year, helped to give me an appreciation for good literature. In addition, in his classes he shared his philosophy of life and in general impressed me greatly. Although he probably did not remember me well and certainly had no reason to do so, I recall that when he died many years later, I thought that I had lost a great friend.

It was difficult, also, to forget Dr. Robert L. Moore, though he certainly had passed his prime when I knew him. He was tall, white haired, rather regal in his bearing and puritanical in his habits. He always wore wing-tipped collars. This revered patriarch had been a long time President of Mars Hill College and probably was as influential as anybody up to the present in molding the character of the college. I had no idea until later how sacrificial and frugal Dr. and Mrs. Moore had been in their life style, living on a modest salary and giving most of their income to the college. Dr. Moore had retired from his arduous responsibilities as President, and had been succeeded by Dr. Hoyt Blackwell, a very able and dedicated man whom I have already mentioned. However, Dr. Moore was still teaching Greek, classical Greek, that is, and I took his Greek classes for both years.

I remember well a happening in Greek class involving one of our class members, Ronda Robbins, from Lenoir, North Carolina. Robbins was about three years my junior and one inch taller than I though somewhat more slender. He had a deep bass voice, and like me, what he knew of music was mostly of the shaped note variety--though the shaped notes seem not to have had an abrasive effect upon his vocal cords. Because of his name, Ronda was often mistaken for a girl--so long as he stayed out of sight. Also, he had sparse red hair on the fringes, because for some unknown reason he was prematurely bald. Neither of these characteristics seemed to have any negative effect upon his self-confidence, of which he had an abundance.

But back to the Greek class. Dr. Moore liked to stress good--and puritanical--habits to the students. One of his favorite sayings, which he shared with us after exhibiting one of his mannerisms, in this case, pursing his lips and pausing for emphasis, was "Young men" (he tended to ignore the young women), "you can't fly with the eagles by day and the owls by night." In other ways, also, he emphasized the necessity for our getting plenty of sleep--eight hours per night, if my memory is correct.

One morning when Dr. Moore had digressed from his Greek lesson to exhort us about our sleep habits, Robbins raised his hand. "Yes, Mr. Robbins?" he asked. Robbins responded, "Dr.

Moore, you talk about the importance of several hours of sleep. For years I have been doing very well on four hours per night." Said Dr. Moore, "Mr. Robbins, I notice that you don't have much hair?" Not to be outdone, and certainly with no apparent diminution of his intrepidity, Robbins replied, "But Dr. Moore, you should have seen me when I was first born!"

I have mentioned that I did most anything that was to be done on the Mars Hill campus. These tasks included mowing grass, cutting wood, firing boilers, working in the Library and night watching, among others. It was said by some that Dr. Moore, in one of his chapel messages, referred to me when he mentioned a student pushing a wheelbarrow on campus and singing, in the words of a contemporary popular song, "I don't want to set the world on fire." Actually, I remember the remark very well. However, it was not I but a schoolmate, Rucker Turner, who gave Dr. Moore ammunition for that particular day.

One of my failures, for which I felt keen embarrassment (for a brief moment I really wanted to quit and go home), occurred not long after I enrolled at Mars Hill. I was asked by Mr. Bryson Tilson, the Director of Buildings and Grounds, to oversee some students in removing a wooden frame from around a new coal stoker for one of the boilers. Several tons of coal had already been unloaded around this frame, almost submerging it. I did not know how to get the frame out and ended up letting the coal enter it before we could remove it. Actually, I had presided over a fiasco, and Mr. Tilson made no attempt to conceal his displeasure. Some time later I learned that he feared that I would quit school because he wondered if I would make it academically anyhow! So far as I know, I did all right at my other jobs in working for the school.

One of my most distasteful chores was night watching. The night was divided into three periods, I believe, seven o'clock to eleven p.m., eleven to three, and three to seven a.m., and for each of the three periods a student was night watchman. While I had this chore, ordinarily my watch was the first, seven to eleven, the very time which pointed up the considerable differences in the regulations governing the behavior of young men and that of young women.

Concerning women students, the rules were much stricter. Among several other requirements, there was a rigidly enforced curfew of ten o'clock p.m., girls could go up town only once a week, I believe, under certain rather galling conditions, and of course young men and women could not be caught in an embrace or kiss. (Until recently there had been a "ten inch" rule, that is, male and female students had to keep at least ten inches between them).

On one occasion, I reported a young woman who had been up town buying something, only to learn later, to my chagrin, that my report had been the straw which broke the camel's back. On top of several other infringements, that particular violation had resulted in her expulsion.

At another time, Norwood Davis, a classmate who had the second watch, came bursting up the stairs wide-eyed and in considerable agitation to wake me from a sound sleep and implore me to come to his aid. When he went to punch the clock at the rear entrance to the Library just across the street from where I lived, he explained, he had been jumped by three young men. I hastily pulled my pants on and went with him onto the darkened campus.

Fortunately, the young rascals were nowhere to be seen; but we thought their actions serious enough to report to Mr. Tilson, who strode forth in the middle of the night, walked over the campus until he found the offenders, and proceeded to read them the riot act. "Don't you know," said Mr. Tilson, "that attacking a night watchman is a felony? Get off this campus, and if you ever set foot on it again, I'll have you arrested." The three departed posthaste. It turned out that they were from Chicago and were visiting a friend on campus. I never heard of them again.

Without meaning to do so, I made a friend by my night watching. The Treat Dormitory was a white frame building at the very center of the campus, elevated at the front and with a basement in which the college laundry was housed. The dormitory was on the night watchman's circuit and at the door to the laundry was a box where his clock had to be punched.

One night I had exchanged my earlier watch with the student whose responsibilities began at eleven o'clock. In walking my beat I came around the rear corner of Treat Dormitory to punch my clock, when someone took off running from the vicinity of the laundry room. I immediately suspected that I had on my hands an attempted robbery and that the would-be burglar was in flight. I took after him, and although I was not swift enough to overtake him, there was enough light for me to recognize him as a fellow student and call him by name.

"Jack," I yelled as we both ran, "do you want to stop and talk to me, or do you want me to report you to Mr. Tilson?" Jack stopped, and when we had approached each other, he said, "Promise me that if I tell you what I was doing, you won't report it." "I can't make such a promise until I hear what you were up to," I replied.

"Well," he said, "I suppose I don't have anything to lose, so I'll tell you. I've just returned from a baseball trip and I went to a spot below my girl's window to speak with her for a few minutes. So I threw some gravel at her window to get her attention. Now that's all in the world I was doing," he continued. "I don't care what you report about me but I don't want my girl to get into any further trouble. She's already violated some of the college rules and has been campused."*

Then Jack waited for my response. I knew he was on the college baseball team, he seemed to be an honest fellow, and what he said made sense. So I replied, "Jack, when Mr. Tilson gave me this job, I assume he expected me to use my own judgment. I'm going to exercise that privilege. I believe you and I don't intend to report you." From that moment, Jack was my friend.

The kitchen crew kindly prepared a snack for the student who had the second watch, and when I traded with this student, I was able to share his reward. The experience was not too encouraging. In the kitchen were the largest cockroaches I have ever seen, probably more than an inch in length. They seemed big enough to carry off the watchman's lunch or even to kidnap the watchman himself! Fortunately, the lunch was in a sack, which they did not penetrate.

When the first Christmas vacation came, naturally I wanted to go home to Mount Nebo, West Virginia, to spend the holidays with my parents. Since I had too little money for bus fare, I decided to hitchhike, a common means of transportation at that time. So I positioned myself on the highway north of Mars Hill,

---

*To be "campused" meant to be confined to the campus, with all privileges suspended.

U.S.19, I believe, which at that time went from Asheville north through Erwin and Johnson City, Tennessee, and Wytheville and Bluefield, Virginia, to Summersville, West Virginia. Soon I got a ride to Erwin, Tennessee, where I stood by the concrete pavement and thumbed.

Before long, a truck came by with a load of lumber and stopped to pick me up. When I started to take my suitcase into the cab with me, the driver remonstrated: "We don't have room in here for that suitcase," he said. "Put it on top of the lumber." Now, I knew something about trucking, and I did not expect my suitcase to stay on that load of lumber. On the other hand, I did not want to disagree with my benefactor. So I carefully put the suitcase in the middle of the load and in front of the boom chain. Then I got in the truck and hoped for the best.

When we arrived at Johnson City, the truck's destination, which was not very far, I hastily got out and looked on top of the lumber. My heart sank. Just as I had feared, my suitcase was gone! I told the driver of my plight and asked when he would be returning to Erwin. "Not until I unload this lumber," he replied. "maybe in an hour or two." Of course I knew that would be too late. So I thanked the truck driver and quickly dashed across the street to a filling station and asked the attendant if he could drive me back to look for my suitcase. "I'm very sorry," he said. "I'm here by myself and I can't leave the station."

Then he volunteered some counsel. "Anyway," he suggested, "you're not going to find that suitcase. You know that if it fell off where it could be seen, someone would have picked it up by now. If it fell off where it can't be seen, you can't see it either."

What he said made sense, but I felt that I had to try and find the suitcase. After all, it had just about all my clothes in it: my only suit, my few shirts, my ties, my underwear, my socks, and my handkerchiefs. The thought of going home with no clothes except what I had on distressed me. I knew that my folks could not afford to buy me another outfit.

In something of desperation, I started walking back the way the truck had come. Prayer came rather naturally. I prayed something like this: "Lord, you know I can get by somehow without that bag. And I don't expect you to bail me out every time I do something stupid. But it surely would be good to recover that suitcase." Suddenly, as I walked, I began to feel confident. I felt that I would find my belongings.

So I kept walking briskly. Whenever I met a pedestrian or a bicyclist, I asked if they had seen a suitcase on the highway. Always the answer was the same: they hadn't. Finally, after I had walked five miles or so, I reached a little filling station on a hill to my left. I went in and made my usual inquiry, and this time I struck pay dirt! An attendant had seen the suitcase. "I saw the truck pass," he said, "and the suitcase was teetering on the right hand side of the load of lumber. I said to myself, 'It can't stay on till the truck gets out of sight,' but it did."

Now I knew that the bag had fallen off between where I was and where the truck had terminated its run in Johnson City. I quickly decided upon my strategy. I would stop and ask at every house on the way back to Johnson City. The first residence was fairly near. When I knocked, a pleasant gentleman came to the door. He listened to my story and then said that he had not seen the suitcase. "However," said he, "do you see that house across the road and on the hill? That woman up there sees everything! If your suitcase dropped off in sight of her house, she would have seen it. Go ask her, and whatever the result, come back down here and have supper with my wife and me. It will soon be dark anyway. After supper we're going to Johnson City to see a movie. We'll be glad to take you into town with us and put you out on the highway beyond Johnson City to resume your hitchhiking."

I scurried up the hill to knock at the door of the house located at its top. A woman came to the door (surely the same woman my new friend had mentioned), listened to my query, and then answered, "Yes, I saw that suitcase lying on the pavement. About the time I saw it a Greyhound bus came along, and the driver got out and picked up the suitcase and put it on the bus and went on." Excitedly I asked, "Which way was the bus going?" "Toward Johnson City," was her reply.

Profoundly relieved, I thanked the lady, returned to the first house, told my good news to the man who had offered me hospitality, and then accepted his kind proposition. His wife turned out to be just as cordial as her genial husband. So after a delightful dinner, they took me to the bus station in Johnson City where I had every reason to believe my bag would be. When I asked the man in charge behind the desk if they had a stray suitcase, he asked me for identification. So I handed him my driver's license, and he produced the suitcase. He had already opened it and found my name and address in my Bible.

Although the bag was old and flimsy and held together by a belt, it had survived its fall without breaking open. My host and hostess delivered me to a spot outside the city where I thanked them warmly, told them goodby, and continued my hitchhiking.

I have often thought of this experience as a kind of paradigm, a tiny window through which I could peek and see the hem of the robe of God's good providence. Not that God had to take care of my needs while many others suffer. I did not expect that at all. Afterwards, I was to have losses that I never recovered. I know that Christians, like all persons, have no exemption from the world's pain and deprivation. But that incident taught me that no matter what, God loves and cares for me and that ultimately everything will be set straight. A politician friend, who has had his own troubles, has often said to me, "Luther, everything's gonna be all right." And I believe that it will.

Toward the end of my stay at Mars Hill, I became interested in Elizabeth "Lib" DuPuis, a blond girl of about average height and better than average intelligence, with brown eyes and a sunny disposition. I suppose I was attracted to Lib because I always felt very good in her presence. This was not always the case in my interpersonal relationships because my background caused me to feel culturally deficient, if indeed my personality itself did not tend to give me a sense of inferiority. I felt that Lib was attracted to me also, and before we left Mars Hill we exchanged pictures.

Religion, of the Christian variety, was very active on the campus. At the center were chapel services, the Mars Hill Baptist Church, and the Baptist Student Union (BSU). The church was located on the campus and was attended by many students and staff persons. It also included community people as well.

The pastor was William Lynch. His sermons were well prepared, but his mannerisms were somewhat effeminate. He had attended a Northern seminary and was known as a liberal thinker. Although he was roundly criticized as not being evangelistic enough, I found him very helpful, particularly in personal contacts, and considered him a good friend. He came to Southern Baptist Theological Seminary in Louisville, Kentucky, while I

was there, to get a degree which would make him more acceptable to Southern Baptists, and he then took another pastorate in
North Carolina before returning to Mars Hill as a counselor on the
staff of the college.

The President of the BSU was in effect the President of the
Student Body--though this latter office was filled separately. Douglas Aldrich from Florida was elected President of the BSU for our
second year and I was elected Vice-President. One of our unfor-

Illustration No. 23
BSU Officers
(From left: me, Wallace Parham, Henry Anderson, Douglas Aldrich)

gettable activities was a student led revival, in which Doug and I, among others, were preachers for one night each. Out of that revival, many students made decisions to follow Christ and many more renewed their commitment to discipleship. According to the usual criteria, the revival was a huge success. Later, I was to be reunited with Doug at Southern Seminary, and in various times in our later ministries. He married Edna Lou Lamb, a first year student when Doug and I were seniors, and they have remained a very fine and attractive couple.

In addition, there were Sunday School classes in campus buildings. My memory is that this Sunday School was part of the organization both of the college BSU and the Mars Hill Baptist Church. My Sunday School class was a very good one, taught by Professor Spencer King of the history department. Also, there were dormitory and cottage prayer meetings. All in all, there was an intensive religious en-vironment.

I have mentioned that I became pastor of the Linville Falls Community Church. Linville Falls was a little village a few miles from Linville, North Carolina, and on the Blue Ridge. The falls of the Linville River, located almost in hearing of the church, are a famous scenic spot, and the whole area is very beautiful indeed. The congregation was interdenominational: there were Baptists, Episcopalians, Methodists, and Presbyterians, with Methodists predominating.

The little church building was very rustic and attractive. It was constructed entirely from chestnut timber, the trees having already perished in a blight before the building was erected. The inside was paneled with beautiful chestnut lumber and the siding was chestnut bark.

The community's population soared in the summer with the addition of many tourists, and the permanent inhabitants were divided between mountaineers--some of whom were educated and urbane, many of whom were not--and retirees of various sorts. This very interesting mix was represented in the attendees of the church.

The previous pastor of the church at Linville Falls was Haggard "Sandy" Ellis, who later--understandably--went by his other name, Cowen, instead of Haggard. Sandy had recommended me to succeed him upon his graduation, but our styles were quite different. The community was notorious for bootlegging, and Sandy had attacked the problem head on, opposing the bootleggers themselves and gaining their animosity, even to the point of the endangerment of his life.

I decided--and I don't believe it was from lack of cour-age--to approach the problem from within the congregation, particularly since I learned that a nearby beer joint, notorious for bootlegging, was owned by one of the deacons of the church. I visited the beer joint and met the (moonshining) proprietor, and I told the deacon that he would have no peace--obviously he was miserable--until he cleaned up his place or sold it. After I had left that church, I had the satisfaction of receiving a letter from the deacon indicating that he had sold the beer joint. By the way, the beer joint was so close to the church that often when I stood up to preach on Sunday morning, I could hear the juke box belting out, "When my blue moon turns to gold again . . . ."

I spent the summer after I had completed my college work at Mars Hill in the community of Linville Falls where I could work more intensively on the church field. I boarded in the home of a widower by the name of Henry Franklin, who was rather famous as a cook. During that time, I ate a lot of delicious country ham. My host looked as though he had eaten too much of his own cooking.

Before I left Mars Hill, I was ordained to the gospel min-istry by the Mars Hill Baptist Church at the initiative of the Linville Falls Church. An Ordaining Council, consisting almost entirely of Professors and Staff of Mars Hill College, had met with me and examined me as to my call and my understanding of Christian theology.

Mr. B. M. Canup, Bursar of Mars Hill College, questioned me whether I thought that baptism was a prerequisite for par-taking of the Lord's Supper. Obviously, Mr. Canup thought that it was. I answered that it was the *Lord's* Supper and I would not presume to determine eligibility. I also indicated that Paul thank-ed God that he had not baptized certain of the Corinthian Chris-tians. I assumed, I said, that they were baptized by someone else, but the Scripture did not tell us. When Mr. Canup pressed the matter, Pastor Lynch came to my rescue, affirming my answer. So the Council recommended me.

The date of my ordination was June 7, 1942. I remember

very little about it except that I asked Dr. Walt N. Johnson to give the charge to the candidate. Since I had heard Dr. Johnson speak about the immediate presence of Jesus and had read his periodical, *The Next Step*, devotedly for some time, I had great respect for him, although he probably did not know me at all. I think I felt that somehow mystically the spirit of Dr. Johnson would rest upon me. Unfortunately, I was mistaken. The reason for the ordination, of course, was that I intended to stay at Linville Falls Church for the summer and I expected to be doing some baptizing and administering of the Lord's Supper.

Surely enough, I baptized several people in the Linville River that summer. Even some Methodist teenagers wanted to be immersed. And when we did the baptism, with a crowd of church members assembled on the bank of the river, a lad from the community came to confess Jesus as Lord and Savior and ask for baptism. The church accepted him and I baptized him on the spot.

This fellow was the son of a woman who had terminal cancer. His father, who was dead, was said to have killed a man. I had visited the sick mother several times. She had a daughter, Cathy, who was about 19. The place appeared to me to be unsanitary. For instance, I used to sit on the car seat which served as a kind of settee on the front porch of the humble home, and I noticed bedbugs crawling out of the seat while I was occupying it. I had to be careful not to carry some of them away with me. (Of course we had bedbugs , especially when we lived in shanty cars, but I hadn't associated the lack of sanitation with them.)

The daughter was very grateful to me for my visits with her mother, and she wished to find some way to express her gratitude. So she said to me one day, "Brother Copeland, you are so good to spend time with Mama, and I want to do something for you. What about a good fried chicken dinner?" I replied, "Cathy, you are overburdened with the care of your mother. Don't let me hear another word about a dinner!" I wonder if I was as concerned for Cathy as I was for myself! In any case, I learned later that as a pastor, and especially as a missionary, I could not be so squeamish.

I was told of a Mrs. Wiseman who had at one time been a loyal member of the church but had dropped out several months previously. Nobody knew why, or if so they did not share the secret with me. I went to Mrs. Wiseman's home and found her to be a local mountain person, very much like some folks I had known in West Virginia: a salt of the earth type but quite unlettered. I reminded her of what I had been told about her relation to the church and asked her if she would mind telling me what was the problem so that I might be of help.

"I don't mind tellin' you at all, Brother Copeland," said Mrs. Wiseman. "It was that Brother Ellis. He had the gall," said she, "to stand up in that church and say that from now on this church is to be run in a democratic way." She continued her explanation, "Now they's two things I am, from the top of my head to the sole of my foot. One is a Baptist, and the other is a Republican. The very idea, bringin' politics into the church!" I tried to defend the former pastor and explain what he meant, lower case letters and capitals and so forth, but I saw I was getting nowhere. So I simply said, "Come on back, Mrs. Wiseman, and I promise I won't bring politics into the church." She did come back and we got along very well.

A fellow student, John Hodge, was pastor in the nearby Baptist church in Crossnore, where the Presbyterians had a rather famous mountain school and hospital. John was a most unusual fellow. Whereas I had started to college at the age of 24, John had entered high school at that age. Several years earlier he had dropped out of elementary school and had been employed in construction work.

When John became a Christian, he felt called to preach, and he decided he needed to get an education--which in itself was rather remarkable in light of the fact that he was from Rutherford County, North Carolina, where his father was a one-horse mountain preacher who was illiterate, with the obvious result that he could not even read his Scripture lesson. John's brother, Dewey, also, had become a Baptist preacher without a college education.

John drove a school bus in high school and worked in the kitchen at Mars Hill College, where he took three years to get his diploma. Later he was to graduate from Furman University and marry a very cultured young woman who complemented his ministry in a splendid way. She was Vera Witter, who was teaching in the Presbyterian school in Crossnore while John was pastor in that village.

Vera was small and frail and quite accomplished musically, while John was of average size but rough and ready and permanently affected by his mountain culture. Vera was an MK (missionary kid) from India, where her parents, following their parents, had been American Baptist missionaries. The grandparents had begun Christian missionary work among the Nagas. John always butchered the king's English, but somehow because of his wife's upbringing and his unusual ability he was able to hold several successful pastorates in cultured eastern Virginia.

John and I traveled together to our church fields in his Model A Ford sedan. He would drop me off at Linville Falls and then go on to Crossnore. We became fast friends. Once in a while we had a flat tire, and I would simply lift the Ford until he could set the jack under it. Then we would repair the tire and inflate it with a hand pump.

John told me that on one occasion, a mountaineer who lived near Crossnore had earnestly requested him to take the man's wife to a hospital in a town somewhat distant for surgery. John had complied, and at the end of the ride, the fellow had told him goodby with the words, "Well, Preacher, I don't have no money, but I'll meet ye up yander." John opined that he had a notion to tell the fellow, "I probably won't need any gasoline up yander."

During our second year at Mars Hill, Ronda Robbins and I decided that we needed to do something about continuing our college education. We had become good friends and often studied together. It seemed a good idea for us to enroll at the same senior college. At that time, the closest relation Mars Hill had with a senior college was with Carson Newman College over across the mountains in Tennessee. So Robbins and I thought it would be a good idea to go to Carson Newman.

Each of us wrote a rather long letter to the President of Carson Newman, pouring out his heart about his dreams for his future ministry, and concluding with the fact that he had no money and would need to work his way. The President replied to each of us with a very short paragraph, the gist of which was, "If you have no money, I don't know what we could do for you." Talk about getting hit in the face with a sack of soggy grits!

While we were still in a state of shock, Dean R. N. Daniel of Furman University, Greenville, South Carolina, visited our campus with the purpose of recruiting students. Robbins and I each got an interview with him, and we found him most understanding of our situation. He told us that the South Carolina Baptist State Convention provided a scholarship for all Baptist ministerial students with no strings attached as to the place of our future ministries, a remarkably generous provision. Obviously we were eligible. "Come on down," he said, "and we'll find a way." So we began to make our plans to enter Furman.

Why we did not consider Wake Forest College, I have no idea, though I may have known then (possibly it was too liberal for us!) Since Robbins was a North Carolinian, it certainly would have made sense for him to go to Wake Forest. A number of our classmates did.

Chapter Six
PURPLE GARTERS AND BLUEGRASS

Meanwhile, two things happened which had considerable significance for the transfer of Robbins and me to Furman. One was that a number of unmarried ministerial students* at Mars Hill decided to enter Furman that fall. The other was the helpfulness of a fellow whom we knew well who had finished Mars Hill the previous year and enrolled at Furman, Wade Hale, from Walhalla, South Carolina, who was also studying for the ministry. Like us, Wade had worked his way at Mars Hill. It was through his good offices that we were able to rent a two-story house on the edge of the campus, belonging to a Miss Mims from Rome, Georgia. Miss Mims went back to Georgia to live with her sister.

I have often marveled at the faith--or naïveté--of this dear lady in turning her house over to a bunch of college students. All of us single ministerial types from Mars Hill ended up there. Two other Furman men, Horace Buddin and George Bowdler, were already rooming in Miss Mims's house and they remained, independent of the Mars Hill crowd, though they too were studying for the ministry and were cordial.

Since we lived next door to a fraternity house, and since all of our inhabitants were ministerial students, we decided to name our abode "Parsons' Paradise." As such, it became rather well known on campus. In addition to Wade Hale, Ronda Robbins, and me, Dick Heller, John Hodge, Eli Smith, and Bryant Spivey were among the parsons in our paradise.

All of us contributed some money or food or both for the kitchen, and we at Parsons' Paradise provided our own meals. My mother had canned a pretty good supply of foods for me, which was very helpful since I had no money to speak of. Robbins was our chef and I was his assistant. After one semester of this kind of arrangement, we quit the kitchen routine and took our meals in the Dining Hall. "Sarge" Smith, a former mess sergeant in the Army, was dietician and cook. The food was superb, better than

---

*Women were not ordained in those days, so we all were males.

any I have ever found in an institution.

Wade Hale and Eli Smith I was to meet again at Southern Baptist Theological Seminary in Louisville, Kentucky, along with some other Mars Hillians who had gone to other colleges, most notably Wake Forest College. Wade ended up on the staff of North Greenville Junior College in South Carolina. Eli Smith became a high school teacher and counselor in North Carolina. Dick Heller and Robbins went to Southwestern Baptist Theological Seminary in Fort Worth, Texas. Heller became a pastor in Florida. Robbins came to North Carolina eventually for a long pastorate at Apex. Bryant Spivey went to Duke Divinity School and from there into student ministry in South Carolina.

Because of his age, John Hodge never went to seminary. Maybe he took seriously (really, he didn't) the word of his mountaineer uncle spoken to John and me when I visited John at his home in Rutherford County, North Carolina, while we were at Mars Hill: "Ole Hitler will have everybody killed before you fellers ever git out of school."

As of this writing, three of these Mars Hillians are dead, Ronda Robbins, John Hodge, and Eli Smith. In Raleigh, I lived near Apex, where Robbins was pastor, and our two families occasionally enjoyed fellowship together. His wife died just before his retirement, and Robbins didn't last long afterward. John Hodge died, evidently of a heart attack, while cutting wood with a chain saw in the beauty of autumn foliage in the woods near his home in Spindale, North Carolina. I spoke at his funeral. These two died in the 1980s. Eli Smith has died more recently, and Louise and I hear periodically from his widow, Reba, whom I knew, along with Eli, at Mars Hill before they were married and at Southern Seminary afterward. Dick Heller always remembers me, at least on my birthday, and I used to hear from Wade Hale once in a while.

At Furman, as at Mars Hill, there were some outstanding teachers. I was already prejudiced in favor of Dean R. N. Daniel because of his sympathetic treatment of Robbins and me. I ended up majoring in English literature and minoring in history, so I had Dean Daniel for a course in world literature. I enjoyed the class very much and found that it increased my appreciation of good writing. I continued the study of Greek by taking New Testament Greek with Dr. H. W. Miller, a splendid teacher. I ended up with enough Greek for a second minor.

Another favorite was A. T. Odell, with whom I had courses in American literature and Shakespeare. Dr. Odell was a nervous, high-voltage type with a forceful personality. It was his habit to stride into his classroom on time, put a cluster of sharpened pencils and a package of cigarettes on the desk and then light up one of the cigarettes. While teaching, he might sit on his own desk or saunter up one of the aisles to park himself on the desk of a student as he continued to lecture and blow cigarette smoke.

The first semester I had Dr. Odell's American literature course. I soon discovered that I had two strikes against me: I was a ministerial student, and Dr. Odell didn't particularly care for students headed for the ministry. I suppose he thought us too pious, as though when we ate rice we insisted upon Uncle Ben's *Converted* Rice. Secondly, I was playing football, and Dr. Odell disliked football players, because he felt that they were away from class too often and too long and that anyhow the school was putting too much emphasis upon athletics instead of academics. I was lucky to get a B on the course, the only grade less than an A which I got at Furman, I believe.

I particularly remember one encounter I had with Dr. Odell in class. We were discussing Whittier, and Dr. Odell was not very fond of Whittier, especially his poem "Snowbound." He panned Whittier for his romanticizing of snow. Odell opined that snow might be all right when falling and for a brief time afterwards, but soon it got sloppy and dirty and generally obnoxious. When he was in the midst of a tirade about how snow was unattractive, I raised my hand.

Dr. Odell recognized me, whereupon I disagreed with him and said that I found something romantic about snow. "Well," queried Dr. Odell, "have you ever seen snow linger for a long time, say a month or more?" "Oh yes," I replied, "I've seen snow on the ground for about three months in West Virginia where I grew up." I may have exaggerated a bit for the sake of emphasis and in light of the fact that I wanted to have a bit of fun with my professor. As a parting and victorious shot, Odell threw Whittier at me: "Blessings on thee, little man, barefoot boy with cheeks of tan," intoned he.

I learned that Professor Odell, who was a layman but whose father-in-law, the late Dr. W. J. McGlothlin, was an ordained minister and a former President of Furman, had been victimized by a very sad event which had happened to him and his family some years previously. The son of the Odells, when he was maybe ten or eleven, had been run over by an automobile and killed. It appeared that Dr. Odell had never really recovered from this tragedy.

I took Dr. Odell's Shakespeare course in the summer of 1943 and he warmed up to me considerably and seemed to think that I was a good student. The class, as I remember, was on the basement floor of the main classroom building of the Woman's campus, where firecrackers were wont to be thrown around the fourth of July. When one or two landed nearby during Odell's class as he sat near an open window, he came close to apoplexy.

It was in this same class that he told a humorous story about a small church which wanted to call him as pastor. "Apparently," he said, "they assumed that since I was teaching at Furman I was a minister. I turned them down, because I didn't want to hurt them--though as a matter of fact I probably would have done them more good than a lot of preachers." He told us young ministerial students that all we needed to do to get an honorary doctor's degree from Furman was to get a church nearby and start preaching against the school.

One of the most interesting aspects of my year at Furman was my membership in Pendleton Street Baptist Church and especially my relation to its pastor, Dr. Dean Crain. Dr. Crain was a very imposing person, probably about my height but considerably bigger, weighing about two hundred and fifty pounds. He had grown up in a bootlegging family in the Dark Corners section of South Carolina. When he entered Furman with his younger brother Buford, he had prevented students above them in the hierarchy from hazing these two first-year men, by a bold move with a baseball bat. Dean's wit was legendary. When he spoke in chapel at Furman, the building was full and he kept his audience in stitches. I'll spare you the many stories about his life--which you could read in his biography anyway--and confine what I say concerning him to what I experienced or observed.

My friend, John Hodge, and I joined Pendleton Street Church, and we were sometimes--not always--impressed by Dr. Crain's preaching. We declared that we could determine the level of his inspiration by the length of the French cuff extending from his right black jacket sleeve as his arm reached ever upward toward heaven during the progress of his sermon. One Sunday Dr. Crain preached an unusually impressive sermon entitled "The Coming Blackout." Inspiration seemed at an extraordinarily high level: the right French cuff was quite conspicuous. The next day in geology lab, Hodge and I were asked by a fellow student, Jeanne Crain, daughter of Buford, by now a pastor in Tennessee, "What did you think of Uncle Dean's sermon yesterday?" When we praised the sermon highly, Jeanne simply stated, "It was Daddy's. They get together once in a while and trade sermons." John and I quietly remarked to each other that the two brothers ought to confer more often, at least for Dean's sake.

Dr. Crain did not hesitate to inject humor into his sermons. One Sunday a math professor at Furman by the name of Blackwell, who was a deacon at Pendleton Street, was seated fairly near the front of the sanctuary. Blackwell was a fine man, but he had some difficulty staying awake. As the sermon proceeded Dr. Blackwell's head tilted toward the rear only to be caught midway as its owner fought sleep. Finally his neck bent enough for the head to touch something solid, namely, the back of the seat, and Dr. Blackwell entered the dream world. Dean Crain saw what had happened, and he simply stopped his sermon for a moment.

When the sonorous voice which had put him to sleep ceased and all became silent, the hapless professor awoke. While Blackwell was looking furtively around to see if he had been detected, Dean Crain broke the silence. "I see that one of my deacons has gone to sleep on me," he declared. "I never mind it when one of them goes to sleep. I just know I've got too deep for him."

One Sunday evening I was sitting in the choir making as though I could sing. From this vantage point I had an excellent d a frontal view of the congregation. Though I saw nothing amiss, obviously Dr. Crain did. The pastor stopped in the middle of his sermon, and I could see the back of his neck getting redder and redder. Suddenly he extended his long arm to point toward the left rear of the large sanctuary, and he lowered the boom. "You young people sitting under the balcony," he thundered in righteous anger, "quit makin' them faces! And quit chewin' that gum!"

Then he paused, and after a moment something funny

came out of his mouth even in his rage. With an obvious reference to Samson in the Bible, he intoned, dwelling upon the last three vowels: "Many a man has killed himself with his o-own ja-aw bo-one." Nobody so much as tittered, though some of us certainly felt like it. Concluded Dr. Crain, "Now you either straighten up or get out of here!" Nobody moved and Dean went on with his sermon.

Since I was older than most of the students--I became 27 while I was at Furman--I was the object of marital intentions on the part of some young women in the Pendleton Street Church who saw their chances passing them by. One was a Furman graduate who had a good job in a Greenville bank. She was a very nice person and not unattractive. She had two out-of-town friends visiting her on a Sunday afternoon, and she had persuaded me to get Heller and Robbins to pair off with them and the six of us go to Paris Mountain for a picnic. She prepared a nice lunch and we had an enjoyable excursion.

When we returned to Greenville, the two friends departed, freeing my two colleagues who were attending other churches, and this young woman and I went to Pendleton Street Church for the evening service.

Dean Crain, as was his custom on Sunday evening, came out to sit on the front pew before he entered the pulpit. When he looked back in the congregation and spotted me, he dispatched a messenger asking me to come to the front where he was. As I approached, "Brother Coker," he said (he never got my name straight; he always called me "Coker"), "I want you to be in charge of the service tonight. Now I'll do the preachin' but you do everything else: read the Scripture, lead in prayer and so forth." Sensing my reluctance, he volunteered: "Now I know that you're concerned about that young lady back there. She'll get by without you for a few minutes. She's got along without you for more than 30 years."

During the fall of 1942 I played football at Furman. My going out for football had two prominent motivations: I wanted to prove to myself that I was really a man and could rough it with the roughest of them, and I sincerely desired to have a Christian witness among the football players. Since World War Two had decimated his squad, Coach "Dizzy" McLeod was hard up for players so he took me on. I think I made a very good tackling dummy for the rest of the squad. If I had ever known anything about football from my brief and unfortunate attempt to play while in high school, I certainly had forgotten it.

We had a very good first squad, led by Captain Dewey Proctor, and I got to play very little, though I got a letter as did everyone else on the squad, since we were so few. I believe that although my fellow players may have had good reason to doubt my ability, none of them disputed my courage or my strength.

As a football player I heard the song which gave me part of the title for this chapter. "Around her leg she wore a pur-

Illustration No. 24
A Right Tackle

ple garter. She wore it for her Furman man who was far, far away." Purple was a Furman color, and the song was adapted for World War Two. The other part of the chapter title is from the bluegrass country in which the University of Kentucky is located and where I went in the summer of 1944 to finish the requirements so I could graduate at Furman--as I will relate later.

We had a very good football team though we were always decimated. At full strength we only had about twenty-three men on the squad, and we never were at full strength. We always had some injuries, at first from intrasquad scrimmages until the coach saw that we could not afford the risk of such and discontinued them.

We made the tortuous trip across the mountains to Knoxville to play the University of Tennessee, where we were severely beaten. Tennessee had several platoons of players, and one seemed as good as another. I had to go in at right tackle as a sub for the first stringer, who was carried off the field with a concussion, talking quite irrationally. To tell you the truth, I sort of dreaded to go in for him.

The next week we were scheduled to go to Miami, Florida, to play the University of Miami. Coach McLeod tried to cancel the game, since only eighteen of us were able to make the trip, but Miami would not cancel and there was nothing to do but go, shorthanded as we were. Our first team did valiantly, and we acquitted ourselves well in losing. While we waited for the game to begin, I made a macho demonstration of my strength, which I was silly enough to do at times. Sonny Smoak, one of our ends, and I picked up an average car by its wheels on one side, I at the front wheel and he at the rear (they were not nearly as big then as they are now). We probably could have turned it over if we had wished, but we intended no harm.

We fully expected to win the state championship that year, but our arch rival, Clemson, scored a late touchdown to beat us in our final game. Talk about grown men crying. . . .

At the end of the school year, in the spring of 1943, Coach "Dizzy" McLeod sought me out to ask if I would be returning to play that fall. "You're big," he said, "and you're not afraid." Actually, I wasn't that big, about 190 pounds, I suppose, but football players were not nearly as big then as they are now. As I look back on it, I'm sure that Coach's asking me to stay was a mark of his desperation. His prospects for a team were dim indeed, because so many young men were entering the armed services.

Coach McLeod was not successful in getting a team together for the fall of 1943, and Furman did not field another football team until after the War, but I was flattered that he would ask me, and I was especially pleased that he recognized my lack of fear. I felt that I had overcome what I had interpreted as cowardice. I told the coach that I would not be available for football that fall, because I had already decided to take a final summer school at Furman and then enter Southern Baptist Theological Seminary in Louisville, Kentucky.

After Lib DuPuis and I left Mars Hill, and while I was still at Furman for summer school in 1943, I went to Ridgecrest Baptist Assembly with Lib. You remember that I had known her at Mars Hill and thought that I stood in well with her. She lived in Charleston, South Carolina, and was enrolled at the College of Charleston for her bachelor's degree. While at Ridgecrest, at her initiative, we broke off our relationship and I returned her picture. Actually, she thought we could keep each other's pictures and continue to be good friends, but I thought that such a relationship was unreasonable. She had a boy friend in the armed service (whom she later married), and I felt that it was not appropriate to press the issue. I was feeling keenly the fact that I was not in the military.

However, the visit to Ridgecrest proved to have lasting significance for me quite independently of the fact that Lib and I took our separate ways. It was Baptist Student Week, and it happened that Max and Dorothy Garrott, missionaries to Japan, were on the faculty for that week. I attended a small group session that they led, but far more important to me was Max's address to the assembly as a whole.

Max, who was later to be my colleague in Japan, spoke about Christian love. I could see that he was painfully torn between his native and his adopted countries which were locked in a bitter war. Max said that Jesus instructed us to love our neighbor. And Max asked, "Who is our neighbor?" His answer was Japan. "Therefore," declared Max, "we must love the Japanese." Then he indicated that Jesus also taught us to love our enemy. "And who is our enemy?" he queried. Again the answer was Japan. "So we must love the Japanese," Max said.

This kind of message was not popular in 1943. Everything

conspired with American propaganda to nurture hatred of the Japanese. I was impressed not only with Garrott's obvious pain but also with his raw courage. From that moment I began to feel in my innards that God was calling me to Japan. I kept hearing the quiet question within me, "Luther, why shouldn't you go to tell the Japanese of the great indiscriminate love of God, who loves all, Americans, Russians, Germans, Italians, Japanese, equally and infinitely? And why shouldn't you show them that Christians also love them with this same kind of unprejudiced love?" I could not escape this urgent inner voice. And the motive was Christian love, even if I was a poor representative of it.

I worked in the Library on campus, and in addition was interim pastor of Grover Baptist Church, across the state line in Grover, North Carolina, and had bought a Model A Ford with a rumble seat to commute to Grover on Sundays. At Grover I made several friends though, unfortunately, I have not kept up with them and have forgotten most of them.

One couple, at Grover, however, especially impressed me and have remained in my memory. They may have been in their early fifties at the time I was interim pastor. Several years later, the wife wrote me, saying that her husband, who had been a leader in the church, had committed suicide by drowning. As he traversed his daily mail route, he simply walked out into a pond until the water completely immersed his body. In the letter the widow poured out her grief to me. I was profoundly shocked.

I attended the Summer School Session on the Furman campus--well, it was held on the Woman's College campus. Joe Alewine and I roomed together. Joe was a natty fellow, short of stature, with large teeth which were white and well kept. I remember the situation quite well, because of the incongruity of our living on a woman's campus and in a woman's dormitory. There were no showers and the bathtubs were much too short for me. When I bathed, I had to look out between my knees like a raccoon peering out from the forks of a tree.

Across the hall from us roomed a tall, shy fellow who worked in a cotton mill. It turned out that he, unknown to us, was an epileptic. One night after he had retired, he had a seizure. Joe and I thought that it was an attack of acute indigestion or a heart attack or some other ailment of an emergency nature. When he came to, we had already called a doctor (there was no 911 number in those days) and had some cold wash cloths on his abdomen. As you could imagine, he was greatly embarrassed.

At the end of the 1943 Summer School I lacked only ten semester hours of having enough credits to graduate. Before leaving Furman I applied for and was granted special permission from the appropriate committee to waive the catalog requirement that a student take his or her final semester hours--I don't remember how many--at Furman. The committee agreed that I could take my necessary ten hours at any accredited college and transfer the credits back to Furman.

The reason I asked for this arrangement was that I expected that after I enrolled in seminary I would get a pastorate and would not wish to interrupt myself to return for a summer session at Furman. As it happened, I did not become a pastor until my third and final year at Southern Seminary.

During my first summer at Southern Baptist Theological Seminary, I went to the University of Kentucky at Lexington to finish the hours I lacked at Furman. I took for credit courses in Greek and German and audited a course in French. The Greek teacher was Dean of the University and a former member of a Baptist church. He seemed to be a very good man, but for some trivial reason which I do not remember, he had been excommunicated. My courses with him involved reading two of Plato's letters in Greek. I came to know the professor and to appreciate him. I believe he had the unusual name of Jones.

The University of Kentucky was located in the middle of the beautiful bluegrass and horse country, and I greatly enjoyed my brief sojourn there. That summer I was active in Baptist Student Union on campus, and in that connection got to know some other Baptist students. There were identical twin girls who were just entering the university, and I thought it would be fun to go to Calvary Baptist Church with them for prayer meeting on Wednesday evening. After the service a lady of the church approached me and said, "Oh, Mr. Copeland, I'm so glad you brought your daughters with you to church." You can rest assured that I never went anywhere with those girls again!

On another occasion, a young woman--well, not as young as most--who was back in school to enhance her qualification as a public school teacher, invited me to have Sunday dinner at the home where she was staying (it happened that the family she boarded with were gone for the weekend). After she had fed me a good meal, we sat in the swing on the front porch. Obviously, she had designs on me, as she was getting beyond the usual marriageable age. I escaped with no entangling alliances. In fact, I never saw any of those University of Kentucky students again after I returned to Louisville.

Thus by taking two summer sessions, one at Furman and the other at the University of Kentucky, I sped up the process of my higher education by one year.

Chapter Seven
"THE BEECHES" AND THE NEXT SUMMER

In late August 1943, I moved from Greenville, South Carolina to Louisville, Kentucky. I had stashed all my belongings in my Model A Ford coupe. I experienced once more the hospitality of eastern Tennessee as I had in my hitchhiking jaunt of the first Christmas vacation of my college years in 1940.

This time the things I had packed in the rumble seat of my car were in a position where a rain would get them wet. In the late afternoon of my first day of travel it started to rain, and I took shelter under the roof of a filling station which extended out over the pumps. I was somewhere in eastern Tennessee, and although I do not recall my exact location, I remember that there was a boy and his mother in the station. Upon their inquiry, I told the story of where I was going and why, and the very kind lady offered to put me up in their home for the night. The rain soon stopped, and I declined the offer but have never forgotten it.

People in that part of the country, like those of Mount Nebo and its surrounding territory east of the Gauley in West Virginia, were far more openly hospitable and trusting of strangers than folks in areas which were more industrialized. As in the case of our loss of individualism in the homogenization process which the mass media has fostered, we have made some gains but we have also suffered considerable loss in leaving behind these older cultures.

I arrived safely at the Southern Baptist Theological Seminary, called "the Beeches" for its magnificent beech trees. I was assigned a room in Mullins Hall, where I soon became friends with James E. Davidson and Judson Lennon. Davidson was an older man and a second year student. He had a deep, resonant bass voice and probably was a good preacher. He was a native of Alabama and had been married for several years, but his family were in Birmingham, where he had continued as a pastor after entering seminary. I marveled that he commuted back each weekend to his church in Birmingham by train. I have lost touch with him since he finished seminary and returned to Alabama.

Judson Lennon was from North Carolina and a recent

graduate of Wake Forest College. He was several years younger than I, but we hit it off exceptionally well. We enjoyed studying together, and after our first year, since students generally did not have roommates, we arranged to room close together. Judson was to figure significantly in my life later.

Joe Alewine also had come from Furman to Southern Seminary. In Louisville, Joe and I continued to be friends, and he recom-mended me as a second student, along with himself, to share in the generosity of a St. Louis man by the name of Ernest Pohl, who had made a killing on steam irons. I got a check each month from Mr. Pohl, and he came to Louisville to visit Joe and me on one occasion. After Joe finished Southern Seminary, he married and took a pastorate in Alabama. He and his wife had one daughter and they later moved to western North Carolina, where Joe worked as a counselor in high school, and his wife as a musician in a Baptist church. The daughter was killed in a tragic automo-bile accident, a devastating blow to the parents. Now retired, I believe they live in Forest City, North Carolina.

Southern was a good seminary with some illustrious teachers. Among the most noted were two who had recently retired but were still living nearby and occasionally taught classes, Dr. John R. Sampey and Dr. W. O. Carver. Sampey's specialty was Old Testament and he had retired as President of the Seminary, an office which he had held for several years. Sampey was an old "warhorse," fixated on General Robert E. Lee as his hero. Perhaps unintentionally, he let us know by certain remarks that he still had a strong sex drive. Carver taught Missions and Comparative Religions, but he was an unusual scholar, qualified to teach any course in the seminary curriculum.

Older professors included Dr. Hersey Davis, New Testament, Dr. Gaines Dobbins, Religious Education and Church Administration, Dr. J. McKee Adams, Biblical Introduction, and Dr. J. B. Weatherspoon, Preaching. Younger members of the faculty included Dr. Leo Green in Old Testament, and Dr. Cornell Goerner in Missions and Comparative Religion. In between were men such as Dr. Harold Tribble, Theology, Dr. Edward A. McDowell, New Testament, and Dr. Olin Binkley, Sociology and Ethics.

Although the Seminary had some outstanding scholars, its teaching method, for the most part, was antiquated. Most of the textbooks were written by teachers, and students were called on by name to recite, answering the teacher's questions almost always from the textbooks and being graded according to their answers. On tests, one was expected to regurgitate materials from textbooks--or from the professor's lecture notes, since a few of the younger teachers used the lecture method.

Dr. Dobbins turned out reams of mimeographed pages and distributed them in his classes. He had a great deal of exchange with his students. I used to wonder why I resisted Dr. Dobbins' teaching method since he presumably thought, and so did I, that it was progressive. After a while it dawned on me that Professor Dobbins had already decided what the answers were to his questions, and he would keep probing his students until they came up with the right response--indeed, with the correct *word*--to please him. He was not really encouraging independent thought any more than were those who expected rote answers from textbooks.

Not only was there an out-of-date pedagogical method; faculty relationships were strictly hierarchical. There were heads of departments, and assistant and associate professors were definitely of lesser importance. Relations between professors and students, likewise, were far from equal. Teachers tended to be prima donnas. In any case, students usually were reticent to ask for an appointment with teachers because they felt that to seek out a professor would be an intrusion on his time.

Into this staid situation came Dale Moody to join the faculty in my third and final year. Moody was like a breath of fresh air. He was young--I think he was one year older than I--he prepared well for his classes, he did not impose his views upon his students, and he engaged us in dialogue, both inside and outside the classroom.

Probably the professors who were most influential upon me were McDowell and Binkley. I was greatly impressed by these two and developed a friendly relationship with them. Later, I was to join them as a colleague at Southeastern Seminary, along with others from the Southern faculty, Sid Stealey, Leo Green, and Bill Strickland. I believe Strickland was a year behind me at Southern.

McDowell was from South Carolina and was a Furman graduate. I have always thought that he was prejudiced in my favor because I was from Furman. Under McDowell I came to see as never before the revolutionary social teachings of the gospel.

He not only taught the truth about race relations; he lived it. Under McDowell's teaching I saw for the first time how wrong racism is.

Binkley was the son of a preacher in North Carolina. He, too, was a pioneer in race relations, though not as candid as Mc-Dowell in his speaking and writing. His course in ethics under-girded what McDowell was teaching in New Testament. In my final semester, when I was contemplating a June marriage, I sought Binkley's counsel--the only appointment with a teacher I asked for while at Southern--and found him to be most under-standing and encouraging.

As a mission volunteer, I had good instruction from Cor-nell Goerner. I took three of his courses, Missions, Comparative Religions, and a seminar in the Principles and Practice of Mis-sions. In his survey courses, especially the required missions course, he had the reputation of being boring, but my personal concern with the subject matter served to hold my interest. I believe I took the seminar my last year, and I found it to be of great benefit. The enrollment was relatively small, and we used the International Missionary Council's *Madras Series*. Goerner was skillful in guiding our thoughts.

All in all, Goerner was something of an enigma. He was from Texas, and in the pulpit he was quite lively, as you might expect of a Texas preacher. In fact, he was an effective pulpiteer. In the classroom, he lacked animation, and I always felt, also, that he became more conservative both as to missionary principles and theology, after he left Southern Seminary to become a staff member of the Foreign Mission Board of the Southern Baptist Convention.

At Southern Seminary I was able to see Rufus Mosely, whose book *Manifest Victory* I had read a few years earlier. Mose-ly came to Southern just about each year and spent several days on the campus. On one of his periodic visits he attended a class in systematic theology and sat with the graduate students in the "Amen Corner." The regular teacher, Dr. Harold Tribble, was ab-sent and a graduate fellow, Fritz Schlaefer, was in charge. He was discussing various theories of the inspiration of Scripture, in-cluding the plenary verbal inspiration theory, which the Seminary discounted as teaching dictation, in favor of what was called a "dynamic" concept of inspiration, namely, that the Holy Spirit moved people to write but that they then composed according to their own individual gifts and personalities.

Somewhere in this discussion, Mosely held up a hand indicating that he wanted to speak. I recall him as a small, wiry fellow, whose face wore a sort of mischievous smile. He had a habit of rotating a bent right arm before speaking, as though cranking himself up for the effort. Having thus started his motor, Mosely remarked, "You are discounting inspiration by dictation, are you? Well what about Balaam's ass?"

Which reminds me that if you think that ministerial students are all sober and anemic, you are badly mistaken. Take it from one who knows. Southern had a number of unique characters, one of whom was Henry Langford, a Georgian who after he left seminary ended up in Virginia, where he was thought by some to be a failure as a pastor but at the same time amassed a small fortune as buyer of unproductive land on which he planted pine trees. He did the very unusual thing of persuading a dying church to sell its property and give the money as scholarships for needy students at Southeastern Seminary.

I have it on good authority that on a day when Professor Goerner was most tedious and was mesmerizing his students in a required missions class by rotating his key chain, Henry raised a hand. "Yes, Mr. Langford," said Goerner, "what is it?" "I was just wondering," mused Henry, "if everybody in here is as bored as I am." When Dr. Goerner had recovered somewhat from his shock, he issued a challenge: "If you think you can do better with this class than I, Mr. Langford, please come forward and take charge." Henry did precisely that. It must have been merciful, at least for Dr.Goerner, that the period was nearly over.

I was present on two other occasions when Henry expressed his wit for the benefit of his fellow students and, one would hope, of his teachers. One day Dr. Dobbins was discussing miracle and giving the word a prissy pronunciation--though the story by no means depends upon how the professor spoke. In the midst of it all, Henry raised his hand. "Yes, do you have a question?" asked Dr. Dobbins. (He did not call Henry by name, because he never could remember students' names).

Said Henry, "Dr. Dobbins, you're talking about *midicle, midicle* [mimicking Dr. Dobbins' pronunciation]. They performed a miracle recently in Georgia. They took the rear end of a horse and made a governor out of him." (He was referring to the election of Gene Talmadge as governor--not the first or last time that kind of miracle has been accomplished!)

The other exhibition of Henry Langford's wit that I recall occurred in Dr. Sydnor ("Sid")L. Stealey's church history class. I do not remem-ber what it was that Dr. Stealey said that provoked the question--come to think of it, Henry's comment didn't need to be related to anything the professor said--but Henry raised his hand. "Yes, Mr. Langford?" asked Dr. Stealey, resigning himself to Henry's unpre-dictability. "Dr. Stealey," said Henry, "do you know the difference between a Universalist and a Baptist?" Dr. Stealey probably did, on some profound level, but he invited Henry's opinion anyway. Whereupon Henry suggested, "Well, the Universalist says, 'There ain't no hell,' but the Baptist says 'The hell there ain't.'"

But at Southern there were many other funny men besides Henry Langford. Jim Rowles, whom I had known at Mars Hill, worked at the task of being funny and succeeded very well. He was a rather rotund type with protruding teeth, who had grown up as an Army brat. In spite of the preceding description, he was not unattractive. His laugh, which he emitted quite frequently, was an imitation of that of Gildersleeve, a famous radio comedian.

Jim loved to sing, especially for the benefit of the WMU Training School girls, "Jesus Wants Me for a Sunbeam." For the ears of his fellow seminary students, his theme song, with his own revision, was "Take Your Burden to the Lord and Leave Her There." Jim served tables in the Dining Room in Mullins Hall, which meant that he had to get up rather early in the morning. Always, upon rising, he would throw open the window of his upstairs Mullins Hall room which faced a three sided court, and yell out in a loud tenor voice, "Good morning, world!" Jim later became an Army chaplain and then a pastor in North Carolina and Virginia. Upon retirement he went into counseling. He died too young, in his sixties.

The campus did not lack practical jokers. Ivan Hart, a big fellow from Maryland, dressed up a student from Virginia, who was rather small in stature, as his sister. Hart then took this al-leged female into the men's bathroom on the third floor of Mul-lins and introduced "her" to a nude Jim Rowles as the latter emerged from a shower, much to Jim's utter shock.

John Hurt, from Louisiana, for the one year that he was at Southern, was pastor of the Effingham, Illinois, Baptist Church. When the end of the first semester came, John was behind in his studies and fearful of his preparation for final exams. So he asked me to supply for him at Effingham. Several students had churches in that general direction, so three or four of them car pooled on their weekend trips. I remember that John Ed Steely, Frank Norfleet, and I were along, as was somebody else and his wife, maybe Carl and Vera Newland.

As we approached Louisville on Sunday evening, we hatched up a plot which we executed upon reaching the campus. Although the hour was late, we called John Hurt in his upstairs dormitory room from a pay phone on the first floor. The wife acted as the operator. When John answered the call at the nearest phone, the "operator" indicated that John had a call from Effingham. One of us represented himself as the Chair of the Deacons of the Effingham Church (whose name I had given my companions) and reproved John for not coming to Effingham. While John sputtered and tried to explain, the "deacon" persisted, "We didn't appreciate it that you failed to show up, and we liked that fellow Copeland whom you sent. So we decided to call Copeland and let you go." We got so tickled when John nearly fainted that we gave our pretense away.

John himself was quite a clown. He told how, as a pipe smoker, he somewhat dreaded to come to Southern because he assumed that no one else would smoke.* He had already spotted Carl English who roomed nearby, John said, and pegged him as a puritan. In the privacy of his room John was enjoying his pipe, when a knock came at his door. John hurriedly raised the window and with his hands tried to drive out the smoke as best he could. Then he opened the door, and, as fate would have it, Carl English was the man who had knocked. "Have you got a match?" asked English.

---

*After Southeastern Baptist Theological Seminary was founded in Wake Forest, North Carolina, the heart of tobacco country, the word (with appropriate exaggeration) was that "At Southwestern Seminary, smoking is prohibited, at Southern it is tolerated, and at Southeastern it is required."

Like one of my more staid colleagues in Japan at a later time remarked of his own experience, I even said something funny myself. One day I made my way to my usual table in the Dining Hall for dinner. Toward the end of the meal, the waiter brought strawberry shortcake for dessert. Quoting Jacob from the Old Testament, I declared in a solemn voice, "Surely the Lord is in this place, and I wist it not."

Though I am lifting out humorous experiences at Southern Seminary, the truth is that we were serious most of the time, and the seminary community ministered to my spiritual needs. One of my most difficult problems was my uneasy conscience on the question of whether I should join the armed services. After all, many of my friends and acquaintances, and indeed members of my own family, had gone into the military. I was convinced that the cause of the Allies in World War Two was right and that of the Axis powers was wrong. I had pacifist leanings, but I was not an absolute pacifist. I often wondered whether I too should get more directly involved in the War. Often I felt embarrassment if not shame.

While I was in this quandary, Professor J. B. Weatherspoon spoke in the Seminary chapel on the text 2 Corinthians 5:9 about being pleasing to Christ. Dr. Weatherspoon made no such direct application, but I concluded that my conviction that I had been out of school too long to interrupt my education to help out more directly in the war effort was a matter of Christian guidance. My desire to enlist in the military service was an attempt to please those who might be critical of me rather than to please Christ. Of course, I do not judge those who took a different course from mine in regard to this knotty question. The way I decided may not have been right for them at all. As for me, however, right then and there I settled that matter and it has bothered me very little since.

I viewed Southern Seminary as providing a spiritual atmosphere. Therefore, I can enjoy the humor of the following story without in any way agreeing with the persons involved. I have heard this story many times, and I think it happened soon after I left Louisville for Yale.

Three overly pious brethren had entered Southern Seminary and had made a very adverse judgment about the spirituality of the place. When they gathered for prayer, the burden was for revival at Southern. One of them prayed earnestly, "O Lord, bring revival to this seminary! Please set this place on fire! Lord, this is the coldest place I ever saw." Both of the pious brothers had voiced an "Amen!" to the first two requests. Then after the third sentence, about how cold Southern was, one of the brothers said, "Brrr, Lord!"

Since pastorates were not easy to come by at Southern, especially for single students, I worked at various jobs to pay my way. During the first year, I had a job firing the heating plant. Usually, I had the morning shift, from about 5:00 to 7:30, I believe. I had to get up very early, by 4:45, and fire up the furnace. Sometimes I would be asked to exchange shifts with someone who worked evenings, usually so that this student could go on a date. On one occasion I had made such a trade with one of my fellow students. It happened that this guy was one of the few at S.B.T.S. who were subject to occasional epileptic seizures. I never knew whether his epilepsy had anything to do with the outcome of the exchange, for he never mentioned it to me.

Anyhow, the next morning at about six I was blissfully sleeping when someone knocked loudly at my door. When I drowsily answered, in came my boss, a man by the name of Gordon, the assistant superintendent of buildings and grounds, who had responsibility for the heating plant. I awoke rather quickly, when I saw Mr. Gordon, and I discerned right off that he was hot under the collar--as hot, it turned out, as the heating plant was cold. "Why didn't you fire the heating plant this morning?" he demanded in a loud voice. I explained that I had traded with So-and-So.

Whereupon Mr. Gordon came out with a scatological epithet which was about as close to a cussword as you generally heard in those parts. "Shit! Don't you know that you can't depend on him?" demanded Mr. Gordon rhetorically. "Now get up and get that fire going!" It occurred to me to wonder, since Mr. Gordon said that I could not trust So-and-So, why this same Mr. Gordon had entrusted the heating plant to So-and-So? However, it didn't seem the diplomatic thing to ask this question of Mr. Gordon--at least not at that time.

For my second year, I was employed by a filling station owner, a job for which Wade Hale, my friend from Furman days, recommended me. All three of the personnel at the filling station besides Wade and me--the owner, the receptionist, and the mechanic--seemed to be lovers of booze, if not alcoholics. If they weren't drinking something, they had it on their breaths. They sold an inordinate amount of tires, which Wade and I had to mount on wheels. Obviously, their business was very profitable, but Wade and I wondered whether it was legitimate. We never learned. Both of us got pastorates in our final year and left the filling station.

Also, until I became a pastor, I worked at various volunteer tasks in Louisville. One of these was teaching a boy's Sunday School class at the Masonic Home for children on Sunday afternoon. The boys seemed hungry for affection and related very well to me and to other seminary students who visited them regularly. I felt that we had a very fruitful ministry among them.

During my second year, instead of this service I went each Sunday to the Waverly Hills Tuberculosis Sanitorium. A group of us went together in the small Seminary bus, of which I was the driver. Jim Rowles was one of those who went along. He regularly took Hershey's Kisses with him and then bragged about giving the patients a kiss.*

Still another of my volunteer ministries was one which, as I have often reflected, may have been the most valuable of all: street preaching. We preached on every Friday night, in front of a bar on Jefferson Street, in the notorious Hay Market section of Louisville. There was no captive audience. The preacher had to retain the hearers' interest or simply lose them. He had to be prepared for hostile or negative reactions and arguments.

We had a little portable organ which one of the students played, and we sang hymns. Whether because of the nostalgia of the music or for other reasons, members of our audience often came quite contritely to confess their sins and seek forgiveness.

On one occasion, a fellow who was very drunk came to kneel before me and weep. Just about the time he assumed this posture, he "went skidded," as we used to term it, that is, he passed out completely and fell unconscious at my feet. Just at that time, a paddy wagon stopped in front of us, and two big burly

---

*Louise Tadlock was also one of the volunteers, but you'll get acquainted with her later.

policeman got out and, one grabbing each end of the poor fellow, unceremoniously heaved him into the wagon. Feeling some pity for the drunk, I remonstrated with one of the policemen. "You don't have to be so rough," I said. "For all we know, we might be in his place some time." "Brother, *you* might be," replied the cop, "but *I* won't."

I went the next day to visit the fellow, and found him sober and embarrassed. As was our custom, I got his home address, somewhere in Indiana, I believe, and the name of a pastor to whom we could refer him. Though there seems to have been no falsification in this instance, frequently when we tried to do follow up visits in Louisville, we were frustrated because our clients often gave us nonexistent addresses.

On another night, we had set up for our service, not in front of the bar but beside it on a street which intersected with Jefferson. This meant that we were near the back door of the bar rather than the front. An older seminary student, a big stout fellow from Georgia, had just started preaching, when all of a sudden a man came running out the back door of the bar with another man after him. Just as the fleeing man got to where our preacher was standing, the man in pursuit threw a bottle of beer at him. The bottle fell short of its target and landed at the feet of the preacher, breaking and splashing beer all over him. The preacher was quite taken aback at first; in fact, he paled and looked frightened. However, he made a good recovery, and resumed his sermon with renewed vigor, shouting out, "That's what sin will do to you!"

About the beginning of my third and final year at Southern Seminary, I was called as pastor by two churches. Both were across the Ohio river in Indiana and both were affiliated with what was then the Northern Baptist Convention (now the American Baptist Churches, USA). One was the Hebron Baptist Church, a rather strong country church in a prosperous farming community. The other was the Indian Kentuck Baptist Church in the little village of Canaan. Both were near Madison, Indiana.

I thought that each of the two could afford to go full time rather than remain half time, so I persuaded both congregations that they should do so. I elected to stay with the weaker and less desirable of the two, the Indian Kentuck Church, since that commended itself as the Christian choice.

Which means, I believe, that I was at Hebron for about

three months. I found the folks quite devoted to Christ and the church, and I got along well with them. This was in spite of the fact that there was one of my sermons for which no one expressed appreciation. In that particular sermon I made so bold as to suggest that if I owned a piece of land I would ask God whether he wanted me to grow tobacco on it. Since practically all the farmers in the congregation grew burley tobacco, they could hardly have been expected to applaud my sermon.

Also, for the first time I encountered a situation--not a bad idea, mind you--where the church had somebody other than the pastor as moderator, in this case a big fellow by the name of Muse. When I expressed some uncertainty as to who was moderator, Mr. Muse let me know very decisively that he was it, because the church had so elected him. Of course, he was right.

By this time, I had long since sold my Model A Ford to Clyde Bell, a fellow in Summersville, West Virginia,* and had come into the possession of a 1934 Plymouth Coupe. When I had a fellow student from Mississippi, Charles Whitten, help me in a revival, that car seemed bent on turning in the lane to a certain home where there was a friendly family and a croquet court. Usually, to Charles' great amusement, I did not resist the Plymouth. Charles also laughed at the Indiana folks' indicating that they did such-and-such habitually "of a morning," or "of an evening," an idiomatic usage with which I had grown up in West Virginia. Also, many years after he had heard it from me, in his post-retirement years, in a letter to me, Charles quoted verbatim the statement of my semiliterate neighbor from Hookersville days: "As I was caming across the mounting to Mr. Copender's, I met a game rewarder."

At Hebron, I baptized some folks in a nearby creek, one of whom was an exceptionally fine lady, already a Christian, a Presbyterian, who had been baptized by sprinkling as an infant. She sought membership in Hebron Baptist Church, quite aware of the fact that the only way to become a member was to be baptized as a believer by immersion. Though she was resolute in her desire for immersion, she told me that she was deathly afraid of

---

*I came to find out that my brother Lowell thought that I had promised to sell it to him.

water. I gave her every assurance, telling her that I was quite strong and could hold her up. At the time of the baptism, she went into the water with me to where it was deep enough. And then she fainted! Her face turned a pasty white and she went limp in my arms. When I whispered reassuring words to her, she came to and wanted to proceed with the baptism; she did so, without any further difficulty.

I found that many, if not most, of the members at Indian Kentuck were lackadaisical concerning the Church. I'm afraid I was not as understanding and gentle as I should have been, wooing them by the constraints of the love of Christ. Instead, I let what I thought was the zeal of the Lord direct me in my sermons. Especially did I have some trouble with the women. They had a Ladies' Aid Society whose primary concern seemed to be making money for their organization.

When I tried to show them a "more perfect way," namely, a women's group which would be interested in serving the church and community, one of them asked, "And what would we get out of it?" I had some diplomatic women from a Southern Baptist church across the Ohio in Kentucky meet with them to discuss with them how the Woman's Missionary Union tried to get at the problem, but I'm afraid my point of view was not well accepted.

There was a fellow in the community who had come back from World War II with what was then called "shell shock" (and now would be known as Post-Trauma Stress Syndrome or some such fancy name). At times he exhibited some bizarre behavior patterns. One of my profound regrets is that I did nothing for him. I was ill prepared to deal with a person in his condition and I simply avoided him.

I liked to spend time in the home of a deacon--I believe he was Chair of the Deacons--by the name of John Scott. Scott was a bit angular in personality, but he seemed to get along very well with his fellow church members. He and his wife were devoted Christians.

They had two sons, the younger of whom , I suppose, was about three. I related well to the boys and liked to play with them. Particularly, I enjoyed throwing them up in the air and catching them, and they seemed to like this exercise very much. One day I threw the younger one up in the air, unmindful of the fact that we were standing under a chandelier with a spike-like arrangement on the bottom. Imagine my horror to see that the little fellow's head was striking the chandelier! Several stitches had to be taken in his scalp, and I was absolutely shocked and mortified. Fortunately, both the boy and his parents were quite understanding and made nothing of the incident.

When things were not going well at the Indian Kentuck Church, I stopped my car one day and prayed, asking the Lord for a vote of confidence. I probably didn't deserve it, but I was persuaded that God gave it to me.

A full-time pastor, not a student, who had been in a neighboring church field for several years, came to visit my people with me one Sunday afternoon. This guy was quite a cut-up, and the truth is that he knew my parishioners better than I did. When we visited a young couple with a new baby, he led me to speculate as to which of the parents the baby resembled. Quite naively, if tactfully, I noted aspects of the baby's physiognomy which favored each parent in turn. The visiting pastor completely deflated the balloon of my ego by informing me in the presence of both parents that the baby was adopted!

At the beginning of my second year, I met the young woman who was to become my wife. It happened by the confluence of two factors. It might have transpired anyway, but here is the way it actually came about. I have mentioned before that Judson Lennon was my good friend. During our first year at Southern Seminary, Judson was occupied with the problem of how to extract himself from a relationship with a girl back in North Carolina, a relationship which he saw had no future. Therefore, unlike me, he had not made frequent trips across the "Valley of Decision" to the WMU Training School, which was on a contiguous campus, and was not acquainted with the young women in that school. Finally, by the time of our enrollment for the second year, he was free of that troubling relationship. So Judson's liberation was the first factor in my introduction to my future wife.

The second happening came around each fall: the Crescent Hill Baptist Church, the Baptist church nearest the campus, held a reception for new students at Southern Seminary and the Training School. Though Judson and I were not new students, this occasion commended itself as a good opportunity to meet the new Training School girls, so the two of us decided to attend.

The reception, a very nice event, featured refreshments and a long receiving line, with the pastor of the church and the most notable of the faculty and administration of the two schools being the first in the line. The farther you went, the less distinguished were the positions represented. By the time you reached the end of the line, you had just about run out of notables. As we neared the terminus, one of us suggested, I honestly don't remember which one, that we drop in at the end of the line as though we belonged there, from which vantage point we might survey the new crop of girls. Which, of course, is precisely what we did.

Soon Harriet Orr came along with another young lady in tow. Now I had known Harriet at Mars Hill, and she and I had entered our respective schools in Louisville at the same time. Harriet was from Charlotte, North Carolina. She was a very nice, attractive girl, and also quite sharp. She immediately sized up the situation and asked, "Luther Copeland, what are you doing in this line?" I answered quite honestly that the idea was to be able to look over the new girls entering the Training School.

Whereupon I introduced Judson to Harriet and her companion, and Harriet introduced her new roommate to Judson and me, Louise Tadlock, from Oklahoma. Judson and I dropped out of the line to accompany these two young ladies. About two years later, in the summer of 1946, Judson and Harriet were married, and two weeks afterward Louise and I said our wedding vows. Judson was my best man, and Harriet was one of Louise's bridesmaids.

Well, it didn't happen immediately, at least so far as Louise and I were concerned. I had other interests at the Training School, and Louise sometimes dated other Seminary students. Fortunately, neither of us was attached at home. Gradually, our relationship developed, so that by the end of the school year, we had focused our romantic interests upon each other. Louise has told me that she and Harriet used to complain to each other that Judson and I would give them but little advance notice, waiting until about the night before to call them for a date. Actually, Judson and I both tended to procrastinate and not determine our schedules very far ahead of time. We certainly meant nothing by our tardiness.

Also, I really didn't think Louise had more than a casual interest in me. She seemed more concerned with her studies. It took a trick which her friends played upon her and me to cause me to think that she really cared. Louise happened to be gone for a day or so, and in her absence three of her girl friends, including Harriet, decided that it would be nice to invite four of us Seminary students to a picnic in Cherokee Park, an immense city park near the campuses. Since Louise was not present, the girls wrote a note of invitation to me and signed Louise's name.

When she returned and found out what had happened, poor Louise was humiliated. She thought that I would interpret her alleged action as too forward, and that I would have nothing to do with her in the future. On the contrary, I was immensely flattered. Louise Tadlock really likes me, I thought.

Of course both of us very seriously sought divine guidance in this matter. Each of us felt that God had a partner for us and we wanted to be sure that we followed God's plan. Louise has told me more than once that long before I realized it, she knew that I was the one she should marry. Unfortunately, I did not have the benefit of such spiritual insight or prescience.

But let me tell you about Louise. She was born in Las Cruces, New Mexico, the oldest of four daughters, and her early schooling was on the semidesert plains of New Mexico. Although our backgrounds in many ways were very dissimilar, we shared something of cultural isolation in our upbringing, hers of the ranch and mine of the mountains, and both had attended one-room schools for our elementary education.

Her father, John Tadlock, was a New Mexico cowboy who had a physical injury from World War I. He also suffered from manic depression for which he was hospitalized on two occasions. In later life, he developed skills in carpentry and house painting. Her mother was from eastern Kentucky. She came west as a school teacher, met John Tadlock, fell in love with him, and the two were married. When Louise was about 13, the family moved to Tahlequah, Oklahoma, so that the children could be educated at Northeastern State Teachers College (now Northeastern State University). Both parents wanted the girls to get a college education, but the mother was especially committed to it. They were still living in Tahlequah when Louise and I married.

Louise was a tall girl, about five feet eight, with a slender, willowy figure. Although her skin was fair, her eyes were brown, and her hair was brunette, beyond auburn but not black. Her hair, long and with a natural wave, was a striking mark of her beauty. She usually wore a fresh flower in it, enhancing its loveliness. Her walk was most unusual, graceful as that of a doe. I once said of her, quoting from a popular song of the times, "Did you ever see a dream walking? Well, I did." I thought that the color blue was especially becoming to her, and I was particularly fond of a blue print dress which she wore while a student in Louisville.

More pronounced even than her natural beauty was Louise's personality. She was modest to a fault, always self-deprecating. She was sweet and agreeable, very sensitive to the feelings and needs of others. She complemented me at the very points where I was most deficient: my difficulty in feeling and showing affection and my shyness in meeting other people. Louise related to others considerably better than I, and it was always a great benefit to have her accompany me on pastoral visits. She was a devoted Christian and deeply spiritual.

For Christmas of 1945 Louise went home with me to Mount Nebo to meet my family. We greatly enjoyed the time together in the 1934 Plymouth coupe. I'm afraid that West Virginia looked rather drab in its winter garments. We made a trip to Muddlety to see where I had lived longest in my growing up.

In that community was a man fully as bizarre as any of the characters I described in an earlier chapter. He was Mr. Trimble, father of Farley Trimble who had married my sister Vernice. Mr. Trimble was living in a little hut by himself after his wife, who was a few years his junior, had left him (understandably!) and was living nearby with a younger man, Mr. Trimble having given his blessing to this union. Among other eccentricities, Mr. Trimble dyed his very thin white hair with black shoe polish, a result being that the polish was very obvious, as well as unsightly, on his scalp. Another of his foibles was to attach his trousers by means of bailing wire where a belt should have been. As I have warned you, he was bizarre.

I thought the polite thing--not to say the very interesting thing--to do would be to introduce Louise to Mr. Trimble. So it was that we were standing outside the front door of Mr. Trimble's ramshackle abode for the introduction. Mr. Trimble was hard of hearing, so I said in a loud voice, "Mr. Trimble, I want you to meet my fiancée, Miss Louise Tadlock." Mr. Trimble said, "Hah? You say her name is Padlock?" "No, no," I shouted, "her name is Tadlock. It starts with a 'T.'" "Hah? Yeah, well I guess you would need a key," responded Mr. Trimble. So I gave up, saying to myself, "What the heck? I'll soon change her name anyway!"

Meanwhile, in my senior year, the school honored me by granting me the highest office available to a student on campus. I don't even remember the correct title, maybe it was Chairman of the Seminary Council. At the same time, I was chosen by my class as President. In addition, Louise and I studied together for semester exams in those classes which we shared together, even if we were not in the same section. I recall especially that we reviewed together for an exam in one of Professor Gaines Dobbins's classes in Religious Education.

In early June 1946, I went to Louise's home on Summit Avenue in Tahlequah, Oklahoma, to prepare for our marriage. When we went to the Court House to arrange for the blood test and get the marriage license, I was particularly impressed by the fact that most of the town officials were Native Americans. Tahlequah had been settled by the Cherokees as their capital after they had been forcibly removed from their homes in the eastern United States and had completed the very tragic winter journey called the "Trail of Tears" at the instigation of the American government. Fortunately, I found that in spite of the extreme bitterness of their beginnings, the Native Americans of that area of Oklahoma had some compensation in that they were well accepted by the majority culture.

Louise and I were married on her 23rd birthday, June 5, 1946. I had become 30 in January of the same year. The wedding was at the First Baptist Church of Tahlequah, and the reception followed at the Tadlock home. A retired minister by the name of Burton, who was serving the church as interim pastor, performed the ceremony. The church sanctuary was decorated with field daisies, one of Louise's favorite flowers, by her dear friend and mentor, Mrs. Lorena Louise Travis, whose husband was on the faculty and administrative staff of the college.

In the late afternoon we headed for the Seminary in Louisville, where we were to spend our honeymoon in Rice Hall, having rented one of the Rice apartments from a student and his wife who would be gone for the summer. On the way we spent

Illustration No. 25
Our Wedding Picture
(From Left: Mr. Burton, Louise's Sister Wanda, the Bride and Groom,
Judson Lennon, Louise's Sister Winnie, Harriet Orr Lennon)

our first night in a motel near Springfield, Missouri, happy almost
to the point of delirium, so that we hardly noticed that the steaks
we had for supper were very tough. As we continued on our journey the next day, Louise took the wheel to practice her driving,
only to run over a dog. Though the tragic occurrence was un-
avoidable, it was also unnerving. So I drove for the rest of the trip.

To my knowledge, I didn't run over any animals, but I did
get arrested for a traffic violation. We had decided that we should
drive on to Louisville that night, rather than spend money on
another motel. In fact, we didn't have that kind of money. So we
came into Henderson, Kentucky, about midnight, I suppose. The
town seemed utterly deserted. Louise was asleep with her head
in my lap, and I perhaps was daydreaming in the middle of the
night. Ahead of me was a traffic light which was green until I got
almost under it. Then it turned amber and then red. I hastily
looked both ways, and there was no car in sight. So I let off my
brakes and didn't even try to stop. I sneaked through the red light
and assumed no one would be the wiser.

Where in the world did that police car come from? I don't know, but there it was, right beside me, and the city patrolman motioned for me to follow him. His station was nearby, so we soon reached it. By that time Louise was awake and wondering what was happening. Hastily I tried to explain, as I got out of the car to follow the policeman into the building. When the policeman asked why I had run that red light, I started to explain myself, but he cut me short. "Yeah," he said, "if you hadn't been speeding you could have stopped all right."

At that point my newly married exuberance took over, and I said, "Well, you fellows are just doing your job. That's what the taxpayers are paying you for." The fellow behind the desk was writing out my ticket, but he volunteered, "You're unlucky. They happened to be there at the right time." "Hey," I said, "I just got married yesterday, and my bride's waiting in the car. We're on our way to Louisville."

By that time the ticket was completed and the man who wrote it said, "That'll be three dollars." I paid him the money, secretly thanking God that I could cover it. I had visions of paying out all my money, while poor Louise feared that the fine would exceed my very limited resources and I would spend the night in the pokey. She was amazed, and relieved, to see the big cop follow me out the door, slapping me on the shoulder, and saying, "Goodbye, buddy. Be careful."

We arrived in Louisville without any more misadventures, and I began to make further preparation for the revival meetings I had scheduled, in Dupont, Indiana; New Harmony, Indiana; Stephensport, Kentucky; and Fredericksburg, Virginia. In Dupont, Indiana, we had a delightful time serving the Baptist Church, affiliated with the Northern Baptist Convention, the pastor and his wife being Jim and Eda Stertz whom we had known at Southern Seminary and the WMU Training School, respectively. They were a delightful couple, still honeymooning, as were we. We stayed in the home of a lady who was a member of their church. Among other goodies, she served us toast with honey cream for break-fast. It was my first encounter with honey cream.

At Stephensport, Kentucky, down the Ohio River from Louisville, Charles Whitten, whom I have mentioned in relation to my brief pastorate of Hebron Baptist Church, was pastor. Soon he was to marry Indy (Nella Dean) Mitchell, and they would distinguish themselves as missionaries in two or three Latin American countries, in Spain and in Africa. We stayed in the home of a widow woman in Stephensport, Mrs. Dora Gilbert, and we discovered that she had an amazing knowledge of Southern Baptist foreign missionaries. She carefully studied her WMU literature, and she seemed to know all the missionaries by name!

One of the converts at Stephensport was a teenager who was unloved by her only parent, her mother, and was already embarked upon a life for which the community ostracized her. Her name was Inous Henning. At Charles's suggestion, Louise befriended her, and Inous made a profession of faith in Christ. Later Inous married, and had a son, and then grandchildren. This simple woman has kept in touch with us during the years, and her faithful Christian life and strength of character during many hardships have been a blessing to us until this very moment.

My memory doesn't tell me much about the revival at New Harmony Baptist Church, Indiana, except that the church was affiliated with the Northern Baptist Convention and was led by one of my fellow students at Southern Seminary. I don't even remember the fellow's name. I do recall that there was a billy goat tethered in proximity to the church, near a large gully with steep banks. Sometime during the meeting the goat hanged himself and perished. It was not known whether it was an accident or a suicide. I suspected that the goat had heard my preaching and decided to end it all!

Out in the country near Fredericksburg, Virginia, my friend from Mars Hill and Furman days, John Hodge, was pastor of two churches, Shiloh and Oak Grove, and interim pastor of a third. I had a revival in each during the three weeks that Louise and I were there. John and his wife, the former Vera Witter, had their first of three children by that time, Teddy (Theodore Edwin, the Edwin being from my own name), who was just a toddler, still in diapers. On a hot July day while we were staying at their house, Teddy got into the brown sugar and spread it all over his little body except the part covered by his only clothing, a diaper, which also was coated with brown sugar. John unceremoniously turned the hose on him and washed the brown sugar off.

We were impressed with the Christian dedication of this couple, their devotion to each other, and how each complemented the other. John did many of the household chores in addition to his pastoral work. Because of her frail health, Vera of necessity budgeted her energy, but she made fine contributions within her limitations, especially through her music.

We had several professions of faith and therefore several people to be baptized. John did the baptism in the Rappahannock River which flows near Fredericksburg. One of the men to be baptized was somewhat retarded mentally, about 40 years of age, and rather tall and wiry. The river had an attractive beach where John was baptizing, with a large number of the church people gathered there.

The bottom of the river sloped off fairly gently for some distance, when it became steeper, the water, of course, increasing in depth accordingly. John was rather short of stature himself, but he led this tall fellow out into the water to where it was deep enough for the baptism. When he started to put him under, unlike the other candidates for baptism, this guy started crawfishing rapidly out toward the deep. John grabbed him by the belt, lifted him off his feet and hastily dunked him.

When the baptism was over, the two were exactly turned around: the baptized was facing the deep and so was the baptizer. As they walked up out of the water, the new Christian, in spite of the fact that he had almost drowned himself and the pastor, turned to John and said in a loud voice, "I didn't do so bad, did I?" The congregation could not contain their laughter, and the baptism was almost broken up.

I remember that summer as rather idyllic--a kind of honeymoon in which Louise and I got to know each other better. Our God was good to us indeed. The several weeks of preaching and the joy of being with these friends and their church people was good spiritual preparation for our move to New England.

Chapter Eight
THE END OF THE LINE AT YALE

In the late summer of 1946, before Louise and I moved permanently to Yale, we made a trip up to New Haven to look for housing. Being unsuccessful, we had to move there on faith that housing could be found. As we drove about in the 1934 vintage Plymouth, however, trying to find places advertised in the paper, I was something of a deterrent to faster traffic. One genial fellow, noticing my Kentucky tag, pulled up beside us and asked, "Excuse me, suh. Is that the way you all drive in old Kaintucky?"

Finally, on a second trip, a resident of New Haven rented us a beach cottage in Milford, about ten or twelve miles down the coast from New Haven. This rental was a kind of experiment. The beach cottage was not insulated and was heated with a space heater which burned fuel oil. The experiment was to see if we could endure it for a Connecticut winter. If so, the owner could advertise it as a year-round house. It turned out that we couldn't endure the cold, but that wasn't the main reason we felt we had to move about the first of 1947, as I will explain later.

I had been accepted at Yale to do graduate work in Biblical Theology; I had taken Hebrew and Greek and I thought I was well prepared. However, before we arrived, I had decided to change to the History of Christianity, primarily because that was where Dr. Kenneth Scott Latourette's classes were listed. After all,

Illustration No. 26
Uncle Ken Latourette

I had a minor in history in college, I had taken a church history course and two or three missions courses in seminary, and Louise and I were headed for Japan as missionaries. I really wanted to major with the famous missiologist.

When I met with Dr. Latourette, he suggested that I major in the field in which I was preparing to teach in Japan. Since I was slated to offer courses in the field of church history, I felt that the interview had confirmed my plans, though I am not sure that was Dr. Latourette's interpretation.

So I took courses which would continue throughout the school year, and the school year consisted of three terms. I enrolled for Introduction to the History of Doctrine with Dr. Albert Outler; Seminar in American Church History with Dr. Luther Weigle, Dean of the Divinity School; History of the Expansion of Christianity with Latourette; and two reading courses with Latourette, History of Japan and History of Christianity in Japan. In addition, I audited the course in General Church History with Dr. Roland Bainton. I took Outler for historical theology instead of Robert Calhoun because Calhoun was on sabbatical leave that year.

Although my primary registration was in the Graduate School, I had secondary registration in the Divinity School. Also, all of my classes were in the Divinity School and all the professors who taught me were on its faculty. Tuition at Yale was $450 for the school year, which seemed a huge sum of money then. A work scholarship, which meant that I worked in the Library until I got a pastorate, reduced it to $200. For my senior year I had a University Scholarship which took care of tuition.

It was great to be in Yale Divinity School in the 1940s. I may be prejudiced, but I doubt if that school has ever had a more illustrious faculty, before or since. All the men I have mentioned were brilliant scholars and teachers. Latourette's scholarship was impeccable. He was a Baptist and a bachelor, and he always had an informal group of undergraduate students meeting each week in his apartment in the Divinity School. I developed the habit of his students and called him "Uncle Ken," but it took him a while to get accustomed to my name, at first calling me "Mr. Coleman."

But Uncle Ken was unfailingly helpful and kind. After I departed from Yale he always answered my letters in long hand. He was a most humble and devoted Christian scholar, conservative in theology, and with a strong sense of responsibility for an evangelistic witness to undergraduates. Uncle Ken once told me that he never wrote a volume without a sense of call to write that particular book. Even doing his own note keeping and typing, Uncle Ken published more books than I could read!

Outler was relatively young, and he related easily to students. His class was most stimulating. He was a Methodist, and along with Dr. Julian Hartt, the other Methodist on the Divinity

School faculty, he insisted on being pastor of a small Methodist church in the area. Though loyal to his denomination, Outler was quite ecumenical. I viewed him as a truly catholic theologian.

Though I did not have Calhoun as a teacher, I had to take one of his prelims (preliminary exams, preliminary to writing a dissertation, that is). Calhoun was a Congregationalist (later the United Church of Christ). He did not write much, perhaps because he was a perfectionist, but he was a superb lecturer, lecturing without notes (I was told) and writing Greek and Latin on the board as easily as most of us write English. Bainton, whose background was Quaker, also was brilliant. Like Calhoun, he gave fascinating lectures without notes.

Illustration No. 27
With Others at Yale University Graduate School
(From Left, Bill Dolliver, Grad. Student (GS), Professor Bainton,
John Leith, GS, and Me)

Dean Weigle was a Lutheran who had formally joined a Congregationalist church so as to qualify as Dean. He was a splendid man and a fine administrator. As a scholar, he was one of those rare persons with such a remarkable ability and breadth of knowledge that he could teach any course in the divinity school curriculum and do so effectively. He was very likable, and it was most refreshing to hear his booming voice and hearty laugh. And there were others there who were likewise renowned, Richard Niebuhr, Miller Burrows, Clarence Craig, and Paul Vieth easily come to mind.

Although I have used the term "Doctor" rather naturally, at Yale none of these famous professors was called "Doctor" but always "Mister." It was Mr. Latourette, Mr. Bainton, Mr. Niebuhr, and so forth.

Yale for me was a profoundly liberating experience. I was surrounded by persons of other backgrounds, other points of view and other cultures. A premium was put upon reading, and I read more than ever before both in volume and in diversity. In contrast to Southern Baptist Theological Seminary, the teaching was mostly by the lecture method, with an emphasis upon dialogue with students. Also, professors were always available for conferences. I have always been very grateful for Southern Seminary, but it seemed a bit inhibiting compared to Yale.

Certainly nobody at Southern tried to put me into a mold. However, the viewpoints, though somewhat diverse, were nonetheless Southern Baptist. The theological atmosphere at Yale Divinity School was pluralistic but more neo-Orthodox than anything else, probably. It seems to me that I was mature enough to take it in stride. I neither retreated to a narrow fundamentalism nor embraced a radical liberalism.

At Yale I renewed my ties with John Hurt and Ray Brown, both of whom were from Louisiana, and Ray's wife, Caralie, who was from Virginia. All three of them I had known at Louisville. John was quite a sportsman and he and I hunted squirrels together. Also, he was no mean comedian. The dining hall at Yale Divinity School was called "The Refectory." It was especially attractive in that professors sat, one at a table, with students, and engaged them in some very stimulating table conversations. The refectory was not formal, but neither was it entirely informal.

Sitting at table one day for lunch, I became aware of a commotion at the other end of the hall, and I looked up to see what was the matter. Now it happened that we were served beef tongue that day, and you may know that beef tongue is sliced lengthwise and horizontally so that the shape of the tongue is retained. The fuss was caused by the spectacle of John Hurt striding down the aisle with a slice of beef tongue hanging from his mouth, reaching almost to his belt, and with his eyes bugged out as few can bug them.

John married a fellow student named Jane, a nice, attractive young woman from West Virginia. After they finished Yale Divinity School, they went to Louisiana where John became pastor of a Southern Baptist church. They had an autistic son over whom they agonized. John had deliberately gone back to minister to his own people, but he suffered considerably because of his stand on the race issue. He took a job as director of an ecumenical agency in Atlanta, and ended up in the Unitarian Universalist Church where he finally found acceptance before his death. About his friend, Ray Brown, I will have more to say later, since he figured prominently in my life not only at Yale but especially afterward.

As far as churches of the area surrounding Yale were concerned, there was great variety. There were no Southern Baptist churches in New England at that time. There were some Independent Baptist congregations which were very conservative in theology, but most Baptist churches were American Baptist, and among the American Baptists there was a variety which ranged all the way from an extreme conservatism to a far out liberalism.

Although the New England culture was quite different from anything we had known, Louise and I rather enjoyed it. Unlike Southerners, Yankees tended to be unpretentious. They were not so conscious of appearances. Therefore, you did not need to be so overly aware of clothes, and you were expected to be frugal in such things as the car you owned. It is true that there was not the open hospitality and friendliness of the South, but New Eng-landers were by no means unkind. Until fairly recently, we have kept some contact with one or two persons in the Niantic, Con-necticut, church where I was pastor well over fifty years ago.

I was dismayed by the degree of Biblical illiteracy of New Englanders, except fundamentalists. Louise's sister, Betty, stayed with us for a while and attended high school. When a teacher asked students in one of Betty's classes who Judas was, only one girl besides Betty held up her hand. When the other girl was chosen to answer, she said, "He's the man who sold out God."

Louise expected to provide our support. Since she was qualified in home economics, she got a job as a sewing teacher, conducting classes at three or four schools. So she was pretty busy commuting here and there by bus or street car. As there was a good public transportation system, she was able to get about very well. In spite of the fact that we had not planned it that way, Louise got pregnant with our first child. When toward the end of the first semester, in order to be honest, she told her supervisor about the pregnancy, he informed her she would have to quit immediately. After all, a pregnant woman must not teach girls!

So our financial arrangements dissolved like a wisp of smoke in a spring breeze. Fortunately, I had saved up enough money for my first year's tuition, and my oldest sister Bertha gave us a generous donation, citing the fact that in her youth she had intended to go as a missionary.

By this time it was getting cold, and we were hovering around the space heater to keep from freezing in our beach cottage. Since Louise was relieved of her job, it was apparent that I needed to find a pastorate. So I visited Ralph Woodward in the employment office, and he sent me to preach a trial sermon in the Niantic Baptist Church in the small town of Niantic up the beach some 46 miles from New Haven.

I remember that when we reached West Haven on our way back to our cold house in Milford, we had already encountered a very wet snow. Our windshield clogged up with the rapidly falling white crystals, and I got out to clean it off. As I was not wearing gloves, I got my hands cold in the process of clearing the windshield. When I wrung my hands to shake the water off them, lo and behold my wedding band slipped off my finger and landed somewhere in the snow! After a brief and discouraging attempt to find it, we went on home.

On the next day, we woke to find that the wet snow had completely melted. So I dashed off madly for the spot where the ring had disappeared. Traffic had been heavy, including snow plows with chains, and the melted snow had left a rather deep and swift stream in the gutter. Believe it or not, not far from the spot where I had flung it off, I found my ring in the gutter at the bottom of that clear stream of water! I don't know whether the traffic or the melting snow had shifted it there from the center of the road where it had fallen, and it really doesn't matter. Like the woman of whom Jesus speaks who had found the lost coin, I rejoiced. And so did Louise. For a long time the wedding band had rough marks on its edges made by the vehicles which had run over it, but after 55 years it is difficult to find traces of this strange episode.

Well, the Niantic Baptist Church called me. In the con-

Illustration No. 28
Greeting Worshipers after Morning Service, Niantic Baptist Church
(In the Center is Lesley Beckwith; with Back to the Camera Is Axel Anderson)

ference about my coming, among other things I was asked what I thought about church suppers. You see, the women of the church prepared Wednesday evening suppers in the summer, especially for tourists. This could have been seen as an important service for a transient population, but the women viewed it primarily as a money-making scheme. I replied that I was not really in favor of making money that way. Rather, I preferred out and out steward-ship of money. However, I told them that I was not a dictator and had no intention of trying to impose my will on the people of the church. One of the deacons, State Senator Fred Beckwith, told me in his best political tone that the women were going to do it no matter what I thought about it.

Having expressed myself concerning the suppers, I would feel free the next summer to help myself to the delicious ham, baked beans, potato salad, rolls, and pies which the women provided, and to take some of the leftovers home to keep Louise and me from starving!

We moved to a pretty, furnished pastorium and escaped the ravages of a Connecticut winter in the beach cottage at Milford. I learned that the previous pastor had been a dispensational fundamentalist who was a student at Gordon Seminary in Boston. Those staid New England Baptists were shocked one Sunday morning to find that the pastor had placarded the walls of the sanctuary with his dispensational charts. Instead of talking with him honestly and telling him that his beliefs and style were incompatible with theirs, they evidently chose to freeze him out. So they gave him the cold shoulder and he left. I always felt that his failure redounded to my success. The church people compensated for the shabby way they had treated my predecessor by being especially kind to me.

Meanwhile, I was living a very strenuous life, and so was Louise. I commuted every weekday to New Haven for classes. To do so, I had to catch the train about seven o'clock and arrive back at the end of the day after six o'clock in the evening. Although there was no midweek prayer meeting and only the Sunday morning worship service for which I had to prepare a sermon, I had a youth group which met every Sunday evening. I was expected to assume full responsibility for these young folks and provide some kind of a program for them.

The members of my youth group were not bad youngsters but their parents had no relationship with the church and certainly did not desire such. This made it all the more difficult to reach their children. I was surprised to find, also, that these teenagers, mostly middle class but with some privilege and promise, had absolutely no interest in going to college. Even in West Virginia, where there was much more poverty, young people, by and large, were less negative concerning education. It turned out that my most difficult chore at the Niantic church was fulfilling my responsibility to the young people.

At Niantic we had a nice plot for a vegetable garden, and we made use of it. In fact, the year in Niantic was the only time I was serious about a garden. There were a few Brussels sprouts left over from the efforts of the previous pastor, so we entered into the fruits of his labors. We raised the usual vegetables, ranging all the way from lettuce to sweet corn. I bought what were represented as cabbage plants, only to find, to my disgust, that they were broccoli!

Although I knew very little about broccoli and assumed that I did not like it, I found that the fresh broccoli from our garden was really good. Unlike former President George Bush (who probably never had such an experience as mine anyway), I discovered that broccoli is not only nourishing but delicious.

The parsonage was a two-story white frame building, rather typical of the houses of the area. It was near a beach of the Long Island Sound, somewhat rocky and not too suitable for swimming, but we utilized it for that purpose in the summer anyway. The house had a central heating system which used oil. Although the pastorium was provided free of charge, we had to pay the electric and oil bills. I believe the church paid for the telephone. The church was remunerating me only $100 per month, which meager salary we scrupulously tithed.

In addition, I led the church, which manifested considerable reluctance, to participate in the post-War World Mission Crusade of American Baptists, and I felt that I should set a good example by giving a second tithe for that campaign. When we paid the two tithes, utility bills, and my travel expenses, we had very little left for food and incidentals. I really don't know how we survived. Well, for one thing, we became pretty threadbare!

In the midst of this kind of enforced penury, Judy was born. I had naively told my fellow students that she was due to arrive April 27, 1947. Well, surely enough she did--on that very day. In order to afford her delivery, we had to sell our 1934 Plymouth. We got $125 for it, just enough to pay for Judy's arrival. We have often told her and others, therefore, that we traded a car for her.

Of course, Judy was the church baby and was much made over. The good folks of the church gave us a baby shower which was of more significance for us in our poverty than they realized.

Louise Smith lived across the street from us with her brother Ed and his wife and her dog Trixie. When some of the folks were going on about how intelligent Judy was, Louise Smith said, "But she's not as smart as old Trixie!" We have often remind-ed Judy that no matter how much her grades and other evidences of her academic ability may belie it, she's "not as smart as old Trixie!"

Judy was a delightful baby and it was not only the church folks who made over her. We also were very proud of our first child. The one problem was that for several weeks Judy was colicky and kept us awake at night. I had a real problem getting enough sleep, not to mention Louise 's sleep deprivation, for she assumed a great deal more of Judy's care than I did.

One item of the furniture of the church's parsonage was an office type chair with a high back. The chair was very comfortable, especially when it was put in a reclining position. Because of the combination of my pastoral responsibilities and Judy's birth, I had got behind on my reading for at least one of the courses I had with Professor Latourette. When I asked for a few days of grace, Uncle Ken indicated that the matter would have to go to the faculty. Somewhat taken aback by this unexpected seriousness, I withdrew the request and determined to finish the reading on time. To do so meant that I had to sit up at night with very little sleep. One night, sometime in the wee morning hours, I dropped sound asleep in that chair and did not awake until after daylight! But somehow I got the reading finished before the allotted time expired.

Some of the folks in the Niantic church were real characters. I have already mentioned Sen. Fred Beckwith. He was a friendly, outgoing sort, very much the politician. Everything with him was positive. He easily used the adjective "wonderful." Almost everything was "wonderful, wonderful!" He was a little taller than average, slender and wiry. The years had caught up with him somewhat and he walked slowly and carefully. He appeared to be leaning over backward as he walked, and he put each foot in front of the other precisely. He was tactful and diplomatic almost to a fault.

Quite a contrast was the patriarch Byron Clark, who, like Fred Beckwith, was a widower. Without question, Mr. Clark was the most unusual and colorful character I have ever met. I am sure that people who have heard me tell about him in a kind of comedy routine have assumed that I was making him up. I was not and had no need to.

He was somewhat ancient, somewhere in his 80s, which seemed a lot older then than it does now! He was tall, almost as tall as I, only slightly stooped and with little if any excess weight. He had a heavy head of hair and a full beard, more gray than iron gray, sort of a tattletale gray. His face, what you could see of it behind the beard, was weather-beaten. His eyes were milky blue, trimmed in pink. I never knew what his previous occupation was, but at the time I knew him he had several rental properties in Niantic which he regularly visited in his ancient Buick.

I was warned about Byron Clark on my first Sunday in Niantic. "Don't let Mr. Clark get under your skin," I was told. "If he appears to be insulting, just pay no attention to him. That's what we all do." Mr. Clark objected to the organ being played during the Lord's Supper, because he believed that the Supper should be stark and without any frills. In fact, he disliked the organist, Wesley Hoffman, apparently because the latter had once played in bars.

Mr. Clark believed that the Lord's Prayer was Jewish and should be rejected. Everything before the cross, he told me, was Jewish and had no place in the life of the Christian. When I reminded him that according to this principle we would lose all of the teaching of Jesus, including the Sermon on the Mount, all of the healings and such, he held up a large hand and said, "Wait a minute. Wait two minutes. You young fellows are too fast for me. Give me time." After an interval, Mr. Clark changed the subject and we never returned to it. The same thing happened with regard to how blacks were treated in the South. Mr. Clark commended the South on this point, and I disagreed.

Mr. Clark taught a Sunday School class for adults in the sanctuary, and my first Sunday as pastor I attended his class. As soon as the class started, Mr. Clark fixed his eye on me for a moment and then remarked, "I don't know whether it's good or bad to have a preacher in the class." In some embarrassment I assured Mr. Clark that I certainly could go somewhere else and would be quite happy to do so if my presence would in any way be a hindrance. Whereupon he elevated his hand and said, "No, no, I didn't say that, did I? I was only stating my opinion that I'm not sure whether it's an advantage or disadvantage to have a preacher in the class." Not knowing quite what to do, I remained on that Sunday and continued to attend Mr. Clark's class.

I soon discovered that Mr. Clark's pedagogic method was most unusual. He seemed to feel that he had accomplished his purpose if he could come up with a question that stumped everybody, especially the preacher. One Sunday he asked his class if anyone knew who David's mother was. Someone cleverly suggested that she was Mrs. Jesse, but Mr. Clark ruled that answer out of order, quite appropriately, I thought, on grounds that it really did not identify David's mother. When Mr. Clark began to question one student after the other in turn, I searched my mind desperately for the right response to his question but drew a blank. When even the preacher could not come up with the answer, Mr. Clark was ready to dismiss the class in triumph.

After the worship service, I returned home in some confusion and hastened to consult my Bible concordance and dictionary for the correct answer to Mr. Clark's question. Who was David's mother? . . . Nobody this side of heaven knows, for the Bible does not name her!

Let me hasten to say that Byron Clark was never mean to me. He was just--well, different. I could tell other things about him, for I think I became aware of at least most of his foibles. But I will forebear. Only one other story I feel I must tell. Mr. Clark's driving was just as individualistic and cranky as everything else about him. For example, if he decided to drive his old Buick on the left-hand side of the road, he drove on the left. To ride with him was a severe test of one's faith.

Evidently, someone had reported him to the highway department, for one day Mr. Clark came to my home in great agitation. "Mr. Copeland, do you know what they've done to me now?" he asked. Sensing that the question was rhetorical, I paused for a moment, and he gave the answer. "They've taken my driver's license," he declared.

Before I had time to indulge in secret glee, he continued. "You know what this means, of course. I can't visit my rental properties, and neither can I go to church. I don't know why anybody would meddle in someone's private business like this." (I could imagine it was a relative or friend, worried about Mr. Clark and others!) To make a long story shorter, Mr. Clark had come to see if I would drive him to Hartford so that he could confront the Highway Commissioner himself on this important matter. I agreed to take him and we set a date.

And so on a summer morning in 1947, I drove Mr. Clark's Buick from Niantic to Hartford. Upon arriving in the capital city, we went to the government building where the State Highway Commissioner's office was located. Rather than ask at an information desk, Mr. Clark thrust his bearded face between two gentlemen engaged in earnest, and private, conversation. "Where is the Highway Commissioner's office?" he wanted to know. One of the men, after a moment's pause to recover his equilibrium and survey the situation, kindly gave Mr. Clark directions, and at this point Mr. Clark signaled for me to follow him.

When we reached the Commissioner's office, we found a very prim and efficient young woman behind the desk. She asked Mr. Clark, "Yes sir. What can I do for you, sir?" "You can tell the Commissioner I want to see him," said Mr. Clark. "I'm sorry, sir," explained the secretary, "The Commissioner is out of town today, but his assistant is here, and I'm sure he will be glad to see you." "All right." said Mr. Clark. "Let me see him." "Splendid," said the secretary. "Now, would you say that you wish to see him on private business or public business?" "I suppose it's public business," retorted Mr. Clark, somewhat huffily. "They've taken my driver's license and I can't imagine why."

The secretary paused for a moment and then offered a suggestion, "If you will give me your name, sir, I'll have your file ready for the Assistant Commissioner when he sees you." "Well, if you must know, the name is Byron Clark," divulged my companion, his heat index rising noticeably. "Now I happen to know that there's another Byron Clark in Waterbury. The only way I can figure it is that you've got me confused with this other

Byron Clark."

At this point the secretary pulled out Mr. Clark's file and carried it into a private office in the rear where no doubt she reported to the Assistant Commissioner the character who was asking to see him. I heard peals of laughter coming from this inner sanctum. So did Mr. Clark. In spite of his advanced age, his hearing was not at all impaired. He turned to me with the redness of his face--that of it which was visible--registering his anger. "See, that's what they do to you!" he thundered. "These people are my employees. I pay their salaries. But when you expect some service from them, they ask you a bunch of silly questions and then get off to the side somewhere and laugh at you."

Then slowly the muscles of his taut face relaxed and a smile threatened to appear at the corners of his mouth. Actually, he took on the look of triumph I had seen before when he had posed a question in Sunday School class which not even the preacher could answer. "But they don't know which Byron Clark they're laughing at!" Mr. Clark exulted.

Now I know you're eager to know whether Mr. Clark got his license back. So I'll have to tell you the sequel. The official agreed that Mr. Clark should be given a driving test. So I took the street car to do some errands of my own. When I returned, Mr. Clark was waiting for me to drive him back to Niantic. When I asked him about the driving test, he informed me that it was completely unfair.

He was driving and the patrolman observing, he said, when they started to enter a boulevard at which there was a stop sign. When it seemed unlikely that Mr. Clark would stop, the patrolman--in desperation, no doubt--pulled the hand brake, which in those days was in the middle of the floor up front. The patrolman wanted to know why Mr. Clark did not stop, but Mr. Clark insisted that the patrolman would never know the answer to that question since the examiner himself had stopped the car. "Who's taking this test, you or me?" demanded Mr. Clark.

Mr. Clark's daughter, Lillian, a single woman of around 50, made a special effort to take driving lessons and get her license so that she could drive her father wherever he needed to go. Was he grateful? Certainly not. My observation was that in all matters, she got nothing but criticism from him, though she lived with him and took care of him as he became increasingly feeble. I wonder if one of the reasons she never married was that she feared all husbands might be like her father.

The first Sunday Lillian drove him to church, Sen. Beckwith met her in the aisle of the sanctuary with his usual effusion of praise, "This is wonderful! Wonderful! Lillian, I think it's *wonderful* that you drove your father to church!" Byron Clark stood by unimpressed and glowering. "Did you happen to follow her as she drove?" he wanted to know.·

After taking classes for one school year, I took my preliminary examinations for the Ph. D. degree in November of 1947. In some courses, the pre-lims at Yale were oral, at least one or two of them, but in my case all were written. There were six exams, stretched out more than two weeks, given on three days a week, Monday, Wednesday, and Friday, from nine o'clock in the morning to four in the afternoon with the hour twelve to one reserved for lunch. I wrote as hard as I could and usually had to hurry to finish by the appointed time in the afternoon. My good friend, Ray Brown, whom, along with his wife, Caralie, I had known at Lou-isville, preached for me at Niantic while I endured this ordeal. During the weekdays, I stayed with the Browns in their apartment in New Haven, to save the time and energy which commuting would entail.

Professor Outler remarked, half in jest but with a large dose of reality, that the prelims not only tested the Ph. D. candidates' intellectual but also their psychological preparedness for a teaching ministry. For the first week I was unable to sleep at night, but after the weekend at home, I slept very well the second week.

A couple of things happened during the pre-lims. One was what happened to John Peters, a fellow student in the history of Christianity, who, after writing on one of the exams (I think it was church history) for a few minutes after lunch, lay his head upon the desk to rest and clear his mind for a few minutes. Impossible as it seems to me, John went to sleep and did not wake until about fifteen minutes before four! He wrote furiously for the remaining fifteen minutes, finished, and passed. Afterward, he became the organizer and head of World Neighbors, Inc., an ecumenical agency for development projects overseas.

There was yet another episode which affected a number of us. The exam in the history of doctrine was to be given by

Professors Outler and Calhoun jointly. Though most, like me, had not had Calhoun's course, you may be sure that we had obtained his lecture notes and studied them diligently. We entered the room where the exam was to be distributed to us, expecting to pick it up and take it to our own carrels in the Library for writing.

Now we feared Calhoun more than any of the professors testing us, particularly those of us who had not had his course. We waited about twenty minutes for either Outler or Calhoun to arrive with the test, during which time a certain graduate student advised us about the nature of the exam and how to answer it.

Finally, Calhoun arrived, flustered and red-faced, and explained that he and Outler had prepared the exam but that he could not find it in spite of an extensive search. Therefore, he proceeded to write an exam upon the chalkboard for us to copy. We arrived at our carrels to take that particular pre-lim late. In spite of this unsettling handicap, most of us passed the test.

Unfortunately, the student who had tutored us during our anxious waiting was not one of those who passed! His failing this one exam meant that he failed them all. He settled, as was not unusual, for a Master of Arts degree, and left Yale in a hurry.

I passed my prelims on the first try. So I was ready to get my dissertation project approved, which I did right away. The subject, which had been suggested by Uncle Ken, my major professor, was "The Crisis of Protestant Missions to Japan, 1889-1900." According to my memory, Uncle Ken had already approved the project, but it had to go to a committee of the graduate school for their action.

For some good reason which I cannot recall, Uncle Ken was absent, but Dean Weigle reported to me that the project had been approved by the committee, of which Weigle was a member, though Professor Goodenough from downtown, that is, not related to the Divinity School, protested that I did not know Japanese. When Goodenough was reminded that Latourette had written a book on Japan without knowing Japanese, he said "So what?" Weigle emitted his booming laugh as he told me, thus indicating that he deemed the interchange to be hilarious.

To protect myself from those who agreed with Dr. Goodenough, I emphasized the Western, especially American, side of the problem of that decade in Japan, and did extensive research in the correspondence files of major foreign mission boards. This research took me to Boston, New York, and other cities where the mission agencies were located. I also visited the Missionary Research Library in New York, housed at Union Seminary, in addition to the Day Missions Library of Yale Divinity School and the Sterling Library downtown. I believe I spent about a month at the Missionary Research Library in the summer of 1948, at which time Union Seminary kindly rented me a dormitory room and permitted me to eat in their dining hall.

One day during that time I was eating lunch with a group of Union Seminary students. We had introduced ourselves without feeling any necessity to give our denominational affiliations. Actually, all the students except me seemed to know each other. One of them had heard a report from the Southern Baptist Convention, which had just met in Kansas City, Kansas. He asked, "Do you know what the Southern Baptists just did in Kansas City?" After a pause he continued, "They condemned all us ecumenists as Communists and everything else bad," he said. "And then they all got up and sang 'O How I Love Jesus'!" I was very careful not to identify myself as a Southern Baptist.

Meantime, in January 1948, I had resigned my church, and Louise and I had been appointed by the Foreign Mission Board of the Southern Baptist Convention as missionaries to Japan and had enrolled in Yale's Far Eastern Language Institute for the intensive study of Japanese.

Illustration No. 29
About the Time of
Appointment

I think we did not realize how crucial that step was. I had grown up a Northern (later American) Baptist, my last year in Louisville I had been pastor of Northern I had been pastor of Northern Baptist churches in Indiana, and for a year I had served as pastor of a Northern Baptist church in Connecticut. Louise had shared with me the last of these experiences. We could just as easily have gone to Japan under the auspices of the American Baptist Foreign Mission Society. Instead, we had cast our lot with Southern Baptists for my entire career.

It is difficult to know why we made this significant choice. My upbringing had been in small country churches in West Virginia which were affiliated with the Northern Baptist Convention. Consequently, I knew very little about the denomination in that phase of my history. Being educated in two Baptist colleges and a theological seminary in the South afforded me a more intimate knowledge of the Southern Baptist Convention than the Northern Baptist Convention, as well as many Southern Baptist friends.

In addition, I had considerable respect for the zeal of Southern Baptists and their commitment to the gospel of Christ. Of course I did not share the fundamentalist attitude which seemed to prevail among Southern Baptists, but I appreciated their inclusiveness and respect for diverse viewpoints among themselves. I expected that I could work with them with a fair measure of freedom.

Although Louise was not as sophisticated as I theologically, she shared my viewpoint about Southern Baptists. Actually, until we married, her experience with churches had been almost entirely Southern Baptist.

The folks at Niantic Baptist Church were surprised that I had resigned so that the two of us could become missionaries. They wondered why we would take up such an abstemious life. These good folks did not realize that a missionary salary rescued us from the situation of near starvation made necessary by the meager income that they afforded us! Of course, they aimed to be generous, some members giving us items of food from time to time. I am very grateful to them.

From Niantic we moved to an upstairs apartment in West Haven, where we were to live until we left for Japan. We joined the West Haven Baptist Church, also a Northern Baptist congregation, where the pastor, also a Southerner, was unable to occupy his pulpit because of a terminal illness. When he resigned, I served the church as interim pastor until they called another minister.

Our two semesters of language study, January-May 1948 and September 1948-January 1949, were very interesting. Ms. Eleanor Jordan headed our Japanese study. She was young and brilliant, later to be renowned as the developer of the "Jordan method" of teaching Japanese. She taught us the structure of the language in English, while four native Japanese speakers drilled us on the Japanese sentences in our textbook. Only Japanese was used in their classrooms. One of the four was a woman who was especially helpful in teaching the women's way of speaking, which was somewhat different from that of the men.

The idea of having four of them was to insure that a student would not get fixated upon the individual accent or cadence of any one speaker. In our long sessions with these Japanese instructors, we were encouraged to make up sentences using what vocabulary we had. It was fun. Almost inevitably it meant the exercise of a sense of humor even if this quality seemingly was dormant. We were in school all morning and had home work, including listening to records, for the afternoons.

Mrs. Jordan's theory was that, like a child, we should learn the spoken language first and turn our attention to the writing later. Our model sentences in the textbook were in Romanized Japanese (of Ms. Jordan's own Romanization) and not the Japanese script. Louise learned the polite language of Japanese women well and accordingly was complimented by the Japanese. However, she and I always felt that it was too bad that we were sent to Japan and to our work there without the second year of language study at Yale in which we would have learned at least the rudiments of Japanese writing.

Since both Louise and I were in Language School, we had to arrange for child care for Judy. Louise studied hard and took her exam early to end the second semester in December 1948, while I continued language school until the official close of the semester in January.

Meantime, on January 14, 1949, our second daughter, Joy, was born. Joy was a very appealing baby. Both she and Judy were born in Grace/New Haven Hospital, but, unlike Judy, Joy did not have colic. Since Judy was not yet toilet trained, we had a lot of diapers to wash. This was before the day of disposable diapers. I'm sure that with my school work, that is, working on a dissertation in addition to language study, I did not share enough of the parenting duties with Louise. While in language school, I was putting in about twelve to fifteen hours per week on the dissertation, but I gave it the entire summer between the two semesters of language study.

The process of writing my dissertation was rather enjoyable. It was not as laborious as some of my later writing projects were to be, though the research was probably more intensive and complete. At Dr. Latourette's suggestion, I submitted my dissertation to him a chapter at a time. He would take the chapter, read it and then go over it carefully with me. In most cases he did not suggest major revisions. I remember some stylistic suggestions he made, such as that I should not put "however" at the end of a sentence. Uncle Ken encouraged me by his positive and even complimentary attitude.

I completed the dissertation in plenty of time for a committee to review it and approve it before commencement. Accordingly, I was graduated on July 11, 1949, and became a bona fide doctor, though not the kind that can do you any good.*

In this long pilgrimage of higher education, from 1940 to 1949, I had worked hard and had provided much of the schooling by the sweat of my brow, so to speak. However, many others contributed, and I am most happy to recognize them. My folks, parents and brothers and sisters, and some devoted friends, gave money. What my sister Bertha gave me was $500! and once my parents gave me $100! Even five dollars in those days seemed to be a lot of money. For most of my three years at Louisville I was getting a monthly check from Ernest Pohl in St. Louis.

These benefactors gave quite sacrificially. I can neither forget them nor adequately repay them except by trying to be generous myself. And Louise was a most willing and necessary partner, sharing the joys and the difficulties of my pilgrimage at Yale. In it all God had provided bountifully for us.

At long last we were ready to go to Japan.

---

*I am referring here to a story told by Dr. Leslie Weatherhead, noted Methodist preacher in London, who had a doctorate in theology, and who had a son who was a medical doctor living with him. Dr. Weatherhead overheard the maid's part of a telephone conversation, in which she was responding to someone on the other end calling for "Dr. Weatherhead." "Which Dr. Weatherhead?" asked the maid. "The one who does you good, or the other one?"

PART THREE
THE EARLY STINT IN JAPAN, 1949-1956

Chapter Nine
FINDING OUR WAY IN JAPAN

A trip by train across the country, with stops here and there to visit relatives, brought us to San Francisco, where the Foreign Mission Board had arranged to put us up in the Mark Twain Hotel, which in those days was a decent place to stay.

After a few days we left our hotel and set sail for Japan with much fanfare. Those passengers who had friends or family members to see them off stood on the decks holding one end of long paper ribbons while their loved ones on the dock held the other end. These streamers broke as our ship departed, symbolizing our separation from our motherland and adding to the pollution of the waters of the San Francisco Bay. We were filled with nostalgia, especially as we passed under the Golden Gate Bridge and watched that structure fade into the background. We were actually leaving our country! We stopped in Los Angeles for a similar experience though not nearly so exciting.

Our ship was the *President Wilson*, a luxury liner providing no second class, only first and third classes. We were at the lowest level of first class, which meant that we were the nearest to second class which the ship offered. But we had most of the usual privileges of first class, including eating in the dining room, and the food was heavenly! Also, we had various types of recreation, including shuffleboard, a freshwater swimming pool, and deck tennis. The latter was played with a rubber ring tossed by hand, rather than with a ball and racquet which would mean too many lost balls! It was a lot of fun. Children, including our two, were cared for in a special room with many facilities for play presided over by a nursemaid who was generally helpful.

Louise and I had some seasickness for the first three or four days but never enough to cause vomiting or prevent us from at least eating something. However, we had pretty convincing anecdotal evidence that motion sickness has a physical cause and is not merely psychological--though many people will inform you that "it's only in your head." We had been careful not to say anything about seasickness to Judy. Of course, Joy was only about six months of age and would have no knowledge about the malady anyway. Judy was a little more than 2 years of age and was already talking quite a bit, but she had absolutely no reason to know anything at all about seasickness. However, in the middle of our first night out, she woke us by saying, "Mama, I's sick. I need to unswallow"--a very ingenious way to speak of the urge to vomit! Some other Southern Baptist missionaries were on the way to Japan with us, three single women, Annie Hoover, Lenora Hudson, and Lucy Belle Stokes, and a family, Ernest Lee and Ida Nelle Holloway and their two sons, Lee and Bill, about 5 and 3 respectively. We marveled at how well behaved the little Holloway boys were and greatly admired the parents for such successful training.

The Hoshizakis, Reiji (Ray) and Asano (Alice), boarded the ship in Honolulu. Both were Nisei (second generation Japanese Americans). Reiji was from Chicago, though he had lived in California as a child before the enforced removal of Japanese into concentration camps, euphemistically called "relocation" camps. Many of the Japanese so removed were United States citizens. I hope that most Americans recognize the terrible injustice thus foisted upon Japanese Americans. We had known Reiji at Southern Seminary in Louisville. Since Asano was from Hawaii we had not met her before this voyage.

Because of what I have always considered a wrong regulation of the Board, these two fine American citizens, because of their race, were sent out as special appointees and not treated as regular missionaries for about six years, at which time the Board relaxed this policy. All of these missionaries who sailed with us became our good friends.

Since passengers were permitted to embark or disembark at Honolulu, the Hoshizakis had no problem boarding our ship, but we through passengers were not permitted to leave the ship to explore the city for a few hours as we had intended. According to what I heard, there was a seamen's strike, which the crew of our ship would have joined if we had made a normal landing. As it was, since our captain did not allow the dropping of an anchor, a refusal to work on the part of our crew would have been a mutiny rather than a strike.

The Pacific was smooth, except for big but gentle swells, and we had a good voyage, something like a vacation. I must confess that in spite of my Ph. D. degree from Yale, I had retained considerable naiveté. So when the ship's log indicated that Wednesday, after we had departed from Honolulu, would feature "Deep Sea Fishing," I took it literally and pictured in my mind our turning off our motors, with everybody being provided a fishing line which we would cast into the deep. Of course, no such thing happened. We went to bed on Tuesday evening, and the next day was not Wednesday but Thursday!

I worried because I had lost a precious day out of my life. I did not get it back until we returned from Japan four years later, in which case we went to bed on Saturday only to find when we awoke that Saturday was repeated! All the Seventh-Day Adventists on board rejoiced, I was told.

In many ways an ocean voyage is a wonderful experience. Actually, the two weeks on the water which "boat" missionaries enjoyed, unlike the rapid air travel of the later "plane" missionaries, was a most appropriate time to adjust to a new culture, to change worlds, so to speak. Also, every time I crossed the Pacific by ship, I got a new appreciation for the immensity of our planet, set as it is in the huge, unmeasured universe. It is very humbling to see nothing day after day but the expansive vistas of blue water and the curving far horizons—interrupted only by the antics of the flying fish and the dolphins, and on clear nights to look upon the myriads of stars and planets in the uncluttered heavens. I reflected about how marvelous it is that God cares for us creatures, infinitesimal as we are, in the vast universe which God has made and preserves.

In early September we arrived in the port of Yokohama, which serves not only Yokohama but the huge city of Tokyo. There we were met by Edwin and Mary Ellen Dozier, and the Copeland family was taken to the Dozier home in Tokyo for three or four days before continuing on south to Fukuoka where we were to live and work. Unlike the Copelands, all the missionaries who had accompanied us stayed in Tokyo for two years of language study.

The Doziers were unusually fine people and superb missionaries. In fact, we post-War Southern Baptist missionaries were quite fortunate in that our pre-War colleagues were of such unusually fine caliber. In this category there were only seven: two couples, Edwin and Mary Ellen Dozier, whom I have just mentioned, and Max and Dorothy Garrott; and three single women,

Cecile Lancaster, Floryne Miller, and Alma Graves. All of them modeled very well what missionaries should be. The women were not very active in affairs having to do with the common life of missionaries, but the men were especially prominent and all the missionaries were Japanophiles, ready to take the side of the Japanese on any issues which might divide American missionaries and Japanese.

Both by word and example, we were taught that in all things we should forsake our natural American pride and be humble and deferential toward the Japanese. This kind of missionary idealism pleased Louise and me very much, since I had already learned considerable about Japanese culture and missionary history, and since Louise was equipped by nature and by grace to love the Japanese. Nor did these "veterans" try in any way to lord it over us new and untried missionaries. They respected us and tried to make us feel that we were valued colleagues.

Being in the home of the Doziers was a splendid way to get started as missionaries in Japan. Edwin and Mary Ellen were warm and outgoing and they offered us gracious hospitality in spite of their busy schedules. They had three delightful children, Sarah Ellen, Charles, and Adelia Ann.

Of course everything was new and strange to Louise and me. I remember that we were awakened to our first full day in Japan by a strange chanting beneath our window. Someone was calling out in a sing-song voice, "*Natō, natō.*" We were sure that this exotic chant had something to do with religion. When we asked about it at the breakfast table, Edwin smiled and informed us that what we had heard was the sales pitch of a huckster of fermented soybeans! Although an ingredient of a common dish in Japan, *miso shiru*, a soup which we came to like very much, the *natō* itself has a very distinctive and very offensive odor.

Soon our stay in Tokyo ended and we were sent on our way to Fukuoka, the location of Seinan Gakuin, the school where we were to teach. The trip was a long and difficult one. The military train, operated by the Occupational Government, took about 27 hours from Tokyo to Fukuoka. The 700 or so miles may now be traversed by the *Shinkansen*, which Americans call the "Bullet Train," an incredibly fast electric train, in less than 7 hours, even with stops in 4 or 5 prominent cities along the way. There were many tunnels, and the locomotives of that day were coal-fired and the trains had no air conditioning. Since the weather was extremely hot and humid, windows had to be open, so you can imagine not only how fatigued but also how black with soot all of the Copelands became by the time we reached Fukuoka.

At Hakata* station we were met by Thelma Moorhead. She and her husband Marion, with their two sons, Douglas, a few months older than our Judy, and Michael, who had been born about three years before Douglas (later to be joined by a new addition, Margaret, in the following year, 1950), had preceded us by a few months. Marion was teaching in the Seminary, as I was slated to do. Being "green" missionaries together, the Moorheads and Copelands bonded for life.

Illustration No. 30
The Moorheads, Marion and Thelma. Much as We First Knew Them

Fukuoka at that time was a city of about 500,000 (now it has a population of more than 1.3 million but is still viewed by the Japanese as a "rural city"). It is notable that the only privately owned car at Hakata station when we arrived was the Moor-

---

*Originally, Fukuoka was composed of two cities, of which Hakata was one. Therefore, certain aspects of the city still carry the designation "Hakata."

head's Willys Jeep. Just about the only other automobiles were taxis, ungainly beasts which manifested, on their rears where turtle backs normally would be, charcoal burning units. As we drove to our destination, we marveled at Thelma's driving skills as she negotiated the narrow streets of Fukuoka.

Also, we took note of the remaining signs of the devastating war. The city had been more than 60 percent destroyed by incendiary bombs. Most of the buildings which had thus perished had been replaced by very flimsy construction. The ferroconcrete buildings which had escaped the inferno still had the black camouflage of the war years on them. Everything appeared to be very primitive, compared to what was later to become characteristic, and probably compared to what had already been true of Japanese society.

The fact is that for a few years after the War Japan was desperately poor. We were later to learn how the Japanese people suffered for lack of adequate food and clothing and how incredibly prevalent were certain diseases, especially tuberculosis. We were even to hear ludicrous, if poignant, stories of how some Japanese carefully guarded items of food, such as a lone squash on a vine, for example, from the approaching Allied forces, only to learn when the latter arrived that they had no interest in Japanese food and were actually prohibited from eating it, partly for reasons of sanitation.

Thelma delivered us to Alma Graves' house, one of the two large pre-War residences built for missionary families. Alma treated us with great hospitality, and after baths and a good night's sleep Louise and I were ready for whatever new and exciting adventures might await us. We took a walk in Alma's beautiful flower garden, where we noticed a Japanese gentleman walking toward us, somewhat tall for a Japanese, slender, very erect, and dignified looking, with a pleasant smile on his face. I remember that he was dressed in a linen suit, beige in color and nicely pressed. (I always marveled at how the Japanese could look so neat in those days when they had so little).

This man extended his hand to us in the American way of greeting while speaking the words of a Japanese welcome: *"Yoku irasshaimashita! Yoku irasshaimashita!"* Since he had spent some time in the States, I think he used this mixed greeting-- American handshake and Japanese words of welcome--to make us feel at home.

I must confess that up to that moment I had anxieties about going to Japan, worries that I had not revealed even to Louise lest I increase her foreboding. Would the Japanese people welcome us? I knew too well the prejudices of Americans concerning Japanese. Would Japanese have the same prejudices toward us? I felt keenly my responsibility for taking my family into such an unknown situation.

However, seemingly miraculously, in that warm and friendly handshake my anxieties suddenly dissipated. I never worried any more. You see, this man introduced himself as Kawano Sadamoto, Dean of the Theological Seminary (or Department of Theology of the Literature Division of the University) where I was to teach, and therefore my boss! Across the awful chasm of war and the bitterness which it engenders Mr. Kawano had reached out to us with a sincere welcome and his offer of glad acceptance and love. Soon I was to learn that his attitude was representative of the Japanese, especially the Christians.

Illustration No. 31
A Formal Greeting
(Left: Me, and Right: Kawano Sadamoto)

The Kawano family were to become very dear to us in a friendship which lasts until this day, especially through the two oldest children who are daughters, Nobuko and Hiroko. Both parents died rather early of tragic diseases, and the third daughter, Sadako, to whom we were especially close, died of cancer while still quite young. Nobuko remained single and became a professor of religion at Seinan Gakuin University. Hiroko married Tanaka Teruo, who taught English and later became University President and then Chancellor of the whole school as well. Both Kawano Nobuko and Tanaka Teruo are now retired. There were younger children of the Kawano family, a son, Sadao, another daughter, Toyoko, and last of all another son, Yasuo.

Perhaps it is time to tell you something about the structure in which we were to work. As I have already indicated, we had been appointed as missionaries by the Foreign Mission Board of the Southern Baptist Convention. Since we were employed for service in Japan we were automatically members of the Japan Baptist Mission, the organization of Southern Baptist missionaries in Japan, though we were not to have voting privileges in the Mission until we had been in Japan for a year.

This meant that when in 1950 the Mission met in the beautiful resort town of Miyajima, on an island near Hiroshima, we were not eligible to vote, though I was asked to lecture each day--four days, I believe--on some Biblical subject. I chose to speak on the Corinthian correspondence in the New Testament, and I was given credit, along with Max Garrott and Edwin Dozier, with contributing to the harmony which prevailed as tensions had developed amid the efforts of the Mission to absorb new personnel. Members of the Mission numbered about 38 by that time.

At the annual meeting of the Mission in Tokyo in 1951, the first meeting at which Louise and I could vote, I was elected President for a one-year term. I interpreted this action by the young Mission as a remarkable vote of confidence.

Soon afterward, I was chosen by the Japanese at their Convention meeting to be a member of their Executive Committee. Since only about four missionaries were members, I was especially heartened that the Japanese trusted me. Missionary appointments soared so that by 1953 the Board's goal of 100 missionaries in Japan had been reached and still they continued to come. Terrific problems of assimilation accompanied that many new missionaries, especially since there was such a tiny minority of veterans and very few Japanese pastors. Service on the Executive and Personnel Committees of the Mission in those early years helped acquaint me with some of the Mission's difficult problems.

The Japan Mission represented the Foreign Mission Board in Japan, particularly in channeling monies to the missionaries for their salaries and expenses and in paying various subsidies to the Japan Baptist Convention. The Treasurer of the Japan Baptist Mission, therefore, was a staff member of the Board. Edwin Dozier had that position when we arrived in Japan, and he was succeeded by Frank Connely, an "old China hand" who, with his wife Mary, arrived in Tokyo in 1952, after China had been conquered by the Communists. Lucy Smith, also from China, served as Connely's assistant and then succeeded him as Treasurer when he unexpectedly died in Tokyo in 1956.

Although, even in denominations with democratic ecclesiologies such as the Baptists, the structure of foreign missions in general was hierarchical, the Japan Baptist Mission itself was a bastion of carefully guarded democracy. Every member had a voice and a vote and autonomy was considered precious. Decisions had to be made concerning the placement and effective work of missionaries, and the network of committees and local stations helped to protect the democratic ideals.

Paralleling the Mission, and in my judgment much more important, was the Japan Baptist Convention, a small body with its few pastors somewhat dwarfed by the large number of new and inexperienced missionaries. Before the War, Southern Baptist work, which had begun in 1889, had enjoyed the cooperation of Northern (now American) Baptist missions which had begun several years earlier. Accordingly, two conventions had developed, the East Japan Convention of the Northern Baptists and the West Japan Convention of Southern Baptists. For a time the two cooperated in a Union Baptist Seminary; then the militaristic and authoritarian government of Japan forced them into one Convention and later into membership in the *Nihon Kirisuto Kyōdan*, known in English as the United Church of Christ in Japan.

There is still debate as to whether Edwin Dozier, in visiting Japan as a representative of the Foreign Mission Board in 1946, unduly influenced the few remaining representatives of the pre-

War West Japan Convention with promises of Southern Baptist money. In any case, in April of the following year, these representatives met in Fukuoka and acted to withdraw from the Kyōdan and to organize the *Nihon Baputesuto Renmei*, the Japan Baptist Convention, consisting of 16 churches and about 1,100 members. It was this small convention, comprised of what was left of Southern Baptist work after the ravages of war, with which we were to cooperate. Its pastors were few, but they were experienced and able.

Only in 1958, after they became convinced that it was impossible for them to retain their Baptist identity within the Kyōdan, did the churches related to the Northern Baptist Convention withdraw to form their separate organization.

Let me tell you also about the school where Louise and I were to teach. On the rather spacious campus at Nishijin Machi in west Fukuoka were the various departments of Seinan Gakuin ("Southwest Educational System"), founded by Southern Baptist missionary Charles Kelsey Dozier in 1916 (you remember that this was the year that I was founded in West Virginia). Under the educational reform which had been put into operation by the Occupational Government after the war, the school followed the usual pattern of the larger "mission schools" in that all grades were included with the exception of the six elementary grades. The idea, which seems to have been valid, was that the Japanese public school system provided quite adequately for those grades but not for secondary and higher education.

When we arrived in Japan in 1949, education was mandatory from the first grade through middle school, or junior high school. Through college the system was 6-3-3-4, similar to American schools, but there were important differences: even in the elementary grades students went to school for half-a-day on Saturday, that is, five-and-a-half days per week; students cleaned up the grounds at the end of the school day; admission was only by competitive examinations, especially after middle school; the school calendar began about April 1 and closed at the end of March; and whereas our system was controlled by state governments and thus lacked uniformity, the Japanese system was controlled by a national cabinet ministry.

As a rule, the system operated more rigorously than ours until the students reached college, at which time they tended to goof off and give attention to the many extracurricular social activities which the college provided. If asked, the student would explain that he or she needed to concentrate now on "socializing," since that aspect of life had been neglected up until now due to the pressures of competitive exams. I have included both genders, though girls were more serious than boys about their college studies.

The Samidori Nursery School and the Maizuru Kindergarten of Seinan Gakuin enrolled both boys and girls and were located at Torikai in proximity to the Training School for kindergarten and nursery school teachers, which I will mention below. The Middle School and High School were for boys only. The High School had a night department for students who had to work during the day.

The Senior College included departments of English and Theology (the latter of which doubled as a Seminary for the Japan Baptist Convention) in a Literature Division, a Division of Commerce and Economics, and a Division of graduate studies in some of these subjects. The first two years of the Senior College were spent in a General Education course before the student entered upon a major. A Junior College had departments of English and Commerce on the Nishijin campus, and a Women's Training School for kindergarten teachers, which had a separate and small campus in nearby Torikai. The Senior and Junior Colleges were coeducational and along with the Middle and High schools were located on the Nishijin campus (except for the Kindergarten Training School).

Enrollment in the Training School was about 90, in the Seminary about 25, and in the whole school somewhere around 3,500, of whom about 2,000 were in the university, with most of the others in the middle and high schools.

Our first home was a prefabricated aluminum house on the Seinan Gakuin University campus, near the dilapidated pre-War building which housed the Seminary, where I was to teach classes in church history and history of doctrine. Also, it was close to an even flimsier building on the second floor of which I taught one of the courses in religion required of all university students, in this case open only to students who could pass an English test. I remember that while that class was in session, we had an earth tremor, which rather vigorously shook the very insubstantial structure. In spite of the fact that only English was supposed to be spoken, understandably the students cried out in Japanese, "*Ji-shin!*" instead of the English equivalent, "Earthquake!"

The prefab house was small but adequate for our family. It had a small kitchen, one bath, a combination living and dining room, three small bedrooms, and a fourth room which we used as a bedroom for our first maid. The only concession to Japan which I remember in the construction of the house was a Japanese entrance hall (*genkan*) with a shelf (*getabako*) for shoes. We installed a kerosene hot water heater outside the house at the back, we heated the house with a relatively small space heater and some portable Perfection heaters, and we cooked on a Perfection range. All of these stoves used kerosene and we brought them all with us from America.

Our first helper was a Japanese girl who in general proved herself unsatisfactory. After her, we had a succession of helpers, some of whom were very good, at least after Louise trained them, and some of whom never did work out.

The fact that we had a prefab house sent from America was in fulfillment of one of the requirements of the Occupational Government for missionaries entering Japan, namely, that they be provided with homes. Several prefab houses were shipped to Japan, some of which were used for church buildings.

Another directive provided that each person in the missionary family take with him or her one ton of food. Usually, as in our case, this caused special difficulties for missionaries. A policy of the Board's was that nobody could be appointed as a missionary who was burdened with indebtedness. Yet, as a kind of contradiction, the Board advanced us the money to buy this food and allowed us to pay it back as we were able. We repaid the debt to the Board in one year, by reductions from our monthly income. Within about four months the food was gone, for we could not live with provisions stashed away in our pantry while Japanese were in dire need--except for powdered eggs, that is. We were given wrong information concerning foods to bring!

Eggs were everywhere on the Japanese market, though usually they tasted fishy because fish waste was fed to the chickens. But even hungry Japanese would not eat powdered eggs when they could get fresh ones, and it seemed to make no difference to the Japanese that their eggs tasted like the fish that they ate. We ended up giving the powdered eggs to our Seminary dormitory to use, unobtrusively, I hope, as an additive for certain dishes prepared for the theological students. The requirement prohibiting young babies from entering was rescinded just in time for us to take Joy to Japan.

Not long after we arrived in Fukuoka, Kawano Sadamoto brought to our door a fellow by the name of Tsubaki Hachirō, sixteen years of age, with the story that because he had become a Christian he had been expelled by his family who lived near the volcano Mt. Aso, in Kumamoto prefecture. His older brothers, of whom he had several, had threatened to throw him in the live volcano if he did not renounce his Christian faith. He was a student in our night high school, and Kawano requested that we afford him some work to pay for his school expenses.

Thus we began a delightful relationship with Tsubaki, by which we saw him not only through high school but university including seminary. For a time he lived in my office above our garage until he moved in with other seminary students who resided in a little Japanese style house on the Nishijin campus which they humorously called *"Bessō"* or Summer Resort. Tsubaki, small even for a Japanese, was very winsome, almost never without a smile. We came to view him almost as our own son. We procured a bicycle for him and rigged up a seat with which he could transport Judy to kindergarten at Torikai.

For several months, perhaps for the first year, most of our time was spent in Japanese language study. Our teacher was Matsumoto Matsuji, a good man and a deacon of the Fukuoka Baptist Church. Matsumoto Sensei* had a keen sense of humor and was unusually frank for a Japanese. We were told that we got his services because he had been teaching Japanese in a Roman Catholic school in 1949, 400th anniversary of the coming to Japan of the first Christian missionary, St. Francis Xavier, a Roman Catholic. As part of the celebrations, a relic—an arm, it happened—of the saint was carried on a tour of Japan. Matsumoto was asked what he thought of this phenomenon, a query which he answered with his usual candor, and so we procured a language teacher!

---

*Sensei is a title given to teachers and many professional people, including pastors.

When he had taught us for a few days, unsuccessfully fighting sleep as we grappled with the difficult language, we decided that there may have been other reasons why we got him! But he was a fine man, and we were quite fond of him. (I was always a bit put out that although our whole bodies arrived in Japan in 1949, and only the arm of the long dead saint, much more was made over the arrival of that ancient and shrunken relic than over the coming of the Copelands, alive and whole!)

After a while Louise transferred to a female Japanese teacher, Masuda Miyako, a remarkable lady who had been repatriated from Korea after the War. Masuda Sensei had been employed as their language teacher by Marion and Thelma Moorhead. She taught others as well. She was a fervent Christian who considered the teaching of Japanese to American missionaries to be her Christian vocation.

Louise taught English to students in the Seinan Middle School, who, as I have mentioned, were boys, and Bible to students of the same age, some of whom were girls. Her interpreter and general helper in the Middle School was Mura-kami Toraji and a student was Murakami's son, Ryūta. (Mura-kami Toraji was to become a Professor of Education in Seinan Gakuin University and eventually President of the University as well as Chancellor of the whole school. Murakami Ryūta became a Professor of English and later President of the University).

Before long we became so busy preparing talks in Japanese that this chore became our language study. The Japan Mission of the Foreign Mission Board required an examination in Japanese for certification that the Mission's requirements had been satisfied. Both Louise and I passed this test in which a talk was to be prepared in written Japanese. Mine was a sermon, while Louise's was a devotional message. By the time we had been in Japan for the nearly four years of our first term, I was known as a fluent speaker of Japanese, though, as I have informed you previously, both Louise and I thought we had been shortchanged by missing the second year of language study at Yale in which the written language was emphasized. We never learned to read and write Japanese as well as we should have.

One of the most excruciating things Louise had to encounter during our service in Japan was the death of her mother. This tragic event occurred on August 13, 1950, after we had been in Japan about a year. The Tadlocks had just moved back to Fort Sumner, New Mexico, from Tahlequah, Oklahoma, and Mrs. Tadlock had joined the Baptist church to which she had previously belonged. She was being greeted after the service by acquaintances of former days, when she suffered a stroke. Though she survived for a week, she never regained consciousness.

Since the Korean War had already begun, heavily involving planes from the local American air base at Itazuke in Fukuoka, Louise was afraid that if she left she could not get back into Japan. To complicate matters further, she was pregnant with Beth and it was not a good time for her to travel. Though her father offered to pay her air fare, she decided against trying to make the trip home. It was her sad experience on furlough to visit her mother's grave in Fort Sumner to bring some closure to her experience of grieving.

I marvel at how busy Louise was and with what equanimity she coped with her demanding calendar. Sometimes on Sunday mornings she had as many as 100 children in the little prefab house. She was especially handicapped in her missionary work by spending so much time in the home. This was in keeping with a policy of the Foreign Mission Board that the wife should be a homemaker. Like most missionaries at the time, Louise and I agreed with this kind of thinking, though we were to take considerable exception to it later. I am especially embarrassed to remember how blithely I left the management of the home and the care of the children to Louise.

Sad to say, the Board, in agreement with most of its constituency, seems never to have departed from this sexist policy. If anything, it seems more strongly committed to this erroneous way of thinking than ever.

I have mentioned the pitiable poverty of the Japanese in those early post-War years. There were a few beggars, "con" men, and burglars, almost unheard of after Japan's remarkable economic recovery. Americans sent many items of clothing to Japan, which were highly prized and received with great gratitude. Several Japanese, including some seminary students, wore outmoded military uniforms. Once in a while a beggar came to our door, asking for a handout. On one occasion we invited a beggar to have a meal with us, and then, at his request, sent him on his way to some alleged distant city with money for train fare.

When others came to ask for funds, evidently having been told that we were easy marks, we found it convenient to refer them to our Japanese pastor, Rev. Ozaki Shuichi, who knew much better than we how to judge their authenticity and how to deal with them in general. It was good to defer to him anyway!

Once we were visited by a burglar. His coming was not unexpected, since we knew that it was our turn. He had broken into other missionary and American military homes, and on one occasion he had felled a burly military man with a baseball bat. He had broken into Alma Graves' home, near ours on the Nishijin campus, and had taken some expensive gifts which had been given to Miss Graves in light of her upcoming furlough.

Also, the thief had entered the large pre-War missionary home of the Moorheads, at Jigyō Machi, about a mile or so from the Nishijin campus where we lived, while Marion was away. When Thelma heard him downstairs, she hastily put her small children in the room with her, locked the door and left the rest of the house to the burglar. Next morning they could see where he had plundered, and among other things they found missing was a deck of Rook cards! You could imagine that they got some good natured ribbing for that episode. I told them that was what they got for having those "sinful" cards on hand. It turned out that this burglar did silly things like that because he had some kind of mental or psychological illness.

Besides the awareness that it was now our turn, we had another indication that the thief was casing our house: our maid had been startled one night to see him peering through the glass panes in the outside door of our kitchen. Surely enough, that was where he entered. He simply ran a candle in an arc in a corner of the pane nearest the door lock where the key was inserted on the inside. Then he picked out the piece of glass which the candle had broken, turned the key and stepped in. Clever, wasn't he? I thought of taking the key out, but since that would leave the lock easily vulnerable to a skeleton key I had decided against it.

The burglar had what appeared to be an uncanny way of knowing when the missionary men would be away, affording him a safer time to do his robbing. Later we learned that he had a hideout under one of the school buildings from which position he could keep the missionaries who lived on the campus under surveillance. Apparently the intruder chose a night when he thought I was away. I had gone with Moorhead in his car to Kamihonami, a coal mining town across the mountain from Fukuoka, to preach. The mission station wagon, used by several Fukuoka missionaries, was in the shop for repairs and so was not in its usual place in the garage near our house.

When Moorhead had brought me home about eleven o'clock, I had set my relatively new Sears briefcase on the floor near the entrance way (*genkan*). Louise and I did not go to sleep until after midnight, though we were very tired, because we had a premonition that the thief was coming that night.

As was my custom, I had emptied my pockets of their various articles, wallet, watch, change, and the like, and had placed them on the dresser beside my bed. I awoke next morning to see that the closet at the foot of our bed where our clothes had hung was as empty as the shoes in our *genkan*. The sliding doors to the closet were open, and obviously the thief had taken all the clothes in his arms and made his getaway. He had not bothered the items on the dresser beside my bed, which, because of the smallness of the room, was almost like a bedside table.

I theorized that since there was bright moonlight, the burglar could see me lying in bed and that, being surprised, he had hastily grabbed the clothes and fled. However, he had taken time to take the sweater out of my new briefcase, leaving the latter behind, though it was considerably more valuable than the sweater. He had left a trail of hangers and clothes where he had climbed over the wall behind our house.

Of course, we called the police and they came to the house and made their investigation, including fingerprinting, at which time they assured me that they were closing in on the burglar and would soon apprehend him. They said that they already knew who he was, a young fellow in his late teens, alienated from his family, his father being a respected public school principal. The police called one Sunday morning when I had pastoral responsibilities, so Louise was asked to go to the police station and identify the stolen articles.

As nearly as she and I could tell, all the items were recovered. After Louise had concluded that she had identified everything, she was asked if there was anything else. Then she suddenly realized that the thief was wearing the blue sweater which he had lifted from my brief case, though of course it was considerably too big for him. "Oh," she said, "there is one thing more, the sweater he is wearing." Whereupon a policeman unceremoniously took the sweater off the burglar and handed it to Louise. The expensive items stolen from Alma Graves were never retrieved, because they had already been delivered to a fence.

In my eagerness to help the Japanese, I may well have broken the law of the Occupational Government under which we lived and moved and had our being for about three years. At first we had APO privileges, and in that regard we were sought out by a chicken farmer by the name of Morikawa Takao. Morikawa was an enterprising and ambitious fellow, very zealous to be up on the latest in chicken farming. He had learned that at that time New Hampshire Reds were the new sensation in chicken breeds in the United States, and he very much wanted to introduce them to Japan.

The problem was that there was no way that he could order from a company in the United States since Japanese citizens had no access to commercial mail under the Occupational Government. His request was that I order the hatching eggs for him. He had all the information including order blanks; all I needed to do was to fill out the order and write a check to accompany it. He would reimburse me in Japanese currency, and of course the eggs would be sent to me. So I complied with his request, and although very few people were aware of it and even those who knew may have forgotten it, I have the distinction of having introduced New Hampshire Red chickens to Japan!

A separate campus had been purchased for the "Seminary," the Theological Department of the University, at a place called Hoshiguma, and by 1952 the dormitory building for seminary students had been erected there, though the students still had to commute to the Nishijin campus by bus for classes. It was not until 1955 that the administration and classroom building was constructed so that classes could be conducted on this separate campus. Hoshiguma was in a rural setting, about two-and-a-half miles from the main campus in Nishijin Machi, with two beautiful irrigation lakes for rice cultivation and with something of a growing forest.

Two homes for missionary teachers at the seminary and their families, the Garrotts and the Hayses, had already been constructed there, and it was decided that the Copelands would be housed there as well. The lot was fairly spacious. Louise did major work on drawing up house plans.

There was a fairly large kitchen, an expansive living/dining room, a study, a half bath, and four bedrooms with a full bath. Two of the bedrooms had Japanese *fusuma,* or sliding doors between them which meant that they could easily be converted into one large play room for the children. The living/dining room had a wood burning fireplace, and I installed a Ziegler oil space heater with a thermostatically controlled fan in the hall outside the bedrooms. Our heat was fairly adequate. A Japanese *genkan* and *getabako* were constructed at the entrance, and Japanese style living quarters were provided, connected to the house, for the maid. Between the Western style house and the Japanese living quarters was a laundry room.

Chapter Ten
JAPAN: FASCINATION AND DIFFICULTY

On the whole, those early post-War years provided for us a wonderful time to be doing evangelism in Japan. It was very easy to get a Japanese congregation together to hear the Christian message. If you circulated advertisements that at such-and-such an hour you would have a Christian evangelistic meeting, which we often did by means of a loudspeaker attached to a car, and especially if you indicated that the speaker was an American, a crowd was guaranteed. Then the messenger only needed to speak with ordinary effectiveness to have several decisions. Usually, these were indicated on a card on which there were several options listed as well as a place for a person to put his or her name and address. This method, rather than having the Japanese to "come to the front and shake hands with the preacher," seemed to fit in with the Japanese psychology.

The danger in those circumstances was that some would become Christian simply because they were infatuated with things American. Missionaries and Japanese pastors had to be careful lest they admit people into the membership of their churches who were not serious about this most important step. One way to help insure that such was not the case was to require prebaptismal classes for all who had indicated that they wanted baptism and church membership.

For a time I had such a responsibility at the Seinan Gakuin Baptist Church. I prepared for four sessions, and the ones applying for baptism could enter the course at any point. Some attended all four sessions and then presented their public confession of faith (to be read, or spoken extemporaneously, to the assembled church, according to Japanese custom), while others simply dropped out or told me that they were not yet ready for baptism.

I discovered that I was somewhat "conservative" with regard to Japanese culture, more so than some of the Japanese, especially the younger ones. I was afraid that things American would be too hastily adopted to the detriment of the time-honored Japanese ways. For example, I was something of a defender of the Confucian social structure and fearful of the breakdown of the Japanese family system. I was even critical of an evangelistic strategy whereby young people might be baptized into Christian churches without the parents even knowing what was happening to their children.

The spirit of the society was one of intensity in those days. Both Japanese Christians and American missionaries were focused upon rebuilding Japan after the War's devastation. My colleagues teaching in the Seminary, Kawano Sadamoto, Ozaki Shuichi, Miyoshi Toshio, and Kondō Sadatsugu, as well as missionaries Max Garrott, and Marion Moorhead were pastors or associate pastors of churches as well as itinerant evangelists.

The same was true of most of the missionaries who later joined us at Seinan Gakuin University, Tucker Callaway, George Hays, Bob Culpepper, James Wood, and John Shepard, except that some of them lived in a community where they were expected to develop a church in the missionary home. All of these men were ordained, I believe. Also, Shepard and Wood taught in departments of the university other than its Theological Department, and Mrs. Wood, Alma, taught English with her husband. We rarely, if ever, took vacations, partly because of the intensity of the situation and partly because of the example of the pre-War missionary, Max Garrott, who seemed not to believe in vacations!

In those early days, I revealed my ecumenical spirit in various ways, including serving as one of the officers of the Fellowship of Christian Missionaries, an interdenominational group which met annually. Locally, I took some initiative in organizing an interdenominational study group, composed of missionaries, which met monthly at different homes, with members taking turns providing the program. We sardonically called it the KKK for *Kyūshū Kenkyū Kai*, meaning Kyushu Study Society. We included several kinds of Protestants: Lutheran, Episcopal, Dutch Reformed, Seventh Day Adventist, etc., as well as a young couple who were with a faith mission and quite unequipped to deal with an alien culture.

Certain shortcomings of the organization were later repaired. The lack of women members was corrected by the resolve of James Wood. He and his wife Alma, both of whom had degrees in teaching English as a Second Language, came to Seinan Gakuin in 1952 to teach English and English literature in the University. When James was invited to join our group, to his credit he refused unless Alma also was included. Although there were Roman Catholic missionaries in the city, so far as I know no one thought in those pre-Vatican II days of inviting them to be members. Several years after we left Japan this deficiency was eliminated, to the considerable profit of the organization.

I learned also that after the passage of some time the renowned African American theologian, Dr. James Cone, was invited to meet with the society, whereupon the members, noticing his consternation, suddenly realized the inappropriateness of the name, KKK, and changed it!

Like the early apostles, some of us "went everywhere preaching the gospel." I don't know about the others, but I know that in my case it was almost always the same "gospel" since it took so much time to prepare a sermon in the Japanese language. I would preach the same sermon in the several small churches or mission points where I itinerated about once per month: Sasaguri, Amagi, Kasugabaru, Akama, and Koga. All were small villages which I remember well; they were near Fukuoka where we lived. Also, I sometimes went to Ashiya, where there was a small Japanese congregation which met on an American air base. A young woman by the name of Shiota played the organ, and her father was a leader in the small church.

Amagi, so far as I know, is still a mission point. It is a rural community east of Fukuoka and quite conservative. I drove there once a month with an English teacher from the Seinan High School who was quite knowledgeable about the history of the area. I learned a great deal from this man, a likeable fellow who was an earnest Christian and a deacon in the Seinan Gakuin Baptist Church.

He gave me a bum steer on the religious situation of the town, however, and I committed the *faux pas* of telling a relatively large congregation in Amagi that the Baptist mission was the only Protestant work in the community. Soon I was informed by a Lutheran missionary, James Scherer, who lived in Fukuoka at that time, that there was a Lutheran church in Amagi, and I did some sincere apologizing to him.*

The mission at Akama, north of Fukuoka, began in the home of a rather well-to-do man and his family. I have a table given to me by the Akama Mission, with an inscription indicating members of the mission as the donors and myself as the donee. There is in the table a hole for a round pottery charcoal stove (*shichirin*) to cook sukiyaki, a favorite Japanese food of mine.

Every time I read this Japanese inscription, I have feelings of great sadness mingled with the warm emotion of gratitude. A daughter of the home where we met had suffered a rather severe handicap, and although she became a Christian, she committed suicide. I have no way of knowing the depth of her loneliness and discouragement. She must have felt that she was an intolerable burden for her family and that life was too much for her. And so it is that along with my pleasant memories of Akama, there is a profound sense of tragedy.

Both Sasaguri and Kasugabaru developed into strong churches. Recently, I read in the *Baputesuto*, the newspaper published by the Japan Baptist Convention, that in the beginning of the church in Sasaguri I had sought out and purchased the land for the church! If I did so, I have no memory of it.

I do remember, however, that I made a humiliating error in Japanese in connection with a visit to the Sasaguri Mission. I could not drive all the way to the married seminary student's home where the Japanese group met, so I had to park the Mission's station wagon nearby. Accordingly, I stopped at a Japanese home, hoping that the occupants would permit me to leave the car there for an hour and a half or so. Meaning to ask permission, I should have said something like "*Koko ni jidōsha wo tomete, ii desu ka?*" However, I said "*Koko ni tomatte, ii desu ka?*" What I asked of the attractive young housewife who had come to the door was "Would it be all right if I spent the night here?" Noticing her profound embarrassment, I tried hastily to explain myself in Japanese, which I can assure you took some doing!

The Kasugabaru Church particularly profited from the fact

---

*Scherer had been a missionary to China. After his service in Japan, he got a doctoral degree from Princeton University and taught missions for many years in the Lutheran Theological Seminary in Chicago.

that a layman, the late Professor Hiraoka of Seinan Gakuin University, started the work in his home. Also, Christian GIs at a nearby American military base gave the money for the first building of the Kasugabaru Church which was quite small and cute.

Koga was the location of a tuberculosis hospital, a sanitarium, of which there were many, because of the shocking prevalence of this disease in those days (in contrast to present-day Japan). I can hardly remember a Japanese family in which at least one member was not a patient. The Japanese had learned how to cut through the rib cage to remove all or part of a lung and thus to cure or retard the spread of the disease. The sanitarium in Koga had a small Baptist church in it, the Pastor himself being a patient by the name of Yoshihara. His wife was strong and loyal, and helped immeasurably to keep the church work going.

Soon after we had arrived in Fukuoka, the late Ozaki Shuichi, who was pastor of the Seinan Gakuin Baptist Church, sought me out and asked me to be Associate Pastor. I agreed and as a result began preaching about once per month in the Sunday morning worship service with Ozaki interpreting until, after a few months, I was able to preach in Japanese.

Also Pastor Ozaki asked me to begin an English vespers service, meeting at four o'clock on Sunday afternoon, for Japanese persons who knew, or wanted to learn, English. Ozaki was the interpreter of my sermons into Japanese, even after I could handle the language, just to be sure that the message was understood. I remember that after I could detect whether the Japanese was being correctly interpreted, I preached on Zacchaeus, allowing that maybe there were psychological problems for this short individual. When I indicated that I wouldn't know about such problems (being quite tall in Japan), Mr. Ozaki (who was quite short even for a Japanese) faithfully interpreted my words, and then added in Japanese "But I would!"

This episode illustrated Mr. Ozaki's fine sense of humor and got us quite a laugh. So far as I know, that English service, with a change of time, still exists. By the way, Ozaki was a fine interpreter, and I have said more than once that my sermons came out better than the original when he interpreted them.

The morning service was held in the auditorium used by the High School in the red brick building, one of the oldest on the campus, because although the church had its own small building, it was far from large enough for the morning congregations. The vesper service, on the other hand, was held in the church building.

Japanese toilets in those days, called *benjo*, "convenient place" or "convenient places," (the Japanese noun being both singular and plural) were unisex. Many a time I was positioned at a urinal doing my business before I went into the auditorium to preach on a Sunday morning when I was aware that ladies of the congregation were coming in behind me to enter a booth to do theirs. Sometimes I would greet them on the way into the toilet. There seemed to be no sexual content to such encounters whatever. In those days, along with the famous "honey buckets," vessels for collecting the human waste from toilets--a practice which kept the countryside bathed in a certain odor--people "used the toilet" wherever the urge came upon them, especially in rural areas. It is true that women were more modest about this custom than men.

These practices have gradually died out in modern Japan, and only old timers such as I remember them. By the way, evidently the human waste was very good fertilizer; it really grew big vegetables and grains!

I well remember the first time I attempted to give a devotional message in Japanese (a short homily which became a Japanese sermon). I was invited to give such a message at a meeting of Seinan Church women in one of the homes. I was seated in a chair equipped with special runners so as not to damage the *tatami** excessively. The women, including Louise, were all seated on the *tatami*, and I felt somewhat embarrassed, like an undeserving king on his throne, but they insisted and somehow I got through. Refreshments were served, one unfamiliar item being a Japanese confection called *hagi*, or *o-hagi*, since you make it honorific by adding an "o" to an item (generally unrelated to you).

When we were departing, Louise wanted to say some

---

*The reed straw mat, inside of which is rice straw, which is characteristically used by Japanese to floor their living quarters. A mat is roughly 6 by 3 feet, so the size of a room is determined by the number of mats.

polite things, so she remarked to her hostess in Japanese that she certainly liked the *o-hage*. Although the hostess was properly polite, she could not contain her laughter, since Louise, meaning to compliment her, had actually said that she very much liked the "honorable bald head" (vowels do make an important difference in Japan). Of course, I was standing beside her with my bald head, even at that early age (about 34), very much in evidence!

Similarly significant, though so far as I know without such an embarrassing mistake, was the first sermon I preached in Japanese. The location was Amagi and, as was usual, we were seated on the *tatami*, with our shoes off, of course. Men, not in places of leadership, could sit more or less informally, cross legged, while the preacher, and all women, had to sit on their legs in a formal position. (My legs always went to sleep in such situations, and I soon learned to avoid disaster when I stood by subtly encouraging the resumption of circulation of the blood before arising. Fortunately, there were always announcements to be made at the end of the service, just before the benediction, and I used the occasion to rise slightly off my legs, imperceptibly, I hope, to renew the circulation).

On this occasion I was unusually tense, because I had written out my sermon in Japanese Romanization and then committed it to memory. What if I forgot a word? I would be in real trouble because I did not yet know synonyms. Suddenly I realized, by looking at the faces of the listening Japanese that the message was getting through. In spite of my anxiety, the Holy Spirit was overcoming the language barrier and my message, including the emotional content, was communicating. It was a most gratifying experience, which I have never forgotten.

Before long Mr. Ozaki left to become pastor of the Shimonoseki Baptist Church, though he still commuted back and forth to teach in the Seminary. The Seinan Church was several years without a Pastor, during which time Kawano Sadamoto, Max Garrott, and I shared the duties of Interim Pastor. While Max was on furlough, 1952-53, I had most of the responsibilities for conducting baptisms.

In 1952, at Christmas time I baptized 13 Japanese persons. It was quite cold, and the large coal heater which was placed in the middle of the small and very drafty building tried bravely to heat the room but actually made little impression. The water was just about room temperature and the room was very cold since the weather outside was below freezing and the wind off the Siberian snow fields was blowing very briskly, chilling to the bone any who were in its path. By the time I finished the baptism, my legs were almost too numb for me to clamber out of the baptismal pool and make my way to the nearby parsonage, where some of the good women helped me to the bath, which was extremely hot--heated by charcoal--and into which all those being baptized had already entered, one by one since the bath was small, warmed themselves, and then vacated.

While I was pretty successfully nurturing my martyr complex concerning this wintry experience, I learned that at Seinan Jo Gakuin, the Baptist girls' school at Kokura, Moorhead had baptized more than 70 girls in similar circumstances! He had taken a break midway and had poured some hot tea into his baptismal suit!

Besides the extreme cold, one other factor made this baptismal service at the Seinan Gakuin Baptist Church especially significant. I did not know that a journalist was present until the next day when I saw on the front page of the local Japanese daily newspaper an article about the baptism and a picture of me baptizing one of the candidates. The little church building had been decorated for a Christmas celebration, which we had held the night before, and the manger scene had not been removed. The baptismal pool was beneath the pulpit and its platform, so I was baptizing in the midst of straw and under the watchful eye of a cardboard donkey.

The scene looked rather ludicrous, to say the least. However, the headline concerning the candidates, and the article itself, written in Japanese by a reporter who no doubt was not a Christian, recorded it as a remarkable experience: "Not Minding the Cold because of Ecstasy" is a translation of the caption.

I engaged in evangelism quite willingly and wholeheartedly, but never to the extent of trying to overpower anyone. I saw my function as being a witness. Nor did I ever say anything negative concerning Japanese religions, Shinto, the native religion of Japan, and Buddhism, an import from India via Korea and China, which has been in Japan so long and syncretized with Shinto so thoroughly that it has become practically a native religion. Especially since I was later to teach courses in world religions, I have always regretted the fact that missionary work monopolized my time so that I seemed to have little opportunity for direct relations with the religions of Japan.

Even so, I always answered those who asked me about ancestors who died not knowing Christ, that our God is far more loving and just than we can imagine, and that we can commit our dead ancestors to God knowing that they will be treated with infinite love and perfect fairness. I always thought that I had given an adequate answer until one of my students, a young Japanese pastor, told me that he answered in the same way except for an added question: "What are you doing about your living relatives? What about your witness to them?"

As for Japanese who inquired about an actual religion--well, let me tell you how I answered in a real situation. I had preached in special services in the Nagasaki Baptist Church, where a former student was pastor, when a young fellow, a medical student at a nearby university, sought me out and put to me an interesting question. He told me that he actually had no religion (a very familiar statement in Japan) but that his family were Buddhist and that he had respect for Buddhism. He believed that Buddhism conveyed a great deal of truth and goodness. "If I were to become a Christian," he asked, "what would I do about Buddhism?"

I replied that I too knew something about Buddhism and that I shared his respect for it. I indicated that since we Christians confess Christ as Lord, first of all he would need to be sure of his life's commitment. If he gave himself to Jesus, I suggested, he would permit the illumination of this new faith in Jesus to shine upon his Buddhism. In this new light, he would retain much of Buddhism, some of which would perhaps be transformed to new levels of meaning, and other items of Buddhism he would probably see as conflicting with his Christian faith and therefore needing to be abandoned. In any case, he would be the one to decide. He thanked me and departed. I left the city soon, and I never knew whether he became a Christian.

Actually, although I engaged rather unstintingly in evangelism, my major responsibility was teaching. I taught church history and for a while the history of doctrine in the Seminary. In addition, I taught courses in my specialty in the general education division of the University as part of the required courses in re-

ligion. For a time, students, notably Nakamura Kazuo and Hayakawa Satoshi, translated my lectures on church history and history
of doctrine into Japanese and served as interpreters until I felt
secure enough in the language to teach in Japanese. Armed with
the lectures, printed in Japanese, within a few months, I began to
use Japanese only in my classroom. Many is the time when I have
returned to my home from two periods of teaching in Japanese,
fifty minutes each, with my abdominal muscles actually aching
from the strain.

Like most of my American colleagues, maybe all of them,
for a time I hoped that there would be no questions in Japanese,
since I found them very difficult to understand. This was certainly
not a very promising teaching method! Fortunately, I improved.

In addition to teaching, I got into school administration, all
too soon, I'm afraid. I had never contemplated administrative
work, but in preparation for furlough in 1952, Max Garrott resigned the Chancellorship of Seinan Gakuin and the Presidency of
Seinan Gakuin University. Max had carried the school through the
pretty drastic reorganization under the educational reform required by the Occupational Government. He was quite fatigued,
and I agreed that he needed to get out from under the burden of
administration, that, like me, he had resisted.*

Thus, on April 1, 1952, after I had been in Japan less than
three years, I became President of Seinan Gakuin University. Nobody knew better than I how ill prepared I was in terms of the
language and in other ways as well. One thing which made it
difficult if not impossible to decline was that I had determined
before coming to Japan that I would try to do whatever the
Japanese asked me to do, and this resolve was unchanged.

The position of President of Seinan Gakuin University put
me on the Board of Trustees, from which vantage point I soon
learned how difficult it was to procure a Chancellor.** One espe-

---

*In those days the Chancellor of Seinan Gakuin (*Inchō*) and President of
the University (*Gakuchō*) were called President of Seinan Gakuin and
Dean of the University, respectively.

**Both the Chancellor and the University President were required by
Japanese Law to be Trustees.

Illustration No. 32
University Building No. 1
(Where My Office Was as President of the University,
Then as Chancellor of the Whole School)

cially annoying problem was that the Middle School (or Junior High School) was at odds with the High School. The Middle School was said to feel superior to the High School and did not like to recommend that its students seek admission to the latter. On the other hand, the High School felt that it was better than the Middle School and did not like to accept graduates from that school. In any case, there was mutual dislike and badmouthing on the part of certain members of the two faculties.

In mid-1951 the Trustees had brought in a highly respected educator, Dr. Ōhira Tokuzō, an earnest Christian and an emeritus professor at Kyushu University in Fukuoka, a national (formerly Imperial) university, to become Principal of both schools. The Principal of the Middle School, Itō Tsukeyuki, became Vice Principal of the Middle School under Dr. Ōhira. It was hoped that this new system would result in a solution of the problem.

It was in this situation that I was persuaded to become Chancellor of Seinan Gakuin. I insisted that I could accept the office only on two conditions: (1) I would have to be permitted to resign the Presidency of the University and (2) my assumption of this office would be accompanied by the election of a Japanese

Vice Chancellor to help me. The Trustees agreed to these conditions. Accordingly, I resigned the Presidency of Seinan Gakuin University and accepted the Chancellorship of the whole school

Illustration No. 33
As Chancellor, I Gave Many Speeches
(Here I Am Addressing the Dept. of Pre-Education Teacher Training)

in November 1952. A few days later, Kawano Sadamoto was elected Vice Chancellor.

My first secretary in these administrative positions was Kawano Nobuko, who had been a student in my University religion course. After working for one year in my office, she was graduated from Seinan Gakuin University and went to Meredith College in Raleigh, North Carolina, and then to other American schools for further studies. She was the oldest daughter of Kawano Sadamoto. Nobuko was followed as my secretary by Furusawa Kasei, who was also my student but who several years later was to be my fellow professor in the Theological Department of Seinan Gakuin University when I returned to Japan.

Unfortunately, under the administration of Principal Ōhira the problems in the Middle and High schools still festered and refused settlement. Finally, Dr. Ōhira concluded that without drastic action the issue would never be resolved. He developed a plan for a solution which he presented to the Trustees, and they gave it their unanimous approval. Dr. Ōhira's statement called for the resignation of seven teachers in the two schools, most of them teachers in the High School. He listed certain reasons for the dismissals, leaving it up to each teacher to fit the request for his resignation into these official reasons.

I was appalled to learn that as Chancellor, I was expected to call the men into my office and inform them of their dismissal! Up until the present, without doubt this was the most difficult day of my life. Of course, Principal Ōhira consented to be with me for this most distasteful responsibility, and at my request he readily agreed to read the statement. In what I said I chose words which I hoped would make the bitter medicine as palatable as possible, and to assure those being dismissed that the school was grateful for their service and would continue their salaries for one year and do what it could to help them find employment elsewhere.

What we did was major surgery indeed, and as I reflect upon it, I am sure that we could not have proceeded so smoothly had the teachers' union had the strength which it later exhibited. As it was, a Professor from the University came to my office to tell me that he and his colleagues had viewed my election as "the stirring of a fresh breeze" but that my action in this case had seriously disappointed them. I thanked him and then kept silent.

On the other hand, one of the high school teachers who had been terminated, a very good individual who knew that he was dismissed not for any direct contribution to the conflict but because of his incompetence as a teacher, corresponded with me in the most friendly fashion, telling me that he had moved to Tokyo where he had found no employment until he had begun his own school.

I soon left on furlough, leaving the school in Mr. Kawano's hands as Acting Chancellor, and during the year he proposed to the Trustees that the salaries of the dismissed teachers be paid by the school for two years instead of one. They accepted his proposal. Had I been in the administrative office at the time, I would have agreed heartily with this suggestion. Also, Kawano helped to persuade Itō Tsukeyuki to resign as Vice Principal of our Middle School and go to a Methodist institution, Hiroshima Girls' School, as Middle School Principal. I viewed Itō as a fine Christian man but also as a large part of the problem.

If my family and I had any serious cultural shock in Japan, I can say honestly that I was not aware of it. It is true that the language was quite frustrating, but Louise and I coped with it, partly by laughing at our own mistakes, at least usually. We found the process of living in and exploring the Japanese culture a delightful and exciting journey.

The Japanese were almost unfailingly kind to us, especially when they learned that we could speak their language. It was not unusual for a shopkeeper to leave his or her place of business to direct us personally to a location about which we had inquired. When the occupation ended in 1952 and Japan once more had its independence, a few children called us uncomplimentary names, no doubt reflecting what they heard from adults, but such instances were rare.

The Occupational Government, under which we operated until 1952, went unusually well. General Douglas MacArthur was the administrator, and although nominally the occupation was under the Allies, in fact it was almost completely American. The overall policies were remarkably beneficent. I was told that the Japanese were profoundly surprised at the conduct of the occupation, because their own government would not even have thought of dealing with a defeated enemy as kindly as they were treated.

Of course, at lower levels things sometimes caused American missionaries great embarrassment. For example, there were times when drunken and seemingly sadistic GIs insulted Japanese women and generally made themselves obnoxious.

In one instance I performed the marriage ceremony for a mixed couple, the husband being an American GI and the wife a Japanese young woman. The two were living together, the young woman was pregnant, and they asked me to marry them. After carefully interviewing them, I agreed. While I recognized that the groom was socially and culturally inferior to the bride, he seemed pleasant and responsible enough.

The baby was born and soon thereafter the young man was sent back to the States, summarily leaving his wife and child behind. She showed me a letter from him in which he not only dismissed all responsibility for the marriage, but suggested that he had a brother who was coming to Japan who would need to "shack up" with a Japanese girl and that his former wife would be a good candidate! I admired the young woman because she not only renounced her husband and his coarse ideas but also determined to raise the baby herself and not submit it for adoption. I knew that she was assuming a difficult role, for children of mixed races had their problems in Japan.

On other occasions I was able to see policies of the Occupational Government work with positive results. For example, at Seinan Gakuin University we had a certain student, a handsome fellow, rather large for a Japanese, who had suffered the loss of one arm. He had a well-trained baritone voice and sang most impressively. During the few months that I served as University President, this student came to me in considerable distress. His story was that he had been employed in the Provost Marshal's building in downtown Fukuoka and that at the time of his employment he had been told that he was under a certain American sergeant whom he was to obey implicitly.

Things had gone very well until the sergeant had given this Japanese employee a key to the basement where confiscated black market items were kept and told him to get the sergeant some cigarettes. This instruction put the student in a difficult dilemma. He knew that on the one hand it was wrong to get black market goods but that on the other he was expected to obey the sergeant. He opted to do as he was told. Accordingly, he was caught in the act and was fired immediately with no chance to defend himself. He indicated that he could suffer the loss of his job better than to have this matter on his permanent record.

The student requested that I write a letter explaining his situation, a request with which I was glad to comply. So I wrote the Provost Marshal relating the student's story. I was gratified to receive a written response soon thereafter. The Provost Marshal thanked me for the letter and informed me that the student had been reinstated and the sergeant had been "appropriately disciplined." I had no need to ask for further information and I felt a sense of pride in our American military.

General MacArthur, whether by design or by happenstance, proved to be a great administrator of the Occupational Government in Japan. He fit in very well with the Japanese image of a head of government. It is true that his informal attire and his corn-cob pipe were very untypical. Otherwise, he exhibited a Japanese imperial mystique: he was remote from the Japanese public, he operated through subordinates, and his frequently issued directives were in flowery and ambiguous language. The Japanese highly respected him.

An experience which I had in relation to MacArthur's dismissal was in keeping with this evaluation. I was riding in a train beside a Japanese gentleman, whose demeanor indicated that he wished me to respect his privacy. Therefore, I had not attempted to engage him in conversation. (You remember that MacArthur insisted on disobeying President Truman, his Commander-in-Chief, as to the execution of the Korean War.) When we pulled into a train station, my traveling com-panion, as was the practice in those days, raised the window to buy a Japanese newspaper from a vendor. The prominent head-line (which I read over his shoulder) indicated that MacArthur had been dismissed.

The reaction of the Japanese gentleman was one of utter shock and disbelief. He kept muttering to himself, as though no one else were present, *"Taihen! Taihen!"* This Japanese word has a broad meaning, but in this context, I interpreted it as "This is terrible!" As this fellow seemed to indicate, the Japanese had great difficulty accepting the fact that the great MacArthur had been fired by a civilian president.

I personally felt at the time that although it was necessary for Truman to terminate MacArthur as commander of the American forces in Korea, he might well have retained him as administrator of the Occupational Government in Japan. However, for the Japanese it was a salutary lesson in democracy, and I later concluded that it was good that MacArthur lost both jobs because of his insubordination.

For several of us American missionaries the relation to the Allied (American) Occupational Government was quite problematical. We applauded its termination in 1952. To some of us MacArthur's call for "thousands of Christian missionaries" to enter Japan was an embarrassment. It appeared to violate the American concept of the relation of church and state.

When the Copelands first entered Japan in 1949 we were given American military currency, PX privileges, and unlimited hospital care for us and our family. The first two of these soon ended and hospital provisions were eventually closed to us except in cases of life-threatening emergency. Two of our five children were born in Japan. The third Sarah Elizabeth ("Beth"), was born during the occupation, January 14, 1951, in a military hospital in Fukuoka.

The alternative was not very inviting, especially in winter time. Japanese children were born in outpatient clinics which were unheated, and since nurses functioned only as helpers to the doctors and in only a very limited sense as caretakers for the patients, the latter were expected to provide someone, usually a family member, to take care of any of their needs which were not strictly medical, including preparing their food.

Beth was a most attractive little girl, and it was fun to watch her grow up. Though her hair was quite short at birth, she soon developed a beautiful shock of curly hair so blonde as to be almost white, as her daddy's had been when he was a boy (and when he had hair!) Also, like her father and unlike her older sisters, her eyes were blue. She received much attention from the Japanese, partly because she was such a striking blonde.

Beth was very precocious. We noticed especially how fast she was in learning to crawl and walk. When we visited with Melvin and Edith Bradshaw and their boys, Joel and Dicky (Richard, who later became known as "Rick," I believe), who were about the ages of Joy and Beth respectively, we had to be vigilant to keep Beth from stealing Dicky's toys and rapidly crawling off with them. She must have been five or six months at the time. She walked at the age of eight months, setting a record for our children, only Rebecca ("Becky") coming close to it, walking at nine months. For some reason, Beth loved to walk on tiptoe, and it was most appealing to see her tiptoeing about while still quite young, with her abundant and curly blonde hair. Though fiercely independent by nature, she was also very affectionate, often hugging and kissing her parents and assuring us of her love.

Judy, too, was fascinating to the Japanese. She was definitely blonde and her hair was naturally curly. While we lived in the aluminum prefab on the Nishijin campus, she was especially the darling of Seinan Gakuin University students who loved to talk to her and make over her. She enjoyed conversing with the local policemen also, and I remember that at least once she was lost from home and we were extremely worried about her, until we discovered that the police, who had a box nearby, rather easily identified her and delivered her unscathed to our door. Many years afterward Judy told us that she had deliberately left home so that she could be found by the police.

I am often amazed by the profundity of Judy's thoughts and dreams when she was but a child, as she now recalls them. After we moved to Hoshiguma, we began to notice that in addition to being intellectual and bookish, Judy was also dramatic in nature, loving to put on plays for us and the community, plays which she definitely determined and directed. She was highly imaginative, dominating children her own age and younger without ever being in any sense a bully.

Joy had a sunny, bright and cheerful disposition, and we soon knew that we had given her the right name. Even when she became something of a smart aleck as she grew older, her sauciness was often pleasing, though we were never sure what she might say. Her hair was dark, not nearly as black as that of the Japanese, very close to auburn in color. Her prayers were especially, let us say, interesting. One time, while we lived at Hoshiguma, she was reporting one of her prayers to us. (Our children always spoke English to us and Japanese to Japanese guests) She related that she asked God to bless each member of the family, but when she asked God to bless Tsubaki San, God said, according to Joy, "*Ā sō desu ka?*" meaning something like "Oh really?" We found it quite striking both that God gave such an answer, and that God spoke in Japanese to Joy!

I have already mentioned that Joy was just a baby when we arrived in Japan in 1949. Actually, she was less than seven months, and we were not aware of anything particularly unusual about her. After arriving in Japan, however, we soon noticed that as she pulled up on the side of her playpen she seemed not to be using her left hand. Also, when she began crawling, she appeared to drag her left leg somewhat and to use her left arm rather unnaturally.

Becoming quite concerned about her, we took her to an American pediatrician who was available to us in the American military forces. For some time there was uncertainty about her diagnosis. The doctor thought at first that she had been a victim of polio, even though we had no memory of her ever having had such a disease with its characteristically high fever. Eventually it was concluded that her condition was due to cerebral palsy, a light variety which affected only her left limbs and fortunately did not influence her speech or mentality.

Braces constituted a difficult problem. Although in many ways Japanese medicine, which was heavily dependent upon the German system, was considerably advanced, it had done little about prosthetics. A Japanese brace maker created a brace for Joy's leg, but it was ill-fitting and seemed to do her more harm than good. On the advice of an American army pediatrician in the environs of Fukuoka, Louise and I took Joy to Tokyo to see if the American military would let us get a brace for her from their splendid brace shop.

At that time also I got an interview with an Army officer--I don't remember his name or rank--only to be told firmly that we missionaries should not expect to be dependent any longer upon the Occupational Government. I asked this officer what he would do if he were in my place. He replied that he probably would do what I was doing. My rejoinder was that it was embarrassing for me to make the long trip from Fukuoka to appear in Tokyo as a suppliant, but that I was quite willing to do it for the sake of my little daughter. He seemed somewhat sympathetic but was quite unrelenting.

Often you remember too late things you wish you had said in certain situations. I was sorry that I did not think to say to the officer, "You are talking about American missionaries not being dependent upon the United States military. Let me remind you that before the War missionaries had the wonderful facilities of the Episcopal mission hospital, St. Luke's, to depend upon. But now you have taken it over as your own military hospital. This is the very institution, the resources of which I am asking you to make available to me."

At any rate, I could not press my case too vigorously without getting our doctor friend in Fukuoka in trouble with his military superiors. All we could do was to put up with the situation the best we could and ask for an early furlough.

Chapter Eleven
FURLOUGH AND BACK TO JAPAN

When we asked to return to America early because of the need for treatment for Joy, the authorities at the Foreign Mission Board were very understanding and generous, especially our Area Secretary, Dr. Baker J. Cauthen, and the Executive Secretary, Dr. M. Theron Rankin. At first we were granted a furlough beginning in the summer of 1953, one year early, and then it was suggested that we simply wait until after the close of the Japanese school year and commencement at the end of March of that year. This would move our furlough up not just a year but almost sixteen months. The length of the furlough, too, was extended by about the same interval.

Our departure from Fukuoka for furlough was more exciting than we had counted on or desired! By the time we left Fukuoka, my reputation had been enhanced by the fact that I was given exaggerated credit for my role in helping solve the problem of animosity between the Middle and High Schools of Seinan Gakuin. For this or for other reasons, a very large crowd, students and various staff persons of the school, friends, members of the Seinan Gakuin Church, and others, were at the train station to see us off. Louise and I were there with our three little girls, Judy, almost 6, Joy, 4, and Beth, 2. Characteristically, the crowd had sung the Japanese translation of "God Be With You Till We Meet Again." We had been moved almost to tears.

When the train arrived from some other station in Kyū-shū, it was quite long, and the car in which we had reservations did not make it all the way into the station but instead stopped short of the platform. Accordingly, after rather frantically making our way through the crowd back to our car, we had to board the train from track level. I no more than managed to get our 2-year-old Beth on, than the train started to pull off! I hastily scrambled on so that little Beth would not be alone, though she certainly was not upset. Now the train was departing the station with only two of the five Copelands on board! Friends, not knowing what had happened, were waving goodbye to me. Though I cared deeply for them, I certainly was in no mood for farewells!

Fortunately, two Japanese colleagues, who were "take charge"guys, had the presence of mind to understand our predicament and save the day: Matsunobu Yōichi, who was a rather large (for a Japanese) and energetic physical education professor, jumped aboard the train and pulled its emergency cord so that it stopped briefly in the station; and Hayashi Toshihisa, a young and very tall staff member who worked in the University health office and who, like Matsunobu, had a resonant bass voice, grabbed Joy and carried her on his shoulder to the platform on which our car was now located and where she could get on the train.

Others got our bags aboard, and somehow Judy and Louise made it as well. You may be sure that it took us some time to settle down from our experience of panic, though we had a long ride and an overnight trip before we reached Tokyo.

Joy took umbrage at having been hoisted on the shoulder of a stranger and unceremoniously carried through the crowd, and she refused to be mollified. Each time we carefully explained the situation to her, Joy would always respond indignantly as though we had said nothing at all: "Why did that man pick me up and run with me?"

We already knew that when we arrived in Tokyo at least two other factors would make the voyage a very memorable one. First, we were not only on the same ship which had brought us to Japan almost four years earlier, the *President Wilson*; we were assigned to the same stateroom! We have always assumed that this reservation was a pure coincidence. We certainly had nothing to do with it, and so far as we know the same was true for everybody else who had helped with the reservation.

Secondly, Crown Prince Akihito, eldest son of the then Emperor of Japan, who many years later was to succeed his father as Emperor, was to be on board with us. The Crown Prince was nineteen and unmarried, and you could imagine how American teenagers related to him. While on board the ship, we were shocked to hear some of them calling to him across the deck, "Hey, Princey!" Although I have no brief for royalty, undoubtedly I was influenced somewhat by the Japanese attitude. I did not address the Prince directly, but sent him a note which was answered by the Grand Chamberlain, who seemed to be in charge of all the Prince's affairs.

Louise had made identical outfits for our three little girls, and they seemed to be the belles of the ship. Fortunately, all the benefits which we had enjoyed previously were still offered us, including fairly good child care. So we enjoyed the trip home very much--in spite of the fact that the Episcopal bishop nearly spoiled Easter Sunday for us. We had observed him drinking rather heavily the night before, and his sermon was a kind of pusillanimous apology for Christian faith rather than a proclamation of the great good news of the resurrection. The default of the bishop made us glad that when we crossed the International Date Line, Saturday rather than Sunday was repeated!

Frankly, I don't remember much about the rest of the trip except that we traveled by train and that we made some stops here and there to visit relatives. We had settled upon Louisville as our furlough home because I had been invited by Dr. Cornell Goerner to teach at Southern Baptist Theological Seminary during the 1953-1954 term. So we eventually arrived in Louisville, Kentucky, to occupy housing provided by Southern Seminary, on whose campus Louise and I had done our courting a few years earlier.

In the summer of 1953, after our furlough was well under way, I was a speaker at Foreign Missions week at the Southern Baptist Assembly at Ridgecrest, North Carolina. I touched upon several controversial issues, including race, ecumenicity, and the burning of the Revised Standard Version of the New Testament, the last of these having been instigated by a North Carolina Baptist pastor. After the message Thelma Moorhead chided me for trying to include all the current controversial issues!

One of the Foreign Mission Board members (members of the Board of Trustees, not to be confused with Board staff personnel) who heard me took serious offense at what I said, especially about ecumenism. He told a missionary colleague that he was going to see to it that I was fired by the Board. That night when the missionaries were introduced, our Area Secretary, Dr. Baker J. Cauthen, gave me an extraordinarily extravagant introduction. I suspected that this Board member (and possibly others) had vented his indignation to Cauthen and that Cauthen was replying to him and to others who shared his anti-Copeland views.

Of course, adequate and appropriate medical care for Joy was our major concern. Upon investigation, we learned that perhaps the most famous name in the treatment of cerebral palsy was Dr. Winthrop Phelps in Baltimore. So we began the custom of taking Joy to Baltimore periodically during our furlough for Dr. Phelps to observe her and give us the benefit of his counsel.

On the first visit Dr. Phelps confirmed the diagnosis of cerebral palsy which had been given us by doctors whose specialties did not include this particular medical problem. After asking us several questions, he also told us that the brain hemorrhage probably resulted from a birth injury, most likely because of too rapid a birth. That is, the sudden release of the baby's head from the birth canal was the most probable cause of the hemorrhage. For the first time we got adequate braces for Joy's left limbs and we were assured that she was getting expert care.

We were ready, then, to settle in at Louisville. At first, we were domiciled in an apartment in Fuller Hall, but we soon

Illustration No. 34
Visitors at Christmas During Our Furlough
(From Left: Louise's Aunt Gertrude, Betty, Louise's Father,
me , and Matsunobu Yōichi)

moved to one of the multihousing units of Green Tree Manor which the Seminary had recently purchased and renamed Seminary Village, a complex about a mile and a half east of the campus on Frankfort Avenue. During our stay at Seminary Village we were fortunate to have visitors from Japan and from our families. In fact, Betty, Louise's sister, lived with us for a semester while she attended the University of Louisville Soon I was speaking here and there in Southern Baptist churches about missions in Japan while I got ready for teaching courses in the Seminary which I had not taught before, the required course in the history of missions and the survey course in world religions.

Dr. Cornell Goerner, who had succeeded Dr. William Owen Carver as Professor of Missions and Comparative Religions at the Seminary, made sure that I was installed in an office and in other ways was solicitous of my needs. After assuring me that I would be attending faculty meetings, he had to come to my office somewhat red-faced to tell me that he had been out of line since only those who had signed the Seminary's *Abstract of Principles* (confessional statement), that is, who were bona fide faculty members, could attend faculty meetings.

It so happened that the only faculty meeting I attended that whole year was at Southeastern Baptist Theological Seminary! At the invitation of that school in Wake Forest, North Carolina during the spring semester I gave a Missionary Day ad-dress. Since my speech occurred on the day for the regular monthly faculty meeting, President Sid Stealey invited me to attend.

In other ways during my year at Southern Seminary, I was able to contrast the hierarchical faculty structure at Southern with the egalitarian setup at Southeastern, particularly since I was later to join the faculty at the latter school. For example, although I lived some distance from the Southern campus, I had no faculty park-ing place assigned to me and had to compete with students for a place to leave my car. I always thought that the necessity of shar-ing the students' attitude toward parking was good for me. Also, what I had already noticed as a student at Southern was quite ap-parent to me now, namely, that faculty members seemed rather unapproachable by students.

Frankly, although I remember what I taught at Southern Seminary, courses in missions and world religions, I certainly do not recall how many hours I taught. I do remember, of course, that the Seminary obtained my services very economically. Missionaries were on Foreign Mission Board salary while on furlough, with their salaries adjusted (usually upward) for the cost of living in the United States. Therefore, whatever they received as extra income was gravy on their mashed potatoes, so to speak. I know well because I participated in this system, not only as a missionary but later as a professor of missions.

I hasten to say that sometimes churches or denominational entities assumed that missionaries also received a travel allowance for speaking in various places and therefore did not remunerate them for travel. However, this was a false assumption for the sake of which missionaries sometimes were victimized.

My teaching and my presence on the Southern Seminary campus helped in our getting certain students to Japan as missionaries. Among these were Gene and Dorothy Clark, Dewey and Ramona Mercer, Mary Lou Massingill, and Evelyn Owen.

The Clarks lived near us in Seminary Village, and I developed a rather close friendship with Gene. He told me that he had volunteered to go to Japan as a missionary because he felt a call to go there, but that the Foreign Mission Board was trying to get him to go somewhere else where they thought the needs were greater. I encouraged him to stand by his conviction and assured him that the Board would relent and send him and Dorothy to Japan. He did just that and it was my joy to see them and their family in Japan later. Unfortunately, he died in Tokyo of a heart attack in 1981, just short of his 55th birthday.

The Mercers spent a long career in Japan until Dewey's untimely death came just before their scheduled retirement. Evelyn Owen stayed in Japan as an effective single woman missionary until retirement followed by marriage. Mary Lou Massengill also went to Japan as a single woman, a nurse, but a few years later I had the honor of performing the wedding ceremony for her and Wayne Emanuel, an American serviceman whom she met in Japan. Wayne got a seminary degree before the wedding and then joined the bride as a missionary in Japan in 1958. He and Mary Lou served there until their retirement in the 1990s.

In the late spring of 1954, when my teaching at Southern Seminary was drawing to a close, the faculty asked Dr. Goerner to feel me out as to whether I would be open to an offer to accept a position on the faculty as a missions professor. Of course they knew about Joy's physical problem and thought that we might find it necessary to remain in the States. Some of the faculty members were my former teachers and some were former fellow students. I learned later that Dale Moody had become emotional as they discussed the matter. Meantime, Dr. Phelps had told us that if the Board would be flexible enough to allow us to return to the States periodically for Joy's treatment, Louise and I would not need to interrupt our careers as missionaries.

Therefore, I felt that only an emergency need would bring me back for the teaching of missions, and I did not feel that Southern was in an emergency. As a student I had been enrolled in Dr. Goerner's classes, and I knew him as a competent teacher. Although I was aware that Goerner was overloaded, I also knew that Southern was in touch with Herbert Jackson, like me, a former graduate student of Uncle Ken Latourette. Also, Jackson was an American Baptist who had served a few years in India. I suspected that if I did not give the faculty a green light, in all likelihood they would invite Jackson. This proved to be the case and Jackson taught a few years at Southern before moving on to other positions. Therefore it was not difficult to give a negative answer to the Southern faculty.

When Theron Price, whom I knew rather well and who taught church history, suggested to me that if I did not want to teach missions, he would nominate me for a position in church history, I found it even easier to decline. I was convinced that nothing short of an emergency in the teaching of *missions*, not church history, could take me from my place in Japan.

The previous November I had spoken on international missions at the Maryland State Baptist Convention. Dr. Edward A. McDowell ("Dr. Mac," as he was known affectionately by colleagues), who was one of my favorite teachers at Southern and at that time a professor of New Testament at Southeastern Seminary, was also on the program. We had good fellowship together, in the course of which he exacted a promise from me that if I ever entertained any thought of coming back to the States I would let him know so that he could recommend me to President Sid Stealey of Southeastern as Professor of Missions.

For at least two reasons, I could not forget my promise to Dr. Mac. (1) I had a contact from Ray Brown, who, you will remember, was a good friend from my student days at Southern and at Yale, giving reasons why I should consider coming to Southeastern Seminary. At that time Ray was a pastor in Richmond, Virginia, and had no special relationship with Southeastern, but he knew me and he knew Southeastern. (Caralie, Ray's wife, later told me that she remonstrated with Ray for his contact with me, saying, "Now, Ray, let Luther alone. He believes that God has called him to Japan, and you shouldn't bother him." To which Ray gave her his inimitable look and replied, "Woman, did it ever occur to you that God might be speaking to Luther through me?")

(2) I knew that Dr. J. B. Hipps was Professor of Missions at Southeastern and that although he was known as a bright and progressive missionary with a rather illustrious career in China, he had never taught missions. Not only so, he had begun to teach missions when he was beyond retirement age. I interpreted Southeastern as a new opportunity for theological education, continuing the best of the Louisville tradition without the unnecessary baggage of its hierarchical elements, and being located in the progressive environment of North Carolina. Could it also represent the kind of emergency which would call me from a missionary career?

For the Japan Baptist Mission, we bought a red Chevrolet station wagon to drive across the States and then put on a ship as "baggage" and take with us to Japan. We meandered our way across America, visiting my relatives and Louise's here and there. We had a wonderful trip, enjoying the ever changing vistas of the remarkably diverse scenery of our country, and stopping for special sightseeing at such national parks as the Petrified Forest, the Grand Canyon, Sequoia, and Yosemite.

At Glorieta Baptist Assembly in New Mexico, we stayed for several days to help in the first special sessions for the orientation of new missionaries.* Here we were joined by our dear friends, the Moorheads, who, having completed their furlough, were also

---

*These early attempts at orientation were far too brief. Even the more extensive programs of later years depended almost entirely upon Americans (especially missionaries) to the nearly complete disregard of overseas nationals who could have done a much better job of orienting new American missionaries to other cultures.

driving a red Chevrolet station wagon back to Japan for the Japan Baptist Mission!

I discovered that I could not put out of my mind the opportunity at Southeastern and the promise to Ed McDowell. Therefore, from New Mexico I wrote Dr. McDowell, telling him that it would be impossible for me to make a vocational decision away from my colleagues and my work situation in Japan, but that if he and Dr. Stealey could give me another year, I would be prepared by then to give them a definite answer about pursuing further the matter of my teaching at Southeastern. I emphasized that I appreciated the necessity of their moving ahead on this matter and that if they felt that they could not wait on me for a year I certainly would understand.

I gave my Japanese address, knowing that the month or so of our continued journey would give them ample time to give a considered reply. Stealey himself replied in a letter which reached me in Japan, assuring me that the moment I gave the signal he would present my name to the Trustees.

About all I remember about the return voyage on the *President Cleveland,* sister ship to the *President Wilson,* was that it was a delight to cross the Pacific with the Moorheads, and that the woman who took care of our children was a sorehead about whom there was general dissatisfaction on the part of children and parents on board. She seemed interested only in her lucrative trade prospects in Hong Kong. Our children still talk about her cross disposition.

Moorhead entertained the passengers with a skit in which he played a Japanese sumo wrestler with a sheet adorning his ample midriff like a huge diaper. On that same occasion, we and some other missionaries won first prize by a representation of a missionary family, one set of parents playing the role of stern, puritanical missionaries and the others their irascible children. Some fellow passengers, not realizing that all those participating in the skit were themselves missionaries, felt that we were unfairly pummeling the missionaries!

Nor do I remember much about the two years or so in Japan for our second term (almost two years for Louise and the children, about nineteen months for me). However, I recall a trip to Iki Island with Moorhead. Before he and his family moved to Sapporo with Annie Hoover and Suzuki Masana to begin Baptist work on the island of Hokkaido in 1952, he had done evangelistic work on Iki. The latter was a Japanese island in the Japan Sea, about one-third of the way to Korea. Moorhead wanted to revisit the scene of his former labors, and particularly a doctor and his family who lived there and were the mainstay of a developing church.

So Marion and I went to the port of Hakata (Fukuoka) in the summer of 1955 to board a ferry boat for Iki. It happened that two small horses were being transported to Iki, one a bay and the other a sorrel. They were loaded onto the boat by means of a crane and kind of a sling arrangement. First, the sling was secured around the belly of the bay, the crane picked him up, and he was gently lowered to the steel deck of the boat where an attendant waited to receive him. When the bay's hooves touched the solid steel of the deck, he began to thrash about, endangering the attendant in limb and life. So he was again suspended, then lowered to the deck, only to continue his resistance. After this procedure was repeated two or three times the bay elected to go completely limp, allowing his legs to extend out from his entirely uncooperative torso. This action likewise recurred several times, after which the horse evidently decided that he was getting nowhere and it was better to straighten up and fly right.

While this affair was transpiring, I was darting my eyes back and forth to watch the sorrel horse, who in turn was observing the bay. Since I have horse sense (which means I know at least as much as a horse), I discerned what the sorrel was thinking, namely, "When I am lifted up by my belly, I am not going to make a fool of myself like that bay." Surely enough, when it came his turn, the sorrel submitted himself stoically to the indignity of the sling, just as though he had been through this kind of thing before.

For our passage, the Japan Sea was very rough, and I had a miserable voyage. (Moorhead had been a Naval Chaplain and I had heard him boast that though he had been on the boisterous Atlantic, he had never known seasickness) Through a porthole I tried to fix my eye on some stationary cloud, only to find that the clouds also were giddily moving. I was saved from some disaster only by the arrival, after about three hours, of our small boat at a safe harbor in Iki.

But our troubles had only begun. We had to traverse the

island by bus, the seats were all taken, and the bus was built for small Japanese persons and not for my long West Virginia body. I soon discovered that I could not get by with bending at only one place but at two or three. Abetted by the fumes from the fuel, the bus ride did nothing for my aborted seasickness.

Nevertheless, on the following day, which was Sunday, Moorhead and I each preached in Japanese, and we had good services. Several Christian decisions were made and Moorhead was much encouraged by his visit to his old haunts.

Unfortunately, Moorhead and I had boasted to the hospitable physician's family with whom we were staying of how we liked *sashimi* (raw fish), one of the delicacies which the Japanese enjoyed and for which Iki was famous. When we discovered that our hosts had prepared it for Monday's breakfast, we were chagrined but could do nothing but eat it. (*Sashimi* was fine, but for *breakfast?* Ugh!) Not only did they have *sashimi* but the usual toast and eggs for breakfast. Our genial hosts were delighted when we each asked for a bowl of steamed rice for the *sashimi*.

One problem was that soon after breakfast we had to board the ferry for the return trip to our port of origin in Fukuoka. On the way I asked Moorhead, "Did you notice that I put the *sashimi* on top of the other things I ate for breakfast?" He allowed that he did but that he had not attached any significance to my actions. I told him that I was pretty sure that the raw fish would want to get back to the sea before we reached our des-tination, and I wanted them to disturb what else I had eaten for breakfast as little as possible.

When we boarded the ferry, we discovered that the Japan Sea, though it had calmed considerably since our trip to the island two days before, was still acting up. Fortunately, there were only the two of us in a large room with *tatami* floors, and I talked incessantly to keep my mind off the fact of my imminent sea-sickness. Soon I could stand it no longer and made a mad dash for the rail, not bothering to get my shoes from where I had left them at the entrance to the *tatami* room.

After I retched, allowing the raw fish and other assorted occupants of my stomach to join their companions in the briny, Moorhead appeared. He had walked the long way around the boat wearing his shoes and carrying mine. "Did you get some relief?" he asked solicitously, and as I answered "Yes," I thought,

"Uh oh, he's bringing me my shoes with no sign of seasickness himself." Then I happened to notice that he was looking a bit green around the gills. Well, Moorhead suddenly hit the rail and emptied his digestive tract in the waters of the Japan Sea. With some satisfaction, I watched him vomit and then remarked, "Moorhead, you're probably the best friend I have, and I hate to say this, but I must: I never got such satisfaction out of watching someone puke!"

We were really sick, and it took Moorhead and me several days to get back to normal.

When a year had passed since our return from furlough, on a summer evening in 1955 Louise and I determined that we would pray separately about the offer from Southeastern and then report to each other what we felt our decision should be.

After the prayer, our mutual feeling was that we should resign as missionaries and go to Southeastern. For the sake of my teaching of missions, I felt that I should be able to say that I was following my vocation, and that my decision was made on the basis of Dr. Winthrop Phelps's statement about the Foreign Mission Board's flexibility and thus without reference to the needs of our daughter Joy. Louise, of course, had no such necessity and no such conviction. She has always said that it was Joy's needs that were uppermost in her decision.

Actually, all three of the children, as well as their parents, were resisting the fact that they were always under the scrutiny of the Japanese, though Louise and I certainly would not have found that sufficient reason to cut short our missionary career. Sometimes I had to take the girls with me in the Mission station wagon to transact business, and I found it necessary to leave them in the car briefly. When I returned, it was not uncommon to find the automobile surrounded by Japanese who saw these foreign children only as objects of their curiosity. On such occasions, independent Beth was apt to be lying on the floor of the station wagon in order to escape the stares of strangers.

In any case, we stayed another year in order that our responsibilities could more easily be passed to other hands. I was still teaching in the University, of course, and continuing as interim pastor at Seinan Gakuin Baptist Church. By 1955 the Seminary had completed the classroom and administrative building at the beautiful campus at Hoshiguma, where I did most of my teaching.

Illustration No. 35
The Hoshiguma Campus
(Left and Front: the Administrative and Classroom Bldg.; Right: the Dormitory)

Likewise, that year convinced us that Joy really needed to be taken back to the States. She was having an increasingly negative reaction to the attention which the Japanese gave to her handicap, and this psychological reaction was exacerbated by the fact that she was encompassed by persons who considered her an alien (*gaijin*, as the Japanese termed us). Therefore our motives for leaving Japan became somewhat moot. I know now, as I did not know when we made the important decision to return to the States, that I would have left anyway because of Joy's needs.

Soon after we had returned to Japan in 1954, I had submitted to Mr. Sugimoto Katsuji, Chairman of the Trustees of Seinan Gakuin, a letter of resignation as Chancellor. Although the affairs of the school were running smoothly after the big administrative crisis, I found the work of Chancellor burdensome. Moreover, I was sure that if I should resign, Kawano Sadamoto would be chosen to succeed me, and I was convinced that a Japanese, and not an American, ought to be the Chancellor of the school. Unfortunately, Mr. Sugimoto had chosen to "pocket veto" my attempt to resign and did not even communicate it to the Trustees!

Now, however, the fact that I was accepting a position at Southeastern Seminary gave a special urgency to the matter of my resignation, and when I gave Mr. Sugimoto this new informa-tion, even he, as Chairman of the Trustees, could no longer ignore the matter. Therefore, the Trustees voted to accept my resignation as of November 9, 1955, and they elected Mr. Kawano to become the new Chancellor, with his term to begin the day after my re-signation took effect. In that meeting one of the Trustees, Rev. Yuya Kiyoshi, the old and revered pastor of the Meijiro-ga-oka Baptist Church in Tokyo, gave expression to his wisdom and sensitivity by remarking that Copeland, in spirit, was already in Southeastern Seminary.

When I sent a letter to each Southern Baptist missionary in Japan, explaining my resignation as Chancellor of Seinan and my acceptance of a position at Southeastern, almost to a person my fellow Japan missionaries seemed to understand and gave me their blessing. However, "Uncle" Frank Connely in Tokyo, who had spent many years as a missionary in China, mildly rebuked me and told me that I would never be happy in my new position. He told me that if he had known of my coming return to the States, he would have nominated me to succeed Dr. Baker J. Cauthen as Orient Secretary. As it was, he said, he and other mis-sionaries had felt that my place was at Seinan. In any case, Dr. Winston Crawley, whom I respected highly, had become our new Area (Orient) Secretary, and he was to perform this job very commendably.

Of course, I remember well the birth of our fourth daugh-ter. It was difficult for Louise to go to the Baptist Hospital in Kyoto for the birth, since she would be leaving at home a needy hus-band and three relatively small daughters. Moreover, she would have to allow time for the birth and then time for sufficient care for her needs at the hospital before she was discharged, a total of about three weeks at least. We seriously considered having the birth in a Japanese clinic, but as I have indicated previously, this involved great difficulties. We ended up talking to a military doc-tor who was our friend, who then called the ob-gyn who looked after the military wives.

This Army physician said he would be glad to deliver the baby if Louise would do the birth the way he did for military personnel in areas somewhat distant from Fukuoka. His method was to examine the expectant mother fairly close to the time the birth was to occur and then to set a date for the delivery with the understanding that he would come to the home on that day and give the pregnant woman an injection of a drug to induce labor. We agreed and also asked him what we would need to have in readiness. He replied that all we needed to provide was plenty of hot water and a table for the delivery. He would bring a delivery kit in his Jeep, along with his nurse.

So, after examining Louise at an appropriate time, he set the day, March 15, 1956. Early on that morning, we carried the kitchen table into one of the bedrooms, heated plenty of water, and greeted him and the nurse. So we had the setting for an intercultural, international, and interreligious event: a white Jewish doctor who was an American, an African American nurse, a Japanese domestic helper, and a fellow missionary, Lenora Hudson, to care for the new mother and the infant! The doctor gave Louise the injection, and within forty minutes labor had begun. Before noon, the baby was born, and the Jeep with its doctor and nurse and delivery kit had departed.

Everybody did his or her part well, the doctor and his nurse, Lenora and the Japanese maid, Louise and the new infant. Everybody, that is, except the father! Louise wanted me to be in the room when the baby was born. The doctor took a dim view of this suggestion and let me know emphatically that if I fainted I was on my own since all of his attention would be given to the mother and baby. I felt a bit doubtful myself, but since I had never fainted, I assured the doctor that I would be all right. Louise asked me at a crucial moment to give her a little anesthetic which I managed to do.

However, when I saw the blood involved when the infant was ready to emerge, I had to hold on for dear life to keep from fainting! In fact, if I had not been able to lean against a wall, I am sure that I would have fallen flat. Fortunately, since the attention was not upon me, my predicament escaped the notice of the others. I was so embarrassed that for many years I told no one about this event which had so bruised my macho self-image. Finally, I even mustered up the courage to tell Louise.

Since this fourth birth was another daughter and not a son, my Japanese friends came by to offer me their condolences.

"*O-ki no doku Sama*," they would say, meaning literally "It's a poisoning of the honorable mind," but in free translation "It's really too bad." I always made it a point to contradict them, responding, "Oh no, she's a precious gift from God and we are very grateful for her." I even made a pun about her in Japanese: "*Musuko de aru beki desu keredomo, musume de aru* Becky *desu,*" meaning something like "Becky was supposed to be a son but she is a daughter." The play upon words is between *beki*, Japanese for "supposed to be," and Becky, which are pronounced about the same.

Chapter Twelve
RETURNING TO THE STATES THE LONG WAY

Soon thereafter, on April 2, 1956, after the school year had ended, on my way to the States, I set out on a sixty-day tour of other countries in Asia and Europe where Southern Baptists had work. I don't recall whether it was Dr. Cauthen or Dr. Crawley or both of them who suggested it, but since I was to become a teacher of missions, the Foreign Mission Board paid my way on this extended trip.

First of all, I decided to visit Korea and then come back to Tokyo (since I had visited Taiwan in 1955, I did not revisit it on my return to the United States) and thence to Hong Kong and Macao, the Philippines, Indonesia, Singapore, Malaya, Thailand, India, Jordan, Egypt, Italy, Spain, and Switzerland on my way to the States. (I did not visit Israel because of the difficulties in getting a visa for Israel with visas of Arab countries in my passport, though I visited Jerusalem and the surrounding "holy places," since these were in Arab hands)

Louise and the children were to leave Japan in time to meet me in Louisville, Kentucky, so that we could drive to Wake Forest on Tuesday, June 5, which was Louise's birthday and our tenth wedding anniversary. For the drive and for our transportation needs afterward, I had purchased a 1954 Ford from a fellow missionary to Japan, Tucker Callaway, who was on furlough in Louisville. Of course, our new home, Southeastern Baptist Theological Seminary was located in Wake Forest, North Carolina.

Leaving Fukuoka was a *very* sad occasion. I kept saying to myself, "Seinan! what a wonderful school! Seinan Church! what a dear Church! Fukuoka! what a good place to live! Japan! what an unusually fine country!" A large crowd of friends from Seinan Gakuin and the Seinan Gakuin Baptist Church came to the station to see me off. After they sang the school song, Mr. Kawano Sadamoto led them in a *banzai* to *"warera no aisuru sensei"* (our dear teacher). I was profoundly touched when he told me a tearful goodbye. I fought hard for self control, and lost.

As the train pulled out I was looking most eagerly in the sea of faces for those of Judy, Joy, and Beth. A missionary wife had brought them to the station, and they were excitedly waving goodbye. The parting was doubly hard because I was not only leaving Japan. I was also separating myself for two months from my family. Becky was only a little more than two weeks of age and a little sick, and Louise was not yet strong. Therefore, Lou ise and Becky did not come to the station to see me off. A dear Japanese friend who taught at Seinan Gakuin University, Matsunobu Yōichi, one of the two who had been very helpful when we left on furlough in 1953, accompanied me on the train as far as Moji. I was most grateful for this special act of kindness.

I spent about a week on the way to Tokyo, stopping at Kyoto to be examined by our Baptist missionary physician, Dr. James Satterwhite, and for visits with Jim and Altha and the Satterwhite children, and with Coleman and Jabe Clarke. They showed me the sights of Kyoto, especially Buddhist institutions which I had never had—or taken—the opportunity to visit before. It was especially important for me to see the Headquarters of the Eastern Division of Jōdo Shin Shu, the Buddhist denomination which teaches salvation by faith in the great Buddhist personage, Amida, Lord of the Western Paradise.

Jim Satterwhite, who was a great jokester as well as a fine physician, was not above a bit of scatological wit. During his examination of me, he put a rubber-gloved finger up my anus, and had the nerve to ask how it felt. While I paused to seek the right response, he answered his own question, saying, "I know how it feels. It feels just like someone has his finger up your ass."*

With Coleman as my tour guide I also visited Omi-Hachiman, where I renewed ties with Dr. Merrill Vories and observed for the first time his remarkable enterprises, an architectural firm, Mentholatum salve and Airwick factories, schools and a tubercular hospital, all of which were offering a splendid service to the Japanese, while affording Vories and his staff an income "according to their need," and helping to develop a number of

---

*Jim and Altha have been in the States for several years, having settled in Florida. Sad to say, Jim has something like Alzheimer's disease which has robbed him of his wonderful memory and made of him a different person. Altha has honored him by writing a book about him with an apt title, *The Good Doctor.*

self-supporting churches in the area.

Dr. Vories, a Methodist, had come to Japan about 1900 under the auspices of the YMCA, with convictions that he was to develop a Christian work in an area where the Christian message was unknown, and that his work was to be self-supporting. Trained as an architect, he had given up his architecture to follow his missionary vocation, only to find that it would be most useful for him in Japan. So he had developed his architectural firm and then his other institutions. One of my joys in Japan had been getting to know Dr. Vories. He had visited in our home, and I had listened with fascination as he told many stories concerning his career in Japan. He did most of the architectural work for our school.*

I also made a side trip to the Grand Shrine of Isé, the most famous and probably the most important of the Shinto shrines in Japan. It is here that Amaterasu Ō-Mikami, the Sun Goddess, is worshiped. The shrine is torn down as another is built every 20 years, to escape the pollution of death, since Shinto has a strong taboo against death. Shinto has its impressive characteristics, particularly its stark simplicity. The Isé shrine building, for example, has almost no adornments. It is constructed of new wood, unpainted; and the grounds afford beautiful surroundings, with cryptomeria and camphor trees of enormous size and age, and with many maples and cherries, the latter almost in full bloom at the time of my visit.

From Isé I made my way to Tokyo, where I spent the weekend, procuring visas, worshiping at the Chapel Center, and visiting a meeting of Baptist women of Southeast Asia and the Pacific. There were women from Japan and Okinawa (which was still several years away from being returned to Japan), Hawaii, Taiwan, Hong Kong, the Philippines, Malaya, and Thailand. It was an impressive gathering. I was especially moved by the spirit of reconciliation between the women of Japan and those of the Philippines, whose people had suffered a great deal under Japanese colonial rule during the recent War.

---

*If you want to know more about this remarkable man, see his book, *A Mustard Seed in Japan*. Vories took the Japanese name of Hitotsuyanagi, the surname of the Japanese woman he married, the first instance of a Westerner marrying a Japanese woman of the nobility.

On Monday morning I caught an early plane for Korea, where I spent a week sightseeing, enjoying Korean food, speaking several times and observing the work and situation of missionaries, particularly Southern Baptists. There seemed to be a general complaint about the resurgence of nationalism, after several decades of harsh Japanese colonialism.

Our own Southern Baptist missionary work was relatively new, and the missionaries included a few old China hands and some new appointees. On the other hand, the Korean Baptists had existed for several decades although they had only recently achieved relations with the Southern Baptist Foreign Mission Board. Lack of mutual understanding, among other factors, had thrust the work into a severe crisis.

John and Jewel Abernathy were transferred to Korea in 1950, as the first Southern Baptist missionaries, after a long career in China. They were in Korea only briefly before being evacuated to Fukuoka because of the outbreak of the Korean War. John seems to have fit very well into the "episcopal" role played by a former Baptist missionary who had no relation to Southern Baptists. Abernathy, who was unable to use the Korean language, was accused of being overly dependent upon a certain Korean leader. I was told that the Korean Christians wanted to receive the money directly from the Board and administer it all themselves. How the Southern Baptist work is plagued by money!

I felt very sorry for the young missionaries who were thrust into the work without adequate preparation because of their inability in the language and their lack of knowledge of the people and their culture. Mutual distrust between missionaries and Koreans clouded the atmosphere, and I felt that the Korean Mission of Southern Baptists was in for trouble.

On Saturday, I was able to meet with a former student in Japan, Kwon, a native Korean, who, while in Japan, had assumed the Japanese name of Yoshikado. This fellow seem-ed lonely and was encountering considerable difficulty because of his Japanese connections. He had dual citizenship, both Korean and Japanese. He told me that since he had run into difficulty with a Southern Baptist missionary, he had quit teaching at the Korean Baptist Seminary to accept the pastorate of a Korean Baptist church.

On Monday, April 16, I returned to Tokyo by air, where I was *very* busy Tuesday and Wednesday getting visas, travelers' checks and the like. I was very happy to receive a letter from Louise which I read and reread several times. Then late on Wednesday evening, my host while in Tokyo, "Uncle" Frank Connely, took me to the airport where I was to depart for Hong Kong. I was also accompanied by a former student, Ms. Matsuo Sadako, who was then on the staff of the Japan Baptist Convention. It was very good to see her again. I was to learn later that she left her job in Tokyo to attend Southwestern Baptist Theological Seminary in Fort Worth, Texas, where she met a fine Hispanic fellow whom she married.*

To Uncle Frank and Ms. Matsuo I had to say good-bye in the airport, because I had to go through immigration by myself. Since I knew the procedure quite well and could speak to the staff persons in Japanese, I was the first one to board the plane. I think the walk to the plane was the loneliest of my life. I was departing from Japan all by myself. I thought of family and dear friends and of the beautiful wooded mountains and neatly laid out rice paddies I was leaving behind as well as the culture and language which I had entered into with considerable youthful excitement. A great wave of sadness engulfed me, and when I sat down alone, I secretly wept.

I arrived in Hong Kong on Wednesday, April 18, and found the missionaries most gracious. They helped me to have a busy whirl of activities, including several delicious Chinese dinners, a bricklaying for the Henrietta Shuck School, shopping and picnicking, as well as consulting about college administration, since Christians in Hong Kong, including missionaries, were considering starting a college (which, by the way, they did, and Hong Kong Baptist College has become a rather important institution. What it will become since British control has ended remains yet to be seen).

From Hong Kong I made a side trip to Macau, which at this time, of course, was still a Portuguese Colony. I was especially interested in the remaining facade of Saint Paul's Cathedral

---

*Many years later Louise and I were to meet this fellow in connection with American Baptists and to discover that he was a very successful business man in upper New York and quite devoted to the cause of moderate Southern Baptists.

(Roman Catholic), which had been built in 1602 by Japanese artisans. The impressive ruins of this church had inspired John Bowring's hymn, "In the Cross of Christ I Glory."

I also had a look at the grave of Robert Morrison in the British East India Company cemetery. Morrison was the first Protestant missionary to China, having arrived in Macau in 1807. His wife preceded him in death in 1821, and was the first person buried in this cemetery, along with an unborn child, since she was pregnant at the time of her death. Two other children and her husband later joined Mrs. Morrison here for their final resting place. I was struck by the youth of many of the Europeans, the markers of whose tombs may be found in this British graveyard. Cholera and other diseases took a terrible toll on their lives.

Although I kept a diary for most of this trip, I will spare you the details of my journey. However, I will take the privilege of relating certain incidents of special significance for me.

On April 21, Saturday evening at 7:20, I arrived by plane in Manila, the Philippines, only to find that no one was at the airport to meet me. Of course, I had notified a missionary, Ted Badger, of my arrival time. I took a taxi to the only address I had, which, I suspected--correctly, as it turned out--was an office and closed on Saturday night. Finally, I found someone who knew Ted Badger, and I sent word to Badger that I had gone to the Hotel Lun-eta. After laundering my dirty clothes, I finally got to bed.

Next morning, just after my breakfast, Ted Badger called to offer a somewhat casual apology, explaining that since he had been deeply involved with the itineraries of two dignitaries who were on the staff of the Southern Baptist Sunday School Board, he had been late getting back from Baguio. Frankly, I think he had completely forgotten about me! Nevertheless, since I know how "visiting firemen" can disrupt the busy schedules of missionaries, I understood. Believe me, this was not the only time I was not met by missionaries whom I had informed of my arrival. Nor, as you will discern from what I am about to relate, was it the worst experience I had in the Philippines.

On that same Sunday morning I went with Dr. William House, one of the Sunday School Board dignitaries, to a Chinese Baptist church for a Vacation Bible School commencement followed by Sunday School and morning worship. There I met Theresa Anderson, a single woman missionary to the Philippines, who, along with several others, had been transferred from China because of the Communist takeover. I had assumed that my remark to Theresa that I knew her brother Henry from Mars Hill days had gained me some rapport with her.

If so, it turned out that Ms. Anderson certainly had a strange way of communicating rapport! Later, I sat across from her at a luncheon including House and several missionaries, at least one couple, James and Zelma Foster, whom I had known from Louisville days. When Miss Anderson learned that I was on my way to Southeastern Seminary to assume a teaching position there, she completely surprised me by coming out with, "Oh, so you're a quitter! I didn't know we had a quitter in our midst. Have you really left the ranks?"

It is unlikely that Ms. Anderson knew anything of the circumstances of my leaving Japan. In humiliation and anger, I responded, "I do not consider myself a quitter, nor do I believe that I am leaving the ranks." Very diplomatically, Dr. House asked me, "Dr. Copeland, I imagine that the decision to leave Japan was the most difficult choice you have ever had to make, wasn't it?" I replied affirmatively, and the tension was relieved.

That I was deeply hurt is indicated by the fact that although I have long since forgiven Theresa Anderson, I still remember the incident as though it happened yesterday. I have often pondered the fact that her father was at that very time a Professor of Missions at New Orleans Baptist Theological Seminary, having left a career as a missionary in China to take that position. Were there some hidden connotations concerning her father which would help explain his daughter's attitude?

Certainly, when I had opportunity to reflect upon this experience, I made my own the words of the Apostle Paul: "But with me it is a very small thing that I should be judged by you or by any other human court. I do not even judge myself" (1 Cor. 4:3). Miss Anderson's words reminded me that many persons, unlike most of my colleagues in Japan, would misunderstand and misjudge my motives since they had an inflated and fallacious idea of the missionary vocation, and that therefore I needed all the more to be sure that I was appropriately humble. Be that as it may, her words rankled in my heart and hovered over my several days in the Philippines and all of my journey to the States--indeed over my life for many years--like a dark cloud.

In various other countries of Asia I had delightful fellow-ship with Southern Baptist missionaries I had known in other years, some of whom were dear friends, such as Judson and Harriet Lennon who were in Thailand for a long missionary ca-reer. Some were British or Australian Baptists, and still others, such as Winburn Thomas and his Japanese American (Nisei) wife, were non-Baptists and ecumenists. Having begun as a Presbyterian missionary in Japan in the late 1930s, Thomas was at that time in Indonesia in an ecumenical role. Later he was to be located in New York in a position, I believe, with the Presbyterian Board of Missions. Both Thomas and his wife are now dead.

In mid-May I spent about a week in the Arab countries contiguous to Israel. In Lebanon and Jordan, I enjoyed good companionship with Southern Baptist missionaries. Then I pro-ceeded to Jerusalem and surrounding cities which were under the control of Jordan in those days, Bethlehem, Bethany, and Jericho, as well as the Jordan river and the Dead Sea. In Jeru-salem I visited the so called holy places, the Church of the Na-tivity, the Via Dolorosa which Jesus trod on his fateful journey to the Cross, and the Church of the Holy Sepulchre. Especially at the last of these, I was distressed by the competition and disputes of the various Christian groups, Armenian, Coptic, Greek Orthodox, Roman Catholic, and Abyssinian.

As loci of the cross and resurrection of Jesus, Gordon's Calvary and Tomb look more authentic than the traditional sites, but who knows about the real locations? For the student of church history there is much of interest here. Many locations are made holy by association with the life of our Lord. On the other hand, they are made occasions for idolatry and superstition if not un-seemly rivalry. So reverence mingled with disgust in my mind.

Because of problems for a traveler with visas from Arab countries in his passport, I bypassed Israel. In Cairo, Egypt, I was frustrated because I could not get in touch with Mr. Seddik Girgis, who was in charge of the only Baptist effort I knew of there, a very tiny work indeed. I had written Mr. Girgis in advance and asked him to meet my plane, and I had him paged in the airport and waited all morning in vain for him to show up. Maybe he didn't get my letter. I had no way of reaching him by telephone, so I finally gave up.

I went to see the Sphinx and the Gizeh Pyramids and

marveled at the engineering feats of several millennia ago, over 2 million stones averaging more than 2 ½ tons each were in the Cheops Pyramid alone. No mortar at all was used to hold these stones together. How such huge building blocks were transported across the desert from the distant hills and raised to such heights is a mystery indeed! Unfortunately, in Cairo I was annoyed because most everybody seemed to want to sell me something or else to receive a tip.

In Rome I spent about 2 ½ days, getting acquainted with missionaries, staying at the orphanage conducted by the Moores and seeing a few of the many sights of that ancient city. I liked Roy and Lillie Mae Starmer very much, and I think they returned the compliment--after they learned that I was a real Southern Baptist. It seems that Mrs. Alice Moore had told them that she did not know whether I was an Independent Baptist, member of the Church of Christ, or what!

Roy and their daughter, Sandra, took me to see the famous St. John Lateran Church where I observed the ancient baptistry, designed centuries ago for immersion but now used for sprinklings, and the famous Santa Scala ("Holy Stairs") which the faithful ascended on their knees and thus attained merit, a practice which repelled both Martin Luther and a contemporary Luther whom I have known pretty well for several years! I learned also that the Baptist Mission in Italy had only been organized as a mission the previous year, 1955. Prior to that time, all negotiations with the Foreign Mission Board had been mediated through Dewey and Alice Moore. That mission had problems, and no wonder!

On Monday afternoon, May 21, I went sightseeing, along with the Charles Cowherd family, missionaries to Indonesia, with Dr. Dewey Moore himself as our guide. It was a most interesting tour. We saw the ancient Roman Forum and the Coliseum, and the dark, evil-smelling dungeon which almost certainly was the room where the apostle Paul awaited execution and wrote the "Prison Epistles." Then we saw the site on the Appian Way where the apostle was said to have been beheaded, the Church of the Three Fountains, and the famous Catacombs. Afterward, we had dinner in the home of the Moores.

The next day, Tuesday, May 22, about noon, I departed by plane to Barcelona, Spain, where I was met by Charles and Indy

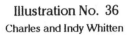
Illustration No. 36
Charles and Indy Whitten

Whitten, friends from Southern Seminary days. I had delightful fellowship with them and their three children, both in Barcelona, where I participated in the Seminary Commencement, and in Madrid, where I was speaker at the midweek (Friday evening) prayer meeting of Second Baptist church.

I was well impressed with the Spanish Baptists. In spite of the fact that Protestants in toto were a very small minority, these Baptists had a very buoyant attitude and no evidence of a martyr spirit. At the midweek prayer meeting of the Second Baptist Church of Madrid, held across town in the building of First Baptist Church because their own building had been padlocked by the governmental authorities, I was surprised by the fine attendance--in spite of a driving rain. (The speaker had nothing to do with the turn out, since the audience did not know who was to speak until they arrived.) Particularly, seminarians were much more spontaneous and less inhibited than were their Japanese counterparts.

As one of many sightseeing spots in Madrid, I saw an old synagogue, closed during Inquisition days in the sixteenth century when Jews were forced out of Spain, and later converted into a museum. I was reminded of the great tragedy of the frequent and widespread persecutions which have beset the Jews and the possibly even greater tragedy of the fact that it was usually Christians who were persecuting them.

On Saturday, May 26, I bade farewell to the lovely Whitten family and departed by air for Zurich. Because of a defective fuel pump on the plane, I was forced to stay over Sunday in Rome, thus delaying my arrival in Rüschlikon, Switzerland, near Zurich, until Monday. For my one night at the International Baptist Seminary in Rüschlikon, I was entertained rather royally, especially by Dr. Theron Price, then on sabbatical leave, who was teaching church history at Southern Seminary when I spent our furlough there, 1953-1954. I was also visited by a Japanese fellow, about whom I have quite a story to tell you later.

Though my trip from Switzerland to the States was of short duration, it was filled with tension because of what happened to me in Rüschlikon. I had accepted Price's kind offer to drive me to the airport in Zurich, where I was to board an Air France plane for Paris. When we were about halfway to the airport, I remembered that I had left my briefcase at the Seminary in Rüschlikon.

Theron told me that we had already come too far to return to the campus without missing my plane, but he graciously suggested that if it were feasible, he would be glad to go back to Rüschlikon after I had boarded a plane in Zurich, pick up the briefcase, and put it on the next flight to Paris. When the clerk at the Air France desk assured us that the briefcase could be sent to Paris on the next flight, I accepted Theron's offer and looked forward to recovering the item in Paris.

I spent the night in Paris, did some sightseeing, and leisurely went to Orly Airport, fully expecting to recover my briefcase there. However, a customer representative of Air France looked all over the airport and then reported to me that he had failed to find the briefcase, but that he would continue to look and if he found it would send it on to me in London.

With some misgivings I flew on to London, where my two days in that city were a complete wash out so far as sight-seeing was concerned. I was thoroughly preoccupied with pestering Pan American Airlines, with which airline I had bought my through ticket, about the briefcase in Paris. Pan Am had a defective computer, or whatever kind of fast communication they had with Paris in those days. The personnel of Pan Am also made negative remarks about Air France, telling me that if it were any other airline they could retrieve my briefcase, but since it was Air France I had just as well forget it. Finally, after two nights in London, I boarded a Constellation on Thursday, May 31, and left for New York on schedule, without the briefcase!

I was due to arrive in New York early enough on Friday to retrieve my freight, which I had shipped from Japan before I left, see it through customs and arrange for its transportation by truck to Wake Forest, North Carolina. Unfortunately, we hardly got airborne when we discovered that the landing gear was defective and would not retract. So we returned to the London Airport, fixed that problem and took off again.

Soon our crew learned that we had a bad storm on the eastern seaboard of the States and that New York was fogged in. Therefore, we determined to make a stop at Reykavik, Iceland, for refueling. When we approached New York, we were informed that it was still impossible to land there, so we were sent to Montreal. When we were almost ready to land at Montreal, we were told that New York was now clear and that we should proceed there for landing. When we reached the vicinity of New York, we learned that the city was once more blanketed by fog and we were rerouted to Syracuse!

At long last, we flew from Syracuse to New York City on Saturday instead of Friday, to encounter the surliest customs and immigration officials I had dealt with anywhere on this long trip. After some bickering, Pan American agreed to put me up in a hotel for the weekend.

I was at the steamship company as early as feasible on Monday morning, June 4, only to be told by the official that he could not let me have the freight which belonged to me since I could not produce the bill of lading, the reason being that my important papers were in the lost briefcase! Believe me, I pled my case as earnestly as possible. Finally, he relented, saying, "Well, I know that the stuff belongs to you. So I'll bend the rules and let you have it if you will sign the release for it." At that point I was ready to sign anything, even with my life's blood; so I inked the document and headed for customs where the freight was held.

I told my tale of woe to the customs official, including the fact that I had to arrange for my freight to be shipped to Wake Forest, North Carolina, and then catch my plane that afternoon in order to meet my family in Louisville. He was very hard-boiled, telling me that I should shut up and only talk in answer to his questions, and that in any case it was close to lunch time and that nothing could be done until his crew had eaten their lunch. So I cooled my heels while I waited for them to partake of their repast.

After what seemed to me an everlasting wait, the lunch was ended and the men were ready to return to work. The official told them to open a certain crate, and he instructed me to tell him what was in it. My problem was that my revised lists were in the missing briefcase* and I had to depend upon secondary lists that were defective. I could only hope and pray that I had the right information. So I took a stab at identifying what was in the box. Very fortunately, my information tallied with the crate's contents and I was home free.

The customs official ordered his crew to close up the crate and then moved to the side where he could speak to me privately. He looked at his watch and said, "I believe you can make that plane schedule, can't you?" I allowed that I could. Whereupon, with a furtive glance about, he said that he had to be hard-boiled around his crew in order to retain their respect! I could have hit him--but I didn't. Instead, I hastily arranged for a trucking company to convey my freight to Wake Forest and I sped to the airport to catch my plane in order to be in Louisville in time to meet the plane of my family on that very day.

On the next day, Tuesday, June 5, 1956, which, as I have indicated, was Louise's birthday and our tenth wedding anniversary, we were ready to drive from Louisville, Kentucky, to Wake Forest, North Carolina.

To this day I carry a burden of guilt that I allowed Louise to shepherd those four girls by plane all the way from Fukuoka to Louisville: Judy, 9, Joy, 7, Beth, 5, and Becky, only a baby of some two and a half months. I keep telling myself that it seemed the only way, since obviously Louise could cope with the situation better in Japan, while she was regaining strength from Becky's birth and where she had domestic help and a ready made support system, than she could have done in our own country.

Also, she has told me that the three older girls were real troopers. It was after this trip that Louise became known to the children as the "jet propelled lady" because of the speed required for these kids to keep up with their mother in the airports.

---

*After about a year at Southeastern, I retrieved the briefcase. What happened was that Max Garrott, soon after I had been gone for a few weeks, had picked up a letter from Air France addressed to me in Fukuoka indicating that the briefcase was in Paris, but Max, with typical absent-mindedness, failed to forward the letter! When I finally received it, I thought surely it would be too late, but I contacted Air France anyway and they sent me the briefcase!

CHAPTER FOUR
THE SOUTHEASTERN YEARS, 1956-1976

Chapter Thirteen
SETTLING IN AND STAYING

Southeastern Baptist Theological Seminary was located on the campus of Wake Forest College, which had been founded more than 100 earlier than the seminary and around which the town of Wake Forest had developed. By 1950, the college had decided that for certain inducements it would move to Winston-Salem, about 100 miles to the west. Therefore, it sold the campus to the Southern Baptist Convention, which in turn established Southeastern Baptist Theological Seminary while the college was still in Wake Forest.

The following year, 1951, Seminary classes began, though the Seminary was confined to one building, the Religion Building, while Wake Forest College occupied the rest of the campus until its already decided departure. When we moved to Wake Forest in the summer of 1956, the seminary had already graduated its third class and the college was in the process of relocating in Winston-Salem, with the result that when classes began that fall, for the first time the seminary had the whole campus to itself.

Upon our arrival from Louisville by automobile, for about two days we were put up in Gresham's Motel, located on U.S. Route 1, a few miles south of the town of Wake Forest. This motel was a somewhat seedy facility, which has long since been replaced by a little shopping center.

From Gresham's Motel we moved to the Ruby Reid house on White Street in Wake Forest, which its owner, Miss Reid, had donated to the Seminary at her recent death. This house had no furniture, and neither did we; it was exceedingly run-down (we may have been, too!). The house was soon to be razed in favor of a bank building for which the Seminary had sold it; and it was very dirty. The Seminary was pressing us to find other housing as soon as possible, and in fact gave us a deadline of three months.

Two other teachers, both younger than I, had arrived at the seminary along with their small families at the same time we relocated. One was moved from Arkansas, where he was dean of a Baptist junior college, and the other from Missouri, a tenured teacher at a Baptist senior college. The former was placed for some time in a more or less permanent Seminary house from which vantage point he and his wife had the leisure of looking for more long-term housing. The latter arranged for rental property for a while and then built a more spacious house.

As Louise soon discerned, President Stealey had no understanding at all of missionaries who, unlike other teachers, were living abroad at very low salaries. In our case, we had absolutely no savings and had to trust the Seminary to look out for us since we were living in faraway Japan and had no way of caring for our own interests.

Eventually I was to discover that President Stealey was known as a "horse-trader"--though he also had his good traits, which I will point out later. Not only had he failed me in the matter of housing. He had also snookered me with regard to placement in the faculty ranking and salary scale, though I had tenure from the beginning. Promotion was more or less automatic, once your rank was determined.

From Japan I had, by letter, entrusted my ranking and salary to President Stealey *and the faculty*, assuming that the latter had some say in the matter. It turned out that only the President determined faculty status, though I was never notified of this fact. It was also true that rank determined salary. After the passing of two or three years, I learned from Dr. Ray McKay, Professor of Preaching, that Stealey had at first pegged me as an Assistant Professor. McKay had been to Japan on a preaching mission while I was there, so when he had learned where Stealey was placing me, he went to Stealey in some indignation and told him that in light of my position in Japan, he simply could not consign me to such a low status. Whereupon President Stealey, according to McKay, changed my designation to Associate Professor.

Several years later, I learned that I was placed one year in rank, and therefore in salary, behind two other colleagues,[*] one of whom was about my age and had only a brief experience of teaching and the other of whom was younger and had taught

---

[*] The older of the two signed the *Abstract of Principles* when I did, along with two other colleagues. The other had signed about three years previously. The *Abstract* was a confessional statement which Southern Seminary had adopted about a century earlier.

about the same number of years as I. Neither of them had any more publications to his credit than did I. President Stealey alone was responsible for ranking and therefore for this inequity. Since I was to be a member of the faculty of Southeastern Seminary for almost twenty years, the sum that I was penalized each year until I finally reached top salary, which did not occur until near my departure time, amounted to several thousands of dollars, which we certainly could have used!

Salaries at the seminary were abysmally low, and all of us staff members had to try and supplement our income otherwise, which usually meant supply and interim preaching. Though they were more lucrative, I usually did not seek interim pastorates because I felt a responsibility to represent missions whenever possible, which meant a wider circulation than an interim ministry allowed. However, occasionally I did accept interims. Two of them which I remember with special fondness were the First Baptist Church of Rocky Mount, North Carolina, and the First Baptist Church of Danville, Virginia, particularly the latter, where I served as interim pastor for about nine months, 1959-1960.

Nor, on principle, did I agitate for higher salaries. I had told myself when I left Japan that I would never complain about salaries lest I be misunderstood as having left international missions because of dissatisfaction with the low pay. As a matter of fact, as I have often said, the only place I know of that was anywhere near Christian in the remuneration of employees was international missions as I knew and experienced the system. All missionaries received what they or their families needed on a more or less equal basis. I found this system profoundly satisfying. Also, I have *never* made a vocational move on the basis of salary.

After a diligent search for housing in Wake Forest, we were able to purchase a very large residence with a spacious lot at 330 South Main Street. We cashed in a life insurance policy for about one thousand dollars, the Wake Forest Savings and Loan Association afforded a first mortgage loan, and the Seminary generously supplied us with a second mortgage loan; so we had a home.

The property belonged to a college fraternity, and since there was a house provided for the fraternity on the new campus in Winston-Salem, they could offer the old residence at a bargain price, $4,500, to be exact. The problem was that the fraternity had no incentive to maintain the property and had let it run down, with the result that it cost us more than three times its price to make necessary repairs and renovations. So our mortgages had to cover these extra costs.

The house was immense indeed, with high ceilings in all its rooms, most of which were very large. Even after our extensive renovations, there was a spacious kitchen,* a separate dining room, an unusually large living room, a den and two bathrooms, as well as several huge bedrooms. We were able to have a master bedroom for ourselves and a room for each child--even after Luke was born in 1958--as well as to rent one room to two seminary students. There were attractive pillars on a large porch which extended about halfway around the house.

The considerable repairs inside included refinishing the floors, oak on the first floor and pine on the second, renovating the bathrooms, redoing the wiring and plumbing, and putting on new plaster and wall paper. When the carpenter disappeared under the house to repair the girders so the house would not collapse under our weight, I thought we would never get him out of there, so extensive was the unseen work that he had to do. This house was to be our home until we moved to Raleigh in 1967. The children loved it, as you might imagine.

Even so, during the first winter, when we had a severe cold spell while I was at Mars Hill College participating in a Religious Emphasis Week, water pipes froze and we discovered that there was no insulation at all between the plaster and the siding. Louise had a terrible time in my absence, and the next two summers I was engaged in putting aluminum siding on over the wooden clapboards to make the house livable. Insulation consisted of aluminum foil building paper under the new siding, and it seemed to be adequate. After I installed the aluminum siding, we had no more problems with pipes freezing.

---

*Actually, there was a building behind the house which had once been a separate kitchen. I later tore it down and constructed behind the house a large deck with a concrete floor upon which I mounted a steel railing which I acquired from the Seminary. It was from the old Wake Forest College cafeteria.

Heat for this massive, two-story house was supplied by a large coal furnace in the basement, for which we were able to buy coal from the Seminary at the latter's own cost, which was a very good reduction. The basement was no more than a hole in the ground large enough for the furnace and its accouterments, with a sump pump to take out any water which flowed into the basement when we had hard rains.

In order to improve this dungeon and to keep from being overly depressed when I visited the place to service the furnace, I built a concrete floor and installed an automatic bin-fed stoker, after which I surrounded the basement with a masonry wall. Some digging and moving of dirt was involved, and although the area enclosed was relatively small, the masonry work took a lot of time and effort since I was utterly inexperienced at it.

But let me get out from under the house and discuss theological education. After all, it was as an educator that I came to Wake Forest. There were certain important advantages in joining the faculty at Southeastern Baptist Theological Seminary, some of which, at least, were not lost on me in making the decision to come there. Chief among these was the fact that Southeastern was a new seminary, with the opportunity to form its policies and determine its atmosphere *de novo*. This was a very exciting and attractive feature indeed!

A second significant benefit was that Southeastern was located in a progressive environment, the southeastern area of the States. Moreover, Wake Forest College was in the background, Duke University was in nearby Durham, and the University of North Carolina was relatively close in Chapel Hill. All three were known as liberal institutions. Certainly the setting of Southeastern was more conducive to progressive theological education than was true of any seminary of Southern Baptists.[*]

Still another benefit, certainly for the teachers, I learned about later and I have already shared with you, namely, that rank and salary were more or less automatic. Unless one really messed up, he or she would advance one step each year until attaining

---

[*]Which at that time numbered five: Golden Gate, New Orleans, Southeastern, Southern, and Southwestern. Midwestern was founded later, in 1958.

the apex of the scale.

In many ways we at Southeastern insisted that theological education must be holistic. We refused to have "heads" or chairpersons of departments. The curriculum was divided into four areas, and an Academic Policy and Procedure Committee had a rotating representation of the faculty (and later the student body, as well) from all four of these divisions. Also, unlike all other Southern Baptist seminaries, we resisted the pressure to divide into separate schools, schools of religious education, music, and theology. It was expected that all graduates would be well versed in courses in Bible, theology, and church history. In fact, a great deal was made of the "classical body of divinity," which featured all of these along with the Biblical languages.

All of us thought of ourselves as students, and there were no artificial barriers between faculty and students. In fact, students were always welcome to enter our offices, and faculty publication suffered accordingly. In the late 1960s we tried to anticipate student-led educational revolution by putting students on committees which previously had included faculty only and by drastically reducing the core curriculum in favor of greater student choice of courses.

I developed a great variety of courses in missions at Southeastern, ranging all the way from a required course which was a kind of introduction to international missions* to a course in home missions. Because of my own background, I usually favored a historical approach. Also, my perspective in the teaching of missions was ecumenical. I never taught a course in Southern Baptist missions, because I thought that such a denominational approach could too easily disregard what the whole church has done in fulfilling the mission of our Lord.

Likewise, I believed that the teaching of missions should avoid any hint of American ethnocentrism or nationalism, majoring on what the nationals did, whether Japanese, Indian, African, or whatever nationality, rather than what the missionaries had accomplished. Much of what I taught was based on my experi-

---

*The term "international missions" came to be used by my successor, Dr. Alan Neely. It was more appropriate than the old term, "foreign missions," which I ordinarily used.

ence in Japan as well as my research and reading.

Illustration No. 37
In Front of Binkley Chapel
(To My Right Is Paul Medling [Son of Missionaries I Had Known in Japan],
on my Left is Hayakawa Satoshi, a Japanese Pastor)

Much was made of practica and internships, courses
especially in home missions and various kinds of ministry which
took students off campus during the summer or during regular
semesters. A conversation with the late James ("Jimmy") Duncan, resulted in my initiative at our school in beginning a Seminar
on Urban Studies in certain metropolitan areas off campus, especially the Washington area where Duncan was editor of the District of Columbia Baptist Convention's paper. Tom Bland, who
taught courses in Ethics and Sociology, collaborated with me in
this course and took full responsibility for it after I left the Seminary to return to Japan.

This Urban Seminar was offered in the summers, for the
first two years, 1966 and 1967, in the Washington, D. C. area but
more commonly in the metropolitan area of what was called the
Triangle: Raleigh, Durham, and Chapel Hill. Almost immediately,
it became very popular. It was based on the conviction that seminarians needed to be oriented to the growing urbanism of our
society since most were from rural or small town backgrounds.

The Home Mission Board cooperated with us and provided scholarships for our students as well as personnel for our faculty, that is, staff persons from the Home Mission Board who served as teachers or facilitators along with Bland and me. Likewise, persons in the employ of the Baptist Joint Committee on Public Affairs helped us teach the course and Jimmy Duncan and others gave invaluable support and helpfulness when the seminar was taught in Washington.

Together with the Home Mission Board in Atlanta, I offered a summer practicum in home missions, which was generally conducted in New England. After my leaving, George Braswell, who began teaching missions and church history while I was still at Southeastern, greatly expanded the offering of such practica. In addition, I developed area studies, following the then division of the world of the Foreign Mission Board of the Southern Baptist Convention, and teaching the course on Eastern Asia myself.

For the graduate programs of the seminary, the Master of Theology degree and, later, the Doctor of Ministry degree, I developed two seminars, one in Christianity and the World Religions and the other in Missions and Theology.

In the standard degree program, the Master of Divinity, I did not develop offerings in world religions beyond an introductory course. Actually, I felt somewhat deficient in world religions, since I had no graduate work in this very broad field. George Braswell, who had a Ph. D. in anthropology from Chapel Hill and had experience among Muslims in Iran, became much more of an expert on the religions, especially after I left Southeastern.

For a few years, 1957-1963, at my suggestion, I believe, though the others involved were in hearty agreement, Pope Duncan in Church History, John Steely in the History of Doctrine, and Copeland in the History of Missions, put together a massive required course in the History of Christianity, in which we tried to incorporate all the above mentioned areas. At first, the course was taught for four semesters, for three hours each; later it was reduced to three semesters, four hours each. The book by Kenneth Scott Latourette, *A History of Christianity*, was the textbook. George Shriver, a young Ph. D. in Church History, and Missions Professor Emily Lansdell were brought into the teaching of this course after they joined the Faculty.

The idea of such a comprehensive course seemed to be

good, but it never worked out well. One problem was that the history of Eastern Christianity was usually left to the Professor of Missions. I had enough background to manage this area, but I think that Lansdell had some problems with it. The integration of the immense amount of material was pretty much left up to students, with the result that the really good students were able to synthesize its contents and appreciate the course, while the others were left floundering and complaining. Actually, the course was never really team-taught as it was supposed to be. Each professor attended on those occasions when he or she was slated to lecture, and generally did not show up otherwise. In no cases did the three teachers lecture or dialogue together.

The proverbial "straw that broke the camel's back" for me was that I was increasingly being known as "Professor of Church History." Since for the sake of my sense of vocation, I wanted to be identified as a teacher of missions, the new label greatly disturbed me. So I suggested to the other professors that we go back to the old system of separate courses, and they reluctantly agreed.

I taught a course on the history of the ecumenical movement, but when I presented it as a new course, the title was changed by the Faculty to "A History of Christian Cooperation." However, I not only taught ecumenics, I also practiced it in so far as I had opportunity. For example, in the summer of 1960, I took a couple of seminars at the School of Theology of Boston University with Dr. Nils Ehrenson, a noted Lutheran scholar and staff member of the World Council of Churches. For this summer curriculum, I received an ecumenical scholarship. Also, I enjoyed associations with fellow Baptists from several lands as a member of the Commission on World Missions and Evangelism of the Baptist World Alliance, 1970-1975.

Even more significantly, I put a premium on fellowship and theological discussions with theologians from many different denominations, first as a member of the National Faith and Order Colloquium, from its beginning in 1967 under the sponsorship of the Commission on Faith and Order of the National Council of Churches of Christ in the USA, and then as a member of that Commission itself, 1970-1975.

Also, I was active in certain professional societies, which of course were ecumenical, especially the Association of Professors of Missions, of which I was Vice President, 1970-1972, and

President, 1972-1974; and the American Society of Missiology, 1972 to the present, and a member of the first Executive Committee of the that society, 1972-1975.

In these capacities, I proposed a second Edinburgh World Missions Conference to be held at an appropriate location in the seventieth year since the original conference, that is, in 1980, to do for our time what the Edinburgh World Missions Conference 1910 did for its generation. I wanted a broad ecumenical conference, including the various branches of Christianity, and with special attention to representation of the non-Western Churches, which had been, for the most part, planted by the various missionary efforts of Western Christians. According to my memory, I did not indicate a location, but I certainly did not have Scotland in mind.

To get the idea off the ground, I had already corresponded with Dr. Emilio Castro, then Executive of the Commission on Mission and Evangelism of the World Council of Churches. Dr. Castro made efforts in this regard but reluctantly concluded that the time was not yet ripe for such an inclusive conference (probably it still is not). From my standpoint, it was unfortunate that Dr. Ralph Winters, then at Fuller Theological Seminary, was able to get a 1980 Conference on Frontier Missions, taking my idea in quite a different direction from what I intended.

I also participated in what is now the National Association of Baptist Professors of Religion, attending some of their meetings, submitting articles for publication, and serving on the editorial board for a few years until 1975. At that time I had to resign all such positions, and certain memberships, in order to return to Japan in early 1976.

Soon after I came to Southeastern, I began to hear how wonderful the fellowship was at this school. It is certainly true that the nonhierarchical character of the relation of faculty members and staff with each other and with students made for a better fellowship than would otherwise be expected. However, having worked for several years in the Japan Baptist Mission, I knew that the fellowship at Southeastern, though commendable, left something to be desired.

For one thing, we always had trouble getting students to attend chapel. Such services of worship, as well as classes, were not held on Monday, since we allowed students with pastoral or other ministerial roles to have a long weekend for ministry in their churches. The other four days, Tuesday through Friday, were given over to the usual fifty-minute classes and thirty-minute chapel services, except for those few occasions each semester when we had special lectures, for which the chapel time was extended to fifty minutes.

I have already hinted at one of the reasons why it was difficult to have a community spirit. Many of our students, especially those who were married, had pastorates and lived in proximity to their churches. They commuted to the campus for classes and some of them lived in Seminary dormitories for part of the week except for weekends. It was understandable that for such students the necessity of contributing to a community of learning would not be a high priority.

Although I was aware of this problem, I still chafed greatly at the poor chapel attendance. More than being embarrassed when only a few students showed up when we had special chapel speakers from off campus, I was distressed because I believed that the problem of sustaining good chapel attendance boded ill for the future of worship in the churches where our graduates were filling pastoral and other roles.

I worried that churches led by persons who did not appreciate worship for its own sake--that is, who cherished worship only when they were leading it--would not be taught to esteem the worship of God. In addition, there were students who lived on the campus who did not attend chapel regularly. Some of them might, or might not, have taken their studies seriously, but they certainly had a low estimate of chapel worship. For all of my years at Southeastern I was concerned about chapel attendance, but I never saw any solution to the problem.

If the difficulties in sustaining community worship were not enough to call into question the vaunted fellowship of Southeastern, a dramatic event contributed measurably to convincing us that our Southeastern fellowship was somehow deficient. This occurrence was the death of Bob Daniel at his own hand. Robert T. Daniel, Professor of Hebrew and Old Testament, accompanied by Stewart A. Newman in Theology and Philosophy of Religion, had come to Southeastern from Southwestern Baptist Theological Seminary, Fort Worth, Texas. The two were among the first members of the Faculty.*

Daniel was a very meticulous fellow, always choosing the earliest period of the day for his classes, for example, and arriving not just in time for his classes but before the hour. He had contracted a disease of the urinary tract for which he had received treatment, including a stay at the Baptist Hospital in Winston-Salem. Presumably, he was well on the way to recovery.

In spite of the fact that his doctors gave him assurance to the contrary, apparently, Daniel became convinced that he had cancer. In May of 1959, after he had followed his usual pattern of turning all his grades in on time, Bob's wife, Alberta, returned home from an errand to find Bob in the living room with his head blown off by his shotgun which he had placed in his mouth and then pulled the trigger.

As you might imagine, Bob Daniel's suicide was a profound shock to all of us at Southeastern. Much soul-searching occurred, most of it in private. I don't remember that I heard any exaggerated claims for our fellowship after that tragedy occurred.

Of course there were other deaths or serious illnesses of staff members which affected the Southeastern fellowship, but none of them were suicides and most came after the person involved had retired, as in the case of J. B. Hipps, who died in 1968. Some had resigned, such as Emily Lansdell who left the faculty in 1962 to marry and died of cancer in Georgia in 1973, while still in her late fifties. Others died in the midst of their careers at Southeastern, such as Raymond B. Brown, Distinguished Professor of New Testament, and Dean during much of my tenure at Southeastern, whose death occurred in 1977; and Ellis Hollon, Professor of Philosophy of Religion, in 1979. Hollon had been one of my students, and Brown was a dear friend. However, both of these died after I had left South-eastern in early 1976.

Outside controversies among Southern Baptists also affected our fellowship, usually serving to draw us more closely together. The most important of these to occur while I was at Southeastern were the Elliott controversy of 1962, followed by the

---

*Other members were J. Leo Green, Professor of Old Testament; J. B. Hipps, Professor of Missions; W. C. Strickland, Tutor in New Testament; and Marc H. Lovelace, Visiting Professor of Archaeology.

revision of the Southern Baptist confessional statement, called the *Baptist Faith and Message*, in 1963, and the contention surround-ng the publication of the *Broadman Bible Commentary* in 1969.

Ralph H. Elliott, a professor at Midwestern Baptist Theological Seminary, got into trouble because Broadman published his *The Message of Genesis* in 1961, a book which greatly agitated Southern Baptists, most of whom thought the book was liberal. Actually, in the spectrum of general theological scholarship, the volume was somewhat conservative. The problem was that in the book Elliott used historical critical methods, which, so far as I know, were employed in all Southern Baptist seminaries but not generally communicated to the public. This made Biblical scholars all the more vulnerable if they published what they really believed.

Since he was transparently honest, Elliott refused to use the "doublespeak" urged upon him by certain Baptist scholars, notably a mentor who had taught Old Testament to Elliott at Southern Baptist Seminary. Also, after Broadman, under heavy criticism, had agreed not to reprint his book, Elliott refused to promise not to seek a new publisher for the controverted volume on his own initiative, though he agreed not to republish the book if the Midwestern Trustees requested it. Apparently so that they could not be accused of book-banning, the Trustees made no such request, but rather fired Elliott for refusing "to come to a mutual working relationship with the administration."*

It is likely that all of us at Southeastern took the side of Elliott in this sorry affair. The problem was that we were embroiled in an internal dispute usually referred to as the "Bultmannian controversy" and felt that we could not afford to be diverted into the defense of a colleague in another seminary. I remember that Ralph visited our seminary once and was treated by the faculty as a celebrity. Though he is younger than I, he has remained one of my heroes.

On one occasion, just after Elliott had been fired, I was two hours or more between planes in the Atlanta airport when I

---

*For further information about the Elliott controversy see Ralph H. Elliott, *The "Genesis Controversy" and Continuity in Southern Baptist Chaos: A Eulogy for a Great Tradition* (Macon, GA: Mercer University Press, 1992).

ran across Dr. Herschel Hobbs, then President of the Southern Baptist Convention and by virtue of that office a member of all boards of the convention, including, of course, the Board of Trustees at Midwestern Seminary. The late Dr. Hobbs, who also had some time on his hands in Atlanta, had been deeply involved in the Elliott controversy and had helped manage its solution.

Hobbs invited me to have coffee with him in an airport facility, whereupon he proceeded to talk for a long time in defense of the Elliott dismissal. I listened in silence, and then when he paused for my reaction, I responded by saying nary a word. Since there was nothing further to be discussed and the time for my departure was nearing, I thanked him for the coffee and took my leave.

In the aftermath of the Elliott controversy, there was a clamor for the revision of the Southern Baptist confessional statement, the *Baptist Faith and Message*. Though this demand was made predominantly by conservatives, the actual revision went against them.

The article on Scripture was significantly altered at two points, both of which were contrary to a conservative interpretation: the Bible was recognized as the "record" of God's revelation and Christ was indicated as the criterion for interpreting the Bible.* The article on the Church was changed from an exclusive emphasis upon the local church to include a recognition of the universal church. I am told that two New Testament scholars who figured in these revisions were related to Southeastern: E. A. McDowell, Professor of New Testament at Southeastern, and Ray Brown, then teaching at Southern Seminary but later coming to Southeastern as Professor of New Testament.

In spite of the less conservative guise of the *Baptist Faith and Message* after its revision, there was an increased tendency to require agencies, especially seminaries, to affirm this confession, an attempt which was recognized by many Southern Baptists as a step in the direction of creedalism.

The controversy which attended the publication of the *Broadman Bible Commentary* was even closer to home. John I

---

*These revisions were undone by the Southern Baptist Convention at its June 2000 meeting.

Durham, who taught Old Testament at Southeastern, was one of the editors, several of our professors contributed commentaries on various books, and I contributed a general article, "The Christian Mission and the People of God." My article was not really controversial, and since it was in the last volume, it is doubtful if it was widely read.

In any case, it was the commentary on Genesis, in the first volume, which came in for the harshest condemnation. The author was Dr. G. Henton Davies, a British Baptist and a distinguished scholar of the Old Testament. Though considered conservative by most Christian scholars, Davies' treatment of Genesis was condemned by many Southern Baptists, with the result that the Sunday School Board of the Southern Baptist Convention withdrew Volume 1 and substituted for it a volume containing a new commentary on Genesis written from "the conservative viewpoint" by Clyde T. Francisco, a Professor of Old Testament at Southern Baptist Seminary in Louisville, Kentucky.

The reaction of the faculty of Southeastern Seminary was to continue to view Henton Davies with friendship and respect and to invite him back for chapel messages and visiting professorships. If they possessed copies of the *Broadman Bible Commentary*, they probably kept the original Volume 1 which contained Davies' commentary on Genesis and did not honor Francisco by accepting a copy of the revised volume, though some had been Francisco's teachers, his colleagues, or his students.*

These Southern Baptist controversies were to increase in stridency and effectiveness until they reached their zenith in 1979 and succeeding years, during which time one by one the agencies were taken over by fundamentalists. Southeastern Seminary was the first to be captured. But I'm getting far ahead of my story.

Soon after coming to Southeastern, I was invited to teach in the summer session at the Carver School of Missions and Social Work. This was the former Woman's Missionary Union Training School from which Louise had graduated in 1946. The President when Louise studied there, Dr. Grace Littlejohn, had retired and

---

*Francisco was on the faculty of Southern when I was a visiting teacher there, 1953-1954, but I surely did not exchange my original volume for the revised one.

was succeeded by Dr. Emily Lansdell, a former missionary to China.

Dr. Lansdell had led the school to make several alterations, among which was calling the school by a new name, signifying a change in character and honoring Dr. W. O. Carver, a Professor at Southern Baptist Theological Seminary and a longtime teacher at the old WMU Training School. The new name was the Carver School of Missions and Social Work. The school had also become coeducational, though the male students were very few. I think that I taught at the Carver School in each summer session, 1957-1961.

Meantime, Dr. Emily Lansdell resigned in 1958, and I was invited by the Trustees to succeed her. After careful consideration, I wrote the Chairman of the Board indicating that unless three conditions were met I could hardly consider the offer. These were (1) That there be assurance of at least as much emphasis upon missions as upon social work, especially since I had no qualifications in the latter field; (2) That the school be developed as a kind of finishing school for missionaries, that is, all persons appointed by the Southern Baptist Foreign Mission Board would take a year of orientation at the Carver School; and (3) That the Foreign Mission Board pledge continuing support of the school.

Since Dr. Baker J. Cauthen, then Executive Secretary of the FMB, indicated that he would treat the school as one of the seminaries, obviously the second and third of the conditions, which were closely related, could not be met. Therefore, there was no way I could accept the offer.

Southern Baptist Theological Seminary tried to get me to join the Faculty each time they had a vacancy in my field, until I finally made a trip to Louisville in 1969, at their expense, to confer with Dr. William Hull, Provost of the school and Dean of the School of Theology, about the position. The tentative offer at that time, which waited upon my positive reaction, was that I occupy the Carver Chair of Missions and World Religions. Again, after careful and prayerful reflection, I withdrew my name before the offer was made official. Up until then and for a few years afterward, I thought that my place was at Southeastern.

Chapter Fourteen
TAKING A STAND

There was something very exciting about teaching in a progressive environment and a new context. At Southeastern, we

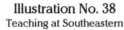

Illustration No. 38
Teaching at Southeastern

tried to be as far out front as a Southern Baptist seminary could be. My own theory was that we should keep the strings which controlled us stretched pretty close to the breaking point. Though two or three of our teachers were known as conservatives, we were generally considered a liberal seminary within the Southern Baptist context. Nevertheless, the faculty prized our diversity and sought to prevent any one theological viewpoint from dominating. Our approach to Biblical studies was quite open to historical and critical methods. Most of what I had learned at Yale seemed appropriate at Southeastern.

Of course, in those days the matter of race was the most prominent social issue. We arrived in Wake Forest only four years after the famous Supreme Court decision which had desegregated the public schools. Many facilities were still segregated, and the notorious "Jim Crow" laws were yet operative in the South.

On this question, as on others which I will discuss below, the Seminary adopted a progressive stance. As soon as we had possession of the whole campus (which occurred the year I came to the Seminary), we accepted students into our classrooms and dormitories as complete equals. Though some teachers were more prominent on the racial issue than others--Edward Mc-Dowell and Olin Binkley, for example, had long been known as pioneers with regard to race--I cannot think of any who was reactionary.

My own conviction with regard to what I should do about race, a premise upon which I had already begun to operate, was that the church itself was my particular area of influence. I had profound respect for those who mixed it in the secular arena, facing the hate mongers, the unscrupulous and sadistic law enforcers, and the trained dogs. It is possible that my choice of an ecclesiastical setting for what little I could do for African Americans was a rationalization of my doubt that I had the courage required to seek justice in the secular world. In any case, for better or worse I felt that my own priority was the community of Christians, which, by the way, was by no means free of radical racists including Ku Klux Klanners.

Even in these more enlightened times, I feel that we still have work to do in the churches. It is often pointed out that the hours given to Sunday School and worship constitute the most segregated time in our society, and I have said more than once that until we are willing to "blacken" our churches and their ministry we will continue to be segregated. In other words, we have a profound cultural division, and we need consciously to try to overcome this schism by accepting at least aspects of minority cultures rather than always expecting minorities to take on the majority culture.

By various means I tried to implement my racial vision. In my classrooms, when it seemed appropriate to discuss race, I sought to bring the judgment of the Bible and of Christian ethics on the matter. Occasionally I invited African American civil rights leaders to visit my classes, and they usually shocked some of my more conservative students.

Both within the seminary and in speaking or writing to Christian audiences on the outside I rang the changes on the contradiction of supporting a message of racial equality represented by the words and actions of missionaries beyond our country's borders, while upholding a system of inequality in our own nation. I insisted that to deny by our practice at home what we preached abroad was to hang a millstone around the neck of the Christian mission which threatened to pull it under the turbulent waters of our world.

Once in a while I had evidence that my message was getting through. For example, a woman in an eastern North Carolina church where, as was my custom, I had hit the racial question hard early in revival services, related to me a very revealing dream. She dreamed that she died and went to heaven, she told me, and there she saw Jesus. He was unbelievably beautiful, she said, with a most attractive smile. When he saw her, however, his face clouded and he looked profoundly sad. "I'm sorry," he said, "but we can't let you stay." The dear woman was crushed, and she cried out, "But why? Why can't I stay?" "Because you do not love Negroes," he replied. "But I do! I do!" she cried, and seeing an old Negro man, bald and with a fringe of white hair, she ran to him and threw her arms around him. At that point, she said, she awoke. I interpreted this story as an expression of the troubled conscience of the South.

More often I got the cold shoulder or even hostility, often in the form of letters. In 1957, not long after I came to Southeastern, I was invited to write an article, somewhat like an editorial piece, for a young adult Sunday School quarterly. As usual, I approached the subject of missions from the standpoint of the racial contradiction. I did not think that I had written anything radical at all.

Nevertheless, I got some hot letters* about it, including one from a fellow Baptist in Louisiana in which he ended his letter by saying that as a Baptist he was exercising his right to tell me that my attempt to integrate his little girls into a mixed society

---

*On a long and hostile letter from a fellow in Florida, my oldest daughter, Judy, who was then ten years of age, wrote in her own handwriting, "I wish I could tear this letter."

"STINKS," and that he would go to hell before he would see it realized. "Just keep your ideas out of print in our Sunday School Books," he admonished me.

Not being accustomed to getting that kind of letter, I hardly knew what to do about it. I decided, however, that I would answer it, but as briefly as possible. Fortunately, because of a rather extensive trip, I did not have to answer immediately. When I returned to my office, I answered something like this. "This is to acknowledge receipt of your letter of such and such a date. I pray that God will bless you according to his infinite wisdom and love."*

I thought that would be the end of the matter, but it wasn't--quite. A few days later I got another letter from my critic, enclosing an editorial from the Louisiana Baptist state paper, the then editor of which was quite reactionary on the race issue. The enclosure would indicate, said my correspondent, that the people of the South would not accept my ideas. The only way he could understand integrationists, "foreign missionaries included," he wrote, was that they "have one or more half-breed children running around the world somewhere."

Pretty obviously, he was nettled by my indication that I would pray for him, since his letter instructed me as follows: "Don't bother to answer [when I read this phrase, I heaved a sigh of relief!] or pray for me--as a Baptist I'll pray for myself." I felt that my accuser's words had put me in an ethical dilemma. I said to Louise, "What do you do about a fellow who, in spite of his obvious need of prayer, specifies that he doesn't want you to pray for him? Should you pray for him anyway?"

On occasion, as my files reveal, I argued with denominational editors about softening my meaning on racial matters without my consent. Even some pastors resented my speaking on the race issue in connection with world missions. Apparently, along with many other leaders, if they intended to do anything about race relations, usually it was by a strategy of "gradualism."

**I was not so unkind as to answer as did another person about whom I heard, who responded as follows: "I am now sitting in the smallest room in my house. Your letter is before me. In a moment it will be behind me."

That is, they expected that as they ministered to their flocks, they would slowly and gradually get across a Christian way of dealing with race. And they did not appreciate any outsider coming in only briefly and stirring up waters which he had no responsibility to try and calm.

They certainly had a point. I never adequately resolved this conflict between my prophetic conviction and my sense of concern for the pastoral viewpoint. One minister who was a casual friend from our days at Southern Seminary noticeably cooled toward me after, at his invitation, I spoke at his church and related the race question to world missions.

Another fellow met me at the airport and, after we reached his church on Sunday morning for a missionary sermon, informed me that I should not speak about race. Actually, I was both confused and relieved. But I have sometimes wished that I had not been so sensitive to his position and had asked him to take me back to the airport, explaining that I could not preach when someone told me what I could not or should not say. By the way, in my judgment neither of these two was a racist.

Perhaps the most serious racial problem, at least the one closest to home, was within the Wake Forest Baptist Church whose building was located within the seminary campus on land which the church had purchased from the college several years previously when the college was still there. Most of us on the Southeastern staff were included in the membership of this Church, along with many persons from the community. Some Seminary folk were even Deacons.

In the fall of 1962, two Africans, both mature men with several years of pastoral experience, enrolled in our Seminary. Since their background was Southern Baptist missionary work, they had very little in common with the local African American churches and wished rather to become members of the Wake Forest Baptist Church.

On a September day in 1962, President Sid Stealey, as he was prone to do, rather than inviting me to his office to make a formal request, encountered me on the street on my way home, stopped his car, thrust his head out of the window and asked me as Professor of Missions, to take responsibility for the spiritual needs of these African brethren.

On the following Sunday, instead of risking taking them to

Wake Forest Baptist Church where they might suffer some embarrassment, Dean Olin Binkley accompanied me and we took them to Pullen Memorial Baptist Church in Raleigh for the morning worship service and to Binkley Memorial Baptist Church in Chapel Hill for supper and evening worship.

Meanwhile, these African Baptists' desire for membership became a matter of concern to some of the members of Wake Forest Baptist Church and there was a decision that a special meeting of the Deacons be called for Wednesday evening, September 19. Since I was a Deacon at the time, I received a notice of the meeting, and I came prepared to offer a motion. After explaining the situation as well as I could, I presented the following motion: "That this Diaconate recommend to the church in conference that the church go on record as follows: no person shall be debarred from attendance or membership in the Wake Forest Baptist Church because of race." When the vote was taken, the Deacons unanimously approved the motion.

Then all hell broke loose. I can imagine that when fellow Deacons, especially persons not related to the Seminary, tried to explain the matter to their families and friends, the reaction was one of shock and strong negativity. It was said that since I had "mesmerized" the Deacons, none had dared oppose me.

Though one or two townspeople quite gratuitously offered me their support, for which I shall always be grateful, I had visits from a lay member of the Church who was a community leader and from my Pastor, both representing others, asking me to withdraw my motion. The community leader insisted that he did not want his children to grow up in an integrated church, to which I countered that I also had children and I did not want them to grow up in a church which denied the Christian gospel. My Pastor quoted to me Reinhold Niebuhr to the effect that politics is the art of the possible, and I responded that it was very disappointing to me that my Pastor was sitting across the desk from me trying to get me to compromise the very gospel that he himself preached.

The following Wednesday evening we had a called Conference of the Church to take action on the resolution that the Deacons had passed. The Church building was packed as I had never seen it before in spite of a pouring rain. A seminary student stood to say, "My God, I have never seen such a crowd in a

Church during a rainstorm aiming to shut people out when you can't get them to come to welcome people in!"

By then all the Deacons had deserted me and I had to present the resolution alone. I explained the situation and insisted that I had no intention of leaving the Church. However the Church decided the matter, I stated, I would stay with it because I loved it.

Dr. S. L. Morgan, a retired pastor, read a statement which he and Dr. W. C. Cullom, retired Chair of the Religion Department of Wake Forest College, had prepared. It was remarkably progressive, so far as I am concerned, right on the money. Since that time, I have been careful to point out that age does not necessarily mean that people have grown increasingly narrow in their viewpoints. At that time Dr. Morgan was in his late eighties and Dr. Cullom was in his nineties.

A substitute motion was presented, which had the blessing of President Stealey, to the effect that anybody would be acceptable as a member who had any connection with the Seminary. The aim of this substitute motion was to preserve the Church from an anticipated clamor for membership on the part of local African Americans--though the future revealed that this fear was quite unfounded. Dean Binkley spoke briefly, to the effect that he had never known of such a double standard for membership in a Baptist church. After several people had expressed their sentiments, it was pointed out that this motion would allow membership to the several local blacks who worked for the Seminary. Of course, this is not what the Church wanted, and chaos immediately ensued.

The substitute motion was withdrawn, and an interim measure was passed by which the African brethren could be welcomed as members on the same basis with other persons -- but as special cases. These two students took their time in presenting themselves, however, and the matter dragged on for some time before they finally asked to join.

In the meantime, a very humorous incident occurred. At a Church conference, the matter of the membership of the two African pastors came up. A very short fellow stood to speak, stating very strongly that if "those niggers" became members of the Church, he and his wife would leave.

When he ended his short speech, his wife stood up. She

was as tall for a woman as he was short for a man, giving them a kind of humorous appearance as being unequally yoked in marriage. The wife indicated that she was a daughter of the South and that it was not natural for her to accept Negroes into church membership. But she also had always been a member of the Woman's Missionary Union and had loyally supported missions to Africa, she said. The two Africans, as products of Southern Baptist missionary work, had a right to belong to Wake Forest Baptist Church, she opined, and "if they join, we are not leaving this Church!" She sat down, her husband said nothing in response, and when the two Africans later joined, the couple *did not* move their membership nor cease attending the Church's services.

Finally, in January 1965, after my family and I had been on sabbatical leave for a year in India, 1963-1964, the constitution of Wake Forest Baptist Church was revised so that nobody was voted on immediately upon presentation of himself or herself for membership. Rather, a vote of the Church was deferred until a business meeting, during which interval the applicant was to be met and oriented to the meaning and responsibility of Church membership by a committee consisting of the Pastor and several Deacons. The revision had the advantage of stating the requirements of Church membership positively rather than negatively as my motion had done. This was the way church membership was handled when we left the Wake Forest Church in 1967 to move to Raleigh, though I suspect it was simplified later.

Meanwhile, a group of members departed and formed another Baptist church within the town of Wake Forest. Although its name was Community Baptist Church, a wag on our faculty said that it should be called the "Lakeview Baptist Church" because it was led by Dr. I. Beverly Lake, a retired professor at Wake Forest College and former head of the Law School. In my judgment, the late Dr. Lake was a brilliant man with a noteworthy blind spot concerning race. After the college moved, he remained in Wake Forest and became a famous politician and then a member of the North Carolina Supreme Court (as did his son and namesake).

Incidentally, when this small schism occurred, Dr. Lake attended the new Baptist church but never moved his membership there. Ultimately he returned from the Community Baptist

Church and resumed his place at Wake Forest Baptist Church where his membership had remained.

When the Community Baptist Church was organized, I predicted that in after a few years this new church would have a pretty good reputation and be ashamed of its origin. In spite of my record to the contrary, in this instance apparently I proved to be a good prophet.

With regard to the ecumenical issue, we at Southeastern seem to have been quite conscious of our fellow Christians, in spite of the fact that we were somewhat isolated in the small town of Wake Forest. We had a succession of non-Southern Baptists as guest lecturers, and we soon developed the tradition of a dinner during Thanksgiving week with the faculty of Duke Divinity School where President Stealey had once studied. Each year the place of the event alternated between the two schools, and a member of the faculty being entertained would present a paper.

In a study course book, called *Frontiers of Advance,* which I produced for publication at the request of the Foreign Mission Board in 1964, I included a brief treatment of the ecumenical movement. Although I viewed what I wrote as factual and objective, it caused quite a storm in the Southern Baptist Convention. Dr. Baker J. Cauthen, in his position as Executive Secretary of the Foreign Mission Board, once more was called upon to defend me, which he did, I was told, on the basis of the claim that he thought that he and I believed about the same with regard to the ecumenical movement, namely, that "everyone should have both the courage and the courtesy of his convictions."

Some Woman's Missionary Union circles in Oklahoma refused to use the book and even sent it back to Baptist Book Stores. Of course, I received several letters about it, most of them taking issue with me.

One letter which especially impressed itself upon my memory was from a woman who wrote that she could not understand why what I had written about the ecumenical movement had so upset people, since she thought that I had just stated facts and was not trying to plead a cause. She ended by saying that the ecumenical issue could not be discussed in the Baptist church to which she belonged but could be treated dispassionately in her local chapter of what in those days was a rather popular right wing organization, the John Birch Society!

Some of the Southeastern Seminary Trustees became concerned about my ecumenical stance. One of them, a pastor from New Mexico, visited my class in "A History of Christian Cooperation." It happened that I was not lecturing that day but had a student report on some of his research on Roman Catholicism. I regretted the fact that the Trustee turned up unannounced and that the student who reported was somewhat uncomfortable in his presence, but I saw no reason to deny the Trustee access to my classroom. Later, he visited me in my office to ask me about my view on ecumenism. This Trustee left without agreeing with me, but he did not seek my termination.

Not only did I teach ecumenics, I also practiced it in so far as I had opportunity. I was in the unenviable position of being ecumenical in conviction while belonging to a denomination which was anti-ecumenical. I have already mentioned my study at the School of Theology of Boston University in the summer of 1960, my membership on one of the Commissions of the Baptist World Alliance, and my participation in efforts of the Faith and Order Commission of the National Council of Churches of Christ in the United States of America to draw in groups that were outside their orb, such as the Southern Baptist Convention. I am told that Albert McClellan, staff person of the Executive Committee of the Southern Baptist Convention and Editor of the *Baptist Program*, recommended me for this latter responsibility.

When I resigned my membership on the Faith and Order Commission in the summer of 1975 in order to return to Japan a few months later, I had participated directly in the work of the Commission for about nine years, a service which had included several committee assignments. Members of the Commission's staff, including Bill Norgren, Sister Ann Patrick, and Jorge Lara-Braud, were unanimous in their expressions of appreciation for my service to the Commission--though, of course, they may have been prejudiced since they desired to move the Southern Baptist Convention toward greater ecumenicity. My view was that the SBC should join such agencies and give our witness from within.

My stance on the Southern Baptist "invasion" of the "North," where American Baptists were at work, was likewise controversial. In most cases Southern Baptists were indifferent or else hostile toward the presence and structures of other Christians, including other Baptists. I argued that we Southern Baptists especially should unite with the American Baptist churches and their denominational structures so that we could both learn from these other Baptists and contribute to their growth rather than to develop our own denomination at their expense.

Much was said about Southern Baptist congregations as "New Testament churches." I even remarked that if we Southern Baptists found a "New Testament church" in the north, we probably would erect a Southern Baptist "New Testament church" across the street from it! I referred to our conviction that our program was superior as a "cultural idolatry."

Particularly, I ruffled some feathers by an address I made at a Convention-wide Woman's Missionary Union confer-ence at the Southern Baptist Assembly at Ridgecrest, North Caro-lina, in the summer of 1959. Some of the women upon returning home reported to their pastors what they thought I had said, though my remarks about the Southern Baptist work in the North constituted only a small point in a much larger address.

Concerning this speech, I received one or two negative letters from Southern Baptist ministers, one of which was from a Southern Baptist pastor in Boomer, West Virginia, who assumed that I knew nothing about American Baptists. If I did, he allowed, as "a good SBC man you could hardly approve of their positions and deviations from the Baptist movement." If I did not know about them, of course, I had no business speaking about them. In either case, I did not belong in a Southern Baptist seminary, and my critic wrote that I should join a fellowship of those with whose beliefs I agreed.

Of course, I did not take this brother's counsel, choosing rather to determine my own place of work. I replied indicating that this pastor was working in "an area dear to my heart," and I proceeded to tell him of my background growing up in West Virginia in American Baptist churches where I first heard the gospel, and of the (then) membership of my parents in an Ameri-can Baptist congregation in Mount Nebo, West Virginia, where they lived. Only later did I learn from a cousin who was an Amer-ican Baptist that this fellow was a "sheep stealer," that is, he was stealing members and churches out of American Baptist asso-ciations and adding them to his Southern Baptist work. I had caught him red-handed! (Incidentally, my cousin mentioned the name of this pastor; I did not ask anything about him at all.)

On the issue of women in ministry, we at Southeastern were certainly too paternalistic in our early years, but soon after I came to Southeastern I recommended to the President that we invite a woman, Dr. Emily Lansdell, to join our faculty as my colleague in the teaching of missions and world religions, which she did in 1959, after a year of special studies at Union Seminary in New York.* Also, we were not against the ordaining of women for pastoral ministry. In fact, we admitted them to the Master of Divinity (previously Bachelor of Divinity) course on the same basis as men.

When Addie Davis, a student from Covington, Virginia, was ordained by the Watts Street Baptist Church in nearby Durham, I participated, along with Dr. R. C. Briggs, Professor of New Testament at Southeastern Seminary. Perhaps other Professors at Southeastern would have been involved if it had not been for the pressure of other commitments. The year was 1964 and Ms. Davis has the distinction of being the first Southern Baptist woman to be ordained to the ministry. (My role in her ordination may be my only claim to fame!). All of us at Southeastern shared in this honor, and Briggs and I took some of the flak in Southern Baptist state papers.

---

*At that time, Dr. Lansdell, who had been a missionary to China, was President of The Carver School of Missions and Social Work in Louisville, Kentucky. In 1962 she married a widower--Dr. J. B. Weatherspoon, one of my teachers at Southern Seminary in Louisville who was now retired and a visiting professor at Southeastern, 1959-1963--whereupon she resigned her teaching post at our seminary. To my knowledge, Dr. Lansdell was the second woman to teach in a non-religious education or non-music position in a Southern Baptist theological seminary, following Dr. Helen Falls, who was moved from the School of Religious Education to the School of Theology at New Orleans Baptist Theological Seminary as Assistant Professor of Missions in 1956.

Although William Shinto taught as a visitor at Southeastern, 1958-1959, the invitation to him to become a member of our faculty at Southeastern in missions did not come until after Dr. Lansdell resigned. (On this point, Alan Neely's article in *Servant Songs*, edited by Thomas Bland, Jr., p. 172, is in error.)

It is important to say that Ms. Davis was unable to find employment as a pastor in the Southern Baptist context. Instead, she turned to American Baptists and had a distinguished career as a pastor in New England.

Beyond these expressions of a progressive spirit in my interpretation of Christianity, there were other quite significant evidences of this breadth of perspective. I had always tended to side with the underdog, probably having learned this from my parents, particularly my mother, and from many other sources. These earlier insights had been broadened and deepened by several college teachers, and especially by seminary teachers such as McDowell and Binkley.

When, as a result of liberation theology upon missiological studies, I first detected a new emphasis upon God's championing of the poor, the underprivileged, the oppressed, I began to read the Bible with new eyes and to find fresh support for my views on race and class, with the result that these convictions became even more meaningful. I increasingly became active as a volunteer and a contributor of funds, not only to help the racially discriminated against but also the homeless and other deprived persons. I must confess, however, that the combination of the heavy demands of my job and the practical needs of a large family hindered these impulses until after I retired.

Somewhat similar has been the conviction that God has a way of saving those who never hear the Christian gospel, or who hear what purports to be the gospel but for whatever reasons reject it. I have always found it hard to believe that God assigns to hell those millions of persons who are outside the usual places or situations where the Christian message is heard and believed. Many years of studying, reading, and teaching missions has but made me more convinced than ever that God, who loves all equally, does not act so capriciously.

Often I have been content to ask "thought" questions of students and challenge them to find their own answers on this matter, queries such as this: "How would you answer if a young Christian should ask you about the eternal destiny of his or her grandmother, someone who had been a strong influence upon him or her for good but had died without ever hearing about Christ?" More and more, however, I have expressed my own conviction, especially to students, and have tried to deal with the motive of missions accordingly.

I have said repeatedly that I could not believe in a God who callously condemns millions of persons to eternal damnation simply because no missionary ever reached them. Even I am not that cruel, and if God is less ethical than I, I cannot voluntarily worship such a one. I take seriously my confession that the One who meets us in Jesus Christ is truly God.

More recently, too, I have developed as an environmentalist. For a long time I had been impressed by such Scriptures as Paul's words in Romans 8 about the creation. A long time ago, I preached an Easter sermon setting forth the cosmic dimension of salvation, one point of which was that we have in store a remarkable transformation of the universe, that God is not in the business of a cosmic wastage but a cosmic salvation.

Although I am not sure of the chronology, in the 1960s I began to feel keenly the pressure of this important issue. Of course, I paid attention to the pioneer contribution of Joseph Sittler on the relation of Christian theology and the environment. Experiences of my year in India, 1963-1964, heightened this concern.

In the late 1960s, when Nicholas Zernov was a Visiting Professor at Duke University, I invited him to lecture in one of my classes. I was profoundly impressed when he pointed out that Eastern Orthodox Churches have always believed in the transformation of the material universe and that their bounteous use of the elements in the sacraments--water in the trine immersion of baptism and bread and wine in the Eucharist--were foregleams of that profound change. I found Zernov's thought very congenial to my own.

For a time, I intended to write a book on how environmentalism is inseparably related to Christian theology, but never got around to it, and, of course, considerable literature has been produced on this subject by now. In the meantime, I have insisted that the ecological message and practice of Christianity constitute for us a newly recognized dimension of the Christian mission. So far as I know, I was the first missiologist to write that missionaries need to be earthkeepers, all of us in a general sense and some in a particular sense,* but this happened after I resigned at Southeastern.

Before I left the Seminary in Wake Forest, however, I firmed up my opposition to capital punishment. It has grieved me very much that North Carolina, a state for which I have much respect and affection, has continued to execute persons. It has seemed to me that Christians, of all people, because of our alleged compassion and reverence for life, should unite against the death penalty.

Similarly, I gradually became an advocate of gun control. The violence of American society has convinced me that we need to correct this aspect of our culture and that one of the ways to do it is to regulate guns. Also, we need to be known in the world as a peaceful nation, not as one which has a love affair with guns. Although I have given up hunting, I have no quarrel with those who use guns for that reason, if their hunting is done for economic reasons and *if they truly respect the environment.*

I think the reasoning of the National Rifle Association (NRA) is seriously flawed in various places, nowhere more evident than in their use of the Second Amendment of the Constitution to bolster their belief. I even wrote a song after retirement, entitled "Salute to the NRA."

I regret that it took me so long to see that the Vietnam War was wrong. It was not until the decade of the 1960s had almost spent itself that I decided that I must oppose this War. I will say more about it when I discuss my sabbatical in Chicago.

---

*See my *World Mission and World Survival*, 121-123, and *A New Meeting of the Religions*, 90.

Chapter Fifteen
THE BULTMANNIAN CONTROVERSY

It is painful to try to reconstruct from my inadequate memory and from my insufficient notes, the first major controversy to beset Southeastern Seminary, a controversy in which I found it impossible to maintain a neutral stance. I had respect--and still have--for colleagues on both sides of the question and was particularly grieved when some in the opposing camp resigned and went elsewhere.

The controversy may be dated from a Faculty Club discussion, which I believe occurred in the spring semester of the 1959-1960 session. It centered around the teaching of a New Testament teacher, R. C. Briggs, who had been at Southeastern since 1957. In the Faculty Club discussion, it appeared that three members of the New Testament Faculty, Briggs, Harold H. Oliver, and William C. Strickland, were aligned against their more senior colleague, E. A. McDowell, Jr., and intimations were made that anyone--meaning especially McDowell--who did not accept the stance of Rudolph Bultmann in New Testament studies, was hopelessly out of date.

Red flags came up immediately, not only because it appeared that three colleagues were opposing one, but because it was interpreted that, in addition to Briggs and Oliver, "Bill" Strickland, who was known as a devotee of Archbishop Temple, had been converted to the Bultmannian view.

Moreover, those who taught systematic theology were incensed because it was being said openly that this discipline of theological studies was outmoded and would soon die. In addition, certain members of the Faculty were upset because it seemed that colleagues outside the New Testament area were adopting the Bultmannian theology.

The latter was based upon existentialist philosophy, especially the thought of Martin Heidegger, who emphasized the moral and emotional situation of the human being and the necessity of choice. Existentialism was popular in Europe, Japan, and other places after the end of World War Two. Thus Bultmann, known as an existentialist, carried his theology considerably beyond his methodology for interpreting the New Testament. For him, in keeping with existentialism, the central aspects of the gospel story, for example the cross and resurrection of Jesus, are to be understood quite individualistically and subjectively.

Personally, I first began to take this problem seriously when I was taken aback by a question of a student in one of my missions classes. I believe this incident occurred in the fall semester of the 1960-1961 session, though I made no note of it. In a free-wheeling discussion, this student wanted to know "how we as Southeastern graduates are to communicate our Bultmannian theology to the Southern Baptist churches we serve as pastors?"

I answered that I was surprised to hear that a student should feel that graduation from Southeastern would mean acceptance of a Bultmannian theology since I myself was not a Bultmannian. I was deeply troubled because for the first time I felt that our school was being identified with a particular theological stance, and one that Southern Baptists would consider very radical at that.

Some time later, a Southern Seminary Professor of Theology, the late Dale Moody, visited our campus and met that evening with Briggs and the Southeastern Faculty members who sided with Briggs. The next day, the first thing Moody said when he saw some of us who were identified with the other side was something like "Well, I didn't know that Southeastern Seminary was the home of Rudolph Bultmann."

Was Bultmannism, unlike Bultmann himself, Messianic in nature? Was it bent on converting others to itself? I have never felt that Briggs himself was Messianic, though *in our context* I believe that the Bultmannian movement was indeed Messianic. In other words, I saw it as a kind of academic imperialism. I am convinced that a peculiar set of circumstances combined to make Southeastern Seminary especially vulnerable to Bultmannian theology at that time: a disabled President who could not cope adequately with this crisis, an increasing stridency of the conservative Southern Baptist constituency who owned and controlled the Seminary, and a strong revulsion of students and Faculty against this growing fundamentalism.

President Sid Stealey has often been psychoanalyzed by persons like me who are nonspecialists; so please take my assessment with a large grain of salt! Dr. Stealey had many good things going for him. He had been one of my respected teachers at Southern Seminary. He possessed a keen mind, a high regard for scholarship, and great skills as a communicator. His instincts were democratic and his wisdom was practical. He related well to most audiences. His varied experiences as pastor and teacher enabled him to be an acute interpreter of Southern Baptist affairs. Much more could be said on the positive side of the equation.

On the other hand, Dr. Stealey, though still in his sixties, was increasingly a victim of ill health, and the controversy within his Faculty seemed further to debilitate him. Much of his administration was by hunch, especially when it came to the employment of staff, and his judgment about persons was never as valid as he seemed to think. He played Rook with what came to be a faction in the Faculty which sided with the so-called Bultmann disciples. It was generally known, also, that his theology had differed from that of his very narrow preacher father and that because of this difference the latter had rejected him.

For some reason, Stealey had an inordinate attachment to Bill Strickland; he looked upon Strickland as a son and could not permit himself to be in the situation of seeming to side against Bill. This paternalistic affection for Strickland made it difficult for President Stealey to deal objectively with a controversy which rather directly involved this younger colleague. Consequently, Stealey was prone to throw this hot potato to the Faculty for solution without adequate guidance.

I have already mentioned the controversies within the Southern Baptist Convention which were increasingly rancorous. When the Convention met in Miami in June 1960, an attack was made upon a theo-logical school which was identified as Southeastern Seminary. It was rather obvious that some leaders of the Convention considered Southeastern to be liberal, and that this young seminary would need pretty good protection from the Administration and Trustees if we were to survive.

Two years later, at its meeting in June 1962, in San Francisco, the Convention affirmed faith in the entire Bible as the "authoritative, authentic, infallible Word of God." To some of us Faculty members whom President Stealey happened to encounter in the cafeteria, he indicated his difficulty with this phrase and his deep concern with the direction which the Convention was taking. Like most if not all of the Faculty, I thoroughly agreed with the President on this matter.

A letter which came to Stealey soon afterward from the President of the Convention, a copy of which was supplied to Faculty members, indicated that no new creed had been imposed upon us and that the structures of our Seminary (including our confessional statement, the *Abstract of Principles*) had been left intact.

The 1960s are remembered as an age of protest. Within the Southern Baptist Convention, both on the part of teachers and students, there was a noticeable spirit of resistance to the fundamentalist tendencies of the Convention. Among our students there was a kind of youth rebellion, an anti-institutional attitude, which took a significant number of seminarians out of the ministry in a formal sense and into secular occupations. The theology of the Convention and its churches was interpreted as fundamentalistic and was rejected, both by students and Faculty.

Regrettably, there was also an immaturity on the part of many young Southern Baptists which eagerly seized upon a radical theology as a means of protesting fundamentalism. A colleague spoke of this kind of alleged liberalism as "fundamentalism standing on its head." That is, it had exchanged a set of rightist theological tenets (fundamentalism) for leftist ones (Bultmannianism) without any change in the dogmatic, fundamentalistic mentality, except that, if anything, it was even more condescending and elitist, disdainful of those who did not agree with it even if they were basically liberal.

I believe that there were some among us with this attitude, certainly a coterie of students and probably a few Faculty members. This sort of person naively identified with the Bultmannian theology as the most readily available means of protesting the fundamentalism of the Convention. Bultmannianism was the opposite of what was being rejected: it was new; it was non-Southern Baptist; it was German; it was radical. Therefore, it was to be affirmed.

I have no way of knowing how Briggs and his Faculty colleagues taught the New Testament. There are indications that they did not distinguish between the historical-critical method and the larger corpus of Bultmannian theology. It was the latter and not the former which was in question at Southeastern. I know that according to a press release in the *News and Observer,*

December 30, 1964, he identified the problem as the protest of several Faculty members against the use of "the historical-critical method of interpreting the New Testa-ment" on the part of Briggs, Strickland and Oliver.

Though Rudolph Bultmann certainly was one of the founders of form criticism, which by that time had been generally accepted as a part of historical criticism, the "historical-critical method" had been utilized by Biblical scholars long before Bultmann came upon the scene. So far as I know, nobody on our Faculty objected to the use of historical-criticism in Biblical studies but only to the radical Bultmannian theology.

Early in the dispute, I had spoken favorably of Bultmann in a Faculty meeting, indicating that I had no problem affirming his basic intent which was to "address the gospel to modern man." I spoke positively of "heretics," who, as I saw it, generally had served the cause of Christian faith better than had the "ortho-dox." I said that I would welcome Bultmann as a fellow member of Wake Forest Baptist Church, though I admitted that I doubted that he could be employed at a Southern Baptist seminary.

Our administrators, President Stealey being the foremost, insisted that the matter be resolved by Faculty discussions. The first of these talk sessions involved only the Faculty members in Biblical and theological studies, which, of course, did not include me, since I was in the historical area. Many of us felt that the whole Faculty must indeed close ranks and deal with the issue, since it was exceedingly hazardous to refer it to the trustees.

After Faculty members had bloodied their heads in a series of long discussions by the whole Faculty, the word was dropped, perhaps inadvertently, by Briggs that he had entered into a "pact of silence" with Strickland and Oliver where their Faculty colleagues were concerned. That is, the three of them were not going to discuss their theology with fellow teachers.

I was deeply hurt by this disclosure of the refusal of these three men to discuss their theology with us, and I concluded immediately that it meant a measure of distrust which rendered attempts by the Faculty to get at this problem useless. I remember that after this word was divulged, I went to Briggs' office to tell him that if the pact of silence continued I thought it inevitable that he confront the Trustees. He had experienced a successful encounter with Trustees at Union (Tennessee) University before coming to Southeastern. Possibly he thought he could win at Southeastern as well, though I never heard him say so.

At any rate, in the spring semester of 1961, President Stealey sought the counsel and aid of the Trustees. In a statement which he read to the faculty dated April 7, 1961, he indicated that it seemed to him "that the administration can no longer be useful alone and that the counsel of the Board is necessary."

I have notes on a report which as a Faculty member I made to the Instruction Committee of the Board of Trustees of Southeastern Seminary (the committee which had to do with academic affairs) at their request on May 16, 1961. I called attention to the development of the problem, much as I have above, and suggested that there were "three contributing factors": (1) the emergence of a radical theological viewpoint, with intimations that those who disagreed were hopelessly out of date, a viewpoint which as a tiny minority–for example, one Professor--might have been contained; (2) a basic distrust of the Faculty on the part of some, as not intellectually equipped to discern issues or else not spiritually competent to deal with them as a Christian fellowship; and (3) inadequate leadership on the part of President Stealey, who was in ill health and seemed confused about what to do concerning the controversy.

I closed my discussion by indicating that in this situation I welcomed help from the Trustees and suggesting that the Committee take time to talk with each member of the Faculty individually. I believe that they did so, if not at that particular time, then later.

Somewhere along the way, I think it was in the 1961-1962 session, two Trustees who lived in North Carolina (both of whom are now deceased) came to the campus and requested of the President that he circulate a carefully phrased questionnaire to members of the Faculty individually, a crucial question of which asked whether the Faculty member believed that a radical theology was being taught by one or more members of the Faculty. President Stealey acceded to their request, though he later indicated that he had made a major mistake in doing so.

The answers revealed that the Faculty was split into two groups, about equal in size, one group answering affirmatively and the other negatively. Most of the doctoral degrees from northern schools were held by Faculty members answering affirmatively and it was especially galling for some of us who did so to be known as fundamentalistic in spirit, since we had always prided ourselves as being somewhat liberal in the Southern Baptist context.

In 1963, with the controversy still unresolved, Dr. Stealey retired as President of Southeastern Seminary, effective July 31. He was succeeded by Dr. Olin T. Binkley, who had been a member of the Faculty since the beginning of the school and had been the first Dean of the Faculty since 1958. Educated at Wake Forest College, Southern Baptist Theological Seminary, and Yale University, receiving the Ph. D. degree from Yale in 1933, Binkley was uniquely fitted for his role in saving Southeastern Seminary in the Bultmannian Controversy and for his continuing work as administrator.

Not only did he have impeccable educational qualifications; Binkley also had a background of experience which augured well for his future as a seminary administrator. Upon receiving his Ph. D. at Yale he had become Pastor of what came to be the University Baptist Church of Chapel Hill, 1933-1938, and the last two years at Chapel Hill he had been a Lecturer in Sociology at the University of North Carolina. From there he had gone to Wake Forest College, where he served as head of the Religion Department, 1938-1944, and from Wake Forest to Louisville, where he taught Ethics and Sociology at Southern Seminary until he moved to Southeastern in 1952.

In each of these three places, Binkley had served with marked distinction, receiving the highest praise from students, colleagues and others who knew him. There was no doubt about his impressive gifts: he had a brilliant intellect, intense respect for scholarship, convincing skills as a teacher, a profound humility, sincere piety that easily communicated itself to others, a pastoral way of seeing persons and situations, unusual qualities of loyalty, confidentiality, friendship, and much more.

Some of us felt very keenly that the only hope for resolution of the crisis was Binkley's election as President. On a rainy evening I drove to Greensboro to impress upon a Trustee whom I considered a friend that Binkley simply must be elected. It turned out that Binkley was the unanimous choice of Faculty and students to succeed Stealey. Probably, my trip was unnecessary.

Before I left on sabbatical leave for India in July of 1963, and after Binkley had been elected but before he had officially become President, he worked out a scheme which he thought would satisfy both sides in his new administration. Binkley proposed that Pope Duncan become Vice President with responsibilities for publications, public relations, and alumni affairs, and that I become Dean. Both Duncan and I agreed to this arrangement. Binkley elected not to take a written poll of the Faculty on this question, nor to ask for a public decision. Rather, he called members of the Faculty to his office individually to give their assent or refusal of his proposition directly.

The results were quite surprising, certainly to Binkley. All of the Faculty members on my side in the controversy agreed to Binkley's proposal. All of the teachers on the other side refused to approve the proposition because they insisted that Duncan should be Dean, in spite of the fact that President Stealey had committed to Duncan and John Steely "especially the work in recruiting of students and in supervising publications" as of November 1, 1962, at the resignation of Ben Fisher as Administrative Assistant.

I interpreted what certain members of the Faculty had done as a rejection of me as Dean and an expression of a somewhat jaundiced view of the work designed for Duncan. Though Binkley, according to my memory, never broached the matter of the Deanship with me again, Duncan indicated to me his disappointment with what his compatriots had done to him. Later that year, Duncan resigned to become dean of a community college in Brunswick, Georgia. Shortly thereafter he assumed the Presidency of Georgia Southern College at Douglas. This launched him on a distinguished course as a college administrator which issued in his service as President of Stetson University from 1977 until his retirement in 1987 and assumption of the office of Chancellor.

Meanwhile, Faculty members knew that as early as 1961 the Trustees had raised questions about the teaching of three New Testament teachers, Briggs, Oliver, and Strickland. According to a press release of the Trustees after Brigg's resignation, which appeared in the *News and Observer* February 18, 1965, the Board had begun a "process of inquiry and counsel" on February 15, 1962, which was to be completed by February 18, 1965, three years in the future.

According to this press release, Briggs met this deadline

by choosing to resign rather than to continue in this procedure. Therefore, on October 19, 1964, he had met with President Binkley and arranged for his resignation to take effect January 2, 1965. He was afforded two years of salary and fringe benefits, an action which the Board defended for reasons that Brigg's resignation was conditioned upon it, that he was a full Professor with tenure and with no plans for immediate employment, and that they and the Administration wished to be just and generous. After teaching for a year at the Divinity School of Vanderbilt University as a visiting Professor, Briggs became a member of the Faculty of a consortium of theological schools in Atlanta, Georgia, where he finished out his teaching career in the 1980s.

Harold H. Oliver resigned in the summer of 1965, to accept a position on the Faculty of the School of Theology of Boston University.

In spite of my plea to him to remain in his teaching post at Southeastern, William C. Strickland resigned in 1966, to become head of the Department of Religion and Philosophy at Appalachian State University in Boone, North Carolina. Two years later, he became Dean of the College of Arts and Sciences of that University, a very responsible position which he retained until his retirement in the 1980s.

Simultaneously with Briggs, Denton Coker, Professor of Religious Education, resigned to follow Duncan as Dean of the community college at Brunswick, Georgia. Later, he became President of one of the colleges in the University of Georgia system. He ended up as Assistant to the Chancellor of that system.

Eventually, and for various reasons, one by one the other Faculty members who had sided with Briggs, Strickland, and Oliver, except for two, resigned and left Southeastern. The fact that these two Professors continued until death or retirement is testimony to the rigorous efforts to maintain academic freedom at Southeastern until the final tragedy which overtook the school in 1987.

Binkley steadfastly refused because of the "strictures of confidentiality" to discuss Brigg's resignation beyond what was said by the Trustees in their press release of February 18, 1965, namely, that Brigg's resignation was at his own initiative and was accepted with regret. Briggs himself spoke to the press at least twice,* insisting that he resigned not at his own initiative but at Binkley's and for two reasons: a protest by several Professors of the use of historical critical method by Briggs, Oliver, and Strickland, and "deterioration of faculty morale and interpersonal relationships."

As I stated to a professor at another school who knew both men, how one interprets this resignation depends in part upon whom one believes. I prefer to believe Binkley, although I do not thereby impugn Briggs's truthfulness, for which I have considerable respect. It is entirely possible for two persons to remember and interpret the same event differently, especially if they are complex personalities, a category in which I would put both Briggs and Binkley.

Now for some summary statements: (1) I repeat that the controversy was not about the use of historical criticism in anyone's teaching of Biblical interpretation. Never, in my almost twenty years as a Faculty member at Southeastern, have I heard any teacher suggest that this method be abandoned or even criticized.

(2) There was a certain Messianic quality about the Bultmannian theology, at least as we experienced it. We heard overtones of Bultmannian Messianism at other schools, but I am only concerned with what we confronted at Southeastern. At the end of the controversy, President Stealey, perhaps overemphasizing my role, remarked to me that I had "stopped the juggernaut," albeit with methods which he would not have used. Though he did not specify those methods, I took his words at least as a recognition of the Messianism we faced.

Though Southeastern Seminary became identified as a Bultmannian school, I believe that Briggs himself did not intend to be Messianic. It was natural, possibly inevitable, that he accept the defensive wall which was thrown up around him by certain Faculty members and students. As I have indicated, there was a unique confluence of factors which made for what some of us sensed as a Messianic movement or an academic imperialism at Southeastern: a weak and disabled President who could not ad-

---

*According to press releases in *The News and Observer*, December 30, 1964, and *The Raleigh Times*, February 24, 1965.

equately deal with the problem; an increasing stridency on the part of the sizable body of fundamentalists within the Southern Baptist Convention; and a strong move, especially in our part of the Convention's territory, to resist this harshness.

(3) There was the problem of academic freedom involved. Naturally, for a Professor to be called in by a Trustee Committee and questioned about his theology, and then to resign under pressure, would connote to him and to others that his academic freedom had been infringed. Particularly, when communication broke down, some would conclude that their theology was threatened by an unwillingness, even on the part of colleagues, to tolerate their theological convictions.

On the other hand, there was the belief of several members of the Faculty, of whom I was one, that the presence of a radical theology with which the school was becoming identified was itself a serious threat to the academic freedom of all us who taught at Southeastern.* The educational enterprise to which we had committed ourselves with great hope and enthusiasm was mortally imperilled. In other words, the dream of progressive theological education in the most favorable climate for it in the territory of the Convention was seriously threatened.

Beyond this threat was the specter of a school where one theological viewpoint dominated. I have said more than once that I was against a reducing of theologies to one, even if it were mine which came out on top! I simply believe that theological education cannot be done well in a situation of less than theological pluralism.

(4) I am convinced that by the insightful and diplomatic actions of certain Trustees and Administrators, chief among them being Olin T. Binkley, Southeastern Seminary was saved from a far greater catastrophe than it actually experienced. Along with Faculty members, they put careers and identities on the line and endured considerable misunderstanding and calumnies from

---

*In the midst of the controversy, at President Stealey's behest, I produced a paper on academic freedom in the denominational seminary. My paper was later published in several of the state Baptist papers. For example, it may be read in the *Religious Herald* (the Virginia paper), February 14, 1963.

those who should have been their friends. By their heroic efforts the life of the school was spared for about another quarter of a century. They had no way of knowing that a far greater threat was lurking just over the horizon and that well before the century was over their beloved school would be captured and its character radically changed for the worse.

(5) In similar fashion, it was remarkable that our controversy, which lasted for about five years, did not receive more attention by the press than was actually the case. Of course, if our school had been older and better established, such lack of notice would have been more difficult. Even so, the fact that the press was not consulted speaks well for the restraint which was exercised by all those involved, on both sides of the controversy. Of course, it is not a matter of surprise that at the end there was a flurry of press activity, some of which was encouraged by faculty members resigning.

This relative lack of press coverage is all the more remarkable in that Southeastern Seminary, unlike other Southern Baptist seminaries, was in such a small town. For the most part, Faculty members had children in the same schools, were members of the same Church, shopped at the same stores and in many cases had the same neighbors. Inevitably, the families of Faculty members from both sides met each other and their mutual friends in the course of their normal activities.

(6) With all the painful memories which this recounting of a tragic experience has resurrected, it is pleasant to remember that even in an atmosphere of distrust and division, in which the Faculty was divided into two opposing camps, with few exceptions the canons of civility and decency were observed by colleagues on both sides of the controversy. Of course, there were great strains upon fellowship. Not more than one or two Faculty members and very few Administrators were able to maintain real neutrality. But, in spite of reports to the contrary, courtesy never failed us, and we never stopped speaking to each other. I believe that this fact has a positive word to say about Christian character under stress.

Finally, the controversy was over, though it had overtones for many years. Certainly it marked its major participants for life —I know that it has left its permanent scars upon me. I felt that for the first time I had experienced the rupture of a Christian fellowship, and that I could do nothing to stop it. In fact, in retrospect, I think that perhaps I tried too hard. Nothing I attempted would work; conversely, whatever I tried seemed to make matters worse.

If I had it to do over again, would I react differently? Honestly, I do not know. For good or for ill, I acted according to my character. Let's leave it at that.

Chapter Sixteen
FAMILY AND PATIENTS

As I have indicated, a prime motivation in our return to the States from /Japan was concern for Joy's health. We had known vaguely of Duke University Hospital and Medical School in Durham, North Carolina, and had hoped that we could get the kind of help we needed there. If so, since Durham was only about 22 miles from Wake Forest, we would not find it necessary to continue the long trips to Baltimore.

However, we were hardly prepared for what we found when, very soon after arriving in Wake Forest, we took Joy to Duke. There we met Dr. Lennox Baker, a physician who, we learned, was quite renowned in the field of therapy for cerebral palsy patients. After examining Joy, Dr. Baker indicated that she should by all means be admitted to the "State Cerebral Palsy Hospital," which was on Erwin Road, close to Duke Hospital. For the first time we learned that such a hospital existed, that it was in Durham, and that Dr. Baker was its Medical Director!*

You may be sure that Joy was admitted to this special hospital right off. She was to stay there for a year, her second grade being taught by teachers who came to the hospital each week day during the school year. Louise and I, and her sisters, visited her every Saturday, taking her out for a picnic in a city park or for lunch in a nearby café if the weather indicated. She made her adjustment with a minimum of problems, better than did her parents, and she did well with her school work and her exercises. We have nothing but praise for that hospital.

In the middle of her year there, Dr. Baker operated on her foot, to lengthen the heel cord and to relocate some muscles on the top of her foot, after which she received some physical therapy. From that time on, Joy has not needed a leg brace, and she walks with a very slight, almost unnoticeable limp. Dr. Baker did not do surgery upon her arm because he thought that surgery

---

*Dr. Baker became quite prominent in Republican politics. A few years ago he died and the hospital now bears his name.

would accomplish too little. Years later, when she was taking a Master's degree at the School of Social Work at Chapel Hill, she had two operations for cosmetic purposes at the hand clinic at Memorial Hospital of the University of North Carolina. This surgery improved the looks of the hand but not its usefulness.

I was inordinately proud when our son was born on November 9, 1958. We named the boy John Luther, for both of his grandfathers as well as for his dad. Like me, however, he was not a junior, though we added some confusion by calling him "Luke," a nickname by which I was known by my family and most others who knew me in my growing up. Our son was sometimes called "Little Luke" to distinguish him from me.

To demonstrate my exuberance at getting a son, I wrote a letter to a friend capitalizing on the choice of a Pope at about the same time as Luke's birth. In that missive I allowed that I had built a fire in our fireplace, sent the proper smoke signals up the chimney and then announced in a loud voice, *"Habemus filium!"*-- which is, being interpreted, "We have a son!" (Instead of the *"Habemus Papam!"*--"We have a Papa [or Pope]!"--of the Roman Catholic Cardinals announcing the election of the Pope.)

In addition, when certain missionary friends in Japan sent me a huge paper fish (a carp), I hung the thing on a pole at the back of our house on Boys' Day, a Japanese holiday. This act conformed to Japanese custom, but it also caused bemusement on the part of neighbors and most others who saw the strange object flapping in the breeze.

All his big sisters liked to dress Luke as a girl and pretend that he was indeed of the feminine gender. He cooperated in this charade, I presume because he was not old enough to know better. I must admit also that his beautiful blond curls made him an appropriate object of gender confusion. When people began to mistake Luke for a girl, I decided that something had to be done. So I took him to my barber and had the curls cut off. I think Luke was two at the time. I still get flak about this decision from Luke's sisters and from his mother as well, though I cannot imagine why.

Luke was an adorable child, always even-tempered and cooperative. His large blue eyes and his natural honesty and innocence added to his charm. We were surprised to learn from his first-grade teacher that he had used some "profanity" at school. When the teacher questioned him he readily admitted that he had used a "cuss-word." What happened was that when threatened by a fellow first-grade student, who, we were told later, was a bully, Luke had told the boy that if he did not stop, "I'll beat the hell out of you!" Since he was always big for his age, he looked as though he could back up his threat all right! And more has been expected of him in school and otherwise, than is justified.

It also turned out that he had a special gift for writing letters and expressing gratitude, a gift which stood him in good stead when his parents returned to Japan in 1976, leaving him to take his last year of high school, not to mention college, alone.

Becky (Rebecca), also, was a very charming child. Louise and I decided long ago that we did a much better job of parenting Becky and Luke than we did the earlier three. After all, the first three were born in intervals of about two years, while between Beth and Becky there was a little over five years. No doubt when Becky came along, we were more relaxed and had less parental anxieties and uncertainties than before, because we had already practiced on the other three.

Becky tended to be an extrovert, an athlete, and a tom-boy, though she says that she learned how to hit a ball from Joy, who, of course, could only ise one arm. When Becky was little, she was something of a monkey, climb-ing most anything around, including the outside of the long staircase of our Wake Forest house which she ascended while still a toddler. When we dis-covered her, she had caught her head between the last step and the second floor, from which perilous position I had to extricate her. She frightened us even more when as a toddler she escaped from our house and was found running down the middle of the busy South Main Street on which the house fronted.

Also, unlike their older sisters, the youngest two of our five children had no particular problems with Wake Forest. Luke was born while we lived there, and Becky arrived there as a tiny baby. Judy, Joy, and Beth were 9, 7, and 5, respectively, when we came there from Japan. The drastic change of cultures was most dif-ficult for Judy. For about a year she used to cry at night when we put her to bed and berate us for bringing her and her sisters from their home in Japan to such an unfamiliar and unlovely place. Her memories of Wake Forest are more negative than those of Joy and Beth, although her classmates, for whatever reason, were more accepting of her than were those of these two sisters who were nearest to her in age. Judy was always introspective, intellectual, and absorbed in her own world.

Like most other places, Wake Forest was cliquish, and our children never seemed able to break into the major clique. It probably did not help that they moved to the Southern United States at the time when the racial crisis was at its most crucial, that they had never learned racial prejudice, and that their parents identified with African Americans in their struggle for justice. Joy not only suffered from exclusion, she also became the butt of cruel jokes because of her handicap. Though we have forgiven them, it is difficult to forget the cruelty of some of her masculine classmates.

Two or three years later, as I remember, the atomic bomb scare resulted in a sort of bomb shelter craze in America, of which Louise and I made light. In fact, we found unappealing the idea of shutting even neighbors out of our shelter. However, this fad seemed for a while to penetrate our culture, perhaps affecting the schools.

So we were somewhat touched to discover that our daughter, Beth, who at the time was in the third or fourth grade, had tried to make a haven for our family out of the dirty basement of our Wake Forest home. She had taken from the kitchen bottles of water and items of food, such as slight portions of loaves of bread which were as yet unused, and had hoarded them on the masonry wall under the house to create a cache that might see us through a crisis.

It was during the years at Southeastern, also, that Louise became dissatisfied with her role and the way I had handled it, and that we worked out the matter in ways that were good for both of us, certainly for me.

Although I had tried since the beginning of our marriage to be deferential to her, the truth was that I was oriented to male sexism and that I was more fixated on my own distinctiveness than hers. Therefore, I had found it too easy to take advantage of her compliance and I had done so in several ways. In addition, I was by nature and upbringing very reticent about expressing affection to others (I don't remember ever seeing my father and my mother kiss each other), whereas she had been influenced by a family which was at least normally demonstrative for folks in our culture.

Louise had no problem about the primary role of care-taker within the home while the children were still around. When they entered school, however, she began to look for outside em-ployment. While Luke was still in kindergarten, she had a day-care center in our home for one year. Then she became a teach-ers' aide in the local elementary public school for a session.

In spite of her major in home economics and her prev-ious teaching experience, Louise did not want to take up teaching again. Happily, she ended up deciding upon social work as a vocation. For her to commute from Wake Forest to Chapel Hill to take a Master of Social Work (MSW) degree at the University of North Carolina, she would need to travel NC 98 to Durham, which was a dangerous road upon which she had already suffered an accident. Therefore, for her sake, as well as for the benefit of the older children, we decided to move to Raleigh.

Soon after we came back from Japan, I had renewed my interest in hunting and had taken up rabbit hunting as a hobby. A student had given me a young female beagle of mixed breed, so I commenced hunting on Saturday with some fellows who lived north of Raleigh, and I soon bred my little hound, whom we call-ed "Brownie," to a pure bred beagle. We kept one of the pups and the children named him "Tubby."

After we moved to Raleigh, we procured another dog which was half beagle and bred her to Tubby. She and the pups seemed not to be good rabbit dogs, so I gave them away, and we were left only with Tubby and his mother, Brownie. In Raleigh, we kept them in a pen which I had built in the edge of the woods behind our house.

These dogs represented the only problem worth men-tioning that remained between Louise and me. She had told me more than once that I loved the dogs more than I loved her, a charge which I had always dismissed as ridiculous. Nevertheless, her resentment was well founded: I had pretty much left her with the responsibility of care for the home and a growing family, and the dogs were a symbol of my neglect.

Illustration No. 39
The Family, Not Long after the Move to Raleigh
(From Left, Back Row: Becky, Beth, Judy, and Joy
Front Row: Me, Louise, and Luke)

I had already given up hunting for a number of reasons. Certainly I was influenced by a wife and children who took the side of the little animals and wanted none of them killed. Of some relevance was my own developing sense of environmentalism. As i have said previously, I suspect that I was affected by the sabbatical year in India, where I had a great deal of contact with vegetarianism, on the part of Hindus, many of whom were negative toward meat eating, and of Jains, all of whom are strictly against partaking of any meat products, even eggs. In any case, I was already on the way to becoming a vegetarian, though the trend did not come to fruition until several years later. Even so, I still had two dogs, Brownie and Tubby.

Louise had combined her social work study at Chapel Hill with assuming responsibility for my dogs while I was gone most of the time on my sabbatical leave in Chicago for the school year, 1969-1970. After completing my sabbatical leave in 1970, I was scheduled to conduct a tour to Japan in connection with the Baptist World Congress and the International Exposition in Osaka, and I had already engaged people to accompany me.

Louise, who had taken a job as a psychiatric social worker at Umstead Hospital in Butner, North Carolina, told me in no uncertain terms that she felt that I should make the tour but that she would not take care of the dogs while I was gone. I am sure that this ultimatum carried some of the baggage from the long simmering conflict between us, for which I must assume almost sole responsibility.

Perhaps there was some pique involved on my part, though I do not remember it. After all, it is likely that I could have arranged for someone else to take care of the dogs, but getting boarding care for the beagles seemed out of the question, given the stringency of our budget. In any case, according to my memory, the only option I saw was to have the dogs put to sleep.

Surely it made sense to bring a merciful end to Brownie's life, but Tubby was another matter. Brownie was about 15, a ripe old age for a hunting dog. She had developed an abdominal tumor which almost reached the ground. Tubby was two or three years younger but had contracted some disease, maybe distemper, that had sapped his vitality to some degree, though he had otherwise recovered.

When we were on our way to the vet's for the final solution, Tubby almost disintegrated me by reaching across the back seat of the Ford station wagon in which we were riding and affectionately licking my arm. Perhaps he thought we were going hunting. I patted his head and begged for his understanding. My own background involved putting dogs down when they were no longer useful for the purpose for which one kept them.

My vet had no scruples about putting Brownie to sleep, but he let me know that he saw no reason why he should bring an end to Tubby's life. At my insistence, however, he agreed to inject both dogs with the lethal drug.

So the last remaining major obstacle to my relationship with Louise had disappeared, in so far as I carried my share of responsibility for the family and house work (which I have not accomplished very well). Nevertheless, this episode is very vivid in my memory, and I have carried some guilt, especially concerning Tubby, through the years.

In countless ways, Louise has been of inestimable help to me. Specifically, she has enabled me to release my inhibitions against showing affection to her and to other persons, and she has helped me accept in practice as well as in theory that women are in every way equal to men. Her feminism has had considerable influence on me. I had expressed more truth than poetry when I wrote to a counselor soon after our marriage quoting someone whom I have long since forgotten that Louise "was better by nature than I was by grace." Not only has she shared with me a similar vocation, she has always manifested utmost respect for what I feel called to be and to do. It has been a joy in more recent years to reciprocate by encouraging her to achieve or to continue what she most eagerly desires.

Meantime, we had our problems in having to deal with mental patients before either of us had adequate knowledge or experience. First of all, there was the Japanese scholar who had come to see me at Rüschlikon, Switzerland. I had heard no more from him after that meeting and actually had been absorbed in other things and had largely forgotten about him.

Imagine my surprise, then, one night in early December of 1957, after we had been in Wake Forest about a year and a half, to receive a telephone call from the Raleigh/Durham Airport, informing me that there was a Japanese gentleman there who expected me to come and meet him. I assumed that it was the fellow I had encountered in Rüschlikon, and of course it was. He reminded me that he was to spend Christmas with me, adding that at that time he was to undergo an experience of transformation into a new life.

When we were entering Wake Forest in my automobile, he asked me if I could hear music. The radio was not on, and of course I told my friend, whom I shall call "Tanaka Jirō," that I heard nothing. He said that he certainly could hear music, and he proceeded to inform me, also, that he was distressed because on the plane coming from Europe, voices were beamed at him from the public address system and that he did not know how to answer. I knew that something abnormal was afoot but I did not know yet what to do about it.

Since we had students rooming in our house, and the Christmas vacation at Southeastern Seminary had not yet begun, before I had left Wake Forest for the airport, I had hastily arranged for a guest room at the Seminary for my Japanese visitor. Therefore, when we arrived home, I stopped only briefly, and then took Mr. Tanaka to his room. I knew he was tired, and I suggested that he sleep as long as he wished. Surely enough, he slept much of the next day.

We were somewhat surprised in midafternoon, however, when he appeared at our door with his bags, informing me that he was going to sleep on the sofa in our living room. Also, he proceeded to reproach me for putting him in a room which was specially wired so that voices could be directed at him. I assured him that I had no intention but to offer him the best hospitality possible, that I had no knowledge of special wiring and voices, and that of course he could stay with us, since our roomers were soon to leave for Christmas.

By then, I knew beyond any doubt that I had on my hands someone who was delusional. When I sought the counsel of the specialist in Pastoral Counseling on our Faculty, he told me that Mr. Tanaka was not only delusional but possibly dangerous as well, particularly since we had small children in the home. Moreover, said my colleague, Mr. Tanaka's assertion about some transforming experience at Christmas might actually be a subtle way of talking about suicide.

When I asked my physician in Wake Forest for help, he told me that he would be quite willing to aid me to get Tanaka committed to Dorthea Dix Hospital, the State mental institution in Raleigh, but that this would involve a legal procedure. Thinking that such an action was too traumatic to impose upon my friend, I considered it no further.

Finally, I decided to take the bull by the horns, and try for a voluntary admission to a psychiatric ward at Duke Hospital. In order to arrange it, with considerable reluctance, I had to make use of a delusion of grandeur which Tanaka had shared with me. He had told me that he was to be the center of some important medical experiment at Chicago, where he had previously studied, sometimes representing himself as the director of the project, sometimes as the guinea pig. I suggested that he need not wait until arriving in Chicago to begin the project, since there were well-known medical authorities at Duke. Mr. Tanaka was quite interested and agreed with me that he needed to consult with these famous doctors at Duke.

I decided it was better not to inform Duke Hospital ahead of time but to have Tanaka admitted as an emergency patient. Fred Sandusky, the kindly Registrar of Southeastern Seminary, offered to accompany me on this unusual mission, and I took him up on it.

So the three of us appeared at the admissions office at Duke Hospital to get Mr. Tanaka admitted, or as he understood it, to prepare for his great experiment. Though I tried to be guarded in what I said to the admissions officer, there came a point where I had to use the word "psychiatric," at which time Mr. Tanaka briskly departed from us!

When this development occurred, Sandusky told me that I had as well give up and call the police. But I wanted to make one more attempt. So the two of us went outside and soon found Mr. Tanaka waiting for us. He put me on the spot by saying, "I think of you as my pastor. What do you intend to do with me?" I assured him that I aimed only to do what was best for him, and I said further that I was embarrassed because he had let me down when I was trying to make arrangements for him to enter Duke Hospital for his great experiment. Then he readily accompanied us back to the desk.

My nervousness and anxiety increased markedly when I learned that there had to be a preadmission interview by a psychiatrist. I had no idea how this procedure would go. The young doctor who did the examination first of all asked Mr. Tanaka to tell him about the voices he was hearing. "Voices?" asked Tanaka. "What voices? I don't know what you are talking about." My anxiety just about reached the boiling point. Then the psychiatrist called me aside and said, "He's pretty cagey, isn't he?" I said "Indeed, he is!" I hope the psychiatrist didn't hear my sigh of relief!

So Mr. Tanaka was admitted. They gave him whatever treatment was given mental patients in those days, including electric shock therapy. They also afforded him the most economical rate possible and kept him several weeks. With his cooperation, his travelers checks were used as far as they would go to defray his medical bill. In addition, at my request, the Dean of the Divinity School of the University of Chicago, who was a friend of mine from Mars Hill days, used money his school was holding for a scholarship for Mr. Tanaka to finish paying his medical bill at Duke. Finally the Hospital released Tanaka, with the psychiatrist saying that though he was much better, he could not be completely cured until he returned to his own culture.

I brought Tanaka back to our home, but obviously he had no intention of departing for Japan. Then we discovered that our troubles had only begun. Mr. Tanaka would periodically disappear, on at least one occasion departing from Wake Forest by bus, leaving us with no clue as to his whereabouts. In that instance we were called by the President of Duke University and informed that our Japanese charge was in his home and would we please come and get him.

I spent just about all the hours when not in my classroom trying to get Tanaka back to his own country, all the while giving most of the time I had left to the responsibilities for which I was being paid. First, I arranged for a letter from Tanaka's psychiatrist to the effect that he was no danger to anybody but himself, and that he would hurt himself only if he failed to exercise normal vigilance, for example, in crossing busy streets.

Then I talked to the only major airline at Raleigh/Durham Airport at that time, the result of which conversation was that if they flew Tanaka, somebody would have to accompany him. I even made a trip to Washington, to confer with personnel at the Japanese Embassy. I found, to my surprise, that the Embassy would assume no responsibility for Tanaka whatsoever. At the same time, I talked to the folks at Japan Airlines; they were very nice but told me that Mr. Tanaka would have to be accompanied to Japan, for which cause, I had neither the time nor the money.

Finally, I decided to quit being so scrupulous in what was obviously a desperate situation. First, I procured a generous offer from the Presbyterian Board of Foreign Missions, which had brought Tanaka to the States initially, to pay for his return ticket to Japan in spite of the fact that he had disobeyed this agency and left McCormick Seminary in Chicago to study in Europe.

Next, I contacted the immigration authorities at Norfolk, Virginia, and arranged for one of their agents to meet us, though this official insisted that the conference should be in Durham, not Raleigh. He was very frank with Tanaka, telling him bluntly that he could not hope for recovery in this country. He said further that if

Tanaka left the States voluntarily he could get a visa to return later if he wished, but that if he elected not to go back of his own accord, the immigration authorities would surely deport him, in which case he could never visit the United States again. I thought that Mr. Tanaka took seriously the brutally frank words of the immigration agent. He finally seemed ready to cooperate with me in getting back to Japan.

Accordingly and finally, I called Japan Airlines in Washington (being afraid that I would be recognized at the local airport), and got reservations for Tanaka to Tokyo one way and for me to Seattle and back. At the same time I sent a wire to Tanaka Ichirō, Jirō's older brother whom I liked very much, informing him of his brother's arrival and asking Ichirō to meet him in Tokyo. Also, I called Tanaka's psychiatrist and got a prescription of a tranquilizer for his patient and instructions to try it out on the trip to Seattle. So we drove to Washington in time for our plane. When we boarded, I gave Tanaka a dose of the prescribed medication, and surely enough, he slept all the way to Seattle.

As we drank coffee in the airport restaurant in Seattle, Tanaka told me that it was ironic that he had defended America during the War, when it was costly to do so, and that he had always taken the part of my country when its defense was called for in Germany. "Now," he lamented, "the country that I have defended at some personal sacrifice is forcibly expelling me from its borders." His words made me so sad I could hardly keep from crying. As I write this I still feel their poignancy.

Although I saw to it that he took another dose of medicine before departing Seattle, I was still concerned at a point or two. For one thing, Tanaka did not know it, but my plane departed for Washington a few minutes before he took off for Tokyo. Another source of anxiety was the fact that his plane stopped for refueling in Anchorage, Alaska.

As I walked with him to his gate, I noticed a Japanese gentleman carrying a brief case. I sidled up to him and, out of hearing of Mr. Tanaka, told him that my Japanese friend had recently been sick and that I was afraid that if he got off the plane at Anchorage, the cold night air might not be good for him. Would he please try and prevent his deplaning until they reached Tokyo? This Japanese gentleman seemed pleased to be asked, in Japanese, to assume this responsibility, and he assured me that he would take care of my companion. So I told Mr. Tanaka farewell at his gate, saw him board his plane, walked leisurely until I was out of sight and then ran to catch my own flight to Washington. I returned home safe and sound if utterly fatigued and much older!

As if one mental patient were not enough, in the autumn of 1962, I was made responsible for another, an African from Liberia in West Africa. This fellow, to whom I shall assign the name, Hugh Stanley, came to Southeastern as a student in the fall of l962, sent by the Baptists of his country.

You may know that Liberia was formed by the African Colonization Society before the Civil War and that it has in its population people of African American background as well as Africans whose forebears had no American experience. Hugh Stanley, though living out in the bush, was of African American extraction. As it turned out, it is likely that he never should have been sent to America, since it was too much of a traumatic experience for him.

Stanley had the misfortune of arriving in the town of Wake Forest by bus while the Faculty were away on a weekend retreat. It appears that he was mentally ill when he arrived, for he was found sitting on the street of Wake Forest in a catatonic state. The Business Manager of the Seminary, who reluctantly took charge of Stanley, had him put in the town jail for the night, where the guards removed all his belongings, including his belt and any other items they considered possible instruments of suicide.

Afterward, he seemed to think that the authorities in Wake Forest took his money from him, though he also spoke of being betrayed "by his own people," which led some of us to assume that he had been robbed in New York by fellow blacks before he reached Wake Forest. In any case, the Administration of Southeastern, when we returned from the retreat, sent him to the mental hospital for blacks in Goldsboro, in keeping with the segregated system of mental health which still existed in North Carolina at that time. Also, before he left the country, the Administration refunded some of his money, rather than having him think that he had been relieved of it in the jail.

After treating him for a few weeks, his psychiatrist decided that he was ready to return to Liberia. The Foreign Mission

Board, SBC, had responsibility to return him to his country, and, since I was teaching missions, I was chosen by Dr. H. C. Goerner, Secretary for Africa, Europe, and the Middle East at the Foreign Mission Board, to accompany Stanley to Liberia.

I was also to see as much of the Board's mission work in western Africa as possible while I was at it. Since by that time it was early December and nearly Christmas time and I certainly wanted to return home in time for Christmas, I elected to see only the two countries of Liberia and Ghana, missing Nigeria.

To prepare for accompanying Mr. Stanley, I visited him in Goldsboro and was somewhat relieved that he related to me filially and referred to me as "Father." Although I had hoped that he could have a meal with us in our home in Wake Forest, the psychiatrist strictly forbade it, saying emphatically that Mr. Stanley must not go back to Wake Forest but be taken directly to the Raleigh/Durham Airport.

Since Stanley and I had several pieces of luggage, and since we had to transfer planes in Washington and even airports by helicopter in New York, I had visions of Stanley escaping from me in one of these places. However, he proved to be an ideal passenger, fully cooperative. The only problem was that although the plane trip took a long time, more than one day as I recall, he absolutely refused to urinate. I marveled at his bladder's capacity since he drank everything offered him. I even took him with me when I visited the men's rooms, but he never relieved himself.

I learned that he had anxieties about being reunited with his wife, afraid that he would be impotent. I assured him that his impotency was probably due to his medication and that no doubt everything would be all right when he returned to his home. In spite of my assurances, however, he still did not urinate. Since he was whisked away at Roberts Field in Monrovia, Liberia, I never learned any specifics about how he fared, though I was told later that he recovered. Dr. William Tolbert, who was then President of the Liberian Baptist Convention and Vice President of Liberia, along with his wife,* gave a sumptuous dinner on my behalf and sent me happily on my way.

---

*After he became President of Liberia, both Dr. Tolbert and his wife were killed in a violent overthrow of the government.

Dr. Goerner had instructed the missionaries in Liberia and Ghana to roll out the red carpet for me. So they proceeded to use the time well. The male missionaries in Liberia, Adrian Coleman of Ricks Institute in Monrovia, John Carpenter of a place south of Monrovia, and William Mueller, a new missionary, rented a small plane in Monrovia, and accompanied me on a trip that included most of the mission points in the country. Thus these three missionaries were afforded an opportunity to visit Nimba, a steel mining area on the back side of Liberia where Mueller and his wife were to be located.

When we boarded the plane that morning, the high mogul of the rental company emphasized that since the small airport had no lights, we must budget our time so that we could get back to Monrovia before dark. The problem was that our American pilot, like Windy Blankenship's mule* didn't give a damn about anything. When we stopped for lunch, our pilot excused himself, saying that he had friends at the Episcopal Mission. We saw no more of him for about three hours, at which time we were already far behind schedule.

When we took off from our last stop, which was Nimba, it was already getting dark. Soon the pilot began to cuss his own airport and especially Roberts Field, the large commercial airport which served Monrovia, saying that he could not get in radio contact with Roberts Field and that this was nothing new, since they were utterly inefficient. It turned out that something was wrong with the compass on the plane, and before long it became apparent that we were lost! It was a moonlit night, and we watched what we could see of the terrain below us. My eye lit upon the two fuel gauges and could see that they were getting

---

**Haven't I told you about Windy Blankenship's mule? Windy was a character about whom Pop told various stories. One of them was that Windy once had a mule who was blind. He traded him to a fellow, who later complained that the animal was unable to see. When he turned him loose in the pasture field, said the new owner, the mule walked into a ditch. Whereupon the mule scrambled to his feet and collided with a fence. Concluded the man with some indignation, "That mule is blind!" Windy responded, "Oh no, that mule ain't blind. He just don't give a damn."

dangerously low.

Fortunately, my companions were looking below at the right time. One of them happened to see the beach as we headed out over the Atlantic Ocean. "Isn't that the beach?" he asked, as he pointed toward the white sand, and our pilot admitted that it was. He veered the plane back toward Monrovia, saying that he could now see the lights of Roberts Field.

Actually, what the pilot saw was not Roberts Field, which was not even visible, but the lights of Monrovia itself. He was on the other side of the city from Roberts Field, which, if my memory serves me right, was about 30 miles down the coast from Monrovia, which indicates how far we were off course. The pilot soon got in touch with his own airport in the city and they positioned an automobile and instructed him to come in by its lights. So we landed without mishap and the loquacious pilot quickly made himself scarce and I never saw him again.

One of the missionaries remarked that if one of us had not seen that beach, the males of the Liberian Baptist Mission would have been wiped out along with one Baptist missions professor from the States. As usual, I got pretty scared, but only after some time had elapsed.

Soon I left Liberia for Ghana, where it was the middle of the dry season, and I ate a lot of dust as I went by bus to a far inland mission station, Nalerigu, where I visited with a medical missionary and his family. The missionary was Dr. George "Footsie" Faile, one of my classmates at Mars Hill. I gave a devotional message at Faile's clinic, but the most memorable occasion of the trip to Ghana was a visit to a Chief's compound near Nalerigu, where the very impressive Chief lived, surrounded by several houses for his numerous wives. I was told that only once did he visit the coast, and that when he saw the Atlantic Ocean he said, "I wonder what happens to it when there is a *harmutan*?" (meaning an arid wind off the desert)

With an uneventful flight back to Raleigh, I returned home in time for Christmas, 1962.

Chapter Seventeen
GETTING AWAY: SABBATICALS

I was due to have a sabbatical leave in 1962-1963, which would have saved me from the episode with Hugh Stanley, but I found it expedient to delay it for a year, at the Administration's request, because of the resignation and coming marriage of a colleague in the same teaching area as mine. I have already mentioned this wedding, that of Professor Emily Lansdell and Visiting Professor Jesse B. Weatherspoon. I was assured by the Administration that deferring my sabbatical for a year would not result in a penalty; in other words, my second sabbatical could begin on schedule except for a year later.

Before I found it advisable to cancel my sabbatical plans, I had been given the status of alternate for a Fulbright grant for a project in the Philippines. The next year, 1963-1964, I was fortunate enough to receive a Fulbright Research Grant for India, the provisions of which were very generous. Not only did I receive travel and other expenses, but also a liberal stipend for living costs for me and my family. Although travel for the family was not covered, we were able to buy one way air fares to India via Europe, and then to save up money in India from the living stipend for the sabbatical to purchase plane tickets for the rest of the journey around the world.

Salaries at Southeastern were notoriously low, but the sabbatical policy was remarkably beneficent in that these study leaves provided for a calendar year during which time the Seminary paid full salary.

On the way over, we Fulbrighters had a few days of orientation in Washington, D. C., a time for the family to do a great deal of sightseeing. The orientation was quite helpful, but about the only thing I remember concerning it is that the lecturer was quite witty and kept us entertained with his jokes. Among other funny things, he told us that when he first heard someone talking about the then President of Egypt, Nasser, he thought the speaker was discussing NASA with a Kennedy accent.

Then we stopped in Oxford, England, where we visited with John and Judy Durham; in Germany, where we stayed about two nights with Jim and Eda Stertz and their children; in Greece, where we met my colleague Elmo Scoggin and his wife Hannah on their way back from a sabbatical in Israel; and in Israel, where we stayed one night with Lee and Sarah Bivens.

In England our oldest daughter, Judy, made a famous remark suggesting a new understanding of the death by burning at the stake of some of the martyrs in the early Protestant Reformation: "Probably they were warm for the first time," said Judy. (Our visit was in July but the weather was chilly and drizzly, and at that time Judy was quite cold-blooded). In Greece, Luke, our youngest, then 4 years of age, greeted "Uncle Elmo" with the serious inquiry: "Did you ride your tractor from Wake Forest?"

Thanks to the generous provisions mentioned above, I was able to afford the family a splendid intercultural experience. Even Louise profited greatly from the venture, in spite of the fact that she was very busy with the care of the children and of the household. Judy, our oldest, was 16 and in eleventh grade, Joy, 14, was in ninth, Beth, 12, was in seventh, Becky, 7, was in second grade and Luke,4, was a preschooler. Through various methods, including taking school texts with us, using the curriculum provided for high school students by the University of Nebraska, and some home teaching by Louise, each of our girls was able to advance normally in her respective school in Wake Forest.

In addition, we were able to afford an Indian experience of education for each child: Judy took some courses in a junior college for girls on the campus of the Banaras Hindu University where we were living, Joy and Beth took arts classes in a Hindi language girls' school, and Luke and Becky attended a Hindi elementary school. All of us had a number of Indian friends.

Also, we enjoyed the companionship of an American family from Oregon, Peter and Lannie Hurst and their children, also living on the Banaras Hindu University campus. Peter, who has since died, was a Jewish medical doctor paying his own way and serving in an Indian hospital in Banaras. We also had contact with students from various countries of the world.

For a few days we were put up in an International Guest House, during which time we consumed considerable quantities of goat curry and vegetables and permitted our stomachs to adjust to Indian food, which gave us all dysentery (called "Delhi belly") for a few days. Then we moved into a bungalow on the campus of Banaras Hindu University where I was attached to the College of Indology (Indian Studies). The bungalow was spacious, all on one floor, with concrete floors and thick walls made of brick overlaid with stucco outside and plaster inside. There was a large front yard and a rectangular court yard in the back. The move involved bullock carts and we rented some basic items of furniture, such as beds and chairs.

The house had been occupied previously by an American A. I. D. family who obviously had been provided a much better income than we. Unlike them, we could not afford the usual American amenities. We had no air conditioning or refrigeration and our cook stove was a crude charcoal affair. In spite of the fact that it got pretty cold in the winter months with a little frost for a few nights, we had no heat except for a portable Perfection kerosene heater. We had running water but not hot water, though we had an electrical unit which we could submerge in a tub to heat water for baths. Our oldest daughter, Judy, and I prided ourselves on our cold showers, the only difference between the practice of the two of us and that of most Indians was that these latter showered at a public spigot with most of their clothing on.

At first our lack of modern appliances was a source of some disdain on the part of our domestic helpers, of whom there were several. We soon learned that the employees of the family who had preceded us expected us to take on those who had worked for them as well. Although we had given little thought to the matter, we certainly did not intend to hire *that* many. Nevertheless, when it became apparent that they were depending on us, we overcame our scruples and employed them.

All at once, then, we had a Muslim cook and a sweeper and his wife who were full time, and a part time laundryman and gardener. All except the cook were Hindus from various divisions of the outcastes, or "Scheduled Castes,"* as the Indian government classified them.

---

*The term is from what we may call the "affirmative action" program of the Indian government by which certain seats in the national and state legislative assemblies and designated scholarships in government universities were reserved or "scheduled" for outcastes.

The sweeper and his spouse and their cute little baby boy soon moved into vacant servant quarters in our compound, since the sweeper alleged (maybe it was a pretext?) that a rain had washed away their mud house. As you may have guessed, the sweeper and his wife kept the premises fairly clean by using brooms.

The laundryman was turbaned and otherwise wore a *dhoti*, a typical Hindu type of apparel which I always thought of as a glorified diaper. He got our clothes very clean (if they could bear up under it) by beating them on a stone, and he pressed them with a huge iron fueled by charcoal.

The gardener always seemed to have a problem with Luke. In fact we considered that his actual age was that of a child, although according to his chronological age he was in his early middle years. He was very careful of our potted plants, which he kept outside.

Our cook, Abdul, was a remarkable fellow. He was illiterate but able to converse acceptably in English after we had adjusted to his unusual sentence structure. He had a pretty good English vocabulary, but he threw together the English words which he knew, according to his native tongue, Hindi. Though he probably was older than we, he called Louise "Mama" and me "Daddy." He was scrupulously honest. He shopped mostly in the Muslim quarter where he lived, taking with him enough money, given to him by Louise, to pay for the groceries. When he returned he would always insist that Louise write down the price of each item that he had bought. Thus he would give an accounting of every rupee that he had spent.

It was also a considerable advantage that he was a Muslim, since we were meat eaters in those days, and he could get water buffalo meat for us in the Muslim quarter. We also procured water buffalo milk, which Louise pasteurized and gave to the children to drink. Since Abdul could interpret English into Hindi, and since he was a Muslim and not an outcaste Hindu, he was a natural for head employee. Abdul seemed to enjoy giving instructions to our other helpers, who proffered him considerable respect.

Abdul cooked very acceptably, on our rudimentary charcoal stove. I remember especially the beef (water buffalo) roasts we had and the baked vegetables accompanying. For the great Muslim festival, Id el Fatr, following the fasting month of Ramadan, Abdul and his wife had us come to their humble abode across the city for a sumptuous meal. His devotion to us was a very humbling experience. He spent one night about every other weekend in his own home, doing his traveling by bicycle. When we left India Abdul very much wanted to come to the States with us (he said nothing about his wife accompanying him), having no idea of the complications which his living in the States would involve both for him and for us.

What our helpers did for us at Christmas was quite touching. Over the strenuous protests of the gardener, we had brought in a shrub for a Christmas tree. On Christmas morning we were awakened by some noise outside, and "what to our wondering eyes should appear" but streamers of gardenias and jasmine flowers adorning our entrance way, from the gate bordering on the street to our front door. Then our employees came in to put a garland of these same flowers around the neck of each of our family members. Since they did not share our Christian faith, obviously Christmas meant little or nothing to them. But they knew that it was important to us, so they did what they could to make it meaningful. We were profoundly moved.

In Banaras travel was a problem for us since we had no car. We soon learned that we would have to depend mostly on bicycle rickshas, and our family required three, so we used what resembled a ricksha train! Indian men are notoriously lascivious, getting their garbled knowledge about American women from our movies. In addition, although Joy and Beth were quite young, 14 and 12 when we arrived in India, they were large for their ages and looked rather mature.

Therefore, we had to have a regular--and dependable--ricksha driver to take Joy and Beth to school, so we employed Abdul's nephew, Munowar, and provided for him a cycle ricksha. From his meager income, he paid us back a certain sum each month, with the result that when we departed we left him the vehicle. Munowar was delighted to be ready to go into business for himself as a ricksha driver.

I found it expedient to purchase a bicycle, particularly because I had to make frequent trips downtown to do banking

business, and downtown was about 2 miles away. Since I had
often coveted but never possessed a bicycle as a youth, I had
never really learned to ride the vehicle. For a while, until I knew
my way around, I was quite a hazard to the life and limb of
Indians as well as myself when I sallied forth on my bicycle.

In the entire city, which was strongly Hindu but had a
pretty sizeable Muslim minority (about 30%!), there was no Baptist
church and only two English services, one Methodist and the other
Anglican. Since the time of the Anglican service was the much
more convenient of the two for us, it was in the large cathedral-
like structure of the Anglican Church that we worship-ed each
Sunday morning.

This particular Church was pretty conservative, being affiliated with the evangelical Bible Churchmen's Missionary Society
(BCMS) rather than the regular Church Missionary Society which
was the Low Church Anglican society as contrasted with the High
Church Society for the Propagation of the Gospel. With both of
these two older societies I had been long acquainted through my
study of missionary history. I encountered the much more recently
organized BCMS directly for the first time.

Although the British missionary, who seldom visited, was
very conservative, the minister himself was quite open and we
very much enjoyed his Biblical sermons. He was a graduate student at Banaras Hindu University, an Anglo-Indian (half Indian and
half English), and a very personable bachelor by the name of
Peter Day. He welcomed us to communion, which the Anglicans
celebrate each Sunday, receiving the elements while kneeling at
the altar, though he inquired about Becky, who had been baptized
the year before. Luke, of course, not yet being baptized, did not
take communion.

During the few months we were in Banaras, I was invited
to preach twice in this Anglican Church and was honored to ac-
cept (I was permitted to preach but not to read the Scriptures!).
We became much more familiar with the Book of Common
Prayer than previously and came to appreciate the beauty of its
English.

All of us studied Hindi, though we adults always were
conscious of the fact that we would not be in India long. In any
case, the younger the children, the more easily they picked up the

language. Often Becky served as our interpreter, sometimes to our chagrin, as for example the time we hired a two-wheeled carriage pulled by a very small, scrawny looking horse to convey us somewhere. Being able to converse in Hindi, Becky positioned herself by the driver. Not until that afternoon when he brought some horses to our house did we realize that Becky had engaged him to let her and her siblings ride the horses! Of course, unwittingly we had committed ourselves through Becky, and we had to pay for the rental of the animals. It appeared that from a very early age Becky loved horses!

Illustration No. 40
A Horse Carriage in India

The poverty of India in the mid-1960s was almost overwhelming. Never had we encountered such raw human misery. We were frustrated because people who worked in welfare told us that we must never give to beggars since that kind of naive giving only served to perpetuate the beggary system. Even children were sometimes crippled so that they might be more effective in seeking charity. At first we were anxious because we feared that we were not responding adequately to human need. Then we worried that we were becoming too calloused.

In the servants' quarters of the Professor's bungalow next door lived a family of a Scheduled Caste. Their little girl, perhaps 11 or 12, liked to play with our children, and she usually brought her little brother, Ramji, with her. Ramji was quite pathetic. He was well over a year, certainly old enough to be crawling, if not walking. Actually, he could not even turn himself over. He seldom cried and he never smiled. His eyes were dull and listless. Louise and the girls decided something had to be done about Ramji. So Louise got a bottle and fed him milk, and an eye dropper and administered vitamins. She gave him a bath and exchanged his rags for clean clothes.

Then Louise realized that she had not asked his mother's consent, so with some trepidation she took Abdul with her as interpreter and went to see the mother. To her profound relief, the mother was very grateful. So there began a custom that the big sister brought Ramji to our house every day for his feedings and baths. It was remarkable to see the change that came in a few months. I wish you could see the before and after slides!

Before we left India Louise taught the mother how to do the same for her little boy, and when we departed Louise gave her a supply of powdered milk and vitamins. Since the parents were illiterate it seemed impracticable to try and keep up with them. But we have often wondered about little Ramji, the smallest child of our family. Did he live to become a man? If so, what kind of man? If Ramji survived, he would be almost 40 by now.

I am sure that subconsciously we were comparing India to Japan and expecting to find some familiarity. At first, almost always when we saw an Indian face, we wanted to speak Japanese. At least this was the case with Louise and me. However, we soon discovered by experience that India was as different from Japan as both were from the United States.

For one thing, whereas Japan was a highly collective and homogeneous society, India was communitarian--made up of many diverse communities--and was competitive to the point of individualism. For example, though both Japan and India have their own musical traditions which differ significantly from each other and from the music of the West, the Indian tradition, unlike that of Japan, rivals that of the West in its complexity. However, whereas the Western classical music majors on harmony--symphony orchestras are fairly typical--the Indian tradition emphasizes individual performance and friendly competition between players, certainly not harmony. Although I am not a musician, I have discerned this much about Indian music.

Another point of disparity between Japan and India was the degree of secularization. Superficial reactions are quite hazardous, but I have always thought of Japan as being rather thoroughly secularized, especially in the academic circles where I lived and moved and had my being. And the Japanese people, unlike the Indians, are highly educated.

In India, on the other hand, the circle of radical secularization, like that of education, was relatively small. Most everybody was religious, one way or another. You could practically feel the spirituality in the atmosphere. Indians, in contrast to many if not most Japanese and Americans, really liked to talk about religion. I always felt that Indians were somewhat puzzled by nonreligious Americans. You did not have to agree with Indians about religion. In fact, they rather expected disagreement. What most of them seemed to appreciate was the expression of profound religious conviction without overt attempts to convert, a pattern into which I fit rather comfortably.

Still another way in which Japan and India differed was in the degree of candor with which they expressed themselves. Japanese people are quite reserved and tend to be introverted, while Indians are frank almost to the point of rudeness. In other ways as well the two cultures are very unlike.

For a good reason which I do not now recall, my family and I, upon our arrival in Banaras, were met at the airport and conducted to our temporary living quarters, not by Dr. A. K. Narain, Principal of the College of Indology (Indian Studies) to which I was attached, but by Dr. Netarwala, the Principal of the College of Mining and Metallurgy of the Banaras Hindu University.

The Netarwalas were Zoroastrians, and Mrs. Netarwala was an accomplished concert pianist. She knew Western classical music well. She was delighted to have someone listen with appreciation to her playing, in which Indians usually had no interest. Dr. Narain, with whom I came to have most cordial relations, was a Buddhist. These facts illustrate, though very inadequately, the religious diversity of India.

In fact, India was and still is a remarkable laboratory of living religions. It has been a fertile breeding ground for religions, though each of these indigenous expressions has had difficulty escaping the all-absorptive effects of Hinduism, the religion of something like 80% of Indians. Hinduism is itself indescribably diverse.*

Buddhism developed in the Hindu milieu almost six centuries before Christ, became rather strong in ancient India, and launched successful missionary campaigns to the south and east by which it became the great religion of Eastern Asia. It seems to have died out in India only to be reintroduced in modern times, but it has remained a small minority movement.

Jainism, likewise, was born in ancient India, probably before Buddhism, and has been almost entirely confined to India. Partly because of its rigorous asceticism, it has never claimed more than a small minority of the Indian people. In the fifteenth century, Sikhism emerged as an impressive attempt to combine in one religion elements of Islam and Hinduism.

In addition, in spite of the partition of India at the time of independence in 1947 into India and Pakistan (West and East Pakistan, which, as the result of a later civil war, became Pakistan and Bangladesh, respectively), the latter being a country expressly created for Indian Muslims, India still ranks fourth in size as a *Muslim* country, behind Indonesia, Bangladesh, and Pakistan, in that order. Even so, Muslims, though the largest religious minority in India, are not so sizeable in the vast population of India. Islam, of course, was not born until the seventh century after Christ. It came to India from outside, especially due to successful military campaigns which it waged during the Middle Ages, and converted many Indians, largely by force.

According to tradition, Christianity has existed in India since the missionary work of the Apostle Thomas. Even if one

---

*The population of India at the time of writing is more than one billion, second only to China. This means that Hinduism, mostly confined to India and immigrant Indian communities outside India, is third among world religions in number of adherents, with only Christianity and Islam having more members.

does not accept this tradition as valid--and I am more and more persuaded of its authenticity--Christianity certainly entered India quite early. This ancient Indian Christian Church, affiliated with Eastern Christianity, has been augmented in more recent centuries by missions, both Roman Catholic and Protestant.

In addition, Zoroastrians found refuge in India in the eighth century, during a time of Muslim persecution in Persia, where the Zoroastrian religion had been founded in pre-Christian times. They are particularly prominent in the Bombay area, where they are known as Parsees and constitute a tiny minority. Also, one can find Jewish communities in South India which claim to date back to the time of Solomon!

All of which is to say that for the scholar of religions, India is an intriguing laboratory. Even in Hinduism, though the context is quite different--and the context is very important—one can find most of the expressions of religion which are seen in the world religions. A Hindu philosophy professor even argued with me that Indians did not need to study other religions, since what the various faiths teach and practice can be found within the great storehouse of Hinduism.

In the philosophy department of Banaras Hindu University, I audited a course in Indian philosophy (the philosophy of the great Hindu, Sankara) taught by the famous T. R. V. Murti, and in the College of Indology I audited a course in early Buddhism led by a young Hindu scholar by the name of Mishra. In addition, I developed fruitful contacts with scholars of Jainism and Sikhism. My major emphasis, however, was on the reading of sources on Hinduism and secondarily, Buddhism. On my frequent visits to the University Library, at 10:00 a. m. I stood at attention with other teachers and students when hymns were recited in Sanscrit (which I did not understand) from the ancient Hindu Scriptures.

Dr. A. K. Narain, Principal of the College of Indology, invited me to give four lectures on Comparative Religion in December, 1963. Having accepted, I then had considerable trepidation about what should be the topic of my lectures. Happily, I think, I decided to lecture about the discipline itself. This relieved me of the burden of getting into differences of the various religions among those who knew some of them much better than I. My topic was especially propitious in light of the fact that Dr. Narain was eager to establish a Chair of Comparative Religion in his College, where the subject could be treated as religion and not as philosophy as was usually the case in India.

The lectures were held in the College of Indology and attended by teachers and graduate students from that College and from the Department of Philosophy. The position of moderator of these lecture sessions rotated, and I was somewhat amused to discover that the lecture given by the moderator was usually longer than my own lecture! My method was to close a lecture early and then invite questions and comments.

On one occasion, either the third or final lecture, the moderator was a female Associate Professor who was a devout member of the Ramakrishna movement within Hinduism. She put me on the spot by asking if Dr. E. A. Burtt, a famous American professor of philosophy of religion, was justified in converting from Christianity to Buddhism. I replied that I did not know Professor Burtt personally, but that of course he had a right to put his trust in any religion he chose. Then she asked if I thought it beneficial in general when a person converted from one religion to another. When I asked whether she wanted me to respond as a scholar of comparative religion or as a person of faith, she said that whichever I chose would be all right.

I answered that since my lectures gave my viewpoint as a scholar, I would try to state my view as a Christian. I said that I suspected that everyone in the room felt that it would be beneficial for others to share his or her particular religious viewpoint. I indicated that for me Jesus Christ is everything, and I certainly wished that everybody shared my faith in him.

After the period ended, several of my hearers, including Dr. Narain, came by to apologize for the moderator, and interestingly, from that time on, I felt rapport with various Buddhist, Hindu, and Sikh scholars, some of whom came to my home to discuss religion with me. The female Hindu teacher who had been my moderator invited me to give a lecture in the local service commemorating the centennial of the birth of the great Swami Vivekananda, the "Apostle Paul" of the Ramakrishna movement.

This is but one illustration of the fact of my experience that Indians profoundly respected the expression of religious conviction as long as it did not lead to grabbing them by the collar in attempts to convert them.

The University published the lectures as a small booklet in 1964, some copies of which I still have. Besides that publishing venture, I submitted an article to the *Journal of Church and State* at Baylor University on the development of Neo-Hinduism. It was published in 1967. Quite apart from these modest attempts at publishing, the sabbatical year in India was extremely valuable. It has influenced my teaching and writing profoundly ever since, perhaps more than I am aware.

At last it was time to leave. Dr. Narain had already felt me out about remaining in India to set up a Department of Comparative Religion in his College of Indology. If Southeastern Seminary had not been in crisis, I might have taken him up, for I found his suggestion very appealing. I already knew that there were no such departments in Indian universities, where religion was taught as philosophy. If you wanted to find it treated as religion in India, you needed to look to Christian theological seminaries. To stay in Banaras, where I could give a Christian witness in the very heart of Hinduism, not as a professional missionary but as a Professor of Comparative Religion, exerted a strong pull indeed. Had I stayed, I would have learned not only Hindi but also Sanscrit. But it was not to be, for I gave Dr. Narain no encouragement.

After leaving India, I heard that Dr. Raymond Panikkar, who was much better qualified than I for this task, had accepted the invitation and established the Chair of Comparative Religion at Banaras Hindu University. Dr. Panikkar is a Roman Catholic, son of a Spanish Roman Catholic mother and an Indian Hindu father.

Since Banaras was already getting unbearably hot in May, I settled the family into a hill country retreat in Missourie while I took a side trip to visit Southern Baptist missions in countries in East and Central Africa for about three weeks: Kenya, Tanzania, Malawi, Northern Rhodesia (now Zambia), and Southern Rhodesia (now Zimbabwe). I returned to meet the family in Banaras, from where we began the long trek home, stopping in various places on the way back and enjoying the hospitality of Southern Baptist missionaries everywhere (except Nepal where they were not yet present). We stopped over in Nepal, Thailand, South Vietnam, Hong Kong, Taiwan, Japan, and South Korea (skipping East Pakistan [later Bangla Desh], because we had spent a few days there earlier).

In Japan we stayed for about three weeks, the first week of which was spent largely in preparation for some lectures in the theology of mission which I was to do at the Theological Department of Seinan Gakuin University (the Seminary) at Hoshiguma in Fukuoka, where I had taught before. Of course, those lectures were given in Japanese and required some extra time for preparation. Otherwise, we were for the most part visiting with friends, both missionary and Japanese, except for one week spent in South Korea, where I lectured at the annual mission meeting.

Finally, in late July, we arrived back in Wake Forest, and I was soon engaged in a busy year of teaching and involvement once more in the Bultmannian Controversy.

When we began to think of my second sabbatical, which was due in 1969, it seemed impossible to move the whole family. After all, some of the children were already in college. You will recall that two years earlier we had moved to Raleigh, and Louise had entered the School of Social Work at the University of North Carolina in Chapel Hill. In the spring of 1969 she had graduated with a Master of Social Work degree and was beginning her career as a psychiatric social worker at the John Umstead Hospital in Butner, North Carolina, for which purpose she was commuting to Butner five days per week.

In preparation for the sabbatical I had arranged to be a Visiting Scholar at the Divinity School of the University of Chicago, and had applied to the Association of Theological Schools for a Faculty Fellowship which they had graciously granted. Consequently, I traveled mostly by airplane, commuting to Chicago about every second or third weekend. The University afforded me an apartment in graduate student housing in the city, so I was pretty well set up.

I audited a course with Dr. Pierce Beaver, Professor of Missions and World Christianity, on the history of Roman Catholic missions, in which there were only three students, I believe, a seminar on urban studies with a young professor whose name I do not now recall, and a seminar on world religions with Dr. Mercea Eliade. Otherwise, I read quite a bit and worked on a

redoing of my manuscript on world religions, which I had published as a study course book in 1963.

Dr. Ralph Herring, who had been pastor of the First Baptist
Church of Winston-Salem, North Carolina, and was later head of
the Seminary Extension Department, had asked me to do the
book for a text in the Extension Department. In the meantime, Dr.
Herring died, and Broadman Press elected not to publish the
manuscript.

All in all, the sabbatical was quite profitable for my continued teaching, giving me further confidence in these three areas
of my courses. I used to joke about the utter chaos of the University of Chicago, which, I insisted, could not have existed without
somebody deliberately trying to create it. I soon gave up on trying
to detect any organization of the Divinity School. As nearly as I
could discover, there was absolutely nothing to bring students and
faculty together, no chapel, nothing. It was quite unlike anything
I had known at Southern Seminary, at Yale Divinity School, at the
Seminary in Seinan University, or at Southeastern.

And certainly there was no occasion for Visiting Scholars
to meet anybody except their own teachers. Accordingly, I did not
intrude myself into the affairs of the school--if indeed it had such--
nor into the offices of busy Professors.

The fact that the right hand of the University of Chicago
Divinity School did not know what the left hand was doing was
brought home to me in a rather striking way some two or three
years after my sabbatical year. Dr. Langdon Gilkey, who was a
Professor of Theology at that school, had been asked to give some
special lectures at Southeastern Seminary, and I found it my happy responsibility to preside at one of the occasions when he gave
a lecture in Chapel. In Chicago, I had seen Dr. Gilkey but had not
met him. At Southeastern I mentioned to him that I had spent a
year at the Divinity School of the University of Chicago and that my
closest contact had been Dr. Pierce Beaver. Now I happened to
know that Dr. Beaver had since retired (subsequently, he has also
died). However, Dr. Gilkey asked me, "Where is Pierce now? Is
he still with us?" Obviously, Gilkey knew less about his former
colleague than I did!

Some of my most pleasant memories of that sabbatical
year had nothing to do with my study. By then my mother was

widowed--my father had died in 1966--and I had taken her to Chicago where she was to stay for a while with my sister Faye, who lived in Valparaiso, Indiana, not too far from Chicago. Also, my nephew, Mike Trimble, Vernice's son, was living in Valparaiso and finishing a degree at Valparaiso University. It was a joy to visit occasionally with my mother and my sister, Faye, and her husband, Paul ("Buck") Hanna, and some of the children, as well as with Mike and Loretta Trimble and their first child, John, who was a cute little baby.

Likewise, it was quite a pleasure to drive back to Chicago with Luke and Becky, at the end of my stay there, to take them to the fine museums in Chicago, and to conduct Luke, who was 10 and very interested in baseball, to a Chicago Cubs baseball game with the San Francisco Giants at Wrigley Field. I remember well the trip back with the kids in our navy blue Pontiac Catalina. I was only 54 and quite vigorous in those days.

I got home in time to conduct a tour to the Baptist World Congress meeting in Tokyo and the World's Fair in Osaka, Japan. Though I had only sixteen people, all of whom were very nice folks, I swore off being the guide for tours. I decided to leave that sort of thing to those who really like it, and there are certainly some who do. It wore me to a frazzle, and I did not care for it at all. However, I do remember some bright spots, though I promise not to bore you with all I remember!

One impressive thing was the Baptist World Congress itself, though my tour members and I were not able to attend very many of the sessions. I was to give a major address on race relations, being a substitute for a substitute. Ted Adams, I believe, was the one who was asked to do it, and he was not able to attend. Then Olin Binkley was the first substitute, but Binkley professed to be so busy with administrative duties that he could not travel abroad. So by default, I ended up doing it.

The powers that be wanted my lecture, like all the major addresses, to be interpreted into Japanese, so I was assigned Yagyū (Fred) Nozomu as my interpreter. Since I knew Yagyū, I made it up with him that I would start out in Japanese with him interpreting into English. Then after everybody was thoroughly confused we would indicate that it was all a joke and switch languages. We did so and it went over well--I think.

Another notable happening came at the end of the tour. For some reason I had left Honolulu off the schedule, but it seemed that almost everybody wanted to stop there for a few hours. While we were in Tokyo, I had spent considerable time at the Japan Airlines office getting the tickets changed to include Honolulu. Then, with the exception of one or two people who did not wish to make the stopover, we had proceeded to Honolulu, and I had seen everybody off and arranged to catch my own flight (with my free ticket) afterward. It was late, about midnight, as I recall, and I was feeling relieved though dead tired and was leisurely making my way to the gate. Imagine my surprise to hear my name paged by Japan Airlines.

Quizzically, I went to the desk, only to be told that the economy seats were oversold but that there was plenty of room in first class and, with my free ticket, I was asked if I would mind moving up to first class. I was big about it and acceded. On the huge B747 (Jumbo Jet), I was seated alone in a whole row of first class seats. After I was served a delicious meal, the stewardess asked me if I wanted to lie down and get some sleep. When I assured her that I wanted precisely that, she took up the arm rests, afforded me a blanket, and put me down to sleep--after bringing me a glass of champagne. Being completely fatigued, I was out until we prepared for landing in Los Angeles.

Chapter Eighteen
CHANGES–MOSTLY AT SEBTS

I taught long enough at Southeastern to work under three administrations and to experience two presidential changes. My longest stint under one administration was during the years of the Presidency of Olin T. Binkley. In spite of Binkley's impressive gifts and of his indispensability for solving the difficult Briggs controversy, I have always felt that Binkley functioned much better as Dean than as President. As Dean, he worked under authority, where his remarkable gifts of keen insight, clear headed organization, and fierce loyalty were especially appropriate.

A pastoral demeanor, which Binkley certainly manifested, is better fitted to a seminary dean than to a president. It does not go over so well when characteristic of the chief administrator in his relationships with tough minded faculty members and with trustees, many of whom are themselves skilled administrators, as businessmen, pastors, or former pastors.

In addition, Binkley had a tendency toward paranoia, by which he sometimes made enemies of his friends, and the proclivity to express hope to people, directly or indirectly, for things that he could not and probably should not deliver. I was one to whom he promised certain positions, which I always took with a grain of salt, since my vocation did not depend upon anyone's word to me, even Binkley's. Others may have taken his promises more seriously.

One criticism directed toward both Binkley and his predecessor, Sid Stealey, was that they had a "Depression mentality" which caused them to keep salaries low. I must admit that I too was a child of the Depression and shared this mind set. In addition, as I have noted, I was strongly influenced by missionary salary scales.

After the Copeland/Duncan debacle, Binkley had tried to elevate John Durham to the Deanship and had ended up naming him Acting Dean and later Associate to the President, since the Faculty would not accept him as their Dean. Durham, who had taught Old Testament at Southeastern as a graduate student (Th.

M.), had returned to the Faculty in 1963. He was a graduate of Wake Forest College, Southeastern, and Oxford (D. Phil.) and was a very able fellow and a fine scholar of the Old Testament. Although a Faculty colleague who was opposed to Durham as Dean spoke of the "crisp efficiency" of his work, certain members of the Faculty were not about to approve him as Dean, partly because he was so young.

Accordingly and happily, Binkley turned to Raymond B. Brown as Dean. Brown, in the midst of a distinguished career, had moved to Southeastern from Southern Seminary in 1964, primarily because of his devotion to Binkley and McDowell. He was well prepared in New Testament, with degrees from Louisiana State University, Yale University Divinity School (B. D. and S. T. M.), and Southern Baptist Theological Seminary (Th. D.), and with experience as pastor. Brown had been minister of the Tabernacle Baptist Church in Richmond, Virginia, as well as Faculty member at Southern Seminary. When Binkley presented him to the Faculty as his proposed Dean in 1965, only a year after Brown had come to Southeastern, the Faculty readily accepted him.

Although Brown had arrived for the final stages of the Bultmannian controversy, he was known as a neutral, who had always been quite fair in his presentation of Bultmann. While teaching at Southern and then at Southeastern, Brown made it a practice to give one week to the positive elements in Bultmann and then a second week to point out Bultmann's weaknesses.

Brown himself related that while he was teaching in a downstairs classroom at Southern, he was in the midst of a lecture on Bultmann when a note was lowered to the classroom window from an upstairs room. Brown stopped speaking and retrieved the note to find on it this message: "Bultmann is O. K. with me." [signed] The Man Upstairs.

As a Professor, Brown was very well received by students. To his classroom, he brought an emphasis upon integrity, dramatic qualities, a booming bass voice, the discipline of rigorous scholarship, and a delightful sense of humor. As Dean, also, Brown manifested the same qualities. On social issues, he ventured as far to the left as President Binkley, to whom he was scrupulously loyal, would permit. In everything Brown sought to be insightful, compassionate, and fair.

However, in spite of Brown's scrupulous efforts to handle Bultmann objectively, he was associated with the "anti-Bultmannian" group at the Seminary in Wake Forest, an identification grossly unfair to Brown. His primary fault, I should think, was a large ego which encouraged his tendency to be a clothes horse. In any case, his faults were far outweighed by his assets.

During Brown's tenure as Dean, 1965-1974, along with President Binkley and other Faculty members, he was instrumen-tal in bringing a dozen or so outstanding colleagues to the Faculty. All of these teachers, including several Southeastern alumni, had graduate degrees outside of the Southern Baptist context. Thus Brown helped to strengthen the conviction at Southeastern that the Faculty should represent several non-Southern Baptist gradu-ate schools. He encouraged Faculty members and in general strengthened the academic life of the school.

Illustration No.41
Singing Bass in a Quartet
(Left to Right: Dean Brown, Professors Cook, Scoggin ,and Copeland)

What I considered Brown's only serious mistake as Dean also involved me. This misstep was his introduction of a "Dis-tinguished Professor Fund," made possible by a gift of stock from

Mr. Harwood Cochrane, a member of Tabernacle Baptist Church in Richmond where Brown had at one time been Pastor. Cochrane, who was very devoted to Brown, had developed the Overnite Transportation Company and had become quite successful and wealthy as a business man.

There were those, consistent with our tradition of Faculty equality, who opposed any such special designations as "Distinguished Professor." However, it is likely that an objective critic would admit that the criteria for selecting the beneficiaries were quite well devised and reasonable. Perhaps Brown could have escaped harsh criticism for what was clearly an effort to bolster Faculty morale, if he had not acceded to Cochrane's stipulation that Brown himself be the first of the "Distinguished Professors."

When the Faculty chose me as the initial Distinguished Professor (besides Brown) of the Harwood Cochrane Endowment Fund, I very much desired to decline. I knew how some members of the Faculty felt about this matter and in general I shared their concerns. Nonetheless, I knew that my refusal would be a profound embarrassment to Dean Brown. So I swallowed hard and accepted. Later, I helped persuade Leo Green, the next Faculty member chosen for this benefit, to take it also.

I must admit, however, that the $3,000 to $4,000 stipend each year (the amount varied according to the price of the stock given by Cochrane) was a wonderful help to the Copeland finances at the very time (1974) when our fourth child was entering college.* (I understand that after Randall Lolley became President, this Harwood Cochrane Fund, with Mr. Cochrane's permission, was quietly transformed into a scholarship for students.)

In the later years of the Binkley Administration, the President became more and more remote from the Faculty. So far as I know, his one remaining confidant was Dean Brown, a rela-

---

*We told all of our children that they could choose any college they wished, if accepted. Each of them, except Luke, who did not enter college until I had resigned at Southeastern, chose private and expensive schools, in the following order: our oldest daughter, Duke, the next, Furman, and the following two, Saint Andrews. If they had not had financial help, I do not know how we would have made it. Actually, I don't know anyway!

tionship which was entirely proper since it was within the Administration. Nevertheless, several of us remained loyal to Binkley, partly because we knew that although, like all of us, he had his faults, he was an exceptionally fine and able person, and partly because after all he was the President of the Seminary and we wished to give him our support. On those few occasions when I felt Binkley was mistaken, I opposed his policies and actions both publicly and privately.

Gradually, and especially as the election of a new President by the Board of Trustees became more imminent, it was apparent that the Faculty again was divided as in the former Briggs affair. This time, however, the alignments were significantly different. A number of those who had supported Binkley in the Bultmannian controversy were no longer committed to him, and it was obvious that a new faction had come into being that cut across the old divisions. This new group, allegedly led by one individual,* had determined that no one who was loyal to Binkley should be elected to the new Administration.

At the same time rumors began to circulate which were uncomplimentary to Brown and to the other Binkley supporters. One of the kindest of these rumors was the widely circulated assertion that no one could be elected to the Presidency from within the school. It may well be that this bit of gossip had some foundation. Certainly there was no problem in its being said if it was genuinely believed. Indeed, it may not have been wise to choose an insider. The problem was the surreptitious way in which the claim was communicated and the suspicion that it really meant that no one *loyal to Binkley* could be elected as President. In any case, it was a profound relief to some of us that we did not have to assume that awesome responsibility, especially in the light of what has happened since.

Several months before the election, Faculty members had been asked by the Chairman of the Board of Trustees to write him indicating both qualifications of a future President and the names of persons who might qualify. I had responded, suggesting the following qualifications: "(1) dynamic Christian faith and

---

*This colleague has changed remarkably, though I had predicted that he never would! In his case, I was wrong, and I am glad to admit it.

unimpeachable integrity; (2) understanding of and commitment to excellence in theological education; (3) the kind of acceptance within the denomination which makes for effective leadership; (4) truly democratic instincts and style of leadership--the quality of firmness without autocracy; and (5) a knowledge of and appreciation for Southeastern seminary, its history and traditions, its regional context, and its unique potentialities."

Because of these qualifications, especially the last, I nominated Dean Brown as my first candidate. If the Trustees felt it advisable to go outside the school, I suggested that they consider Dr. Elmer West, then in an administrative position with the Southern Baptist Foreign Mission Board.

I thanked the Chairman of the Board of Trustees for this measure of participation in the election of the Seminary's new President and respectfully urged him to permit the Faculty to react to any candidate they chose before they made a final decision. They honored this request, maybe because it was made by Dr. Randall Lolley after he became a candidate. I have no record of any other communication from the Board.

Also, so far as I know, no Faculty members or students were asked to be members of the Search Committee to select a candidate or candidates for President of the Seminary. This was in spite of the fact that this procedure had been followed recently at New Orleans Baptist Theological Seminary and was characteristically done by universities, though I believe that these latter usually include representatives of alumni as well.

When it was quite close to the time for a successor to President Binkley to be chosen, the Seminary was rocked by another explosive event: a very distinguished teacher, who had been at Southern Seminary a long time, had agreed to allow his name to go to the Board of Trustees of Southeastern Seminary as a prospective Faculty member, and they had unanimously elected him, possibly not knowing that his chief reason for agreeing to come to Southeastern was his devotion to Binkley and Brown. The bombshell was a letter from this teacher to the President, dated March 30, 1974, resigning from his position as a Professor at Southeastern before he ever embarked upon it.

He requested that his letter be shared with "each member of the faculty, each of the trustees, and with your Seminary

Council," the last of which he assumed would include students (I take it that he meant by the "Seminary Council" the Student Coordinating Council).

The principal reasons which this famous theologian gave for his resignation were the following: (1) He had been told by an Administrator at Southern (with whose administrative procedures he strongly disagreed) that this colleague was at the "serious negotiation stage" with Southeastern's Trustees concerning the Presidency of Southeastern.

(2) He had been further upset when he learned that neither Binkley nor Brown nor members of Southeastern's Faculty knew about this matter. He had concluded that persons outside the Board knew more of the proceedings with regard to the procurement of a new President than did anybody within the school.

(3) He had been told by a Trustee that there had been too much emphasis at Southeastern upon the classical aspects of theological education to the neglect of practice. To this suggestion this distinguished theological educator had taken special umbrage, because he saw it as "disruptive" and as downgrading "both the conceptual and the practical aspects of ministry."[*]

(4) Consequently, he concluded that "hidden agenda, power politics methods" were being employed by some of the Trustees in contradiction to the openness and mutuality of true Baptist polity.

This Southern Seminary Professor made it clear that the person chosen by the Trustees to be President of Southeastern Seminary (and by this time it was apparent that it was not the Administrator at Southern but rather was W. Randall Lolley) was not the issue. Instead, the problem was the procedures which the Trustees were employing. This theologian may have been a little too hard on the Trustees. If they believed the false rumors they were hearing, they probably felt that they could not afford to let the whole Faculty know what they were doing.

---

[*]On this score, I may have been the chief villain, since I was the one who had made the motion in faculty meeting that required courses, with certain exceptions, be chosen from the "classic body of divinity," that is, courses in Bible, theology and church history. I had not even included my own course in missions as a required course.

So at their meeting in May 1974, W. Randall Lolley, at that time Pastor of the First Baptist Church of Winston-Salem, was elected to succeed Olin Binkley as President of Southeastern Seminary and he accepted. Lolley was an alumnus of Southeastern with the graduate degree of Master of Theology as well as the Bachelor of Divinity. On both degrees he had the distinction of being graded with nothing but As. From Southwestern Seminary in Fort Worth he had received the Doctor of Theology degree.

In my files I have a letter from Randall, dated May 22, 1974, soon after his election as President of Southeastern, indicating his intention to be fair, firm, and friendly in working together with me and other members of the Faculty. I responded warmly, thanking him for his letter, and indicating that I looked forward to welcoming him and doing what I could to be helpful to him.

I certainly tried to fulfil this promise, even to allowing my name to be suggested to President Lolley for Dean of the Faculty, since Brown submitted his resignation to take effect with Binkley's. Then I discovered that the anti-Binkley faction were against me for their Dean. They carried their opposition to anyone who had been loyal to Binkley to the office of Dean as well as President. It was apparent that certain Faculty members by whose side I had fought what we thought was the good fight in the Bultmannian contro-versy were now against me, though they may have had reasons other than the alleged Binkley association.

So I had the distinction of being the only person who had been turned down as Dean by colleagues for the second time! Of course, it was not that I coveted the office of Dean. I simply wanted to be accepted by colleagues for a job I knew I could do. To be sure, I knew that both times I was rejected there were special circumstances, and I was greatly encouraged by the unwavering support of certain colleagues.

After this debacle, President Lolley, wisely, I believe, found it expedient to go outside the Faculty for a Dean. A committee, on which I served, drew up some regulations for the office, and Dr. Albert L. Meiberg was invited to come from Rochester, New York, where he was a Professor of Pastoral Care at the combined divinity schools of Crozer, Rochester, and Bexley Hall, to assume a similar post on the Southeastern Faculty along with the Deanship. He accepted and arrived in 1975. I was to serve only one semester under Meiberg's leadership before I returned to Japan.

From reports that I have heard, Lolley made an unusually fine President, and it was under his leadership, 1974-1987, that what came to be called the "golden years" of Southeastern's history occurred, and especially when Morris Ashcraft was Dean, 1981-1987. By that time, of course, I was no longer there.

I survived the Bultmannian controversy, which was confined to Southeastern Seminary. I have also lived through a later controversy, which involved not only Southeastern Seminary but the Southern Baptist Convention as a whole. It has affected my life very significantly. To that controversy I shall need to return later.

At the present I need to bring you up to date on what was happening with our family, and especially the move to Raleigh. I have already said that this move occurred primarily because Louise needed to commute to Chapel Hill to take a Master of Social Work degree, and that it was much more satisfactory to commute from Raleigh than from Wake Forest.

Actually, while I was occupied with the second of the Urban Seminars in Washington, D. C., Louise took responsibility for some house hunting in Raleigh. She was very fortunate to find a place in the northwest part of the city which was well suited to our needs and to our financial situation. The owner, who worked for an insurance company, was being moved with his family to Charlotte. It happened that I had preached at his church, the Hayes Barton Baptist Church in Raleigh, and since he knew me, he was especially eager to make the deal attractive financially. So, when I returned from Washington, I added my approval to what Louise had selected, and we purchased this property and moved to Raleigh in the summer of 1967.

Our new home was located in the Oak Park subdivision, less than a mile west of Crabtree Mall and south of Glenwood Avenue (U.S.70). The house was a brick veneer split level, and the lot was large and pie-shaped and wooded on the back. Since the house had four bedrooms, it had space adequate for our family, especially in light of the fact that the oldest girl was already in college and the second was entering that fall. Attached to the house was a double carport with a utility room at its rear. The flat roof over this area was a sun room surrounded by a railing and entered via a door in the master bedroom. There was ample room for me to build a fenced-in dog lot in the rear. So the property met our needs admirably.

It was from this convenient location that I commuted to Wake Forest for the rest of my tenure at Southeastern, and Louise commuted to Chapel Hill for her two-year program of studies, and then to Butner, where she was employed at John Umstead Hospital as a psychiatric social worker.

Two years earlier, Judy had entered Duke University to major in religion. There she distinguished herself, for example, by winning the freshman essay prize for her theme on Joseph Conrad's *Heart of Darkness*. After finishing Duke in 1969, she deferred for a few years her entrance into graduate schools, where she was to receive further significant honors.

In the fall of the year we moved to Raleigh (1967), Joy enrolled at Furman University with a major in sociology. When she finished Furman with honors in 1971, she entered the University of North Carolina at Chapel Hill and received a Master of Social Work degree two years later.

The younger children went to the appropriate public schools in Raleigh. Beth took her junior year at Broughton High School and transferred to Sanderson when it became available in her senior year. In 1969 she entered St. Andrews College in Laurinburg, North Carolina, for a major in English. At St. Andrews she began to compose poetry and won a senior writing award for which the school published a chapbook of her poems. After she was graduated from college in 1973, Beth followed her interest in poetry by enrolling for a Master of Fine Arts program at Bowling Green (Ohio) State University, receiving her degree in 1975.

Becky attended Martin Junior High and then Sanderson High School. After finishing Sanderson, she followed Beth at St. Andrews as an English major. Luke enrolled at York Elementary School in Brookhaven, Ligon Junior High downtown, and then Sanderson High, where he was a junior when I returned to Japan. To all of these schools in Raleigh, our children were bused. Becky and Luke were school bus drivers in high school.

When we moved to Raleigh in 1967, we visited several churches to see which would be best for our children. (Since the two older girls, Judy and Joy, were already in college, they were not involved). We finally settled upon First Baptist Church, Salisbury Street, because that seemed to offer the best youth program. Of course, it did not hurt that Dr. John Lewis, whom I had known at Southern Seminary, was Senior Minister.

It happened that the Youth Minister at that time was exceptionally good. We still believe that Beth profited greatly from that Church experience. She really blossomed, both spiritually and intellectually, and exerted a great deal of leadership, some evidences of which we knew at the time as well as observed later. There are those at First Baptist who still remember the impressive speech that Beth gave as one of the representatives of the young people on Youth Sunday. She was well on the way to becoming the splendid person she later became.

Unfortunately, about the time that Beth entered college, the Youth Minister changed, and the younger children suffered. We learned recently what we had suspected for a long time, namely, that Becky does not have good memories at all of First Baptist. During her high school years, when she needed the Church most, she was rejected by a clique and for the most part ran only with those very few young people who accepted her. Luke seems to have profited from Sunday School, but gained little from the youth experience.

This is the status of our children when we returned to Japan in 1976: Judy, Joy, and Beth were out in the workaday world, though Judy was to follow other professional interests to graduate schools later. Becky was in the midst of her college studies, and Luke had not yet finished high school.

PART FIVE
IN JAPAN AGAIN, 1976-1980

Chapter Nineteen
BACK IN JAPAN

It was the last week of January 1976, when I went back to Japan to become Chancellor of Seinan Gakuin for the second time. As I expressed it to a newspaper reporter, it was like going home again, as though my family had called, saying, "Your folks need you. Come home."

I am ashamed to say that I had mistaken the air express letter which had come from the Chairman of the Trustees of Seinan Gakuin in early December 1974, as being something having to do with the twenty-fifth anniversary of the University, which dated its organization from 1949, the year in which it was recognized by the Japanese National Ministry of Education as conforming to the educational reorganization required by the Occupational Government. I had already received from the school a watch as a token of that celebration. (Of course, as I have already indicated, the school itself was much larger and older, having been founded in 1916, the year of my birth).

Being extremely busy, I had set the letter aside and had forgotten about it until the next day. As I began to accustom my eyes to the terse Japanese of the Chairman of the Trustees, Mr. Sakamoto Shigetake, I could not believe what I was reading! The Chairman was informing me that the Trustees of Seinan Gakuin had elected me Chancellor and wished me to come as soon as possible! Louise heard me yell something unintelligible from the next room.

Of course, I responded to the letter, not giving a definite answer but asking for time to consider the offer. I conferred with the late Ted Adams, who was then teaching as a visitor at Southeastern, having retired as Pastor of the First Baptist Church of Richmond, Virginia. Ted, whom I considered a good friend, was also an experienced counselor. After listening to me very carefully, Ted surprised me by a bit of direct counseling, "Of course, you'll go, Luther, won't you?" he said. Ray Brown's reaction was similar.

In my conversations with President Lolley, I raised the

possibility that the Seminary give me an extended leave of absence, since I was due a third sabbatical--that is, that the Seminary give me the sabbatical and three more years, a total of four years, without salary--but I soon abandoned that idea as being unfair to the school as well as to me. So I simply gave up the notion of a third sabbatical. It didn't occur to me to ask for retirement at the tender age of 60. I think that John Durham, after his separation from his wife, Judy, set that precedent, retiring when younger than 60, I think. Retirement from the school, of course, would have provided certain benefits that I never received.

Knowing that a decision to accept their offer was difficult to make from a distance, the Seinan Gakuin Trustees very kindly asked me to come to the school and look the job over at school expense. I went in February 1975. When I arrived in the early morning at Haneda Airport (Narita had not yet come into being), I deliberately looked for a Japanese restaurant. Finally, I was successful, and I sat down to a typical Japanese breakfast, *miso shiru* (soup made from fermented soybeans), broiled fish, seaweed, rice, Japanese tea--the works! The food was delicious, and it was wonderful to be back in Japan. I really felt at home.

I caught a connecting flight south to Fukuoka, the city in which the school was located, where I spent several days conferring at length with the Trustees and others who might influence me to accept the Chancellorship. Although they mentioned the problems of the Theological Department of the Uni-versity (Seminary) more than once, they assured me that Seinan Gakuin (the entire school) was facing no other difficult question.

I was taken in the school limousine to Dazaifu, a town near Fukuoka famous, among other things, for its plum blossoms. The weather was unusual in that a wet snow of about three inches had fallen. It was strikingly beautiful to see the white snow, in all its purity, on the freshly blooming pink plum blossoms of which there were many. I certainly came away with a good impression, promising to give an answer soon.

Our son Luke was in the most difficult situation of any member of our family. He was in the midst of his sophomore year in Sanderson High School. The three oldest girls, Judy, Joy, and Beth, had all completed their undergraduate college studies, and Becky was finishing her first year at St. Andrews. Quite unusual for a boy his age, Luke had treasured his friendships since elementary school, and he certainly did not want to leave his many high school friends. We were aware that if he should go with us, he would have to leave home and go to a boarding high school in Kobe or Tokyo, where he knew nobody, and then back to the States for college.

We thought Luke was quite mature about the situation. "Dad, it's a wonderful opportunity for you," he said, "and by all means I think you should go back to Japan. Just don't ask me to go with you."

So, mostly at Louise's initiative, we hit upon a compromise. By this time it was near the end of March 1975. In April I would give the folks in Japan a positive answer, but since I was very scrupulous about giving the required semester's notice at Southeastern, I would not resign until the end of the first semester of that year. This would mean not only that Southeastern would be able to proceed with efforts to procure my successor but that I would have opportunity to finish my semester's work at Southeastern and make some preparations for Japan before departing about the end of January 1976. Louise, then, would stay in the States long enough to see Luke through his junior year at Sanderson and to get him settled in a place to live while he did his senior year.

If I had been superstitious, the prospect of becoming Chancellor at Seinan was not very inviting. Although the school had elected a succession of three Japanese Chancellors after my resignation several years ago, only one was reasonably healthy. The other two had resigned because of poor health, after which one had died and the other was an invalid. The last two Chancellors had been missionaries and both had died in office. Nevertheless, I notified the Board of Trustees at Seinan Gakuin of my positive decision.

Now Louise and I had to decide whether to go to Japan as appointees of the Foreign Mission Board of the SBC, as we had done before, or whether I would be directly employed as Chancellor of Seinan Gakuin, receiving a salary from the school as would any Japanese Chancellor. I sensed that the Trustees were surprised when I posed the question of accepting the office as any Japanese would, their having assumed that I would return as

a missionary. This was in spite of the fact that they had not notified the Foreign Mission Board of my election as Chancellor at all.
I interpreted this lack of notification as the attitude of the mature
Baptist institution which Seinan was. The Trustees were auto-
nomous except for certain moral ties they had with the Japan
Baptist Convention. In any case, the Trustees assured me that they
would accept me either way, as a missionary or as a straight out
employee of the school.

Again, we arrived at a compromise. We would return as
missionaries, primarily because we feared that otherwise we
would cause a breach in relationships with fellow missionaries.
Missionaries tend to be very concerned about their equality, and
it would not do for persons who were essentially missionaries to
be in some special category of employment. However, according
to our compromise, Louise would receive her salary the same as
any other missionary, but the school would reimburse the Japan
Baptist Mission for my salary.

So, in August 1975, we were reappointed as missionaries
by the Foreign Mission Board. This way we received the fringe
benefits of missionaries, including such amenities as pension provisions, medical expenses, housing, and a missionary car, while
the school got a bargain financially! What they paid me was far
less than the salary for a Japanese Chancellor.

In fact, from the standpoint of remuneration, our second
stint in Japan was much more satisfactory than the first. When we
were in Japan previously, the country was poverty stricken. In
those early post-War years, the income we received as missionaries was not much, but it was considerably more than the salaries of Japanese colleagues, though they worked fully as hard as
the missionaries and were better prepared to do evangelism in
their culture.

When we returned to Japan as missionaries in 1976, the
situation was quite different. Our salaries now were less than the
remuneration of our Japanese colleagues, which for Louise and
me was certainly more comfortable than the circumstances of
our earlier situation.

I arrived in Japan on schedule before January 1976 had
ended, leaving Louise not only to get Luke located happily but
also to take care of several other matters which proved to be quite

burdensome, such as selling my Citroën car and arranging what to ship to Japan and what to store in the attic of our close friends, Elmo and Hannah Scoggin in Raleigh. Louise's greatest anxiety was about a place for Luke to live, but finally things worked out very well.

It happened that an MK from pre-War days in Japan was living in Raleigh and teaching math at N. C. State University. I had known both this MK, Norman Williamson, and the young woman whom he later married, Lib Tuten, at Mars Hill College. Not only so, but his folks were missionaries who had lived in Fukuoka for a time and as a child he had played on the campus of Seinan Gakuin.

When Louise learned of Norman and Lib and approached them about a place for Luke, they told her that they had a basement apartment which they always rented to college students, but that they would be glad to let Luke have it instead. They had boys of their own and indicated that they would look in on our son without being substitute parents. It sounded like a wonderful place for Luke, as indeed it turned out to be. He was able to develop considerable maturity and master certain domestic tasks, such as caring for his food and washing his clothes, without having parents breathing down his neck. It was here that he was to live while he took his senior year at Sanderson High.

Becky also made a mature and, as it turned out, a life-changing decision. Without any attempts by her parents to persuade her, she chose to take her junior year in college at Seinan, provided the University would admit her to its Exchange Program. Since I was Chancellor of the school, Seinan was quite willing to admit her, though her college, St. Andrews, had no exchange relationship with Seinan Gakuin University.

So Becky enrolled for an academic year in the appropriate courses in Seinan Gakuin University's Exchange Program. Among several classes, one introduced her to the Japanese Language and another to Japanese culture. She fell in love with things Japanese and especially Japanese literature. As a result, in her senior year at St. Andrews, she made a play out of a tetralogy of Mishima Yukio's books, which in English translation is called *The Sea of Fertility*, and then she graduated in the spring of 1978 in her English major. That fall, she registered in Columbia University for

Ph. D. work in Japanese Language and Literature, receiving her degree in 1986.

I met Louise, with the two children, Becky and Luke, at Haneda Airport in Tokyo in early July, and went with them to Nojiri, a resort in Nagano Prefecture north of Tokyo, then to the Japan Mission Meeting in Amagi Sansō (the Baptist Assembly Grounds) on the Izu Peninsula and on to Fukuoka. We sent Luke back to the United States by air in time for him to enroll at Sanderson, and Becky stayed with us for the year at Seinan Gakuin University.

Before Louise and the children arrived, I lived for a few weeks in the home of the Gerald Fielders, who were on medical leave in Tokyo, and then moved to a permanent missionary residence in the Torikai section of Fukuoka, where Louise and I were to live while back in Japan, 1976-1980. (By the way, the Fielders' dog, although I fed him daily while living in their house, resented my presence and did not learn to like me.)

On my first Sunday in Japan, Pastor Kimura Buntarō of the Seinan Gakuin Baptist Church, where we had been members and I had been Associate Pastor previously, surprised me by asking the Church to vote on me as Associate Pastor without having broached the matter to me at all! Later that year he retired and the church was left in the care of four Associate Pastors, of whom I was the oldest and therefore a kind of Chairman. Of the other three, all of them Japanese, two were my former students and now my fellow Professors in the University while the remaining one, an ordained minister and Chaplain in the High School, had done his basic theological study in Tokyo.

The Fukuoka Baptist Church was without a Pastor and asked me to assume some responsibility as their missionary. So I preached for them once a month for about a year, until they welcomed a new Pastor.

Due to the attendance of members of the Faculty and Administration of the school, the Seinan Gakuin Baptist Church had the reputation of being more difficult than it actually was, so it was still without a Pastor when we left Japan four years later. This meant that I had to continue as Senior Interim Pastor until we departed from Japan. As such, I preached once a month and did Baptisms, the Lord's Supper, weddings, and the like.

Illustration No.42

A Baptism

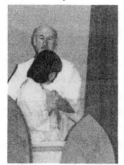

A Wedding

A comical thing happened while I was living alone and awaiting the arrival of more of the family. When I had flown to Japan, a letter had been sent by the Japan Baptist Mission, informing me that I should by all means declare un-accompanied baggage so that I could later recover shipments of freight sent to me. The problem was that this letter arrived after my departure, and when I entered Japan I had blithely declared only the baggage which accompanied me on the flight.

After a while I got word from the Mission office that some freight had arrived in Yokohama, shipped by Louise, of course. Mr. Fukuhara, of the Mission office, kindly indicated, word for word, the letter of apology which I should write and the name, title, and address of the Japanese customs official to whom I should send it. The letter included a profound apology for the trouble caused by my failure to declare unaccompanied baggage and a promise that it would never happen again. Well, it worked, and my freight duly arrived in Fukuoka.

The problem was that unknown to me Louise sent another shipment! When this second batch of freight arrived some two or three weeks later, I had the same situation all over again. Once more Mr. Fukuhara instructed me to send a letter identical to the previous one and addressed to the same official. Once more I complied, and once more it worked! If it hadn't, I don't know what I would have done.

There was another occurrence which was by no means funny at the time. My letters to Louise indicated my absorption in the work at Seinan. In a moment of understandable frustration, Louise sent a letter reminding me of the many problems which I had foisted upon her. Accordingly, I developed a severe case of unrelenting hiccups. After several days, in which a Japanese physician ministered to me with good intentions but with no discernable results, I phoned Louise with my apologies and had the privilege of hearing her calm and forgiving voice. Almost immediately my hiccups were gone.

When I had arrived in Fukuoka and made my way into the Chancellor's office, I was immediately confronted by the pictures of foreigners, American missionary Chancellors, on the walls. Actually the school had elected as many Japanese as Americans to this office, but for some reason they had chosen to exhibit only the portraits of the two Doziers, father and son, Garrott, and Copeland.

I found this deeply offensive and banished the Chancellors' portraits to a basement room where all of them were exhibited, Japanese along with Americans, leaving only the stern countenance of the founder, C. K. Dozier, to grace the wall of my office. Eventually, I added his famous dying words, "Seinan, be true to Christ!" (*"Seinan yo! Kirisuto ni Chūjitsu Nare!"*) in a beautiful exhibition of Japanese calligraphy on the wall behind the Chancellor's desk.

Illustration No. 43

At the Chancellor's Desk Flanked by Two of My Most Favorite People
(On Your Left: Shintani Nobuyoshi, on Your Right: Matsunaga Hiroko)

Although I enjoyed my second stint in Japan very much and had a good laugh at times, I soon discovered that it was not

Illustration No. 44
I Don't Know Whose Joke It Was, But It Must Have Been Good!
(With Hayashi Toshihisa)

the same as before. For one thing, both the language and the culture had changed in the 20 years I had been away. It was more difficult to fit in again. Gone was the old intense, poverty-stricken Japan, and in its place was a new, highly affluent country which was something of a contrast. I said, half jokingly, that I was glad the country was not so intense as before, since I did not have the energy I had when I was young. I am still convinced that a truly Japanese culture still persisted, in spite of the new, which was partly facade and partly something different.

The language had been considerably democratized, and as I look back on it, I am sure that my Japanese must have sounded stilted--except in the academic situation, where the old polite language was still employed. As to my use of the language in general, in spite of the many compliments of Japanese persons, some simply polite but many quite sincere, I knew better. I never reached the level of fluency I had once known, and certainly I did not achieve the promise of my former usage of the language.

Though I had to read Japanese more than ever, I felt even more handicapped than previously in the written language, especially in my writing of it. Fortunately, my three secretaries did almost all of the writing I needed to do, one after the other, Murata Yasuko, Kawachi Megumi, and Matsunaga Hiroko. Each was very different from the other, but each had her strong points and each was fiercely loyal to me. Miss Murata quit after a little more than one year to get married to Inoue Ryūta, and Miss Kawachi resigned after one year to enter Seinan Seminary. Miss Matsunaga stayed with me for the two remaining years.

Of course, not only had Japan changed in the 20 years I was away; I also had changed. In many ways I had become a different person. Outwardly, it was easy to conform to Japanese customs, not only easy but comfortable and pleasant. At a deeper level, it was somewhat difficult. I was much more confident and inclined to follow my own initiative. Even so, I succeeded rather well in conforming to the Japanese tendency to seek and to respect a consensus. It helped that I was firmly committed to democratic procedures. I had a lot of speaking to do: not only sermons at Seinan Church, but also chapel talks and commencement addresses in all the schools belonging to Seinan and the like, and entirely in Japanese.

Perhaps it was good that I was a strong person. I certainly had some difficult problems to confront, most of which the Trustees had not anticipated at the time of my visit almost a year earlier. The most vexing problem was a suit against the school by a pre-War alumnus, Shimoda Riei, who was about my age. The problem was that Seinan University was collecting sizable alumni fees from students each year that they were students, of course before they became alumni, by means of a commission collection process.* The money from these fees was used by the University to undergird the sports program and to finance the exchange program with certain American and French universities.

From the Japanese perspective, the problem was not the collection system itself. It was rather common for schools in Japan to employ it, including the Middle School and High School at

---

*This system was called in Japanese *itaku chōshū*.

Seinan Gakuin, apparently with no objection at all. The point which provoked a severe controversy was the huge amount of the alumni fees which the University thus collected. Of course, Shimoda had been graduated, not by the University, which did not even exist when he finished Seinan Gakuin, but by the pre-War professional school. He claimed, on ethical grounds, that the University was wrong to collect alumni fees from students who were not yet alumni.

I soon discovered that the authorities of the school, including the Trustees, were divided on this issue. On the one side was the President of the University, Funakoshi Eiichi, who had initiated the program. By virtue of his office, according to Japanese law, the President of the University was a member of the Board of Trustees. President Funakoshi had his followers, both on the Board of Trustees and in the University. He was one of several in the leadership of the school whom I had baptized many years previously.

On the other side were such persons as Trustee Sugimoto Katsuji, previous governor of Fukuoka prefecture and a member of Fukuoka Baptist Church. Since as Chancellor, my name was on the suit, along with that of the Chairman of the Trustees, Sakamoto Shigetake, I could not escape some responsibility. Either way I decided, I was bound to make friends and enemies. I determined that before I made up my mind, I would read all the documents I could find which pertained to the controversy, no mean task since they were all in Japanese and I was very busy.

While the controversy swirled about me, I was told that money from these alumni fees had been used to finance a trip to the States by President Funakoshi and Professor Ōuchi Katsumi the primary purpose of which was to further the Exchange Program. Professor Ōuchi, Funakoshi's close friend and English interpreter, had been a student when I was at Seinan previously. He had earned a Ph. D. in International Law from Yale University Graduate School and, like Mr. Funakoshi, was a Professor in the Law School of Seinan Gakuin University. These two denied these reports vigorously and I am convinced that they had the evidence to prove their case.

On the other side were some vicious rumors about the sexual exploits of two of the opposing Trustees. Since these reports had no relevance for the matter at issue, I never investigated them. Funakoshi and Ōuchi wined and dined me, and I believe that they fully expected me to side with them.

My position, which I finally and painfully firmed up after tedious and careful reading, was that the commissioned collection of alumni fees from those who were not yet alumni was wrong if even one victim opposed it. Of course, this eliminated Shimoda since he had graduated several years before the University came into being. However, there were some current Seinan Gakuin University students who strongly agreed with Shimoda. Obviously, unlike Shimoda, these students were themselves victims of the system. Two of them came to my office to inform me of their opposition, and one of them, a student named Ōmatsu Toshiaki, visited me several times. When Ōmatsu, who was a law student, insisted that President Funakoshi and Professor Ōuchi had used funds from the disputed fees to finance their trip to America, I suggested that he use what he had learned in his major to verify or disprove this rumor, believing that he would find it to be false.

When Chairman Sakamoto and I met with Shimoda and his friends who were members of the Executive Committee of the Alumni Association, I discerned that Shimoda was eager to settle the controversy. Unlike the typical Japanese, he was unusually frank, and I thought that as an American I could negotiate with him.

We arranged a meeting for the two of us, at which time I agreed to present his demands to the Trustees with no personal comments. A part of the agreement also was that I make no promise whatsoever as to what the Trustees would do, anticipating that the Trustees would do nothing. Surely enough, when I presented the matter to the Trustees, they elected to take no action. Accordingly, I reported this to Shimoda, and he offered to drop the suit on the basis that he had been heard--if the school would end the commissioned collection system and agree to pay him a considerable sum as a "solatium" for the loss of face that he had suffered.

When I asked him if he was not embarrassed to ask a monetary payment of his alma mater, he replied with some heat that he was not in the least ashamed. He had suffered enough, he said, for a matter that was purely ethical. I referred the matter to the Trustees and they accepted it, solatium and all.

So we discontinued the University's collection of alumni fees and ended this most difficult controversy. This did not mean that the financial support of athletics and the international exchange program ended. In fact, I was committed to both and especially the latter. It meant simply that the University had to find other sources of funding for them, which it did.

Long after the issue had been settled and Funakoshi had ended his term as President and refused on the basis of poor health to allow his name to be placed again in nomination for re-election, I learned to my surprise and chagrin that the law student, Ōmatsu, had initiated a criminal procedure against former President Funakoshi concerning the use of the alumni fees!

Perhaps this constitutes the most poignant memory I have of this second stint in Japan. This was not what I had in mind. When Funakoshi indignantly complained to me that the student should be disciplined, I refused to intervene, arguing that the matter was a problem for the new University President, Murakami Toraji, and not for the Chancellor. President Murakami elected not to take up this problem, but I learned that the student had dropped the case.

On the eve of my departure from Japan in 1980, I telephoned Professor Funakoshi at his home. He was cordial and generous and told me that he had been wrong and I had been right about the alumni fees. Already he was quite ill with cancer, and back in America a few months later I heard the sad news that he had died.

If the controversy surrounding the collection of alumni fees was the most heated, the attitude of persons related to the Japan Baptist Convention (JBC) toward the Seminary (Theological Department of Seinan University) was the longest lived. From what I hear, even now it is not fully settled. The JBC has never given enthusiastic support to the Seminary, though many if not most of the JBC's Pastors are its graduates. Part of the problem inheres in the severe controversy of educational institutions in many different nations, of which the United States is one, which happened in the latter part of the sixties and early seventies.

Students in Japan, including those at Seinan Gakuin University, were particularly difficult to cope with in those days. It seems to be generally assumed that it was this controversy that brought on the heart attack of Chancellor Edwin Dozier in 1969. Because of the charges brought by the students, the three or four missionaries and the several Japanese who taught at the Seminary suffered greatly. All of them I knew rather well. The missionaries I remembered as fellow teachers or at least fellow missionaries and the Japanese I had known as colleagues or as students.

As Chancellor of the whole school and as a Professor at the Seminary, I found various ways to contribute to the well being of this school, which was in the ambiguous situation of being at once the institution which trained ministers for the churches of the JBC and also the Theological Department of Seinan Gakuin University. For one thing, I said a good word for the Seminary whenever appropriate both at meetings of missionaries and of JBC personnel, trying to build bridges of trust from these constituencies to the Seminary.

For another thing, I helped crucially in equalizing the salaries of Japanese personnel who taught in the Seminary (Theological Department of the University) with that of teachers in other departments of the University. In this endeavor I found a doughty ally in Dr. Aono Tashio, a young New Testament scholar who came to teach in the Seminary during my second year. Soon he was elected to a crucial committee of the University Teachers' Union. From this vantage point Aono, who was appalled by this disparity in salaries, greatly strengthened my hand.

From its standpoint, the JBC could point to the fact that because of the very small number of students in the Theological Department, as compared to other Departments of the University, it was still being subsidized by the JBC, since the Foreign Mission Board's subsidy had been phased out in connection with the strong drive for self-support within the JBC (with which movement I was in full agreement)

The Convention argued further that since the Theological Department was in fact the Convention's Seminary, and since the Japanese teachers were all ordained ministers, they should be on the same pay scale with the Pastors of the Convention. A problem was that equality of pay for the Pastors was more apparent than actual. For example, some Pastors had a pastorium and some had the income from a kindergarten, in addition to their salaries.

To me as Chancellor, the stronger argument was that it was intolerable from the standpoint of the school to discriminate with regard to salaries. Moreover, I insisted that the teachers in the Theological Department would not be adequately respected within the University if they did not receive the same pay as other teachers. Eventually, this viewpoint prevailed among the Trustees, though the equality of salaries was accomplished not immediately but in stages.

The ambiguity of the governance of the Seminary remained until after I had departed. There was an Administrative Committee for the Seminary, composed of appointees of the JBC and of Seinan University, which operated independently of Seinan's Board of Trustees. Some time after I left Japan, I was told that this Committee had been discontinued, and I silently agreed.

As administrator of a Japanese school, the Japanese principle of government by consensus was quite congenial to my American concept of participatory democracy. I was happy to operate within its parameters. Two other tenets that I took seriously were that all administrative policies must be reasonable, and that a good administrator in so far as possible anticipated problems and obviated them beforehand. I believe that all of these rules were honored in seeking solutions to the problems discussed above.

In addition, there were other problems which I considered to be at the very heart of school governance and called for even more drastic action than these very difficult ones. One was that somewhere along the way, I don't remember for what reason, the Administrative Committee (*Unei Inkai*) of the school had been discontinued and the Executive Committee of the Trustees (*Jōnin Rijikai*) was functioning in its place, handling the day to day administrative affairs of the school. I did not worry that the Nursery School (*Samidori Kodomo no Sono*) and the Kindergarten (*Maizuru Yōchien*) were not represented, since their enrollments were small and each administrator was a University Professor.

The Middle School and the High School were different; each had a pretty hefty enrollment, about 600 and 1400, respectively, and each had its own Principal, quite independently of the University. The latter, on the other hand, besides the Chancellor, who was a University Professor, and the University President, included the Chairman of the Trustees, who happened to be an emeritus University Professor. All these were members of the Executive Committee whose total membership was seven, I believe. I suggested that the two Principals of the Middle and High Schools be added to this Committee, and the Trustees agreed.

Another matter was even more difficult, for it involved amending the Constitution.* As I recall, there were about twenty Trustees, of whom two had to be chosen from the Council of Deans (*Buchō Kaigi*) of the University. Although the University President presided over the Council of Deans, and both he and the Chancellor were members of the Council, the two Trustees were to be chosen from the membership of the Council of Deans in addition to these officials.

Since the Constitution also required that all Trustees be Christians, these two could not be chosen without seeming discrimination. Those who were not Christians, no matter how loyal they were to the Christian purpose of the school, simply were ineligible. I proposed that all members of the Council of Deans be eligible for election by the Council for these two members of the Board of Trustees, and that the constitutional requirement be changed so that at least three fourths of the Trustees, instead of all of them, be Christians. The Trustees sustained me and approved the amendment.

Of course, these two issues were not solved by anything like a quick vote. They were discussed several times and a consensus reached before the decision was made.

In all of these matters I had not only the able cooperation of some Trustees, including the Chairman, the late Emeritus Professor Sakamoto Shigetake, but also the help of Nakamura Yasuzō, a financial wizard who had retired as Business Manager (*Jimu Kyoku Chō*) but who was so valuable to the school that he was retained as a full-time Trustee. Not only was he a genius at financial matters, he also was able to write reasonable proposals

---

*What needed to be amended was actually the *Kifu Kōi*, the document for receiving gifts, which served as the Constitution.

in beautiful Japanese.

Until his final retirement—which did not come until close to the end of my term—Nakamura was of inestimable help to the Chancellor, and it was very difficult for me to replace him as Business Manager, especially since as full-time Trustee he occupied an office close to my own in the Headquarters Building where his counsel was eagerly sought by many employees of the school. On at least two occasions I tried to procure a new Business Manager, with the blessing of Nakamura, in one case proposing a former Seinan High School Principal and in the other a pastor of one of the Baptist churches, and in both cases I failed.

Some time after I left, the school settled upon the Business Manager of the University as Business Manager of the whole school. While I was Chancellor there appeared to be good reasons not to choose this particular individual, though otherwise he seemed the logical choice, but apparently these obstacles finally dissipated. I was very glad that at last he was selected for the broader responsibilities, though he has since retired and has been replaced.

I had determined, also, that I would do what I could to enhance the position of the female employees of the school. In the academic area, they seemed to do fairly well. At least, some of them were chosen occasionally as Division heads or even Deans of the various Departments of the University. Since at that time both the Middle and High Schools were for boys only, it appeared to be unobjectionable that most of their teachers and certainly their Principals would be men.

The major problem was with the nonacademic personnel, of whom the school had many and among whom women constituted a slight majority but were never chosen as heads of departments. When I was Chancellor, the leaders of the union of nonacademic personnel, the vast majority of whose members were women, were in favor of women's rights, and I was delighted. The problem was that the women tended to be docile and would not press for their rights. I felt that they knew I was their friend and that they appreciated me, but I never felt that I contributed greatly to alleviating their problems.

The one place where I feel keenly that I failed was in getting a Religious Center built for the whole school. Although I proposed this and got the permission of the proper authorities, including the Religious Committee for the whole school and the Board of Trustees, it was never fully approved by the Council of Deans and the University President and it foundered in the University. I insisted that I was not presenting it as Chancellor, but as Chaplain (*Shūkyō Kyoku Chō*) of the whole school, the other hat I was wearing.

To this day I still think it was a good idea and I am not sure why it was opposed. Somehow I must have failed to indicate its real nature and significance. An important part of the Center was to be a museum in which murals and artifacts would communicate the history of Christianity as it spread first of all through Asia and then in more modern times through the Western countries, especially the United States, to Japan. The history of Christianity in Japan itself is very interesting and dramatic, involving much persecution in the early Roman Catholic period. Although Christian museums can be found in Japan, to my knowledge none has such a broad purpose as the one I proposed.

I may well have made a mistake in associating the Center with the one hundredth anniversary of the birth of Dr. C. K. Dozier, the founder of Seinan Gakuin, and naming it the "Dozier Religious Center." I discovered eventually that Dozier was not as popular with the Japanese as I at first supposed, and that George Bouldin, who followed Dozier as Chancellor and took an opposite stand on the Sunday baseball issue, seemed to be more popular than I had thought.[*] It may have been unwise, also, to set forth a budget which emphasized a significant portion to be supplied by Americans, including especially the Foreign Mission Board of the Southern Baptist Convention.

Perhaps this kind of Religious Center would have been more appropriate for the Doshisha University, which was begun by a Japanese Christian (Congregational) and not a missionary, and was the first Christian University in Japan. In any case, if this proposal had been accepted by Seinan Gakuin, I would have felt it incumbent upon me to remain in Japan for a while to help compose the historical murals, though not necessarily to continue as

---

*Edwin B. Dozier, son of C. K. Dozier, the founder, also became Chancellor of the school. Apparently, he was quite popular.

Chancellor.

Although I insisted to the Trustees that I would not accept, they went ahead and put to a vote a second term for me as Chancellor. I was elected on the first ballot, although the election required a positive vote by three-fourths of the Trustees. That I was not elected unanimously reflects the fact that I had made two or three enemies among the Trustees, particularly in the controversy surrounding the collection of alumni funds and in the aborted attempt to get approval for a Religious Center.

I should also mention my teaching. In the Theological Department of the University, I offered one course, an Introduction to Christian Missions. After the first year or so, since I was so busy with the administration of the school with its many difficult problems, I begged off from teaching except for one semester per year. I remained a seemingly respected member of the Faculty of the Department of Theology and faithfully attended their meetings, as well as the meetings of the combined Faculty of the University. I certainly did not concentrate as much on my teaching as I had in the earlier period of my missionary service.

Louise was the main reason that I returned to the States for a regular furlough in 1980 and then retirement the following year. Although I had gone back to Japan with a definite assignment, she had no such clear-cut task to do. She was asked to teach one course in social work in the Department of Pre-School Teacher Training of Seinan Gakuin University. Otherwise, she had to make her own way and she soon discovered that her specialty, social work, was not well developed in Japan.

In addition, she worried about my health, since I was under inordinate pressure and did not take enough physical exercise. She still says, probably correctly, that her insistence that I quit the job added several years to my life. After all, the position of Chancellor did not have a good track record. If it improved so that its life-threatening elements have been ameliorated, I can tell myself that it is because I helped solve some of the difficult problems which so vexed its leaders or had the possibility of causing trouble for them.

Anyhow, Louise is over seven years younger than I, and she reasoned that if she returned to the States she might be able to get a job in social work so that she could continue the career which she interrupted to return to Japan with me. Fortunately, Louise was right. She was able to get her old job back at John B. Umstead Hospital at Butner, North Carolina, and to work there another five years. Since she had followed me so devotedly in my different changes of vocation, it seemed only right for me to follow her this one time. That's the major reason we came back to the States. I returned joyfully, though I was too young to retire.

However, I must admit that when the letter came from Dr. Roy Honeycutt, Provost (later President) of Southern Baptist Theological Seminary in Louisville, Kentucky, inviting me to be Senior Professor of Missions, being alone in my office at the time, I laid my head on my desk and wept tears of relief. A successor had already been chosen for me at Southeastern, and for the first time in years I was about to be without a job.

PART SIX
GRADUALLY HANGING IT UP, 1980-

Chapter Twenty
AN ACADEMIC AND HIS FAMILY

In 1980 we returned to the States for a final furlough before retirement as foreign missionaries. The retirement occur-

Illustration No.45
Louse and Me, Soon After Arrival in the States

ed on March 31, 1981, and we, along with other retirees, were honored by the Foreign Mission Board at an impressive service in the Board's offices in Richmond in October of that same year. We had been under appointment as missionaries to Japan a total of 14 years (although counting language school, furloughs and such we were in that country only about 10 years). The standard for tenure before retirement was 25 years, so our benefits, such as annuities and medical insurance, were prorated for our 14 years at 56%.

With this income, including the amount from my several years at Southeastern Seminary, with Social Security for Louise and me, and with a small pension for Louise from the State of North Carolina since her retirement in 1985, we get along surprisingly well financially. Louise worked for the State 7 years before we returned to Japan and 5 years since, for a total of 12 years. The teaching that I have done, with the important exception of Baylor University, has increased our net receipts very little, since seminaries had limited budgets and their administrators took account of the fact that we were receiving retirement income.[*]

As a matter of fact, the remuneration of missionaries has increased, as it should have, and we were pleasantly surprised that we sensed no great financial sacrifice in giving up two salaries to go back to Japan as missionaries.

In the fall semester of the 1980-1981 session, our furlough year, I was back at Southeastern as a Fletcher Visiting Professor, teaching an area course in Missions in East Asia. I believe that I had about twenty students, including two men from the Republic of Korea. I commuted from Raleigh twice a week for the class and enjoyed it very much.

Some time later I was asked to teach a summer school course on the Founders of Great Religions for Associate Students, that is, those who had only high school diplomas and qualified for courses on a junior college level. Only those whose ages made it difficult if not impossible for them to meet the requirement of a college degree before coming to seminary were admitted, except

---

[*]Of course, my teaching the first year was not on retirement income but on the salary of a furloughing missionary. Also, until 1985, Louise was not retired from the employment of the State of North Carolina.

that this age requirement was waived in the case of seminarians' spouses. These stipulations meant that there were several women in the class. Also, as usual, there were some students whose intellectual level was high.

It would not be until several years had passed and a crisis had occurred before I would be asked to teach at Southeastern again.

My teaching at Southern as Senior Professor had been deferred so that I could honor the previous commitment to teach a semester at Southeastern. Therefore, I could not begin at Southern until the spring of 1981. The late Dr. Carl Bates, who was about two years older than I, shared with me the distinction of being one of the first two nonfaculty persons to be named Senior Professors at Southern. Dr. Bates' field was Preaching. He and I began teaching at Southern at the same time, though he taught more continuously and of longer duration than I. Obviously, he secured more money for the school, for a Professorship in Preaching was endowed in his honor!

The arrangement was that the Seminary and the Senior Professor agree on the need for his or her services. Since both Dr. Bryant Hicks, as a regular Professor, was teaching missions, and Dr. Hugo Culpepper, retired and with the status of Senior Professor, was teaching world religions at Southern, there was not a pressing need for me to teach. Accordingly, I taught in the spring of 1981 and in the two semesters of the 1981-1982 session, for a January term in 1983, and again in the summer of 1984. I was not called upon for more teaching until the Spring of 1986, when Dr. Hicks was on sabbatical leave.

By that time, Dr. John Jonsson, from the Republic of South Africa, had been elected as the Carver Professor of Missions and World Religions to succeed Dr. Culpepper. Since Dr. Jonsson's expertise was in the area of World Religions, the need for my teaching was all the more uncertain. In the meanwhile, I had committed myself to teaching assignments at other schools for about two years, so I retired once more and took my leave from Southern Seminary.

During this time, to accommodate my teaching at Louisville, Louise had retired from her employment by the State of North Carolina in the summer of 1985 at the age of 62. I had already indicated that I would teach no more away from home unless Louise was prepared to accompany me.

From Louisville, after a summer in Raleigh, Louise and I went to Golden Gate Baptist Theological Seminary, where I was to teach during the fall semester of 1986. The Seminary is located in Mill Valley, a town in the very wealthy Marin County, California, close to San Francisco. The campus is on a high elevation over-looking San Francisco Bay, across the Golden Gate Bridge from San Francisco, and is breathtakingly beautiful. It is spacious and natural, just like a park, with raccoons, which visited us frequent-ly at night, especially in search of garbage, and a large herd of deer which we saw daily. The completely furnished house which was provided for us had a wonderful view.

The Southern Baptist churches which we visited for wor-ship and for missionary sermons were quite diverse, some fun-damentalist in theology but others more progressive, some with a kind of whoop-de-doo worship service and some much more staid. San Francisco itself was quite different from any place we had ever been. Faculty colleagues, especially Dr. Francis DuBose, the Missions Professor who had invited me, and Dr. Jerry Stub-blefield and his wife, were unfailingly cordial and helpful, and the students were diverse and friendly. Several people visited us. All in all we had a most profitable and enjoyable time in California.

We spent the spring semester of 1987 at Southwestern Baptist Theological Seminary in Fort Worth, Texas, a school with its own distinctive characteristics, claiming to be the largest Pro-testant seminary in the world. Dr. Justice Anderson, Chair of the Missions Department who, along with his wife, had spent many years as a missionary in Argentina, had invited me to fill in as a national professor, since they had some money in the budget for such a person. By "national professor" they meant a teacher, ordi-narily a citizen of the country, from one of the nations where Southern Baptists had missions, in my case, Japan.

Dr. Earl Martin, who had taken a Master of Theology de-gree under my tutelage at Southeastern and had done some teaching there, was also a Professor of Missions at Southwestern. He and his wife Jane had served many years as missionaries in various countries of Africa. It was a joy to be with these former missionaries as well as others whom we knew on the Southwestern faculty and still others who befriended us there and continued to visit us in Waco, Texas, after we left Fort Worth. The Seminary provided a furnished house for us and did what they could to make us comfortable.

I found the students to be more conservative than any I had ever encountered before. Particularly, some members of a class in Christianity's Relation to the Other Religions attacked me from the right. Fortunately, I had been teaching for many years and knew how to handle myself in such situations.

From Fort Worth, again after a summer spent in Raleigh, we moved south to Waco, also in Texas, where I was to teach courses in Missions and World Religions for two semesters at Baylor University. The school paid me well as a Visiting Professor of Religion and put us up in a lovely guest apartment on the edge of the campus. I had great fellowship with the folks in the Religion Department and in the University in general.

The Fielders were there, Gerald and Jo Beth, Gerald having taught for several years in the Political Science Department. John and Jean Shepard were also there, in a post-retirement situation. John was teaching Sociology as well as Religion. Both the Shepards and the Fielders I had known as missionaries to Japan, and both had taught at Seinan Gakuin University. The Fielders had left Japan because of a health problem of their daughter.

In addition, there were several persons on the faculty who were former students at Southeastern, one of whom, Dr. Dan McGee, was largely responsible for my invitation to teach at Baylor. With all of these and with new friends I had delightful associations.

Although I had wondered how I would relate to college students, after many years of seminary teaching, I found the Baylor students delightfully unspoiled, innocent, and ready to entertain new ideas. I had a wonderful time.

When I left Baylor in 1988, Dr. Glenn Hilburn, Chair of the Religion Department, urged me to stay longer, but I demurred, indicating that I had other things I needed to do (especially going through my papers and discarding many), and that I wanted to quit while people wanted me to stay rather than the other way around!

However, after I left Baylor, I agreed to teach again at Southeastern, 1988-1989, as a Visiting Professor. For the second semester I was a Fletcher Professor once more. I had been sincere in telling folks at Baylor that I certainly did not intend to teach again, but I encountered an emergency situation at Southeastern which drew me back to the classroom. Dr. Alan Neely, who had followed me at Southeastern, had accepted a position at Princeton Theological Seminary. His departure was rather abrupt, so that the Seminary had little opportunity to make provisions for his classes. So I was persuaded to teach again, especially by the importunity of the situation and George Braswell's entreaties.

Already Dr. Randall Lolley had resigned as President and Dr. Morris Ashcraft as Dean because of impossible demands by the Trustees who were now dominated by fundamentalists. The controversy within the Southern Baptist Convention (about which I shall say more later) had now eventuated in a victory for these extreme conservatives. One reason I agreed to teach was to manifest solidarity with remaining colleagues at Southeastern, who were trying to hold out against the fundamentalist takeover.

How I got approval from the powers that be to teach at Southeastern is itself an interesting story. About June of 1988, as I remember, I had been invited by the Dean to teach that fall. I kept waiting for a letter from the President newly chosen by the fundamentalists, Dr. Lewis Drummond, since I was determined that I would not enter a classroom until I had such a letter of official invitation. The weeks hastened by and still I had no letter. I had to order textbooks!

Finally, shortly before I was supposed to begin teaching, I got the letter. It was dated July 17, though it did not reach me until about the third week of August. Later I learned (though I was not supposed to know) that President Drummond had polled the Instruction (Academic) Committee of the Trustees by telephone about employing me as a Visiting Professor, and had obtained a 3 to 2 vote from them, in my favor. Fortunately, only one of them knew me, a very conservative student of several years previous (with whom I had enjoyed a good relation while he was a student), and because of the polling method he had little opportunity to influence the others against me. So I was in--by the skin of my teeth!

In the past it had been possible for the President of the Seminary to appoint Visiting Professors, but the fundamentalist Trustees who were now in control had rewritten the rules with the result not only that the Instruction Committee of the Trustees had to approve the President's recommendation but also that the employment was for only one semester at a time. This meant that I had to be approved for the second semester of the 1988-1989 session as well.

Once more I learned what had happened within the Instruction Committee, this time because the Secretary (an employee of the Seminary) who took the notes made the mistake of sending them out to each Faculty member and then, with considerable embarrassment, had to ask that they be returned! Since I was not a regular Faculty member, I did not receive these minutes, but you may be sure that friends on the Faculty reported them to me, and that indeed some of them copied the notes before they returned them.

I learned that to his credit President Drummond, who had recommended me, defended me to members of the Instruction Committee, indicating that he had known me at Southern, where I had taught as a Senior Professor, and that after all I had been a Southern Baptist missionary. Whereupon my former student (whom I have mentioned previously) declared, "You just don't know him.* You should read some of his writings. He is both an ecumenist and an anti-Southern Baptist." (Of course, I plead guilty to having been an ecumenist for many decades, maybe since childhood, and if I am anti-Southern Baptist, it is only since the fundamentalist victory. Like Will Campbell, I am a Baptist in the South, not a Southern Baptist.)

Once more, I was in by the narrowest of margins, with a 3 to 2 vote. Apparently, the reason that I and another "liberal" got by was the adverse publicity attending the refusal to welcome back Visiting Professors Mahan and Janice Siler, in Pastoral Counseling, because of Mahan's stance for the rights of homosexuals. I was torn between my desire, on the one hand, to stand with

---

*Actually, my acquaintance with Dr. Drummond, except that I knew a little about him and he about me, consisted of no more than the exchange of greetings in the hall.

Mahan and refuse the invitation to teach again, and, on the other, to continue to teach so that I could support my colleagues at Southeastern. That was the last opportunity I had to make that decision, since Southeastern never invited me again.

However, Baylor University did, a few years later. In the spring of 1992, I went back to Baylor for a one semester stint as a Distinguished Visiting Professor of Religion. By that time I was 76 years of age and had lost some of my zest for teaching. Louise and I had as friends John and Gladys Jonsson from South Africa, whom we found to be wonderful people.

As I have already stated, John had previously taught at SBTS in Louisville, where he had succeeded Hugo Culpepper as Carver Professor. Jonsson joined the Baylor Faculty in 1992, about the same time as I. He was doing the same thing that I was doing, and at least in world religions was doing a better job than I. So it wasn't the same as before. I was rather glad to hang up my teaching togs for good.

During these years, not only did I teach, but I also did some writing. Already I had published two or three books, but in retire-ment I have added to this stock. First of all, at the suggestion of Johnni Johnson Scofield at the Foreign Mission Board and Gertrude Tharpe at the Woman's Missionary Union, I wrote a sort of introduction to missions, which served as a program manual for the Missions Education Council, published in 1984.[*] It was also designed to be used by the staffs of the Brotherhood Commission, the Woman's Missionary Union, the Home Mission Board, and the Foreign Mission Board of the Southern Baptist Convention.[**] How much they have actually perused it, I have no way of knowing. Certainly, I should think it has been ignored by the fundamentalists. The next year, again at the encouragement of Johnni Johnson Scofield and this time Steve Bond, who was then Chief Editor of Broadman Press, I published a small book on missions entitled

---

[*]The official title is M[issions] E[ducational] C[ouncil] Curriculum Scope Document. Birmingham, AL: Woman's Missionary Union, 1984.

[**]The two mission boards have had name changes. They are now the North American Mission Board and the International Mission Board, respectively.

World Mission and World Survival.

In 1995, ten years later, I indulged my long existing discontent with the Southern Baptist Convention: University Press of America published for me a historical study, *The Southern Baptist Convention and the Judgment of History.* In 1999, Baylor University Press issued my book, *A New Meeting of the Religions: Interreligious Relationships and Theological Questioning,* which dealt with the theological questions raised for Christians by this new meeting. Throughout my career, I produced a stream of articles, though I am afraid the current has been reduced to a rivulet.

I have always believed that I am more effective as speaker than as writer. Perhaps this is because the personality and emotions are better expressed through oral than the less visible media. In any case, I have spoken from the pulpits of numerous churches and from various other platforms during a long ministry, and usually, I am told, with positive results.

I suppose that since retirement, the most important revision in my thinking came at the point of vegetarianism, a conviction which Louise and I had reached by the early 1990s. Previously, I have hinted that this road which the two of us chose was a rather natural outgrowth from environmentalism. The Lord knows that I was responsible for the deaths, often cruel deaths, of too many animals in my hunting days.

Our vegetarianism came about as a combination of factors, and I cannot be certain which was more prominent than the others. I am sure that health concerns had something to do with it, as did the desire to provide the world's people with food in light of the fact that a terrible waste of protein occurs with the feeding of grains to animals. I am also convinced that our turn toward vegetarianism was in part a reaction to the cruelty foisted upon animals by human beings. I am indignant at advertisements which are flippant in their treatment of food animals, as well as the exploitation of these animals on huge farms. I also believe that the strong vegetarianism of certain Indians had a crucial influence upon me as a result of the sabbatical year spent in India.

If it were not for these various reasons I might still be content with the attitude which I find in the Scriptures, especially the Hebrew Bible which we call the Old Testament, namely, that the whole world, including the animals, is sacred because it belongs to God.* Even so, foods appropriate for the Hebrews were carefully prescribed, presumably, in part at least, for reasons of sanitation. It appears that all slaughters of animals were viewed as sacrifices and that such as were permitted were to be eaten with thanksgiving.

In any case, when Louise and I are eating by ourselves we eat only vegetables, dairy products, nuts, eggs, and seafood. A recent article has reminded me that if everybody ate no meat but seafood, the supply of the latter would soon end, so we may have to give up seafood as well. We are not fanatics and we make it a practice to eat whatever is set before us. I still marvel that Louise manages to make our limited diet so palatable by her choice and creation of recipes.

Meanwhile, something had happened to the Southern Baptist Convention, with which I had identified early in my ministry. Certain agencies of the Convention had kept me in their employ through a rather long career. I had always known that theo-logically and ethically I was in a minority in the Convention, though I had assumed that I was not only tolerated by some Southern Baptists but also respected by most of those who knew me. While I was aware of certain Christian failures of the Convention, I was aware, also, of errors of my own and I respected Southern Baptists for their evangelical vigor and for the prophetic views of a minority.

A fellow missionary in Japan who pretty much shared my views asked me, for his own sake, how I could keep on serving Southern Baptists, knowing that I was at odds with a majority of them. I replied much as I have stated above, with the added assertion that I had always tried to be honest about what I believed, keeping my classroom open to any who wanted to hear what I had to say and sharing what I believed with those who asked me.

Of course, fundamentalists were very strong within the Convention and they sometimes exacted their pound of flesh, but the fact is that the situation has changed. Beginning about 1979, under the leadership of Dr. Paige Patterson and Judge Paul Pres-

---

*One finds the same attitude in the New Testament, especially in the Pauline writings. See, e.g., Romans 14:6 and 1 Timothy 4:3-4.

sler with their intention to "go for the jugular," the Convention underwent a drastic change. Astutely seizing upon a constitutional provision for presidential power to control the membership of boards of trustees of agencies, a provision which had never before been used for political purposes, and apparently employing other means which were even less scrupulous, the fundamentalists grasped control of the Convention.

People who, up until now, had been very much involved in the SBC found themselves excluded from active participation, no matter how conservative they were, unless they affirmed the fundamentalist leaders. A very large number of Baptists were thus barred from any role in decision making. Several employees of agencies, especially the Southern Baptist seminaries, were dismissed or else made so uncomfortable that they resigned. On the other hand, many were allowed to finish out their careers, since the leaders, who were now fundamentalists, knew that time was on their side. If these usual employees were tolerated, the heads of agencies were treated with great cruelty and disrespect, if they did not pass muster with the fundamentalist leadership.

In addition, basic tenets of the Baptist tradition, such as the precious Baptist principle of religious liberty, have been scuttled for the sake of co-opting government to further Christian evangelism or Christian nurture. An example is the school prayer issue. The question is not whether prayer is voluntary. Of course, it is. Nobody can prevent a student from praying.

The problem is that to insist upon Christian prayers concocted or approved by the government, during school time or at school functions, even if the prayers are prepared and voiced by students, is indeed to ignore the rights of non-Christians in a pluralistic society. Moreover, it is to depend upon government to help with an evangelistic task which is specifically Christian. Likewise, to insist upon government approved prayers which are acceptable to all religions is no doubt impossible, since some religions do not even believe in a "god," and, in any case, the likelihood is that the rights of those who believe in *no* religion are thus violated. It is much better to insist upon liberty of conscience for all, even unbelievers, as Baptists have done historically.

This setting aside of Baptist tradition, the exclusion of many, and the inhumane handling of leaders have made it impossible for me to continue as a Southern Baptist. Anyway, I had always thought of myself, not specifically as a *Southern* Baptist, but as a *Baptist*. I had hoped that the dissension of a sizeable group of Southern Baptists would result in some new alignment with the American Baptist Churches, thus, at least symbolically, healing the tragic schism of 1845 over the slavery question which resulted in the formation of the Southern Baptist Convention, a separation which never should have occurred. Such, however, seems out of the question. The power of Southern culture and Southern identity is too strong.

Many people remain within the Southern Baptist Convention, for their own reasons, in spite of the intolerable behavior which I have outlined above. Some have made deliberate and painful choices, believing that their only hope of fulfilling their Christian vocation is to stay with the Convention. For these latter I have great sympathy and profound respect. Still others have left the Baptist fold altogether, believing that it is more important to be Christian than to be Baptist. These, too, I salute, because I believe that essentially they are right: to be Christian is indeed more crucial than to wear any denominational label.

As for me, however, in the present historical situation, though I am always first a Christian and then a Baptist, I cannot cease to be a Baptist. The heritage of Baptists is too precious to surrender. Let me rather be an ecumenist and seek to share my Baptist inheritance with all Christians and indeed with all the universe. Let me complete my race, whatever its length or brevity may be, as a member of a Baptist ecclesiastical structure that is truly ecumenical.

Which brings me to say that Louise and I think we have found such a structure in Pullen Memorial Baptist Church. Pullen is quite active in social ministry and has a strong tradition of being prophetic, which pleases us very much. During the civil rights struggle, Pullen took a strong stand on racial equality. More recently it has taken a courageous position on the homosexual issue. There are several homosexual couples among those who are members. However, the constituency of Pullen is diverse, and the Church puts a premium upon dissent. This congregation is especially appealing to us in that it is related to the American Baptist Churches, USA.

In fact, for a few years Pullen was dually aligned with the Southern Baptist Convention as well as the American Baptists, until it was expelled from membership, not only by the Southern Baptist Convention, but, through separate actions, also by judicatories related to it, namely, the Baptist State Convention of North Carolina and the Raleigh Baptist Association. At present, Pullent is the only predominantly white Baptist church in Raleigh which is affiliated with the Amer-ican Baptist Churches, USA.

The latter has existed since 1814 (with various names) as the first national organization of Baptists in the United States, and from it Southern Baptist congregations withdrew in 1845, primarily because they supported slavery, to form the Southern Baptist Convention. In a certain sense, then, joining an American Baptist church is to go back to our Baptist roots.

Louise joined Pullen two years before I did. I remained in First Baptist for a while primarily because of my relation to the Japanese Christian ministry in North Carolina, which includes a strong Japanese mission in First Baptist Church which I helped to develop. For us to move our membership from that church has been difficult, because First Baptist is a good church and we have many friends there.

To be sure, the decision to leave the Southern Baptist Convention has not been without its pain, though I have transcended the hurt by now. I remember that when I returned from Baylor University in 1988, after fundamentalists had already seized control of Southeastern Seminary, I drove up the driveway to where Faculty members at Southeastern park in front of the Stealey Building. Somewhat unexpectedly, a great wave of sadness came over me, sadness for a lost tradition and for what I thought of for the moment as a lost career. It seemed that all I had tried to accomplish in a lifetime had been obliterated, and I was crushingly grieved. Of course, by now this feeling has passed and a much more objective assessment of my life's work as a Southern Baptist has replaced it.

Now it is time to bring you up to date on the Copeland family, whose privacy I have been careful to guard. Since I have mentioned the college experiences of the daughters, it is appropriate also that I tell you about the youngest, our son, Luke, who is the only one of our children who chose to attend a state university, in his case Appalachian State University in Boone, North Carolina. He entered Appalachian in the fall of 1977 and was graduated in the middle of the 1981-1982 session. Somewhat to the surprise of his parents, Luke had developed an early interest in business, which culminated in a Bachelor's Degree in Business Administration, followed by passing the examination as a Certified Public Accountant.

During college, Luke fell in love with the Boone area and determined that if he ever had a chance he would go back there to work and live. To fulfill the CPA requirements of supervision he worked for two years with a firm in Fayetteville, North Carolina. Then, in 1984, Luke began to seek employment in Raleigh or Durham, assuming that there was no opening in Boone. To his surprise and delight, an employment agency in Durham put him in contact with a CPA firm in Boone which immediately employed him. He has been in Boone ever since.

Our children and their spouses and our grandchildren are a source of great satisfaction to me. In each of them I take great pride and delight. Our four daughters and the one son have grown up to be fine persons. By now they are in the midst of their careers. Our six grandchildren, who are evenly divided as to gender, differ widely in interests and personalities. I am tremendously proud of each one of them. Louise has been a remarkably appropriate helpmeet. Our marriage gets better all the time, and I am far more grateful for her than I can express.

Chapter Twenty-One
PROJECTS AND HOBBIES

After returning from Japan, Louise and I developed several volunteer ministries. Prominent among these was work with
the Japanese who were in Raleigh and its environs, centering in
First Baptist Church on Salisbury Street, where we had become
members again after returning from Japan. This Japanese ministry was started, not at the initiative of the Copelands, but with the
urging of two members of the Church, one of whom was the then
Chair of the Deacons, Caralie Brown.

Early in 1982, Caralie appointed an ad hoc Committee on
Japanese Ministry, of which Louise was one member and I was
Chair. When the Committee surveyed the community, it discovered that the needs of the Japanese were not primarily physical but
cultural and spiritual. Accordingly we started a Japanese American Cultural Exchange program (JACE) which met in the building
of First Baptist Church one a week on Friday morning during the
school year. The continuation of this program is with very good
attendance is testimony to the good leadership of some women
as well as its success.

To minister to the spiritual needs of the growing Japanese
community, since JACE was not primarily evangelistic, Louise and
I began a Bible class, completely in Japanese, with me as the
teacher. Attendance grew from 4 to start with to about 15. When
I was away teaching in several schools, the Nawata sisters,
successively, provided leadership for the class.

In 1990, the Tomonos, Yasushi and Kaoru, a very gifted
Japanese couple, assumed leadership, and the class soon grew
into a Japanese mission of First Baptist Church. Attendance increased to more than 30, though Yasushi itinerated to various
mission points in North Carolina. Two beautiful daughters have
been added to grace the home of this most attractive couple.

Since the couple served all of this state, it was necessary
for us to form a non-profit corporation to support them, and I was
chosen as the first President (though I have since given up this
position). After serving here for nine years, the Tomonos went re-

Illustration No. 46
We Visit with the Tomonos

turned to Japan for Yasushi to assume the pastorate of Nagasaki Baptist in the city where Kaoru's parents are living. Before they left, we were very fortunate to procure the services of another fine Japanese couple to succeed them. I am proud of this Japanese work but now have nothing to do with it.

A few years ago, we sold our house and lot on Pembrook Place in Raleigh at a significant profit* and purchased a condominium in downtown Raleigh. Since the condominium is small, we have had to do some considerable downsizing.

So far as hobbies are concerned, a major one has to do with our mountain property, and I need to fill you in on that. Back in 1972, when I was under considerable pressure at Southeastern, we decided that we wanted to buy some mountain property. It would be an escape hatch for me, quite another world, so to

---

*I have Louise to thank for this good real estate transaction. It was by her initiative that we bought the property, and it was she who decided after I had left for Japan that we should rent the property rather than sell it.

speak, in which I could spend what little time I could get off. It may have been an expression in me, as an individual, of the "myth of the eternal return" about which mythologists speak. That is, I may have been motivated, even unconsciously, by a desire to return to the timber woods and the primitive living of my childhood.

An invitation about the middle of October 1972 to do something at Mars Hill College related to alumni responsibilities--I don't remember specifically what it was--seemed to offer an opportunity to look at some properties. After a kind of vacation at Wolf Laurel, where the College put us up in a ski lodge, and after I had finished my Mars Hill responsibilities, Louise and I, and our two youngest, Becky and Luke, who were with us on this trip, drove on up to the Boone area, since that part of western North Carolina had some special attraction for us.

When we arrived in Boone, we went immediately to the United Farm Agency, a well known real estate outfit which dealt in mountain properties. The agent at United Farm indicated that he had some properties in the Boone area but that they were very expensive. If we didn't mind crossing the line into Tennessee, he suggested, prices were much lower. Since the Tennessee line was only about fifteen miles from Boone on U.S. 421, and since we were already almost two hundred miles from Raleigh, a few extra miles didn't make all that much difference to us. So we let him take us in his four-wheel-drive vehicle to Tennessee.

We were looking for a place of not more than twelve acres or so, considering our budget, and he showed us some pretty places. The problem was access: all of these properties had to have roads built into them. When it was getting well along in the afternoon, he said, "I have one more place I want to show you. It is about 44 acres and has good road access."

I stopped him, indicating that we could not afford such a big place, but he said, "Don't be too hasty. The price is right, the down payment is small, and the owner will finance the balance at 6%. As is his practice, he bought it for the timber, logged it, and built roads as though he planned to develop it."

So we went to look at the place and all of us fell in love with it. It was only about a mile and a half from the little Johnson

County seat town of Mountain City,* though it seemed very private and isolated. The trees were colorfully decked out in their autumnal splendor and the timber was cut so that the scenery was highly visible. It was a watershed, a complete head of a hollow, somewhat in the shape of a horse's hoof, with the line going up the mountain at both ends from a central location and following the ridge around the top. So to make a long story short, we bought it.

We had a tent which we set up on a later visit when we spent a few days there. To store the tent and the few tools which we needed, we decided to build a lean-to. However, the structure grew to a small one-room log cabin, located just under the brow of the ridge. I bought an old army truck with 2 winches on it, so I cut white pine poles and pulled them to the site as logs for the cabin, using only dead ones that were still sound.

I learned that white pines grow very close together in the woods, so that when they are logged, the small poles that are left standing often break from the wind or else simply die--from exposure, it would appear. The lower limbs of these isolated and diminutive trees had already withered from lack of sunshine while surrounded by their larger companions, leaving a puny tuft of foliage in the top somewhat like a crow's nest. It is these poles with a tuft of foliage in the top which die. Of course, if the wind snaps them, as it often does, they die anyway, for white pines never live if they break or are cut above their green limbs. There were plenty of these dead but still sound poles to provide logs for the cabin so that we didn't have to use any live ones.

Louise and I and the children built the cabin (mostly the husband and sire!) as we had time, taking about two summers and a few weekends, vacations, and such. Unfortunately, in my haste I let the thing get out of plumb so that, although the floor is level, the roof line slipped so that it's about four or five inches lower on one end than on the other. The blemish is noticeable; how I managed it I don't know. Undoubtedly, I was in too big a hurry!

Louise has a story which she thinks is very funny about the truck with the winches. The old army truck had a winch on

---

*The property is about 225 miles from where we now live.

Illustration No. 47
The Cabin Takes Shape

the front bumper and another on the back since it had been used as a tow truck. Now I did not need the winch on the back. In fact it was in the way. For a time I thought about leaving the truck in the hands of a friend while I was back in Japan. Happily, I felt better about it and sold the whole truck, afraid that I might lose one of my few friends if I left the truck with him.

While I was toying with the idea of keeping the truck, I had stopped at a filling station to see if the manager, whom I knew very casually, might be interested in buying the rear winch. Though in those days normally I was rather clean shaven, when I went to the mountains I didn't bother to shave regularly and dressed rather shabbily like the hard working mountaineer that I was. Louise says that my grammar suffers when I speak with mountain people, though I insist that I only follow the missionary principle of identifying with the folks.

Well, I had talked with the filling station man about the winch and found him mildly interested. His problem was that a fellow up in Virginia had promised to bring him a winch but, said he, "You can't believe a word he tells you." I told him that I was leaving the country for a few years and "had to git shed of that winch." The man expressed some surprise and wanted to know why I was leaving the country. "Are you in the military or somethin'?" he wanted to know. "No," said I, "I'm goin' to be president of a Japanese university."

When I approached the cab of the truck, I discovered that Louise was all doubled up with laughter. When I inquired what was so funny, she managed to say, "That man was so incredulous when you told him *you* were to be president of a Japanese university that he will think *anybody* who speaks to him about a winch is a liar who cannot be trusted!"

The widow woman who had sold the land to the logger had carved out a four-acre plot in the valley for her daughter and son-in-law and their family. They had built a small and rather attractive house on it, getting their water from a spring above the house. We had a spring, also, at the foot of the mountain, but the water was mineral in nature and not as good as our neighbors'. When the son-in-law decided to move, he gave me the opportunity to make him an offer on the place, but I vastly underpriced it since I didn't really need property with a house on it. As a result, he sold it to someone else, and the new owner later sold it to his brother.

The last year we were in Japan, we were told that the house had burned and was a complete loss; so from that remote distance we bought the four acres of land by mail. We paid more than it was worth to anyone else since we wanted all of the original tract and particularly the water. This later purchase means that this mountain property is close to 50 acres.

After we returned from Japan in 1980, and especially while I was teaching at Louisville in 1981-1982, I built an addition to the back of the cabin. I managed to do this by commuting to

Mountain City from Louisville on weekends and vacations. People must have looked askance at Louise and me meeting for the beginning of weekends, only to take our separate ways after the weekend was over. You see, Louise was working at John Umstead Hospital in Butner, North Carolina, at this time.

The new structure, also built of logs, was a second room which I divided into two: a kind of plunder room on one end and a bathroom on the other. I piped water up the mountain from the spring, using the electricity from the former house, since we had none in the cabin itself. In the bathroom, I had a commode, a lavatory, a shower, and a wood-burning hot water heater.

The cabin itself was furnished very simply, with single beds, home made bunks, and a sleeping loft with a bed made from a foam mattress laid on the floor; a two burner kerosene stove for cooking, a wood stove for heating, and kerosene lamps for light; a kitchen sink, shelves, and some small cabinets. In fact, most of the furnishings came from junk yards. An exception was a dinette set which Joy gave us before she and her family made their series of moves related to her husband's Army career.

To discourage break-ins, of which we had two or three, I beefed up the security of doors and windows. On one occasion thieves took the tent but left the poles for it! I suggested to Louise that we should advertise that the thief who took the tent should please come back and pick up the tent poles.

In addition, together with Joe Sherwood, of Sherwood Hardware in Mountain City, I have supplied several pickup loads of wood to needy persons in or near Mountain City, Tennessee, using a chain saw, cant hook, wedge, and a hydraulic wood splitter So I am back in the timber woods again for as long as I hold out!

Pretty soon after procuring it, Louise and I applied our environmental interests to this mountain land. Perhaps it had to do with the fact that we were growing older. We have kept the place pristine and by now it has quite a bit of marketable timber. We have developed the conviction that even after our deaths this property should not be developed, because to develop it would end the haven for wildlife and mountain plants which it provides.

We tried to get the Nature Conservancy interested in an easement on the land by which they would take care of it and see that it was not "developed," but evidently it was too small for them. Their Nashville office referred me to an agency in Asheville, North Carolina, which seems to be operated by one person. She came to look at the property and then told us that she was interested and would try to find other tracts near Mountain City so that she could supervise a larger acreage. I got tired of calling her and finally gave up.

At this point we have put it in our will, leaving it to the joint ownership of our children, with the indication that we *hope* the land will never be developed. Of course we are aware of the fact that to designate it not to be developed "in perpetuity" does not really mean forever. I know of no way we could insure that it would *never* be chopped up into lots and sold. Of course, we may sell it to someone who will give us assurance that it will not be developed during the new owner's lifetime. As of now we are giving it to our children upon our death and hoping for the best, though we have no way of knowing the long future.

As another hobby, I manage to keep some bees. A number of years ago, when my very close friend, Elmo Scoggin, was unusually depressed for certain good reasons, I suggested that we become partners in beekeeping. This was after Louise and I had returned from Japan and retired as missionaries. So Elmo and I went into beekeeping together.

Already, I was sort of a beekeeper. In fact, the late John Lusby, an African American friend who worked as a janitor for Southeastern Seminary, had introduced me to this new venture a number of years ago, while we still lived in Wake Forest. I bought out a woman in Raleigh who had kept bees, and for a while I had two stands in our backyard in Wake Forest. However, they were in sight of the Community Center which had a public swimming pool, and people thought they were being stung by my bees whether they were or not.

So before I left Wake Forest, I had taken the bee hives over to John's place--of course he lived across the tracks--and he looked after them. This situation wasn't too satisfactory, since now I only bought materials for the bees, brooder wax and such, and had no direct contact with them. However, this arrangement made it convenient when we moved to Raleigh, and especially when we went back to Japan. John cared for the bees, and I didn't have to worry about them. Unfortunately, John died while we were in Japan, and when we returned, his wife, Gertrina (who also has since died), assumed that the bees were her late husband's. She asked me to begin looking after them again, and I did so but before long they died out.

It was at this point that Elmo and I bought some bees and

Illustration No. 48
(Inset: Elmo Scoggin) (Here You See Me Getting a Hive Ready For Occupancy)

started our hobby together. Elmo has an arrangement with a friend in nearby Rolesville, whereby he pretty much shares the friend's farm for any purpose he wishes. This friend, Howard Brown, is a remarkably generous fellow, a fine man. His association with Elmo began several years ago when Elmo became interim pastor of Rolesville Baptist Church, of which Howard is a member. Elmo repeated this service on several occasions when Rolesville Church was without a regular Pastor. Howard has a fish pond on his small farm where Elmo loves to fish. The Brown place appears to be a good home for the bees, except that for some unknown reason there seems to be a dearth of blossoms there for them to work on.

But I must digress to tell a funny story on Elmo. His relationship to Rolesville goes way back, and this story is pretty ancient, too. There was a fellow at Rolesville who had a little café, and some of us who were Elmo's friends at Southeastern went out every afternoon or so for coffee and in this connection visited this man's little eating establishment. While we were drinking our coffee, the proprietor was talking with us.

Now I should say that the proprietor of the café didn't have much to do with the Rolesville Baptist Church (or any other Church, for that matter), but his wife did. So he asked us, "Do you know that feller Scoggin?" "Yes," one of us said, "He teaches with us." "Well," said our host, "He's about the nicest feller I ever saw for an edgicated man." All three or four of us Ph. D.s took notice. We thought that was quite a compliment for Scoggin. I myself aspire to this and other good traits of my friend, who relates easily to people of all social strata.

Which brings me back to my continued narration about Elmo and the bees. Actually, I wasn't much of a beekeeper, didn't know much about a fascinating but complex phenomenon. So it didn't take a great effort for Elmo to surpass me in his knowledge of beekeeping, which he has certainly done. It's a bit embarrassing, but it's a fact.

The other thing to be said is that we had just got started good when some frightening pests attacked our industry, one after the other. First there was the Tracheal Mite, which came from Europe to the States about 1988. This pest is microscopic: it cannot be seen with the naked eye. It gets in the bee's breathing apparatus and eventually cuts off the oxygen, so that the bee dies. The best treatment is crystals of menthol, which are packaged in the right amount for putting in the bee hive. The menthol works best in warm weather. I get different reports on whether it affects the taste of the honey.

A second nuisance is another kind of mite, the Varroa Mite, which arrived about two years later than the Tracheal Mite, I believe. This parasite is big enough to be seen without a microscope, but barely. It attaches itself to the back of the bee and sucks the life juices out of her. Or its eggs are laid in the cell with the bee egg which becomes a larva, at which time it attaches itself to the bee larva and, as with the adult bee, sucks the stuffing out of him or her. (The only male bees are a few drones in the hive. Their only purpose is to mate with the queen. All worker bees, of which there are thousands in a typical hive, are undeveloped females).

Varroa Mite treatment is by means of Apistan strips, plastic strips upon which the chemical fluvalinate is placed, and a new chemical called Apicure, which also is supposed to control the Tracheal Mite once it is released. These medications affect not only the taste of the honey but also poison it; so you can't use them when you are producing honey.

Now, more recently, there is the invasion of the Small Hive Beetle, from South Africa. This is a small beetle, as the name suggests, about the size of a lady bug but more oval in shape, besides being brown in color. They eat bee eggs, and their larvae tunnel through the comb, eating the sealed bee larvae and pupae, pollen, and honey. The beetle larvae look like maggots and they make a gooey mess of the honey which the beekeepers and the bees find repulsive (ugh!). The latest information is that these beetles, like the "killer" bees from Africa, are not apt to bother bees as far north as Tennessee or North Carolina.

Of course, there are other diseases and pests which infest the beehives which have been around for a long time, but I won't bother you with these. I have given you a brief introduction to these newer pests to indicate that beekeeping, which used to be a hobby, has now become expensive drudgery. Elmo and I have never bothered to figure up what we spend on this alleged hobby, but undoubtedly we would be much better off to buy our honey from commercial beekeepers who far surpass us in equipment and professional knowhow to deal with these nuisances. Elmo had already indicated that he wants to bow out this year. How long I can continue the work is quite uncertain.

Well, that about does it for the hobbies. Louise and I do some walking, but it is more for our health than for our enjoyment, though the latter is involved also. Actually being in our mountain place is a hobby for me. Louise says that when we arrive there, she is in the mood for resting, curling up with a book and reading, or else sleeping. She further says that when I reach the place, I am energized, ready for some kind of work which I always find to do. She is probably right. I keep promising that I will spend at least part of my time there reading. But. . . .

Speaking of the mountains, though I am not sure that reunions should be included under hobbies, for our 50th wedding anniversary in 1996, we rented for a few days an old house on the rustic Episcopal Assembly Grounds in Valle Crucis, North Carolina, beyond Boone, and got the whole family together, child-ren, spouses, grandchildren, and a few other relatives who were close to us. It was a wonderful experience! On the last night we were there, our children put on a reception for us which included a book of letters. It was both moving and hilarious.

Without intending to do so, Louise and I started a tradition of family reunions by getting the Copeland siblings and their families together for the first time in 1985. We invited our cousin Jessie Hurt Wood to attend, and out of this small beginning has grown the Copeland/Hurt Reunion which meets annually or semi-annually, usually in some more or less central place in West Virginia, Virginia, or North Carolina. This family gathering by now includes the Hurts on my mother's side, but also the children and other offspring of Aunt Lettie Copeland Gross, my father's only sibling, and some others who usually attend.

In the year 2000, for the first time, the reunion was called off because not enough people pledged to come. What the future will be for the reunion nobody knows, though it is being planned for West Virginia in 2001.

CONCLUSION

Now I have to bring this treatise to a close. I have chosen to do so by a brief mention of what I have promised you in the development of these memoirs, and to add certain things I have learned in a relatively long life.

Fairly early in this volume, I promised you a fuller discussion of my feelings of inferiority, or the contradiction of feelings of distinctiveness and inadequacy. Well, the intimation of distinctiveness has all but disappeared, while the sense of inadequacy has lingered. This feeling of inferiority hasn't been helped by the fact that I have lost just about all of my Hebrew skills and much of my facility in Greek and Latin, not to mention French and German, on which latter two languages I passed a reading test while in graduate school long ago.

I know that there is a sense in which these linguistic losses are justified by the attempt to learn and keep Japanese through the years. One problem, however, is that I have become awkward in Japanese as well, especially as I have grown older and deafer! Even so, I should be able to *speak* Japanese very well, but in the spoken language, too, I have become rather bumbling. When I try to speak extemporaneously, for example, to members of the Japanese Baptist Mission in First Baptist Church, I feel keenly that I am butchering the language.

As a youth, I seemed quite precocious. My high school principal, H. D. Groves, who taught math, once remarked, in a situation where I was not supposed to hear, that I had a better mind than any student he had ever taught--or some such extravagance. A similar remark was made by one of my teachers at Furman. Even Uncle Ken Latourette, my major professor in graduate school and himself renowned as a scholar and writer, told one of my colleagues at Southeastern that I could write anything I set my mind to.

So I embarked on my teaching career thinking I was rather invincible. Plaudits that I received in Japan, particularly in the early period, did not help to dissipate that illusion. Please be assured that I have made my peace with the situation, especially since retirement, more satisfactorily than before.

While I was actively teaching and preaching, I used to have a recurring dream. Sometimes it was directly related to a sense of unpreparedness: for example, I would dream that I appeared at the podium or the pulpit with no idea of what I was to lecture or preach about.

On other occasions, the dream would be less direct: for instance, my dress would be inadequate or inappropriate, say I would appear at the lectern wearing nothing but my underwear! Or often I would be on quite familiar ground making some trip, only to find that the road got smaller and smaller and less and less well known, until it would simply peter out, and I would have no earthly idea of where I was. When I would consult my watch, I would see that obviously I could not make my appointment.

As I have grown older, I seem to be slower in matters of logic. I used to do quite well in question and answer situations, and to pride myself on my critical acumen. I never liked to admit that I had not read some book or did not know the answer to some question, but I felt that I could probe to the heart of a matter and expose its essence. I was always somewhat slow and deliberate, but now I seem to be much more so. If I have time to cogitate on something, I do very well at articulating what I think; but in cases where I have to respond on the spot, usually I do not come off well. It bothers me that I do not appear as sharp as I actually am. It troubles me even more to recognize that I am not as sharp as I once was!

Though you may feel that I am always on top of the world, I am telling you that my feeling of inadequacy never has been resolved, in spite of what it seems that I have accomplished.

Anyone who knows me is aware that I have moved away from the rather conservative politics and theology of my youth. I have become a Democrat and likely am more forward looking than most persons of that party.

Of course, my theology was never fundamentalism, but it was quite conservative. I have become more and more progressive in my thinking, though a true "liberal" would still find my theology rather confining, I suppose. Especially, I am increasingly inclined to be agnostic about many things, including who is saved and who is not, and to take not only other denominations seriously but also other religions as loci of God's revelation.

This has involved a new look at the Bible. Although I believe that I can still affirm the statement that "the Scriptures of the Old and New Testaments . . . are the only sufficient, certain and authoritative rule of all saving knowledge, faith and obedience,"* I have had to work out some additional canons of Biblical interpretation.

Among these tenets are the following: (1) I accept Martin Luther's concept that Christ is the norm by which the Scriptures must be interpreted. (2) Where there seems to be contradiction in the Scriptural teaching on certain issues, I come down on the side of the qualities of love and fairness which seem to me to be central Biblical teachings. (3) I try to read the Bible with the eyes of the poor, and I find that the interpretation is quite different when so viewed. (4) I look for evidences of the influence of the culture of Biblical times upon the teachings of the Scriptures.

(5) I accept teachings and practices from extra-Biblical sources, including, of course, the other religions, so long as these are consistent with what I believe is the spirit of Jesus, even if he did not literally teach or practice them. (6) Though I take seriously the "tradition" of Christian faith and seek to submit my individual ideas to the critical scrutiny of the Church through the ages and the churches of today, since both the tradition and the churches have been and still are sometimes wrong, I must accept the fact that God alone is the Lord of the individual conscience, and that one must swim against the current by oneself, or at least with the minority of Christians, at times.

Human sex, which is one of the strongest drives that we

---

*This Scriptural statement is from the *Abstract of Principles*, 1859, which I reluctantly signed as a Professor, both at Southeastern and Southern Baptist Theological Seminaries. Concerning this fact, let me say the following: (1) I have signed only this one document, and that for the sake of my vocation. I do not like to sign any credo, even one which I have written! (2) Before I signed the statement at Southeastern, I made it known to President Stealey that I saw the *Abstract* as a statement of traditional evangelical faith with a Baptist interpretation, in which stream I stood, and that I understood it as having central doctrines which I affirmed, and peripheral doctrines which I would not like to be held to. I interpreted President Stealey's silence as approval.

experience, I view as a sacrament of love, a sacrament by which love is expressed between two human beings beyond any other professions of love, whether verbal or otherwise, a sacrament by which one receives as well as gives love. Although this sacrament may operate quite well in the secular world, it is all the more fulfilling when seen as a religious sacrament, conveying the divine as well as human love. Although I am certainly a very poor example of this belief, nevertheless I hold to it.

In spite of the fact that I am sometimes pegged—or pilloried—as a liberal, I insist on holding onto my highest ideals, particularly as taught by Christian faith, in spite of all which seems to contradict them. For example, I believe strongly in *koinonia*, an ideal society of sharing, in spite of all the failures to implement this ideal in history. The best human societies that I know have come up short, no matter how Christian or otherwise how religious they have been.

I have been dismally disappointed by some communities to which I have been committed. I have always been an idealist and have sought the perfect society. I now believe that such an ideal does not exist in this life, partly because I myself share in the general imperfection of humanity, no matter how strenuously I seek to overcome my deficiencies.

Nevertheless, it is very important to hold to the ideal no matter what. If the perfect society does not come into being in this life, it certainly will in the life to come. At least this is a basic tenet of my faith. To believe in God is to believe in the fulfillment of our best hopes socially as well as otherwise. Such a society will finally come to pass because God is.

Justice is similar. There are terrible inequities in the world today. For example, there are those who, through no fault of their own, do not have enough food to keep them or (what is worse) their children from starving. There always have been such inequities, and even if we make improvements, probably we will still be plagued by injustices. As I see it, this fact does not mean the lessening of commitment to the ideal of justice and earnest efforts to achieve it. Rather, it means just the opposite. If we are really committed to justice, we will do all in our power to bring it to pass, even if we are discouraged in the process.

The same is true, also, with regard to the natural environment. A large number of species of plants and animals have been lost beyond recovery. We have no way of knowing how much we and our world are impoverished by these losses. Perhaps in other ways as well the environment has been impaired irrevocably. Nevertheless, many of us are committed to saving the environment.

In regard to the history of the universe, the human story is very, very brief. God enjoyed the environment for billions of years before human beings appeared. Or, along with the pleasure of the Creator, the environment enjoyed itself. The instruction in Genesis to be fruitful and multiply, and to subdue the earth and have dominion over it, is always to be considered as subject to the purpose of God. This means that we put careful limitations upon human population, that we enlarge the sphere of our concern to include not only the earth but the entire universe, and that we celebrate the sacredness of all that God has created.

Though I confess that I do not know how it will come about, I stand with the prophet who disapproved of the cruelty or predatory character of our environment and foresaw the day when the wolf would live with the kid, the lion would eat straw with the ox, and there would be no more violence in the earth (Isaiah 11:6-9 and parallel passages). I do not know how the prophet justified the fact that a merciful and loving God created this violent world, and I cannot solve this seeming contradiction myself. But I will bet my life on God's goodness anyhow.

Of course, these are but prominent examples of a more important truth. Many years ago, I think it was while I was in graduate school, I realized that our faith must be eschatological. That is, we have to wait until the end to see God's fulfillment. Nothing that we cherish most as God's sons and daughters is realized in this life. Just as we have individual hope that all that we are will be fulfilled in Christ, and just as none of us who have this hope can settle for less than the character of Christ (1 John 3:1-3), so we hope for the fulfillment of God's perfect social, cultural, and environmental purposes.

In other words, just as we strive for purity of life, even though we know that perfect purity will not be attained in this life, so also we are not content to accept less than God's perfect ideal for society, culture, and the environment. We cherish this hope, not only with regard to ourselves as individuals but also concerning these other three areas, no matter how far beyond what we see of them now the vision of their future may be.

Though I have no way of proving it, I *believe* that in the world to come our own individual imperfections will be done away, many and tragic though they be, and we will appear perfect in the presence of our Creator and Redeemer. I *believe* just as strongly that the world will be perfected, socially, culturally, and environmentally. In neither case do I know how this will be accomplished, but I leave it to God. Meantime, I must continue to work for these ideals.

All of which means that I must be resolute. This account of my life indicates that I have done so on certain issues, always quite imperfectly and with my share of cowardice. What are the issues on which the Christian will have to take a stand in the future? No doubt there are many questions which clamor for our attention and even more yet to come. None of us can anticipate future history.

Nevertheless, in the short future, I believe that the most prominent matter on which we are called to make a commitment is the homosexual issue. And on this problem no doubt there is as much Scriptural ambiguity as there is on the racial issue and the question of women's rights. I believe that it is incumbent upon heterosexual Christians to seek full justice and acceptance for homosexuals in our time, and not to leave this issue for gays and lesbians alone to promote at considerable cost to themselves. Louise, partly because of her personal acquaintance with some homosexuals who are fine persons, has helped me greatly to come to my present position on homosexuality. On this issue, too, so help me God, I intend to take my stand.

As I have grown older, my sense of reliance upon the sheer grace of God has increased. This means that I no longer divide the world into the categories of the "saved" and the "unsaved." I am grateful to be included at all, and I do not quibble about who else may be numbered among the "saved." That is God's business alone.

For me, this saving grace is manifested supremely in Jesus Christ and his cross. True to the voice which I believe addressed me in my youth, I have remained "near the cross." This is in spite of the fact that I have been challenged by a pluralistic view of Christianity's place among the religions. Even if I were to accept the relativism that often seems to accompany pluralism, namely, the persuasion that Christian doctrinal convictions, including the passion of Christ, apply only to Christians—to which belief I do not subscribe—I suspect that I would not be untrue to my earlier faith concerning the cross.

Although the cross (atonement) has been interpreted in many ways and is so profound that it is subject to diverse understandings, it best speaks to me as God's sacrifice for the sins of the whole creation. I think it is entirely erroneous to separate God the Father and God the Son, or God as Ultimate and God as Incarnate, in the cross, as though the Ultimate is angry and the Incarnate appeases the wrath of the Ultimate God. The cross is the action of the one God.

The atonement reveals the love of God for God's creation as the great and necessary sacrifice by which the universe is redeemed. The major religions, as well as primeval faiths, have intimations of the necessity of this kind of cosmic sacrifice. I am profoundly thankful to be included in this marvelous provision for my salvation and I want to share this good news with all the creation so long as God gives me breath and sanity.

I am convinced that for most of us, our God is too small. If God has created everything that is, surely God is interested in all the creation. I often pray that God will make my interests as broad as God's interests.

At least, this is the way it appears to me. And if you do not agree, perhaps you are obligated to come up with your own ideas on such profoundly important matters.

APPENDICES[*]

Appendix I: The Copeland Family Genealogy

Name (Years)	Spouse (Years)	Places of Residence
David Copeland, Sr. (? -1824?)	? (? - ?)	Maury Co., TN
Hezekiah B. Copeland (? - ?)	Annie Kincaid (? - ?)	From Maury Co., TN., to Big Creek, WV
Anthony Copeland (1829-1887)	Mary Ann Rose (1824-1879)	Big (& Smithers) Creek & Gauley Bridge, WV
Winfield Copeland (1853-1943)	Emma Ellen Hill (1855-1880)	Big (& Smithers) Creek & other WV places
(Winfield) Luther Lowell Copeland (1880-1966)	Nannie Cleveland Hurt (1884-1976)	(Mostly) Nicholas Co., WV
Edwin Luther Copeland (1916-)	Louise Evelyn Tadlock (1923-)	Various places, including Japan

Appendix II: The Hill Family Genealogy

Name (Years)	Spouse (Years)	Places of Residence, etc.
Robert Hill, Sr. (1791-1875)	Lettie Estep Hill (1825-1857)	Unknown
Emma Ellen Hill (1855-1880)	Winfield Copeland (1853-1943)	Big (& Smithers) Ck & other WV places
(Winfield) Luther Lowell Copeland (1880-1966)	Nannie Cleveland Hurt (1884-1976)	(Mostly) Nicholas Co., WV
Edwin Luther Copeland (1916-)	Louise Evelyn Tadlock (1923-)	Various places, including Japan

[*]In the appendices that follow, only those that contain the author's bloodline are included

Appendix III: The Hurt Family Genealogy

Name (Years)	Spouse (Years)	Residence, etc.
John Hurt (c.1738- ?)	Anne Garland (? - ?)	Amherst Co., VA
Garland Hurt (1768-1818)	Betsy Ann Tucker (1765-1850)	Bedford Co., VA
Robert B. Hurt (? - ?)	Nancy Hurt (1st cousin) (? - ?)	Bedford Co., VA
John Garland Hurt (1836-1927)	Bettie Ruth Field (1st cousin) (1849-1931)	Fr. Bedford Co., VA to Sanger, WV
Nannie Cleveland Hurt (1884-1976)	(Winfield) Luther Lowell Copeland (1880-1966)	(Mostly) Nicholas Co., WV
Edwin Luther Copeland (1916-)	Louise Evelyn Tadlock (1923-)	Various places, including Japan

Appendix IV: The Field Family Genealogy

Name (Years)	Spouse (Years)	Residence, etc.
William O. Field (? - ?)	Charlotte Ann Matilda Hurt (? - ?)	Bedford Co. VA
Bettie Ruth Field (1849-1931)	John Garland Hurt (1st cousin) (1836-1927)	Fm. Bedford Co., VA to Sanger, WV
Nannie Cleveland Hurt (1884-1976)	(Winfield) Luther Lowell Copeland (1880-1966)	(Mostly) Nicholas Co., WV
Edwin Luther Copeland (1916-)	Louise Evelyn Tadlock (1923-)	Various places, including Japan

Appendix V: Children and Grandchildren of Luther Lowell Copeland
and Nannie Hurt Copeland

Name of Child Birthday (Years)	Spouse (Years)	Grandchild (Years)
Bertha Ellen Copeland 6/18/1904 (1904-2000)	Cecil Bays (1903-1983)	Louise Bays Fox (1942-)
Daisy Dell Copeland, 7/9/1906 (1906-)	Don B. Jarrell (1905-1987)	Phyllis Jarrell Aquino (1929-) Donald Jarrell (1930-) Betty Jarrell Pennington (1932-) Billie Jarrell Bailey (1933-) Jerry Jarrell (1934-) Garnet Jarrell Givens (1939-)
Unnamed Twin (7/9/1906–8/2/1906)		
Vernice DeLora Copeland 3/26/1908 (1908-)	J. Farley Trimble (1913-1982)	Maurice Trimble (1936-) Michael Trimble (1942-)
Garland W. Copeland (1/19/1909-1/29/1910)		
Rita Faye Copeland 9/22/1911 (1911-1986)	Paul W. Hanna (1912-1986)	Janice Hendricks Sible (1939-) George Hanna (1943-) Sandra Bedwell Williams (1945-) William Hanna (1950-)
Lowell Ellis Copeland, 3/4/1914 (1914-2000)	Hilda O'Dell (1919-1979) Ruth Chafin (1929-)	Stephen Copeland (1940-) Warren Mc. Copeland (1942-)
Edwin Luther Copeland, 1/24/1916 (1916-)	Louise Tadlock (1923-)	Judith Copeland (1947-) Joy Copeland Lineback (1949-) Elizabeth Copeland Vargo (1951-) Rebecca Copeland (1956-) John Luther Copeland (1958-)
Robert Warren Copeland, 9/3/1920 (1920-1968)	Louvern McClung (1925-)	Patricia Copeland Pacha (1951-) Cheryl Copeland (1953-1975) Cynthia Copeland (1955-)